Insert

Judge Yohn's Potentially Deadly Blunders

Just as this book was going to press, I discovered some major judicial errors. If seriously considered, these flaws in the December 18, 2001 federal court ruling on Mumia Abu-Jamal's *habeas corpus* appeal are enough to lead to a new trial.

William Yohn is a federal district court judge, known locally for both his legal acumen and his integrity. And over the two years that he pondered the *habeas* appeal filed in 1999, many observers agreed that this judge embodied Abu-Jamal's best hope during what had become a 20-year fight against a sentence of death.

Yohn's ruling overturned that death sentence, though perhaps only temporarily. If his ruling is upheld on appeal, the D.A. has the right to call for a new sentencing jury to reconsider the single issue of whether Abu-Jamal should get death or life in prison without parole. Still on death row today pending that appeal, he could be resentenced to death. Alternatively, if Yohn's ruling suspending the death sentence is overturned on appeal, the original death sentence would be restored, leaving only the U.S. Supreme Court as Abu-Jamal's final arbiter. At a minimum, if Yohn's verdict is sustained on appeal, Abu-Jamal faces the prospect of spending the rest of his days in prison with no further right of appeal. (See Chapter 10.)

In his 272-page ruling (described in one news article as "magisterial"),[1] Yohn invested a level of care approaching what is normally associated with the most cutting-edge high-tech projects. Yet sometimes all the care in the world won't prevent simple yet catastrophic mistakes. In the fall of 1999, the same year that Abu-Jamal's defense filed his federal appeal, a Mars landing craft from NASA crashed into the red planet. No one had noticed a small yet fatal error: a critical measurement had been calculated in feet instead of meters. Yohn made several similarly small mistakes, causing his otherwise meticul⸻⸻⸻⸻⸻ to crash.

Missed by everyone ⸻⸻⸻⸻ these findings are presented here for the fir⸻

Judge Yohn's mist⸻ ⸻rness in the legal

process; they are his alone. Yohn barred several pieces of what would have been powerful evidence for the defense. In doing so, he was adhering to strict rules governing the federal appeals process. Some might rail against these severe limitations—that evidence must be newly discovered, that it must not have been available for admission at an earlier phase of the trial or appeals process, or that it must have been raised and rejected in a lower court. Some will argue for leeway in admissibility where a person's life hangs in the balance. On the other hand, some might argue the converse: with the case having taken already two decades, slain Police Officer Daniel Faulkner and his family deserve justice. But wherever one might fall on the spectrum of this debate, such concerns must here be set aside. Yohn was compelled—just as any other judge would have been—to act within these rules of evidence and procedure. This entire discussion accepts these legal limitations as given. Yohn's errors fall within that framework.

These errors, as will become clear, are focused not on legal loopholes but on questions of constitutional rights central to our commonly held concepts of justice. After discussing these questions, I'll summarize the evidence the defense sought to submit for consideration, review the reasons why Judge Yohn barred this evidence, and then discuss where Yohn erred. The full implications of these errors will then become apparent.

Legal Loopholes
or Constitutional Questions of Justice?

The defense claimed that the prosecution, during the jury selection phase of Abu-Jamal's trial, deliberately removed at least 10, and possibly 11 blacks from his jury. These blacks were legally eligible to become jurors. This included meeting the requirement that jurors be able to vote for the death penalty in the event the defendant is found guilty. If they were purged by reason of race, this would undeniably be a violation of the long-cherished principle enshrined in the Sixth and Fourteenth Amendments of the U.S. Constitution: the right to be tried by a jury of one's peers. While this principle has been the law of the land since 1935, it was not until 1986 that it became a principle with teeth. Prior to that year, defendants had to demonstrate a long pattern of racial discrimination by a prosecutor in order to prove bias. But that year, in a case called *Batson v. Kentucky*, the U.S. Supreme Court ruled that a defendant need only prove that jurors were excluded on the grounds of race in his own case. Such a finding is now sufficient to win a new trial before a new jury.

As Supreme Court Justice Lewis Powell wrote in the majority opinion in the high court's *Batson* ruling:

> Purposeful racial discrimination in selection of the venire [jury] violates a defendant's right to equal protection because it denies him a protection that a trial by jury is intended to secure.[2]

Death penalty advocates criticize *Batson* as a "loophole" that allows guilty people to escape. But the high court approved *Batson* because prosecutors have for years been stacking juries for conviction by weeding out blacks. Prosecutors may purge African-Americans for a compelling, if unjust reason. Namely, a concern that, often with a different experience of the justice system, blacks may be more skeptical than whites of prosecution witnesses—such as the police. *Batson* helps keep prosecutors from such purging.

20th District Court Judge Carol Glowinsky presides over criminal trials in Boulder, Colorado. She states the matter starkly: "The life experience of jurors significantly influences their perception and evaluation of the evidence. When a segment of a community is systematically excluded from jury service, the fundamental fairness of the trial is seriously compromised."

The Evidence: A Summary

But just what was the nature of the evidence that the defense was trying to get admitted? Yohn refused to admit four key pieces of evidence supporting Abu-Jamal's *Batson* claim:

- One piece was a set of data published in the *Cornell Law Review* in 1998, in an article entitled "Race Discrimination and the Death Penalty in the Post-*Furman* Era: An Empirical and Legal Analysis with Recent Findings from Philadelphia."[3] The focus of the study, authored by David Baldus and Gary Woodworth, was that during a 10-year period from 1983 to 1993, race and racism played a powerful role in how juries meted out the ultimate sanction. For short-hand purposes, let's call this the "*Cornell Law Review* study."

- A second set of data, unpublished, focused not on sentencing but on a much earlier stage in the process: how juries were selected. The data were from Ed Rendell's tenure as district attorney in Philadelphia from 1977 through 1986. Collected by University of Iowa law professor David Baldus (lead author of the *Cornell*

Law Review study), this data was successfully used by federal public defenders to overturn another case tried at the same time as Abu-Jamal's, *Hardcastle v. Horn*.[4] We will refer to this material as the "Rendell-era data."

- A third set of data came out of that Rendell-era research and was a subset of it, covering the same time period: 1977 through 1986. This was the record of how one of the D.A.'s attorneys, Joseph McGill, used his peremptory challenges during jury selection. (Peremptory challenges are a certain number of opportunities provided equally to the prosecution and defense to reject jurors without having to offer any justification to the court.) They focused on one question: Did McGill use his peremptory challenges to unfairly skew the racial makeup of juries in the six capital cases he prosecuted? Crucially, one of these six was Abu-Jamal's. We'll call this evidence the "McGill peremptory strike data."

- The defense also offered for Yohn's consideration evidence showing that the pattern of skewing jury composition away from blacks and toward whites was endemic to Philadelphia and continued long after McGill and Rendell had left their posts. This data focused on the years 1987-1991, when a new district attorney, Ron Castille, headed the Philadelphia prosecutors' office. This evidence is important because it puts McGill's actions and the jury-selection practices of the city prosecutors' office into a larger picture, demonstrating clearly that the Rendell-era data was not some kind of statistical aberration. For convenience, we will refer to this as the "post-Rendell/McGill data."

Why Judge Yohn Barred These Pieces of Evidence from Consideration

The core of the defense's *Batson* claim lies in the McGill peremptory strike data: Did prosecutor McGill, by peremptorily striking blacks from consideration as jurors on a routine basis, deny capital defendants generally— and Abu-Jamal in particular—the constitutional right to a jury of their peers?

It is important to keep in mind the first key question for any judge: before evaluating the evidence, it has to be decided whether such evidence can be admitted. Whatever the evidence, Yohn applied three criteria:

- Was the evidence from a relevant time frame?
- Was the evidence new?
- Or if the evidence was not new, had it been raised in a timely manner earlier and then rejected by a lower court?

Solidly grounding his opinion in law and U.S. Supreme Court precedent, Yohn noted that the defense had failed to put prosecutor McGill on the stand to testify about his jury selection process when it had the chance to do so at Abu-Jamal's 1995 post-conviction hearing. Without McGill's testimony, the judge ruled, the defense had failed to establish a legal foundation for later examining the prosecutor's racial jury strike record in a higher court. Yohn ruled that the defense couldn't later raise the issue in the *habeas corpus* appeal because it had already missed its chance. As the judge wrote in his order:

> Specifically, petitioner states that he has identified six other cases in which prosecutor McGill evidenced a pattern of discrimination in the use of his peremptory strikes. He seeks to present that evidence, along with discovery concerning other cases tried by McGill. To determine whether petitioner is eligible for an evidentiary hearing...the court must ask whether the factual basis of this claim was developed in state court and if not, who is to blame for the incomplete record. It is clear that the factual record concerning this claim was not fully developed in state court, and I conclude that petitioner is at fault for the incomplete record. Obviously, this information was available in 1995 at the time of petitioner's [post-conviction] hearing.[5]

This made short work of the defense's McGill peremptory strike data. Yohn also rejected the Rendell-era data, claiming that it covered the 1983-1993 period and was thus not relevant to Abu-Jamal's 1982 trial.

The judge went on to reject the post-Rendell/McGill data, explaining that it covered the 1987-1991 period. Since that is subsequent to Abu-Jamal's trial of 1982, he came to another logical conclusion that it is therefore irrelevant and therefore inadmissible.

If Yohn rejected the McGill peremptory strike data for two reasons (because the defense should have put McGill on the stand and didn't and because the data was available earlier and the defense didn't use it), and if he then rejected both the Rendell-era and the the post-Rendell/McGill data as being from the wrong time period, on what grounds did he reject the *Cornell Law Review* study on sentencing? The judge's reasoning here was twofold. First, again was the issue of timeliness and relevance: Yohn pointed out that the study's data were from the period 1983-1993, while Abu-Jamal's trial was in 1982. Secondly, it had already been submitted late and rejected by the state's highest court. As the judge wrote:

> Petitioner, however, neglects to mention the time period that this study covered, namely 1983 to 1993…Thus, because it did not cover the period of the time during which petitioner's 1982 trial was conducted, I conclude that it is irrelevant to petitioner's Batson claim…In addition, petitioner did attempt to submit this study to the Pennsylvania Supreme Court on August 1, 1998, one year after briefing had been concluded before the Pennsylvania Supreme Court…The state supreme court rejected the submission because of its lateness, as petitioner did not even seek leave of court to file the application to remand. Again, the failure to develop an adequate state court record was the result of the petitioner's own actions. Accordingly, he is now barred from commanding a federal evidentiary hearing to present the Baldus-Woodworth study [*Cornell Law Review* study].[6]

So much for the admission of the evidence of racism presented in the *Cornell Law Review* study.

As noted, these arguments, as presented, were sound and logically based in law. But that's just the start of the story. Because he was badly confused about those studies, Judge Yohn went horribly wrong.

Yohn's Mistakes

In barring the admission of evidence documented above, Yohn made four critical mistakes:

- He confused the Rendell-era data with *Cornell Law Review* study. This led him to assume that the Rendell-era data covered 1983-93, when it actually covered 1977-86. Based on that error he refused to consider the Rendell-era data because he thought it began after Abu-Jamal's trial. *In fact, the Rendell-era data actually include Abu-Jamal's own jury selection!*

- His next mistake was a direct consequence of his first mistake. He confused a subset of that Rendell-era data, the McGill peremptory strike data, which was for the 1977-86 period when McGill worked under D.A. Rendell, with the post-Rendell/McGill data from 1987-91. This confusion led him to reject the Rendell-era data as irrelevant to Abu-Jamal's 1982 trial. Yohn's error here is profound: McGill left the D.A.'s office in 1986 to go into private practice. Thus there could be no McGill data from 1987 or later. *And here again, contrary to Yohn's understanding, the McGill data actually includes Abu-Jamal's own trial!*

• Yohn, because of his confusion about the different sets of evidence, also claimed that the Rendell-era data had been filed too late with the state supreme court and had thus been rejected. He is wrong. The *Cornell Law Review* study was indeed submitted late to the state supreme court, after the court had already concluded hearing Abu-Jamal's appeal in 1998. As such, Judge Yohn could properly claim it should not be available in the *habeas* appeal. But the Rendell-era data, on the other hand, which was assembled by Professor. Baldus on behalf of the Philadelphia Federal Defenders Office for use in the *Hardcastle* case appeal, was separate. Further, the Rendell-era data could not have even been known to the Abu-Jamal defense until the *Hardcastle* case was heard by the Pennsylvania supreme court in late 1998. This was after the state's high court had already ruled on Abu-Jamal's appeal. In other words, the Rendell-era data was new evidence at the time that the defense submitted it to Yohn in 1999. According to the legal precedents and laws governing federal *habeas* appeals, even though it had not been submitted earlier, it was new and therefore qualified for admission.

• As for the McGill peremptory strike data, this kind of information is not something that is readily available, even today, but was only researched by Professor Baldus and provided to the defense for the first time in late 1998.* So the defense could not have presented it, or used it to question McGill on the stand in 1995, as Judge Yohn asserted in his ruling. In fact, prior to Baldus's research, only the D.A.'s office could have possessed such data on McGill's history of racial strikes over the course of six homicide trials. *And if the D.A.'s office had possessed such data,*

---

* Prior to the U.S. Supreme Court's landmark *Batson* ruling, few attorneys bothered to even keep track of the race of jurors excluded by prosecutors, since proving racial bias in jury selection was so difficult, and involved showing a history of such behavior by a prosecutor over a number of trials. As Judge Yohn should have known, such data simply were not available, except as a result of exhaustive and time-consuming research, such as that later conducted by Professor Baldus.

it would have been required under the rules of evidence to provide it to the defense back in 1995.

How did Yohn confuse this important evidence, and what are the implications of his mistakes?

Starting with the *Cornell Law Review* study, Yohn got it partly right: that study did indeed cover capital cases in the 1983-1993 period, and Abu-Jamal's trial was a year earlier, in 1982 (Fig. 12, p. 176j). Yohn also noted correctly that the state supreme court did reject consideration of that study because it was filed as evidence by the defense after the conclusion of the high court's hearing of Abu-Jamal's earlier appeal. Yet even with regard to that study, Yohn still had it wrong on two counts. The study in question wasn't about jury *selection*; it was about racial bias in *sentencing* in Philadelphia. This tiny misunderstanding led Yohn to an incorrect conclusion about the *Cornell Law Review* study's relevance. While the jury decided on Abu-Jamal's death sentence on July 3, 1982, his formal sentencing didn't take place until a hearing before Judge Albert Sabo on May 25, 1983. *As such, contrary to Yohn's understanding, the Cornell Law Review study, while it might have been filed too late in state court, at least should not have been rejected as irrelevant because Abu-Jamal's sentencing was actually included in the study!* (In fact, from the point of view of supporting Abu-Jamal's *Batson* claim, the *Cornell Law Review* study isn't that important a piece of evidence. But it played an important role in this drama. Because it was excludable on grounds of lateness, and because Yohn confused it with the Rendell-era data, it led the judge to exclude the Rendell-era evidence.)

Turning to the McGill peremptory strike data, Yohn confuses it with the separate post-Rendell/McGill data that had nothing to do with McGill. As noted above, the post-Rendell/McGill evidence involves a second set of jury selection data for a later district attorney's administration. Yohn mistakenly believed it referred to data concerning McGill's own jury selection history.

But this can't be, and Yohn clearly misunderstood what the defense was saying. McGill left his job with the district attorney's office to go into private practice in 1986—before the time period of this data. There is not and never can be any jury selection data on prosecutor McGill in the 1987-1991 period. As Yohn should have realized, the McGill data had to be earlier—during the time he prosecuted Abu-Jamal—and as such that data is also highly relevant to the question of whether McGill deliberately excluded blacks from his juries, and from Abu-Jamal's jury in paticular.

Here are the two paragraphs written by the defense as they appeared together in Abu-Jamal's *habeas* petition. They may shed some light on how Yohn confused the issues:

> The evidence establishes that the Philadelphia District Attorney's office continued this consistent policy and practice of striking African Americans and women from venires in later prosecutorial administrations. A review of juror strikes in 80 capital cases prosecuted between January 1987 and April 1991 indicates that the Philadelphia District Attorney's office peremptorily struck African-American venirepersons 58.20% of the time (465 strikes of a possible 799 jurors), while striking other venirepersons only 22.13% of the time (254 of 1,148). This translates into a strike rate against African-American jurors throughout that district attorney's administration that was more than two-and-one-half times greater (2.63) than for non-black jurors.
>
> Petitioner has determined that, throughout the period covered by *the study* [my emphasis], Prosecutor McGill peremptorily struck African-American venirepersons 74.14% of the time he had an opportunity to do so (43 strikes of 58 prospective jurors). By contrast, McGill exercised peremptory strikes against venirepersons who were not African American in only 25.30% of his opportunities to do so (21 of 83, or 25.3%). Consequently, McGill was nearly three times more likely (2.93) to peremptorily strike an African-American venireperson called for jury duty in a homicide prosecution than a venireperson who was not black.[7]

Clearly, the first paragraph, which immediately follows information about the Rendell-era data, refers to additional data on jury selection practices during the subsequent, post-Rendell period at the district attorney's office. This all takes place after McGill had already left the D.A.'s office. In contrast, the second paragraph clearly concerns specifically McGill's jury selection practices, which were earlier. These had to be for the period of his tenure as an assistant D.A., a period that naturally includes Abu-Jamal's trial. There is no transition sentence between the paragraphs to make it clear that the defense had switched from discussing the post-Rendell/McGill-era data to discussing the McGill peremptory strike data, the latter having had to come from the earlier Rendell administration period. As mentioned earlier, the two paragraphs obviously can't be saying the McGill data came from 1987-1991 because McGill wasn't a prosecutor then. The "study" referred to in italics at the start of the second paragraph clearly is a reference to the McGill strike data. But it is easy to see why Yohn, who had only court records and defense and prosecution briefs to guide him, became confused by these two paragraphs.

In other words, there were three sets of evidence submitted in Abu-

Jamal's *habeas* appeal petition which Yohn had ruled inadmissible, at least partly because he felt they were irrelevant, based upon the dates covered by the data. But contrary to the judge's assertions, the *Cornell Law Review* study, the Rendell-era data and the McGill peremptory strike data all included Abu-Jamal's case, making them timely and highly relevant.

The question now remains, how grave are these mistakes? Do they warrant the Third Circuit Court of Appeals ordering a full hearing on the defense's claim that Abu-Jamal's constitutional right to a trial by a jury of his peers had been denied? At such a hearing the defense would be able to make its case, and if McGill were called to testify, he could be questioned about his record of exclusion of blacks from capital juries.

Could the Evidence Swing a New Trial?

Had the evidence that was erroneously barred been considered, its impact clearly should have led to an evidentiary hearing before Judge Yohn—and clearly to a new trial. The core of the argument is McGill's history of selecting largely white juries in homicide cases. The evidence is compelling:

1. It is a fact, not a matter of opinion, that in a city that was 44 percent African-American, Abu-Jamal's jury was initially composed of nine whites and three blacks, along with four white alternates. After the controversial removal of one of the black jurors on the first day of the trial, and her replacement by one of the white alternates, the jury that convicted and sentenced Abu-Jamal was composed of ten whites and only two blacks.

2. It is a fact, not a matter of opinion, that in Abu-Jamal's trial, prosecutor McGill used 10, and possibly 11 of his peremptory challenges out of a total of 15 that he exercised, to remove black jurors who were otherwise acceptable for seating on the panel.

3. The McGill peremptory strike data covers a total of six cases between 1977 and 1986 including Abu-Jamal's. Over the course of that period McGill struck African-American jurors 74 percent of the time. In contrast, he struck potential jurors who were white only 25 percent of the time.

4. Under McGill's boss, District Attorney Ed Rendell, the Philadelphia district attorney's office, over the period 1977-1986, including the trial of Abu-Jamal in 1982, struck black jurors 58 percent of the time, compared to only 22 percent of the time for white jurors. Looked at another way:

> ...the odds that a juror would be peremptorily struck by the Philadelphia District Attorney's office during the administration in which Jamal was tried increased by a factor of 575 percent if the juror was black.[8]

Yohn's Tragedy

The implications of the data presented by the defense are clear: Abu-Jamal should certainly receive a hearing on his so-called *Batson* claim—one at which the defense and the prosecution can openly make their arguments. There, the defense can clarify for the judge the issues and the evidence, so that the kind of confusion that plagued Judge Yohn's decision on this particular matter can be dispelled. The evidence of racial bias in jury selection during the administration of District Attorney Ed Rendell, and in the trials prosecuted by Joseph McGill, including Abu-Jamal's specifically, is damning. It is hard to believe that its careful consideration by a fair-minded judge would lead to anything but a new trial. Indeed, this very same evidence has already proved its power, having led to a reversal in the *Hardcastle* case.

The defense has a serious and convincing claim that has yet to be heard and tested in the crucible of courtroom argument.

"These mistakes certainly more than open the door for the Third Circuit to review Judge Yohn's opinion, because there are factual errors that require rectification and a reconsideration of his opinion," says Bill Goodman, legal director of the Center for Constitutional Rights, and an expert on federal *habeas corpus* procedures. He adds, "If there's real evidence that there was a systemic pattern of racial bias in jury selection in the D.A.'s office and by the prosecutor, a reviewing court has to look at that evidence."

Fortunately, Judge Yohn left the door open for the defense to appeal his rejection of the *Batson* claim. Alone among all the 20 constitutional claims raised by Abu-Jamal in his *habeas* petition and rejected by Judge Yohn, the judge certified this one for appeal to the Third Circuit Court of Appeals. For whatever reason—perhaps his own apprehension that he may not have correctly understood some of the evidence—Yohn felt that this particular issue deserved further review by the higher court, including arguments by attorneys for the two sides. In legal parlance, he "certified" this one ruling for appeal, meaning that although the judge rejected this claim along with 19 others, on this one claim the defense has a right to a hearing before the Third Circuit Court of Appeals. Given his errors, his call for further review is certainly justified.

It is now up to Abu-Jamal's defense team to grasp and skillfully present these errors to the Third Circuit Court of Appeals. If the evidence is admitted, the defense must then convince that court that this *Batson* claim warrants a full evidentiary hearing. Or alternatively, that the evidence already submitted in the *habeas* petition, properly understood, already makes the case for an overturning of Abu-Jamal's conviction.

With his life hanging in the balance, it is hard to predict whether Abu-Jamal can succeed in overcoming these confusions and having his *Batson* evidence of race-based jury selection fairly and carefully considered in a federal court. That outcome will also say a great deal about the state of America's capital punishment system, and more importantly about its vaunted claim to providing justice for all. Judge Yohn's rejection of that claim represents not justice, but a potentially deadly tragedy.

As Philadelphia Defenders Office attorney David Zuckerman, who helped develop much of the data at issue, says, "Judge Yohn was confused. He could have avoided making those mistakes if he had granted a hearing on the issue, where Jamal's lawyers could have explained things to him."

It is a tragedy the judge could easily have avoided, and one that can still be rectified.

Killing Time

An Investigation Into the Death Row Case of
Mumia Abu-Jamal

Dave Lindorff

Common Courage Press   Monroe, Maine

Library of Congress Cataloging-in-Publication Data is available from
the publisher on request.

ISBN 1-56751-228-3 paper
ISBN 1-56751-229-1

Common Courage Press
Box 702
Monroe, ME 04951

(207) 525-0900; fax: (207) 525-3068
orders-info@commoncouragepress.com

See our website for e-versions of this book.
www.commoncouragepress.com

First Printing

To all those on America's death rows,
living and dead,
who were wrongfully convicted and condemned
to state-sponsored
execution.

Contents

Foreword

W hen I was approached in 1999 by Common Courage Press editor Greg Bates to write this book, I had only a passing knowledge of the case of Mumia Abu-Jamal. I agreed to take on the assignment because, as an opponent of the death penalty, I thought it would be a worthwhile project. I also knew that Abu-Jamal was a journalist, and, as another of that persuasion, I wanted to understand how a person who makes his living telling stories could wind up with a murder rap.

I had no preconceived opinion about Abu-Jamal's guilt or innocence. But knowing that Common Courage Press had already published a book of documents on the case edited by his defense counsel Leonard Weinglass,[1] I warned Bates that if I was to take on the project, I had to be free to come up with whatever conclusions my own research led me to. He agreed to these terms without hesitation.

Over the course of the next several years, I pored over the transcripts of the trial and the subsequent hearings in the case, including the voluminous transcripts of the Post-Conviction Relief Act hearings, which ran longer than the original trial—a total of in excess of 13,000 pages of material. I also tracked down and interviewed witnesses on my own, including some who testified at the original trial and some who have yet to take the stand.

I received some cooperation from the prosecution's side: Joseph McGill, who litigated the case for the District Attorney, was gracious with his time. Joey Grant and Hugh Burns, two assistant D.A.s who were prominently involved in the PCRA hearings, also granted interviews.

On the defense side, I was unable to speak with Abu-Jamal, who also declined to answer questions I put to him via express mail (a continuation of his long-standing policy of refusing to discuss his case). I was able to interview his lead appellate attorney, Leonard Weinglass and his chief legal strategist, Daniel Williams, while they were still working on his case and subsequently, but have never been granted an interview by his subsequent legal team of Eliot Grossman and Marlene Kamish.

Pam Africa and the MOVE organization, while eventually unwilling to talk with me, were initially helpful, and assisted in locating for me a nearly complete set of copies of Abu-Jamal's PCRA transcripts, as well as some other background material, for which I am grateful.

The purpose of this book was to examine a case which has been a troubling puzzle since the story first broke that a promising young black Philadelphia newsman had been arrested in the shooting death of a young white police officer on the morning of December 9, 1981. The act itself seemed to make no sense, and seemed terribly out of character with the prior life history of the suspect.

Having finished my investigation, I am left with many questions, among them:

- In a city that boasts some of the finest legal talent in the country, including some very left-leaning progressive attorneys, black and white, why did Abu-Jamal, a man who as a journalist knew just about everybody who was anybody, select for his trial a young attorney with little death penalty experience? And why, when he lost confidence in that attorney, did he try to defend himself in such a life-and-death matter?

- Why did the district attorney's office, fresh out of a decade of terrible racial troubles and just free of a mayor who had been exacerbating racial tensions, choose to prosecute this case as a first-degree murder, when the evidence of premeditation was so minimal, and the prior record of the defendant was so benign?

- Why did the state, in its intense desire to win, resort to such over-the-top tactics, which included eliminating most blacks from the jury, blocking a critical defense witness from testifying, and resorting to dredging up the 12-year-old political statements of a then 15-year-old boy in order to clinch a death sentence (not to mention probably manufacturing—or allowing police witnesses to manufacture—evidence of a confession)?

- Why later, during the appeals process, did the state so want to execute this particular prisoner that it would resort to underhanded means, such as the illegal intercepting and reading of the defendant's mail communications with his attorneys, or the arrest right in the courtroom of a defense witness?

- Why did a respected defense attorney decide to go against his client's wishes, and apparently against the wishes of the lead attorney in the case, and publish an inside account of his defense strategy, leading to his firing—and the firing of the lead attorney—at a critical moment in Abu-Jamal's federal appeal process?

- Why did Abu-Jamal, who had a well crafted appeal pending before a federal judge, suddenly decide to change tack and build his strategy around the claim that someone else (a career criminal and self-described mob hitman) had killed Faulkner, especially since this was a strategy and witness he had expressly rejected two years earlier as being not credible?

I don't know the full answer to any of these questions, or even to the central question of who shot Officer Faulkner, but having researched this case to the best of my ability, I am convinced that to this day justice has not been done in this case.

Any state or country that has a death penalty statute on the books has an awesome and terrible responsibility to make sure that it *never* makes a mistake. American law requires that in any criminal trial, a defendant be found guilty *beyond a reasonable doubt*. That standard holds true whether the crime is the theft of an auto or murder in the first degree. But when it is murder, and when the penalty is not a few months in the slammer but death, the bar must be higher still. Surely we need to be more rigorous in avoiding error in a capital murder case than in a case of car theft. After all, even a reasonable error is an error; in a capital case an error can lead to a wrongful death at the hands of the state.

But a higher bar isn't what we have. The capital punishment system qualifies its jurors to exclude anyone with qualms about execution. Its right of appeal is ever more limited. Its racism is undeniable. And because of the state's obsession with killing this particular defendant, the bar was, if anything, lower than for a common felony case.

It is not enough for the prosecution to claim, as Philadelphia District Attorney Lynne Abraham, a leading advocate of capital punishment, does, that the courts have ruled and that's all that matters. As will be demonstrated in this book, judges can have biases, judges can be corrupt and unethical, and judges—even federal judges—can make mistakes. As Supreme Court Justice Antonin Scalia put it in one of his opinions, "Judges, it is sometimes necessary to remind ourselves, are part of the State..."[2] Prosecutors (and defendants), he might have added, can likewise be corrupt and unethical, and can make mistakes.

No one comes out untarnished in this story, but it is my hope that the reader, after patiently making her or his way through this story, will agree with me that the case of Commonwealth of Pennsylvania v. Mumia Abu-Jamal needs to be retried.

I have not, in this volume, attempted to interview any members of Officer Faulkner's family, or any spokesperson from the Fraternal Order of Police. The reason is that this book is about Mumia Abu-Jamal's guilt or innocence, not about the feelings of relatives or friends of a victim. It has become standard, in the coverage of capital punishment cases, to interview the relatives of victims, as though they somehow represent the "other side" of the story. Despite their legitimate suffering, however, they do not. Family members of murder victims seek justice. And they deserve to see the day it will be done. But their proximity to the victim does not give them any special ability to discern the guilt or innocence of the accused. That is a question of evidence. Sometimes family members may possess pertinent evidence—especially if they witnessed the crime or knew the assailant prior to the event. Certainly in this instance, any evidence possessed by the family would have come to light years ago, as they have been vigorously involved in the case. Because they have not shed any light on the case, and it seems unlikely that they will do so, I conducted no interviews with them.

For the same reason, I have not attempted to interview members of Abu-Jamal's family. It was not my intention to make an argument that this prisoner, by virtue of his qualities as a journalist and as a human being, deserves to be free after two decades on death row.

My sole purpose in this project was to determine whether Mumia Abu-Jamal was wrongfully convicted for the murder of Officer Daniel Faulkner.

In the spirit of full disclosure, I want to note that while I was working on this book, my publisher, Common Courage Press, was approached by Abu-Jamal's then attorney Daniel Williams. He was trying to find a publisher for his controversial book on the case (later published by St. Martin's Press). As mentioned above, Common Courage also did publish, in 1995, a book on the case by then lead appellate attorney Leonard Weinglass, under the title *Race for Justice*. I am also a founding member of the National Writers Union (UAW/AFL-CIO) and am a member of the steering committee of the NWU's Philadelphia Local, of which Abu-Jamal is a member.

I want to thank the librarians at the *Philadelphia Inquirer* and the *Daily News*, the Philadelphia Free Library reserve room and Temple University's Urban Archives for digging up old clippings which ensured accurate footnotes in this volume. I also want to thank friends and colleagues, too numerous to mention by name, who offered encouragement in this project. In the category of special thanks, I want to mention Linn Washington, who took the time to read carefully through the manuscript and offer detailed criticism, and who generously shared his own voluminous files on the case. Also my family, who enthusiastically supported me in the researching and writing of this book, even when it took me away from responsibilities at home and caused me to cut back on my income-producing work as a free-lance writer. And especially my wife Joyce, an in-house editor who has never let me get away with an unjustified conclusion or a confusing piece of writing, and my brother Gary, who came through with a brilliant cover drawing of the subject of this book.

A word of appreciation is in order too for Common Courage's libel attorney, Mel Wulf, a true reporter's attorney who knows how to vet a project without destroying the story.

Finally, I want to thank my editor, Greg Bates. Through delays, the bankruptcy of the company that distributed his press's books, the collapse of a barn and the death of his father, Greg has stuck by this project and encouraged me to finish, and has honored his pledge of full editorial freedom to reach whatever conclusions my research suggested.

Without all the help I received, this book could never have been written. But I hasten to add that any shortcomings or errors are entirely my own.

This book was published with the assistance of a grant from the journalism division of the Fund for Constitutional Government.

Chapter One

Shoot Out

In a city notorious for its bad drivers, what was it that prompted Daniel Faulkner to make the fateful decision to pull over a battered blue Volkswagen that morning on Dec., 9, 1981? Was it driving the wrong way on a one-way street? Was it the non-regulation wooden bumper with the license plate hanging askew? It was 3:45 a.m., cold, and not the best part of town—13th and Locust Street in those days was an area of after-hours bars, prostitutes and drug dealing. Not the ideal time or place to have to get out of the warm squad car and check license and registration documents. But that's what the job was. Besides, Faulkner had already made one such stop an hour earlier without incident, just a few blocks away. And this time, he initially didn't give any indication he expected trouble either. Faulkner had called in to let headquarters know he was stopping a car, but he didn't request any back up. Then, a few moments later, he reconsidered:

> Car 612: I have a car stopped…12, 13th and Locust
> Police Radio: Car to back 612, 13th and Locust.
> Car 612: On second thought send me a wagon 1234 Locust.[1]

With this request for a paddy wagon, what had started out as routine traffic stop now looked like it might end in an arrest.

It had already been a busy night for 25-year-old Daniel Faulkner [Fig. 1, p. 176a], a five-year veteran of the Philadelphia Police force. A quiet evening at home spent paying his monthly bills and talking with his young wife Maureen had ended with the start of his shift. Early during his patrol of his Center City beat in the Sixth District, Faulkner had received a call about a young black girl who had been raped. He picked up the distraught youngster and brought her, crying, to Jefferson Hospital for treatment. He had arrested a suspect as well. What a mess this world was, with little kids getting raped—half the time by members of their own family! Faulkner liked kids and enjoyed playing pick-up games with children of his neighbors.

Married just two years earlier in the fall of 1979, he and Maureen were deciding whether to have a child. He had requested and received a transfer to the Sixth Precinct so he could be nearer to his wife—unusually good treatment for a relatively junior cop. He may not have had a lot of seniority, but he had ranked third in his class at the police academy. The neighborhood leader of the Muscular Dystrophy Association, he was the kind of cop parents hope their small children would turn to if they got lost or needed help crossing the street.

The VW had halted behind a Ford sedan, pointed east on the south side of Locust Street. A young black man in dreadlocks got out of the Beetle. Faulkner, not waiting for backup to arrive, exited his cruiser.

At six feet one inch tall, Faulkner was a much bigger man than the VW driver was. Alone on the dark street but aware that backup was on the way, he started running through the usual traffic stop drill. It didn't look like anything particularly dangerous, though a cop always has to be on guard in a neighborhood like this, crawling with drug dealers, pimps, whores and johns from all walks of life. Faulkner asked the young driver, Billy Cook, for his license. But instead of responding as asked, Cook took a swing at him, striking him in the side of the face and throwing him off balance. Angered, and now concerned about his own safety, Faulkner grabbed his assailant with one hand, and with the other used his police-issue flashlight—a long metal device of considerable heft—to help subdue Cook, striking him around the head and shoulders. [Figs. 3, 4, 5. p. 176c]

But this focus on Cook proved fatal. Unbeknownst to Faulkner, another man, also black, had run diagonally across the street from a nearby parking lot. This second person packed a short-barreled .38 caliber revolver. Drawing up close to the preoccupied cop, he fired one shot into the officer's back. The thump of the projectile jarred Faulkner almost before he heard the bullet being fired. Knocked forward towards the curb by the impact of the bullet, he spun around in mid fall. Instinctively reaching for his pistol, and now battling for his life, he fired off a round at his assailant. But when that failed to fell the man, Faulkner realized he was in serious trouble. Standing over him, one foot astride each side of his body, his attacker held his pistol in both hands and leveled it, execution style, at the young cop.

Despite his serious wound, Faulkner was not about to give up. A soldier before he had joined the police force, and trained to react quickly, he rolled from side to side. His assailant fired a deadly fusillade. Faulkner managed to avoid several rounds. But at last, wounded already and with his energy spent, he found himself staring straight up into the black hole of the stubby barrel.

He never heard the fatal shot. The exploding lead projectile hit him square between the eyes, turning his brain into pulp and ending his life instantly.

The shooter himself, gravely wounded by the policeman's one defensive shot, which had pierced his right lung and cleaved his liver before lodging next to the lower spine, staggered off a few feet, slumped onto the curb, and sat, bleeding internally and from the chest. His spent gun fell to the sidewalk beside him.

Sirens began to wail, and the flashing lights of approaching squad cars and police wagons soon turned the whole block into a strobe-lit stage like a set for the final scene of West Side Story.

Under these pulsing, blood-red lights, a young white cop lay on his back, dead on the street in a spreading pool of his own blood. His killer, a promising 27-year-old radio journalist and former Black Panther activist, sat nearby, critically wounded. Not far away, the initiator of the incident, the VW driver—who was also the brother of the injured shooter—stood staring in shock and horror at the unexpected results of his seemingly minor traffic violation.

That, in a nutshell, is the case of Mumia Abu-Jamal, a.k.a. Wesley Cook, as it was so dramatically presented to the jury back in June 1982 by Philadelphia assistant district attorney and ace homicide prosecutor Joseph McGill at the conclusion of Abu-Jamal's trial. The killer was there, his gun with five empty cartridges was there, and witnesses were there. The cop is dead. You can't get a more textbook example of an open-and-shut case. The deliberate murder of a good cop just doing his job, by a man with a history of cop-hating, cop-baiting, and with a passion for guns. The case was the very embodiment of that exalted standard, "beyond a reasonable doubt." The panel of ten white and two black jurors had little trouble convicting Abu-Jamal of first-degree murder and sentencing him to death.

Mumia Abu-Jamal's case is the best known of any inmate alive on death row today. The details of the prosecutor's case have met with well publicized rebuttals and counter-charges. Yet the full story has never been told, and crucial elements come to light for the first time in this book. Elements that might hold the key to whether Abu-Jamal's 20-year-long bid for retrial is justified. Beyond that, a close look at his case provides an eye-opening view of how—and how well—the U.S. court system carries out its mandate to assure that justice is done. The view is not pretty.

Even before McGill offered his dramatic presentation of what he thought had happened to the jury, problems began to seep into this seemingly ironclad case. As in many murder cases, witnesses had credibility problems and prosecution and defense witnesses gave contradictory testimony. These issues deserve a forensic review when a man's life hangs in the balance. But the prosecution's case raises more pressing questions.

This was an extraordinary case, a cop killing (one of only two such deaths in the line of duty in 1981) that instantly mobilized the entire investigative apparatus of the Philadelphia Police Department. Detectives from virtually every division and precinct were assigned to work on it. A phalanx of detectives and regular cops out to get justice for one of their own who had been felled in the line of duty interviewed over a hundred witnesses. Yet despite such intense motivation and the application of all these resources, routine tests that are carried out in most run-of-the-mill shooting cases were never done. Abu-Jamal's gun, according to prosecutors and police, was never tested to see if it had even been fired recently. (Or if it was tested, no record of that critical test was ever disclosed.) Further, as the bleeding suspect lay in a police van for nearly half an hour before being brought to the hospital, he was within easy reach of a test kit officers could have used to wipe-test his hands to verify whether he had fired a gun. Incredibly, that test was never conducted (or never reported), either.

Some of Abu-Jamal's defenders have asked if the gun might actually have been planted beside him (an all-too-common modus operandi of the Philadelphia Police Department in those days). Was Faulkner actually shot by someone else with an entirely different weapon? Simple tests mysteriously omitted in one of the department's most notorious cases would have gone a long way to proving or disproving these suspicions.

The questions go beyond issues of simple omissions in extraordinary times. Several people claimed to have seen Abu-Jamal (or in some cases witnesses described an unidentified black male), firing, or at least looking as if he was firing, at Officer Faulkner. Yet there was no testimony at the trial as to how Abu-Jamal himself came to be shot. Nobody said they saw it happen. Why is this fact relevant? After all, there was no dispute at the trial that Abu-Jamal was critically injured by a police bullet fired from Faulkner's gun. Doctors removed that bullet from his back later that morning. But the issue is pivotal. Some evidence suggests that Officer Faulkner fired the first shot, rather than the second. Prosecutors, without any solid evidence to back them up, allege Abu-Jamal fired first. But if Abu-Jamal did not fire the first shot, but rather was shot first, it is far harder to sustain the charge of first-degree murder that put Abu-Jamal on Pennsylvania's death row for over two decades.

Just as central, Abu-Jamal and his attorney never argued a simple point which might have spared him from the death penalty: assume for the moment that Faulkner fired at Abu-Jamal *after* being shot in the back. Abu-Jamal, or whoever it was who put the bullet into Faulkner's forehead at nearly point-blank range, far from trying to deliberately murder Faulkner, could have been simply shooting wildly, in a panicky attempt to protect himself from an armed policeman liable to shoot again. It's not an argument for innocence. But it might have averted the death penalty, which requires premeditation. (Premeditation in Pennsylvania law can occur in the split second before the trigger is pulled, as long as the intent, at the moment of the action, is to kill. But in this scenario, the shooter might have been firing wildly, in an attempt to prevent his target from firing again.)

And that raises the third glaring problem with McGill's script of the shooting incident. According to prosecutor McGill, Faulkner fired his one shot at his standing assailant as he was falling. But the bullet in question entered Abu-Jamal's chest at a point near the right nipple, traversed and pierced the right lung, and ran downward through the liver, before coming to rest near the lower spine. The path, uninterrupted by any evident contact with bone, was towards the back and downwards in a completely straight line. Yet in McGill's scenario, a falling Faulkner had to have been aiming upwards, not downwards at Abu-Jamal. It takes a lot of peculiar circumstances all working together seamlessly to get a lead slug to travel the trajectory it did in Abu-Jamal's body if the person shooting fired from a position below him. It would take a gun being awkwardly held high in the air and yet somehow aimed downwards, Abu-Jamal leaning over at a peculiar angle, and a bullet veering because of an odd tumble. The far simpler explanation is that a standing Officer Faulkner fired the bullet at a slightly bent-over Abu-Jamal. But that simply doesn't fit with McGill's story line, or with a first-degree murder charge.

Then there are the problems with the witnesses.

Both of the prosecution's key witnesses—the ones who claimed to have actually seen Abu-Jamal shooting the officer—had grave issues of credibility. Cynthia White, a young black prostitute with the street name

"Lucky," was the only witness presented by the prosecution who claimed to have actually seen the whole shooting incident from start to finish. But White, a prostitute and a drug user, was particularly vulnerable to police pressure designed to get her to say what they wanted her to say. And as Abu-Jamal's lawyer at the trial showed during her cross-examination, her account of what had happened shifted suspiciously over the course of three or four sequential sessions with police detectives to eventually square with McGill's crime scenario. At the last session, she was under additional duress: the police had arrested her. For example, in her initial account the morning of the incident, she describes the shooting as having been a rapid series of shots, like "firecrackers" going off, after which the officer fell. But several days and interviews later, she is saying there were "one or two" shots, then the officer falls, after which the shooter fires "three or four" more times at the prone officer.

The pressure on a prostitute doesn't even have to be overt. To be able to operate freely on the street, prostitutes in a city like Philadelphia depend upon lax enforcement—and in many cases upon payoffs to corrupt cops. And cooperating with the police can lead to exactly the kind of benign neglect needed to go about plying their trade unharassed. Indeed, after the initial trial (and at one point, even during the trial but not in front of the jury), some prostitutes who said they knew White testified that she was well aware of the benefits of cooperation with law enforcement in this case, and of the penalty for non-cooperation. There was even very credible testimony during a post-conviction hearing from another prostitute who knew White that White had been offered a deal in return for her testimony: freedom to walk the street. There is also the very peculiar fact that the police, who brought every other witness up to the paddy wagon to view and try and identify Abu-Jamal—even some who couldn't identify him—did not bring White to the van. Instead she was whisked away immediately to Homicide for questioning. The prosecutor also successfully blocked defense efforts to have White try to pick the defendant out of a police line-up. Did the police know she hadn't really seen anything and thus, wouldn't be able to identify him?

Far from being the occasional arrangement between a corrupt cop and a hooker, two major Justice Department probes of the Philadelphia Police Department during the 1980's and early 1990's demonstrated that bribing and extorting prostitutes and eliciting false testimony from them was common police practice. The revelations which are presented in Chapter 2 led not only to arrests and convictions of more than 50 officers and their superiors, but to the overturning of over 100 cases, including some for murder, as tainted police testimony was thrown out.[2]

Further doubt about Cynthia White's testimony comes from another witness, Dessie Hightower. This young black accounting student, who had been walking to his car with a friend at the time of the shooting, is arguably the single most credible of all the major witnesses to the incident. He had a clean record and nothing to gain from any testimony. Moreover, he actually volunteered himself to police as a witness after hearing the shots. He says he saw someone run away, and felt convinced that the police, whom he says were kicking and hitting Abu-Jamal, "were beating and arresting the wrong guy." Hightower, a shy but straight-speaking African-American man who now works as a caterer, was interviewed in early 2001. He told this reporter that on walking up to the scene, he saw no young black woman there at all, raising questions about whether White's claim to have witnessed the shooting was true.

It would be vital to any investigation of this case to interview White about whether she modified the truth of what she saw or whether she struck a deal with police and fabricated her entire claim to have been present at the shooting. But one simple fact makes this impossible: she's apparently dead. A fatal drug overdose in 1992 ended the possibility of her being questioned during the crucial post-conviction relief act hearing in 1995.[*]

The other witness who, at least on the stand, if not in his initial statement given to police during the investigation, identified Abu-Jamal as the shooter, was a young white cab driver, Robert Chobert. In initial statements to police, Chobert said he saw the shooter run away from the scene. He said also that after that happened, he got out of his cab and walked over to the fallen officer. But later, under questioning on the stand, Chobert altered his account to say that it was Abu-Jamal who was the shooter—the same Abu-Jamal who was sitting beside his gun only a few yards from the dead officer. Yet that raises a question: is it likely that Chobert really would have gotten out of his cab and walked over to the scene of the crime if the man he thought had shot the cop was still sitting nearby, gun close at hand? No one asked him that at the trial.

Whatever the not-so-subtle alterations in his testimony may be, Chobert had other problems that remained hidden from the jury. At the

---

*Abu-Jamal's defense teams have raised some doubts about whether White is really dead. They suggest she may have been given a new identity and hidden away by police, perhaps informally. There was testimony during the PCRA hearing that the fingerprints of the dead person identified as White didn't conclusively match those known to be White's.

time of his testimony in the 1982 trial, Chobert was serving five years' probation for throwing a firebomb into a schoolyard—for pay. The defense attempted to have this information disclosed to the jury. But presiding Judge Albert Sabo rejected this effort, arguing arson for profit is not a *crimen falsi*. That is, since arson for profit, in Sabo's view, wasn't a crime of falsehood, it didn't bear on whether a witness was telling the truth. Had Chobert been on probation for burglary, check kiting or even for rigging the meter in his cab—all crimes involving deception or lying—the defense might have had a point, Sabo suggested. If that were the case, the jury should be told about it so it can properly weigh his character in deciding on the merits and truthfulness of his testimony. But because the crime was arson of a school for profit, Sabo judged this irrelevant to his integrity as a witness. The jury never heard a word about it.

Chobert's issues with integrity didn't stop there. At the time of his testimony and at the time he was a witness to the shooting, Chobert was driving his cab with a suspended license resulting from a DWI conviction. These facts were also kept from the jury. They also raise another doubt about Chobert's claim to have witnessed the shooting: would a cabby on a suspended license have parked and hung around behind a police car to update his logbook?

In fact, at the post-conviction hearing, Chobert testified that at the time of his trial testimony in 1982 he had actually asked prosecutor McGill whether the D.A. could help him get his chauffeur's license back. The jury, of course, missed all this. When I interviewed McGill, he insisted that Chobert's request was an innocent response to his own casual and routine request of prosecution witnesses, made after Chobert's testimony: "Is there anything I can do for you?"

McGill may have been entirely honest in claiming to have extended a common courtesy to a witness who had just endured a difficult time on the witness stand. But whether the D.A. was attempting to influence the witness's testimony isn't the point, or at least the only point. At issue is the mindset of the witness. Had jurors known Chobert was driving his cab illegally, they might have concluded that he was giving favorable testimony in the hopes that the prosecution could help him get his license back. While the context McGill supplies—if correct—gets McGill off the hook for possibly suborning perjury, it makes Chobert's testimony no less suspect. Information about his suspended license, had it been made available to jurors, could well have influenced how much weight they would have given to his account. As it is, they had no idea of either fact—that he was a convicted arsonist, or that he had been driving on a suspended license while out on probation for felony arson.

In any event, by the time McGill made his summation to the jury, he was clearly aware that Chobert was hoping for some assistance with his license problem. But with these facts of arson, a DWI conviction and illegally driving a cab all safely hidden from the jury's view, McGill was free to highlight Chobert's testimony as being particularly credible. And indeed he did. Here's a guy with no axe to grind, he suggested to the panel. Referring to the time Chobert was first interviewed by police less than an hour after the shooting, he asked rhetorically:

> What motivation would Robert Chobert have to make up a story 35 to 45 minutes later?[3]

Problems with the witness Dessie Hightower's testimony that didn't fit the prosecution's story, Cynthia White's credibility problems and Robert Chobert's record as a drunk-driving felony arsonist who wanted his license back all were compounded by several other issues.

In Faulkner's pocket, police investigators found a duplicate driver's license application form—a document that may be used in lieu of a license while someone is waiting for a duplicate to be issued, and which was filled out in the name of Arnold Howard, a Cook family friend. The defense knew of the document, which was on an evidence list, but did not know during the trial that it had been found in the officer's possession, a critical piece of information. But the prosecution failed to pass that detail along to the defense, which was left to assume that the document was just another piece of flotsam collected from the cluttered VW Beetle by police investigators. Nor did the defense know, until after the trial, how seriously the police had initially treated that license application and its implications. After all, since it is highly unlikely that Faulkner would have searched the car and picked up the document, particularly since he had a hostile and combative driver on his hands (and no witnesses said he had done so), he must have obtained it from someone. Yet why would Cook, who had his own license to show, have handed over such a document? Did it come from someone else in the car? Regardless of how it found its way into Faulkner's pocket, the application's very location there does strongly suggest one point. The prosecution claims Billy Cook took a swing at Faulkner out of the blue, with no warning. But in order for that application to get into Faulkner's pocket, more must have transpired than was reported by McGill's witnesses. We don't know any more, though, because the whole issue of that document never came up at the trial.

What became clear since the trial is that early on in the case police investigators had ascribed a great deal of significance to that application. Police almost immediately tracked Howard down at his home and brought him to Homicide for grilling as a possible suspect or witness in the case. They clearly seemed to be assuming at the time that the document in Faulkner's possession meant Howard had been in the car with Cook. Howard, however, explained at a post-conviction hearing held 13 years after the initial trial that police realized this was false. He was allowed to go home after police had questioned him because he was able to produce a receipt from a night market way across town showing that he had been far from the scene of the shooting at the very time it had occurred. He also said in 1995 that he had loaned his license application document to Kenneth "Poppi" Freeman. This was Billy Cook's close friend and business partner in a sidewalk vending stand located in the area of the shooting.

Police also subsequently questioned Freeman, who owned a gun. They even went to his house and arrested him in February 1982. But apparently, no charges were brought against him. Nor was he ever called in to testify during the trial. Could Freeman have been the person Hightower and several other witnesses say they saw running from the scene?

Billy Cook's private attorney is Daniel Alva, a prominent lawyer in Philadelphia's legal establishment. He says his client told him, within days after the shooting, that Freeman had been with him in the car that fateful night that Officer Faulkner stopped him. This claim would have explained the license application in Faulkner's pocket. It also may explain the sudden decision by Faulkner to call for back-up if he realized that two people were in the vehicle he was stopping. But the jury never heard this information either. Instead they were assured by the prosecutor that there were only three people present during the shooting: Billy Cook, Officer Faulkner, and Abu-Jamal. One reason the jury never heard about the possibility of Freeman's having been at the scene is that the police and prosecution never disclosed their initial suspicions concerning the significance of the pocketed license application. Another reason is that Billy Cook, who at the time was himself charged with felony assault of Officer Faulkner, had been advised by attorney Alva not to testify at his brother's murder trial, lest he be charged as an accomplice.

Questioning Freeman could have shed a great deal of light on the case. But he too died later, under suspicious circumstances. On May 13, 1985, a police helicopter bombed the communal home of a back-to-nature group called MOVE, in the process burning down an entire neighborhood and killing a number of women and children trapped by police gunfire inside the house. On that same day, police allegedly found Freeman, a Wharton School alumnus, naked and bound in a vacant lot, allegedly dead of an overdose of drugs.

Despite real questions, including those of police investigators early on in the case, the jury went into deliberations on Abu-Jamal's fate convinced that there were only three people present when the shooting happened.

Other evidence also never made it to the jurors' ears, some for good reason. One source was a high-ranking police supervisor. Alfonzo Giordano was a former captain of the so-called civil defense unit of the Philadelphia Police, a "red squad" that for years had harassed the Black Panthers and other radical groups. Giordano, who certainly would have known of, and probably readily recognized Abu-Jamal, claimed that he had heard Abu-Jamal confess to the crime.

Giordano, a long-time favorite and confidante of former police chief and former mayor Frank Rizzo,[4] and an inspector in the Central Division police district at the time of the shooting, was on the scene within minutes. He claimed in initial police investigative reports that he opened the doors to the police wagon where Abu-Jamal had been placed, in order to look at the suspect. While checking him out, he says he noticed an empty shoulder holster and asked where the gun was.

> As I stepped into the wagon, I had to turn around so that I could get over the defendant, and I reached down and pulled his jacket open.
> As I did, my right hand touched the shoulder holster which was under the left armpit, and my left hand felt something wet over on the right side.
> As I pulled my hand out, I noticed there was blood on it. I asked him if he had been hurt. He did not respond. I asked him at least one other time if he had been injured. He did not respond.
> Then I asked him where the gun was that went in the holster, and he stated that he dropped the gun beside a car after he shot him.[5]

That claim, that Abu-Jamal had inadvertently acknowledged shooting Faulkner, was leaked immediately to the local media, fanning the flames of anger in the city's white community. As *Philadelphia Bulletin* columnist Adrian Lee wrote scarcely a week after the shooting:

> The reported admission is exceedingly brief. It doesn't go to

the question of motive still puzzling Homicide. But it is quite clear and it would seem to dispel any doubts, manufactured or otherwise, left by the ballisticians' initial finding that the shattered slug in Faulkner's head was so "deformed" that it couldn't be matched up with alleged killer Abu-Jamal's snub-nosed .38.

The report: "He (Abu-Jamal) admitted shooting the police officer in a brief comment to Police Inspector Giordano," of Night Command, the senior officer on duty at the time.[6]

But Giordano's report of a confession never did make it into the courtroom. Within days of his testimony at a pretrial hearing, Giordano voluntarily resigned from the department, having learned that he was under investigation for bribery and extortion by the U.S. Justice Department. Several years later, he pleaded guilty to federal charges of tax evasion relating to $55,000 in income. The federal prosecutor explained that this referred to income earned from extortion during the years 1979 and 1980.[7] His corrupt activities predate the Faulkner shooting.

But another report of a confession that has become a central piece in the case eclipsed the police wagon confession. Several police officers and a hospital security guard claimed that Abu-Jamal shouted out, not once but twice in the hospital: "I shot the motherfucker and I hope the motherfucker dies!"

It was a bloodthirsty statement, allegedly shouted only a few feet away from where doctors were still frantically working on the body of Daniel Faulkner in a futile attempt to save him. But there are problems with this reported confession as well. Despite the witnesses all being trained in law enforcement, this confession was not reported to investigators for more than two months following the shooting.

The fact that these witnesses somehow forgot their training and failed to report the confession for months is made all the more remarkable by events and statements made at the time. I interviewed Dr. Anthony Coletta, the emergency room physician attending Faulkner nearby. He stated categorically that Abu-Jamal, about to go into shock from blood loss and internal bleeding, and with his lungs filled with blood, would not have had an easy time shouting out anything. The confession, at least in the manner proclaimed, while possible, was not likely from a medical standpoint, he insists. More importantly, he says that though he was in the vicinity of Abu-Jamal at all times, he heard nothing. "I can't say what happened outside the emergency room, but from the moment he came through the hospital door into the emergency room, I was with him, and he said nothing," says Coletta.

Another piece of evidence at variance with later accounts of the confession comes from one of the officers who claimed, two months late, in February, 1982, to have heard the "blurt-out" hospital confession. Police Officer Gary Wakshul had ridden with the suspect in the van to the hospital and then stayed with him until he was operated on to remove the bullet from his back. Wakshul wrote later in his official report on that night, "The negro suspect made no comment." On several subsequent occasions when asked by police investigators whether there was anything else he could recall about his time with the suspect, he replied with an unambiguous "no." Judge Sabo prevented the jury from hearing about Wakshul and his written reports. Thirteen years after the trial, at a Post-Conviction Relief Act hearing, the defense did point out that the veracity of the confession was challenged by Wakshul's written report. Yet Judge Sabo ruled that the omission and the belated recall was reasonable, given how shaken the officer may have been after the fall of a brother officer.

Perhaps. Except a second officer suffered an identical memory lapse followed by a similarly miraculous recall. Officer Garry Bell, a close friend of Faulkner's, had been with Abu-Jamal in the hospital entrance. His December 16, 1981 witness statement to police investigators concurred with Wakshul's notes, making no mention of a "confession." Then, two months later, he recalled hearing what can only be described as a startling and, one might say, "unforgettably" damning confession.

Despite the alleged "blurt out" supposedly occurring while Abu-Jamal was surrounded by uniformed cops, the first inkling prosecutors claim they had that Abu-Jamal confessed at that time came in early February 1982, two months after the shooting. A round-table meeting of officers who had been with Abu-Jamal during his trip to the hospital and assistant district attorney McGill had been called following a brutality complaint filed by Abu-Jamal. He had charged that police had savagely beaten him during his arrest.

McGill asked the assembled cops, did any of you hear Abu-Jamal say anything? In earlier questioning by investigators from the police department's office of internal affairs or when initially questioned by detectives as witnesses in the case, none reported any such confession. This time McGill got a different answer. Hands went up. Two officers repeated the same overheard confession, word for word. Later, when Wakshul was testifying as a defense witness during Abu-Jamal's PCRA hearing in 1995, Dan Williams had him read a statement he had made 64 days after the shooting to a police internal affairs investigator. Asked why he had waited two months to report hearing a confession, he had told the investigator "I didn't realize it had any importance until today."[8] Such an assertion by a trained law enforcement officer is so ludicrous that it fails to pass a laugh test. The second cop, Bell, claimed that he had been so distraught by the shooting that he forgot to mention the confession. As a retired police detective from another urban police department, who requested anonymity, commented about these excuses, "This sounds to me like a classic case of manufacturing evidence to convict someone. If there is one thing that every police officer learns in training, it's that a blurt-out confession is gold. And as for being in shock at the killing of a fellow officer, a blurt-out confession by the killer is the one thing that would jolt you out of any kind of shock."

But before we jump to conspiracy theories, the prosecution produced another witness, who was not a cop, yet who also claimed to have heard the same confession. Jefferson Hospital security guard Priscilla Durham reported having heard the confession when questioned by internal affairs investigators in February, 1982. But then, while on the stand at the trial in June, during cross-examination, she testified that she had reported the confession a day after it allegedly occurred, not to police but to her supervisor. Durham testified that the supervisor wrote down her report on a sheet of paper, but said that neither she nor her supervisor brought that information to the attention of police. That written document she described was never produced in court. Nor, curiously, was the supervisor, who has subsequently died of natural causes. Instead, the prosecutor, who immediately after her surprise testimony sent an officer over to the hospital, presented the court with a typed version of the alleged report. Durham herself disavowed the paper, insisting that her statement had been written, not typed. The defense protested that there was no establishment of authorship and authenticity. Nonetheless, Judge Sabo allowed the prosecution to include that typed sheet as evidence because Durham claimed it was like what she had written. It was, he ruled, for the jury to decide whether it constituted a valid piece of evidence.

Durham meanwhile, wasn't quite as unassociated with the police as it first appeared. At the time of the shooting, it was later determined, she knew not only several of the arresting police personnel but also Faulkner and his partner, both of whom she concedes she had had coffee with on occasion.[9]

McGill, in an interview, told me that the matter of the authenticity of the typed statement is a "red herring." He, like Judge Sabo, insists that it was fair to let the jury decide on its validity.

Returning to the officer who wrote that Abu-Jamal made no comment and then months later reported hearing the confession, Judge Sabo denied the defense the opportunity to call Wakshul to the stand. His testimony could have raised doubts about the confession, since he would have had to explain the contradiction between his early statements to investigators and his delayed "recollection." Sabo instead accepted the prosecution's assertion that Wakshul was "on vacation" and "out of town." He then denied a defense motion to delay the trial for a few days until Wakshul could be brought in to testify. Wakshul did finally testify in the 1995 post-conviction hearing. At that time, it emerged that during the trial in 1982, he had indeed been on vacation. But, crucially, he had stayed in town during the trial, on instructions, waiting at home in case he might be called to testify.

Suppose the jury had been presented with the conflict between Wakshul's written statement the day of the shooting that "the negro male made no comment," and his two-months-later claim that Abu-Jamal had shouted out "I shot the motherfucker and I hope the motherfucker dies." Might at least one member of the panel have rejected the damning confession? As it was, they were left with the unauthenticated typed report of a confession, uncontested by other evidence or testimony.

If the prosecution's story seems full of problems, the alternative scenarios offered up by the defense are also problematic.

The most common argument made by those calling for Abu-Jamal's execution, and echoed by many skeptical observers of this case, is that for 20 years, neither he nor his brother ever told their side of the story about what happened that morning back in December 1981. Abu-Jamal did insist from the beginning that he was innocent of the charges, but it is true that until 2001, nearly 20 years after the shooting, he never gave an account in public—or even in private to his various attorneys—as to what actually happened. (He did finally give a brief account in a declaration filed in 2001 while a federal judge was considering his federal *habeas* petition. But, as we will see in Chapter 9, he says only that he was shot by a policeman while crossing the street to aid his brother, and then lost consciousness.) But accusing Abu-Jamal of not talking about what happened—which even some writers on the left have done—is unfair. Defendants in this type of case only very rarely take the stand and give a statement. Most are specifically advised by their attorneys not to do so. Once they have testified, the prosecution is free to question them, and it is easy for a clever prosecutor to maneuver the defendant into a position where she or he has to plead the Fifth Amendment against self-incrimination. That can be as devastating as a confession in the mind of a juror. So Abu-Jamal's refusal to take the stand during his trial cannot and should not be held against him. Some, including his one-time appellate attorneys Leonard Weinglass and Daniel Williams, have argued that he should have told his story outside a courtroom, to a sympathetic journalist, but even that can pose legal risks, other experienced defense lawyers say.

At the trial, Abu-Jamal's attorney, Anthony Jackson, tried to highlight statements by some witnesses, made to police during questioning following the shooting, which suggested that one or even two people had been seen running from the scene immediately following the shooting. As mentioned, one of those who at least initially told police the shooter had run was taxi driver Chobert, though on the stand, he backed off that claim. There are enough claims of someone having run off by a variety of witnesses, some of them highly credible (Dessie Hightower, for example), that it does seem likely that someone did flee the scene. But there are also problems with the theory that someone other than Abu-Jamal shot the officer.

Firstly, and most importantly, there is the question of why neither Abu-Jamal nor his brother Billy Cook immediately pointed the finger at another shooter—perhaps Freeman according to one popular theory among Abu-Jamal supporters. (Brother Billy Cook apparently didn't even try to tell police it was someone else while police were beating and arresting his injured brother.) While Freeman, a close friend, was alive, it might be argued, albeit rather improbably, that both the Cook brothers were loyally protecting him, even at the risk of Abu-Jamal's possible wrongful execution. But once Freeman was dead in 1985, there would have been no reason not to finger him as the killer and to explain exactly how it happened—something the defense is only doing now, more than 20 years after the trial.

Similarly, if it had been some other person, unknown to either Abu-Jamal or Cook, who had done the deed (as the defense is now also claiming, 20 years later), why wouldn't either man have said so back then? In 2001, Abu-Jamal's lawyers produced an affidavit signed by a man, Arnold Beverly, who claimed that he, and an unnamed second man, had killed Faulkner as part of a "hit" organized by corrupt police who thought Faulkner was going to rat on them to the FBI. This claim is discussed at length in Chapter 9. Suffice it to say at this point that if this claim is correct, why wouldn't Abu-Jamal, and his brother, who certainly would have seen the whole thing, have reported it to police right away? Billy Cook, when police arrived, reportedly said, "I had nothing to do with it,"[10] not, "The guy who did this ran off into the subway entrance."

This issue of Abu-Jamal's reluctance to talk becomes harder to explain in light of more recent actions. In 2001, two decades after the incident, both he and his brother filed sworn affidavits suggesting that he is wholly innocent and that someone else, or perhaps two or more other people, possibly including Freeman, were the killers. Why didn't they make those claims earlier?

Indeed Cook, in his affidavit, while saying that he didn't actually see the shooting, does claim that later on Freeman told him he had been part of a conspiracy to kill Faulkner. If Cook is willing today to suggest that his former partner may have been the shooter, why wasn't he willing to say it in 1982, when his brother was facing a first-degree murder charge? Or in 1985, after Freeman was dead. Or in 1995, at his brother's post-conviction relief act hearing, when his execution date was at one point only ten days away? Moreover, his statement about Freeman seems extremely far-fetched. It's one thing to suggest that in the heat of the moment, Freeman or someone else might have shot Faulkner. It's another to say that it was a planned execution. How could Freeman have known Faulkner would stop Cook's car? How could he have known it would stop on Locust between 13th and 12th Streets? How could he have known whether Faulkner would be alone? How could he have known whether he would be frisked before he had a chance to pull his weapon?

Cook's attorney, Alva, explains his client's reticence about coming forward saying that Cook was scared, and with good reason, and that he initially had advised him not to talk. Back in 1982, he explains, Cook was afraid of being charged in the crime because of his fight with Faulkner, and indeed he was ultimately convicted of assaulting Faulkner and sentenced to six months in jail. Later, Alva says Cook quite understandably feared harassment or even death, following the torching of his street stand in early 1982 and later the mysterious death of his partner Freeman, not to mention the record of police harassment of witnesses who came out in support of Abu-Jamal. "He once told me he was confident that his brother, who had the support of all those movie stars and famous people, would escape death row," Alva told me. "Then he asked, `If I get on the stand and say what I saw happen, who's going to come to my defense?'"

That said, Cook loved his brother Abu-Jamal—a man who took care of him after their father's untimely death, and whom he so admired that he sometimes adopted his birth name, Wesley, after Abu-Jamal chose a more African name. It strains credulity to imagine that Cook would have allowed Abu-Jamal to suffer through the setting of two execution dates, and to exist for 20 years in the living hell of a super-max penitentiary death row, if he had information that could have helped save him.

Abu-Jamal and a team of attorneys he hired in the spring of 2001 are now making a new claim. It is itself as fraught with problems as the original scenario put forth by the prosecution. A sworn affidavit was filed at that time with the federal court in Philadelphia which was considering Abu-Jamal's *habeas corpus* petition by Beverly, a 51-year-old African American with a long criminal record. Beverly claims that in 1981, corrupt Philadelphia police hired him as a known mob hit man. Faulkner, the story goes, was suspected by his colleagues of ratting on them to the FBI, which at the time was investigating corruption in the district. So Beverly was given the job of killing Faulkner.

Beverly says that on that morning in December 1981, he arranged to be in the area, and that when Faulkner, during a stop of Cook's vehicle, was shot by "another guy," he stepped in and administered the *coup de gras*. Beverly also claims that Abu-Jamal was shot crossing the street not by Faulkner but by another unidentified police officer. Beverly says that as police cars began to converge on the scene, he, as previously arranged, ran into the subway entrance and down the tunnel. There he was met by another policeman who then drove him to safety. As Beverly states:

> I heard a shot ring out coming from east on Locust Street. Faulkner fell on his knee on the sidewalk next to the VW. I heard another shot and it must have grazed my left shoulder. I felt something hard on my left shoulder. I grabbed my shoulder and got blood on my hand.
>
> I ran across Locust Street and stood over Faulkner, who had fallen backwards on the sidewalk. I shot Faulkner in the face at close range. Jamal was shot shortly after that by a uniformed police officer that arrived on the scene.
>
> Cop cars came from all directions. Foot patrol also arrived. I saw a white shirt getting out of a car in the middle of the 13th and Locust intersection just as I was going to the speedline [subway] steps.
>
> I left the area underground through the speedline system and by prearrangement met a police officer who assisted me when I exited the speedline underground about three blocks away. A car was

waiting for me and I left the Center City area.[11]

Abu-Jamal attorney and investigator Rachel Wolkenstein discovered this witness in 1992, though Wolkenstein claims he didn't actually confess to having been the shooter until 1999. Following this new account, Abu-Jamal now claims that he was shot in the street after Faulkner had already been slain.

There are a number of problems with this mob hit-man scenario. First, as mentioned above regarding Cook's claim about Freeman, how did an allegedly premeditated murder come to take place during a chance traffic stop? Mob assassinations are often carefully planned and carried out, and this seems an unlikely set of circumstances for a hit man to use. This plot, in order to work, required having Faulkner turn onto Locust. Yet he did so not out of predictable routine but by chance as he followed Cook. But to complicate matters further, Faulkner, a little earlier in the evening, had stopped another man, Albert Magilton (later a prosecution witness to the shooting), whom he apparently suspected of planning to break into a car. Had Faulkner made an arrest at that time, he never would have even made it to Locust Street to stop Billy Cook. He would have been at Sixth Precinct headquarters booking somebody. There were, in other words, too many variables in Faulkner's free-form tour of duty, for the scenario as described by Beverly to have worked. Anyway, why would Beverly, already wounded himself by a gunshot, risk delivering a fatal blow to a wounded target when none might be needed? (It wasn't as if someone was monitoring his performance to determine whether he would get paid, and Faulkner was already shot, and for all he knew, dying.) Finally, it seems extremely unlikely that a group of corrupt police would choose to execute a colleague in a busy locale where any number of witnesses would be on hand to see and report on what happened. It also seems improbable that they would involve so many people in the carrying out of such a heinous plot. Police have killed their own. And there are a couple of cases of Philadelphia police officers who were talking to federal prosecutors being subsequently shot and killed. But the standard modus operandi for police executions has been for them to occur in a dark part of a park or alleyway, out of view of anyone—often with the officer's own gun used so as to make it look like a suicide.

Beverly's story strains credulity further because of the tale of his escape. Why would such a craven group of corrupt cops, having succeeded in hiring a lowlife mob hit man to rub out one of their own, actually help him to escape, leaving him alive to eventually tell his story? How much easier, once he was in the subway tunnel, to have shot him, leaving investigators with a nicely tied up tale of a cop killed by a mobster, who was then killed by his own people. End of story. Beverly, who has multiple convictions, reportedly also has a history of mental problems, which would tend to make his testimony further suspect.

Abu-Jamal, in his affidavit, actually offers little new information. He claims he was filling out his taxi log after letting off a fare when he heard shots. Looking up from his work, he says he saw his brother staggering around. He says he began running across the street, and at that point claims he was shot, after which he recalls falling in and out of consciousness until he was awakened by an assault by arresting police officers.

The difficulty with his account, spare as it is, is that most of the witnesses in the case say that they saw Abu-Jamal, or someone in any event, running across the street *before* the shooting began. Abu-Jamal claims he heard "what sounded like gun shots," *prior* to his getting out of his cab. The account leaves him some wiggle room. The common disorientation and general fogginess of memory of those who suffer a physical trauma might explain the discrepancy in the sequence of events. Abu-Jamal, who at a minimum had his head slammed into a light pole by police during his arrest[12] and who also suffered major blood loss from his shooting injury, surely had plenty of trauma. Plus he says he heard not shots, but what sounded like shots, so he could presumably say later that maybe they were backfires or something. But the reversal of order between the shooting and the crossing of the street still casts a shadow on the credibility of his account.

Where then, does that leave us?

Both sides in this intensely scrutinized and debated case, which has become a focus of international attention and emblematic of the struggle over America's growing reliance on the death penalty, have resorted to exaggeration and falsification of the facts.

On the pro-execution side, groups such as the Fraternal Order of Police (FOP, a trade union and lobbying organization which represents Philadelphia police) and Justice for Police Officer Daniel Faulkner claim that Abu-Jamal was never really a critic of the police as a journalist. This is an important issue: they are trying to challenge the defense contention that the police and district attorney had reason to want to "get" Abu-Jamal.

In fact, however, it is undeniable that the former Philadelphia Black Panther Party chapter's minister of information long harbored a suspicion that police were a threat to minorities, and that, moreover, he reported on their abusive treatment of the mostly black members of the MOVE organization. There have been other lies, too. Even Faulkner's widow, Maureen, has made a false claim: that Abu-Jamal smiled when her late husband's bloody shirt was shown in court. Not possible: court transcripts show that at the time of that presentation, Abu-Jamal had been ejected from the courtroom.

On the pro-Abu-Jamal side, many supporters have continued to insist that the bullet removed from Faulkner's brain was a .44 caliber, not a .38 caliber. This is important because Abu-Jamal's gun, legally registered to him and discovered at the scene, was a .38. It's easy to see why the defense made this claim: a notation by the medical examiner who removed the projectile from Faulkner's body stated in his report that it was a .44 caliber bullet. But that is the only such evidence. In fact, in 1995, the defense's own ballistics expert George Fassnacht testified that the slug recovered from Faulkner's head appeared to be a .38. Whether that bullet—or the one that was fired into Faulkner's back—came from the gun registered to Abu-Jamal was never established. But the fact remains: it is simply untrue to say it was a .44 caliber. slug.

There is real significance to the medical examiner's misidentification that could be useful to the defense, however. It's not that it proves the slug was not from Abu-Jamal's gun. Rather, it is that Abu-Jamal's lawyer, Jackson, failed to notice the notation at the time, and never attempted to bring it to the jury's attention. Had he done so during the 1982 trial, it might have raised a reasonable doubt in their minds. The defense team, in support of Abu-Jamal's federal *habeas* claim that Jackson's representation of Abu-Jamal was incompetent, cited this oversight.

Abu-Jamal's supporters also continue to describe Jackson as a court-appointed attorney, implying that he was forced on the defendant. In fact, Jackson was introduced to Abu-Jamal following his arrest by friends who knew him as a skilled solicitor with a history of challenging the police in brutality cases, and he was initially hired by Abu-Jamal's family with the defendant's approval. He was court-appointed because Abu-Jamal was an indigent defendant and needed the court to pay his lawyer's bills, but he certainly wasn't forced on him initially. The problem was that as the trial date approached during the spring of 1982, it became clear to both Abu-Jamal and his attorney that Jackson was not up to the task of defending the case. But at that point the court would not allow Jackson to quit or Abu-Jamal to fire him.

Some Abu-Jamal supporters, including his new appellate attorneys, have also continued to make the same false claim—even in a petition to the Common Pleas Judge Patricia Dembe in 2001. Namely, that a biased white juror named Edward Courchain, who replaced a black juror removed by Judge Sabo early in the trial, became the jury foreman. Courchain did not become foreman, however; just a regular member of the jury.

Even Amnesty International, in its investigation and report on this case, made the error of claiming that there was only one black person on the jury which convicted and sentenced Abu-Jamal, when in fact there were two.

Shearing away these and other innuendo and misstatements of fact by both sides, serious doubts about the prosecution's claims concerning what took place on December 9, 1981 remain. Yet it is on that version of events that the justification for meting out the death penalty rests. The shaky nature of the prosecution's scenario is good reason to challenge both the sentence of death, which Abu-Jamal has been facing for 20 years, and the conviction for first degree murder which gave rise to the sentence.

As of this writing, Abu-Jamal sits in the same death row cell, his death sentence at least temporarily lifted by District Judge William Yohn, but his conviction upheld. He is now awaiting a decision from the Third Circuit Court of Appeals on dual appeals of Judge Yohn's decision on his *habeas* petition, one by him and one by the Philadelphia district attorney. How did the process, with the conviction on such shaky ground, get to this stage? A close look at the original trial, the series of appeals and the background of this case is revealing. These include three key elements in the unfolding of events. There is the politics of the city in which he grew up and began working as a progressive journalist. Second is the police department in Philadelphia, which, it will become clear, was rife with corruption, maintained a secretive "red squad," and possessed a long record of attacks on black people. Lastly is Abu-Jamal himself from his development as a young kid in the projects to a prominent and promising, if controversial, figure in the city's journalism world.

Any real understanding also requires a look at the way Abu-Jamal has conducted his own defense. He faced Judge Albert Sabo. During his tenure, Sabo was one of the most pro-death penalty jurists on the bench in America with, at the time of his retirement, the greatest number of death sentences of any sitting jurist in the country. He had sentenced 31 to death;

29 of them were non-white. He was an undeniable friend of the prosecution. As will become clear, the trial can be seen only as a travesty of justice. Yet Abu-Jamal is to some extent—as his nemesis, prosecutor McGill, puts it—also "the architect of his own destruction." His sometimes combative and often disrespectful behavior during the initial trial, his troubled relationship with his problematic attorney, Anthony Jackson, and his later handling of conflicts within the Free Mumia support movement, were all contributing factors. But what may prove to have been one of his most self-defeating moves came in 2001 with his decision to fire his prominent progressive defense attorney Leonard Weinglass, death penalty defense expert Daniel Williams, and the team assembled around them. He replaced them with two untested lawyers with virtually no experience in death penalty litigation.

Indeed, Abu-Jamal seems to have demonstrated remarkably bad judgement—or bad luck—in his choice of lawyers, and in his decision to accept their often ill-conceived advice. He started out by selecting an inexperienced lawyer, Jackson, to try his case. His first appellate lawyer, Lesley Gelb, was less than stellar. He got bad advice from attorney Rachel Wolkenstein, who in 1999 first urged him to adopt the Beverly strategy. He got bad advice from Marlene Kamish, who urged him to fire Weinglass as well as Williams over the publication of Williams' book, and he got bad advice from Kamish and Eliot Grossman, who apparently convinced him that Beverly would somehow shake loose his stalled case. It did, but what it shook loose was much of his support and his financial backing.

Many have come to see Abu-Jamal's well-crafted commentaries and writings as searing reports from a judicial wilderness. How did such a thoughtful, insightful person come to make what appear to be such grievous moves in his own defense? How did a journalist who seems to have an excellent ability to read people in his professional life, make so many poor judgements about the people he hired to defend him? These are questions still begging answers.

There are no winners in this wreckage.

Faulkner, by all accounts an excellent and honest cop and loving husband, is dead, leaving a young life wasted and a family bereft.

Abu-Jamal—son, brother, father and grandfather—cannot even touch his progeny through the heavy panes of Plexiglas of the gratuitously over-secure visiting room reserved for death-row inmates at the SCI-Green supermax prison near Waynesboro, Pennsylvania, where he is incarcerated. Having had to face an appointment with a fatal needle twice, and having been locked down every day in a solitary 8'-by-12' windowless cell for the past 20 years, he has already paid a heavier price than have many convicted murderers. Yet in that time he has managed to write an immense number of probing and disturbing essays on the sadistic netherworld of America's burgeoning prison gulag, as well as remarkably informed essays on national and global issues and events.

Abu-Jamal's original attorney, Anthony Jackson, a once promising progressive black lawyer, was "destroyed" by the case, according to former associates, who say he turned to heavy drinking and other intoxicants, leading to his disbarment in 1990, officially for financial irregularities involving the handling of clients' funds.

Among his subsequent attorneys, Leonard Weinglass and Dan Williams have been viciously attacked (by Abu-Jamal, his supporters, and his current defense team) as craven money grubbers and charlatans. Weinglass because of his legal fees and the money he earned from speaker's fees talking about the case at university campuses and other venues (although this is actually the traditional way "movement" lawyers have earned their keep while defending clients with limited resources). And Williams because of a controversial book about the case he published in 2001 (*Executing Justice: An Inside Account of the Case of Mumia Abu-Jamal*, St. Martin's Press).

Witnesses who have dared to come forward after the trial to support Abu-Jamal have been harassed or had their reputations sullied by the prosecution. Consider Veronica Jones, a former prostitute who was arrested right in Judge Sabo's courtroom in 1995. She testified then that back in 1982 police had tried to bribe her to say she'd seen Abu-Jamal shoot Faulkner. Immediately, the prosecution invited officers from New Jersey to arrest and jail her (with Judge Sabo's acquiescence) right off the stand for missing a court date on a minor check-kiting charge. Or consider Dessie Hightower, a witness who claimed he saw someone flee the shooting scene and who, after voluntarily coming forward with his story, was forced to spend six hours being interrogated at police headquarters, and to take a police lie-detector test. No other witness faced this test. Later, prosecutor McGill publicly outed Hightower as a transvestite,[13] a pure act of intimidation or retribution, since, true or not, this information had absolutely no bearing on the credibility of Hightower's testimony.

Even former prosecutor McGill himself, though he had the satisfaction of winning a high-profile case, was left unable to give out his home address to strangers and now feels, as an attorney in private practice, that he has to privately vet reporters before he can even talk with them. A congenial man who bears an uncanny resemblance to the jovial traveling patent medicine man in The Wizard of Oz, he grumbles that he cannot vacation in Europe because his role in this case has made him an international pariah there.

Abu-Jamal supporters like dedicated progressive activist Jane Henderson of the Quixote Center have been publicly accused by Abu-Jamal and his other more ardent backers of financial improprieties. Journalists, myself included, who have sought to look open-eyed at the case without presupposing Abu-Jamal to be a wholly innocent saint or prophet, have been slandered. (My appellation of record among Abu-Jamal's MOVE supporters: 'Mumia pimp'.)

In the end, the big loser has been justice. However one weighs the various contradictions detailed above, there is no way to claim that Abu-Jamal received a fair trial—or a fair appeal either—in the state court system of Pennsylvania. Consider the relative strengths of each side. The Philadelphia District Attorney's Office assigned one of its star prosecutors, a man who has won almost every jury trial he has served as an attorney in (all but three of about 150 by his own estimate), and who had multiple death penalty murder convictions under his belt. At his disposal were the investigatory resources of one of the nation's largest police forces and prosecutorial agencies. Defending Abu-Jamal in this life-and-death matter was Anthony Jackson. A young attorney who had never been the lead counsel in a death-penalty case, who had just begun his private practice, he was provided with at most only a few thousand dollars by the court and private sources to hire expert witnesses and investigators. Worse, he had a reputation in the Philadelphia legal community at the time for drinking and possibly using cocaine. 'I wouldn't have hired Jackson to handle a parking violation,' says one prominent Philadelphia barrister. To his credit, Jackson realized he was in over his head and, after being denied his request for a second attorney to assist him, unsuccessfully tried to get the judge to release him from the obligation of defending Abu-Jamal.

It would be an incomplete description of the relative strength of the opposing sides without noting that the jurist Abu-Jamal faced, Albert Sabo, was widely viewed in the Philadelphia bar and even within the prosecutor's office, as a friend of the prosecutor. "When you got Sabo, you essentially had a second prosecutor on the bench," opines Jack McMahon, a former assistant district attorney from the homicide department, where back in 1981 he was a colleague of McGill's.

As if the scales of justice weren't tipped enough, Abu-Jamal had more legal and political guns arrayed against him. The Fraternal Order of Police took a vociferous and pro-conviction stance early on in the case, and went on to lobby for his execution. While it did not have a formal role to play in the trial, its presence has been enormous. Judge Sabo, a sheriff before he became a judge, had for 16 years been a member of the organization. More important was the organization's power at the ballot box. At the appellate level as well as at the trial level judges in Pennsylvania are subject to election and periodic reelection. For the most part, those who win are the favored candidates of the FOP. Even at the state supreme court—one of only a handful of such top state benches where justices must face regular election contests—Abu-Jamal had to have his appeals issues considered by five FOP-endorsed judges (a majority of the panel). Even more outrageous, the appeals were considered by a Supreme Court that included Justice Ronald Castille. In addition to any electoral pressure he might have felt from the FOP, Castille had been district attorney at the time it was contesting Abu-Jamal's initial appeal to the state's high court. Nonetheless, he declined to recuse himself from consideration of Abu-Jamal's appeal, and voted to reject it.

Certainly it is true that that some of the mistakes at the original trial were made by Abu-Jamal himself. Consider his decision to offer up a political diatribe as his final statement to the jury mulling his fate without even submitting it to his attorney for prior vetting. This constituted a disastrous legal error and a gross misreading of the psychology and politics of the jurors. So too, almost certainly, was his decision to try and represent himself at the trial. Capital cases are not just complicated. A defendant must build a solid record on which to base any appeal, including attempting to get the prosecution to make errors that can later be used to overturn a conviction. With the defendant's life on the line, this is hardly a task for a novice. If inexperienced lawyers shouldn't try it, even less should an untrained defendant make the attempt. Right from the outset, this decision led to his wasting some critical peremptory juror challenges. Indirectly, it also led to his being absent for much of his own trial (because Sabo frequently threw Abu-Jamal out of the courtroom—mostly for asserting his right to act as his own attorney after Sabo had denied it). When the judge ordered Jackson, against Abu-Jamal's and the lawyer's own wishes, to resume the role of lead attorney, Abu-Jamal certainly hurt his case by viciously attacking, undermining, and at times refusing to cooperate with his own lawyer. A lawyer who was already handicapped by not having been preparing to serve as lead attorney. Yet even if Abu-Jamal and his various attorneys, from Jackson to his current team of Marlene Kamish and Eliot Grossman, have made legal errors, technical or judgmental, this hardly seems reason to justify his execution, or even his imprisonment for life.

When all is said and done concerning this troubling case, Abu-Jamal remains a compelling figure—an obviously brilliant, charismatic and politically committed man who has bravely survived the unrelenting assault of a prison system designed to crush its victims. A man who has so far outlived a legal and political death machine hell-bent on his destruction (including outliving the judge who handled his case, Albert Sabo, who died in May 2002).

Whatever happened on December 9, 1981, I hope the following chapters make clear that this case cries out for retrial. A trial in which the forces on both sides are far more fairly balanced in expertise and resources, and over which presides a judge who holds justice as a conviction, not a conviction as justice.

Chapter Two

"Get Their Black Asses!"
Rizzo's Boys
and a Culture of Police Spying and Brutality

Alfonzo Giordano, Gary Wakshul, Edward Quinn, Thomas Ryan, Louis Maier, Joseph C. Gioffre, Richard Herron, Bernard Small, James Carlini, John DeBenedetto, Joseph DePerri, James Martin, Andrew Kelly, Joseph Alvaro, Abe Schwartz, John Smith and Leo Ryan have three things in common: all were Philadelphia policemen with careers ranging from a lifetime to as few as five years. All played roles in the arrest or investigation of Mumia Abu-Jamal following the shooting death of Police Officer Daniel Faulkner. And all were disciplined, indicted for crimes, found guilty of committing acts of corruption or brutality, or resigned from the department under a cloud of suspicion after being named by corrupt officers. Such acts extended to the manufacturing of evidence designed to frame suspects. Many of these acts occurred prior to Faulkner's shooting, meaning that by the time of their involvement with the Abu-Jamal case, some were already corrupt.

Corruption problems with the Philadelphia Police Department are well documented and pervasive, and it might seem unavoidable that a few bad apples would end up playing a role in Abu-Jamal's case. But in the entire course of the arrest and trial of Abu-Jamal, only 35 police officers' names get mentioned. Nearly a third of them were members of this rogues' gallery. Many more, whose names may not have come up in Abu-Jamal's case, played key roles in the investigation of his case, as they were higher-ups in the department's Homicide division or were in charge of major investigations for the department. Indeed, in the late 1970s and early 1980s, the entire chain of command of both Homicide and Vice were being investigated by the FBI. These were the very units that were investigating Abu-Jamal's case. Vice officers, because the nature of their work had them concentrated around the Center City "red light" district that included Locust and 13th streets, were heavily involved in his arrest. Moreover, many lower ranking officers who were corrupt ended up not being charged with crimes because they had turned state's evidence and were providing evidence to the FBI against senior officers. A total of 13 street-level cops were government witnesses in the corruption case.[1] Many corrupt officers were also never indicted, despite testimony that they were corrupt, because the U.S. Justice Department didn't feel it had enough evidence to convict them.

What does it mean when that many morally and ethically challenged individuals—most of them working within the same chain of command within one police district—are involved in the same criminal case? When, in the case of Deputy Police Commissioner James Martin, they were overseeing that entire department? Possibly nothing. But what are the odds that such a high percentage of crooked or vicious cops—over a third—would coincidentally be working on the same case? Perhaps the entire police department in Philadelphia has the same percentage of crooks, sadists and ethically deficient individuals, making these statistics a plausible random distribution of corruption. But even in Philadelphia's notoriously corrupt department this seems unlikely, and the number should raise a few eyebrows. It is almost as if, like flies to honey, corrupt cops were attracted to the case (perhaps looking for ways to win points by helping to convict the defendant). Whatever those odds, a far more serious issue arises: the jury deciding Abu-Jamal's fate never heard about it. What does it mean when the jury weighing a defendant's life or death hears nothing about this corruption and brutality? Once again, possibly nothing. But jurors must judge the moral integrity of those testifying in order to properly weigh the validity of evidence presented. Arguably, when jurors lack such information, their resulting decisions are based on "facts" that may not have been honestly represented, or which weren't really facts at all. This is particularly true in a death penalty trial, where jurors, already narrowly selected from a pool of people which has been systematically purged of those opposed to the death penalty, tend to be more inclined to trust the word of authority figures and people in uniform.

In 1981, at the time of the killing of Officer Faulkner and the arrest of Abu-Jamal, the Philadelphia Police Department was without doubt one of the most corrupt and out-of-control big city law enforcement operations in the nation. Two years earlier, in August 1979, the U.S. Justice Department had sued the city. In an unprecedented move, it charged Mayor Frank Rizzo (who had been police commissioner prior to his election) and 18 top-ranking police officials beginning with the police commissioner, with condoning systematic police brutality—the first such charge against an entire police department in American history. The case was dropped in December 1979, not for lack of evidence, but on the grounds that this was outside the jurisdiction of the Department of Justice. But that was not the end of federal concern about a Philadelphia police department run amok. At the time of Faulkner's death, the U.S. Attorney's Office in Philadelphia, with the blessing of the U.S. Justice Department in Washington (then part of the ardently law-and-order Reagan administration), was again focussing on the Philadelphia police. This time with a probe of corruption in the Sixth Precinct and the entire Central Division. Again, this was the very jurisdiction where Faulkner's shooting took place. The new federal probe, which had not yet been made public but had become common knowledge out on the street and in the ranks of the police department, was to become the biggest police corruption case in the history of the nation. By 1982, the first indictments began to appear. Over the course of the next few years, more than 30 officers in the division were convicted, including a deputy commissioner, division commanders, district captains and a number of inspectors and lieutenants, as well as rank-and-file officers.

As previously mentioned, a third of the 35 police who played a role in Abu-Jamal's arrest and conviction were nailed by federal and city prosecutors as corrupt for incidents that preceded the shooting. Looked at another way, more than a third of those nabbed and punished in the Justice Department's 1980s dragnet were in some way involved in the prosecution of Abu-Jamal.

Consider the picture: the killing of a white police officer, allegedly by a young black man who was both a one-time Black Panther leader and, as well, an African-American journalist who dared to be critical of the police. The very juxtaposition of such a politically charged criminal case and a corrupt police department, is surely one of the single most suspicious aspects of the whole Abu-Jamal story. "Just visually, it's troubling," says Alan Yatvin, a Philadelphia attorney who specializes in civil rights and civil liberties law. "If cops were convicted of something, it should have been brought to the attention of the defense by a factfinder. They could have been motivated to do something in order to avoid conviction. It's always troubling when you have an environment where people in uniform feel that they can get away with lying, and the level of corruption that they had in Philadelphia in the 1980s and 1990s is staggering."

Covering the downtown Center City area of Philadelphia, the Central Division has always occupied a preeminent position in the city's law enforcement establishment. In this area where the most visible police presence is located, the Central Division protects City Hall, the state and federal courts and the city's main business interests (including nationally-known tourist attractions like the Liberty Bell and Independence Hall). For career climbers in the department, it is also an important stepping stone. The district, particularly in the 1960s, 1970s and 1980s, was also the scene of a lively vice trade, including prostitution, drug dealing and gambling—the kinds of illegal activities that spring up wherever the easy money is. It was the kind of place that is also the most conducive to corrupting good cops and attracting already corrupt ones, and it seems to have done just that—with a vengeance. In case after case, involving foot patrolmen, vice squad officers, elite highway patrol officers, sergeants, detectives, lieutenants, inspectors, captains and even top officers, federal prosecutors found extortion, witness and evidence tampering, payoffs, consorting with prostitutes, obstruction of justice and myriad other crimes being committed.

This was the place where Frank Rizzo, the anything-goes, self-described "Cisco Kid" of the Philadelphia Police Department, first made a name for himself as a bare-knuckled, crime-busting cop's cop, before going on to become first Philadelphia's police commissioner and then later the city's law-and-order mayor. A second-generation cop and high school dropout from the tough South Philadelphia Italian-American neighborhood, Rizzo worked his way up through the ranks to become police chief and mayor. He spent several crucial and formative years as head of the Center City police district. There, he reportedly took an almost perverse personal delight in joining in police raids of vice joints and gay coffeehouses, wielding the big baton that he kept on him even when dressed in a formal tuxedo. (He'd stick it in his cummerbund.)

It's never been proven that Rizzo was corrupt in the classic sense of being on the take. Rumors persisted that throughout his career as a cop on the beat, as a senior officer, and as chief of police, he always had an "understanding" with the Philadelphia mob. Namely, keep the violence and gang warfare out of his city, and the Cisco Kid would leave the mob's vice and gambling operations alone. And certainly, while there were few busts of Philly's mob during the Rizzo years, there was very little mob violence of the type that bloodied the streets in nearby Newark and New York City during a notorious series of "Long Hot Summers" in the late 1960s. Be that as it may, Rizzo certainly seemed to have no such understanding with the prostitutes of Center City, nor with the coffeehouses which catered to the city's gay and beat community. During his tenure, they were harassed mercilessly. Yet that never stopped rumors that Rizzo, the "family values" moralist, was propositioning prostitutes in the district.[2] In any case, he had no such understanding with the city's black population.

Rizzo's climb up the political ladder began in Center City in May, 1952 when then Commissioner Thomas J. Gibbons made him division captain. Rizzo immediately set out to bust the colorful late-night coffee shops that had sprung up catering to Philadelphia's alternative community of beatniks and homosexuals. Right from the start, he made it clear to his subordinates that legal niceties weren't necessary. As Rizzo biographer S.A. Paolantonio writes in his generally sympathetic book *Frank Rizzo: The Last Big Man in Big City America*, in a raid on one of these coffee houses, the Humoresque, Rizzo personally "twirled his blackjack inside the club to menace the patrons." Rizzo told owner Melvin Haifetz, "If you defy me, I'll hang you from a chandelier."[3] Rizzo's official raids were halted by court order. But that didn't stop Rizzo from going after the clubs in a less obvious manner. In one case, he stationed a dozen plainclothes officers outside a club called the Factory to scare off patrons. During those years, Rizzo gained the reputation out in the broader Philadelphia community as a tough guy willing to break heads—and rules—to fight crime. Within the city's 7,500-man police department, he was seen as a leader who defended his men whatever they did, and who expected them to be as tough as he was—and completely loyal. As Paolantonio writes:

> To many beat cops and highway patrolmen, the two elements of the force that Rizzo favored, the Big Man had become an object of worship. He stood up for what he thought was right and for his men—no matter what. "He was idolized," said Pete Evangelisti, a patrolman under Rizzo's command at 12th and Pine.[4]

Rizzo carried this Wild West attitude of cops being above the law over into his approach to policing the African-American community, for which he clearly harbored little affection. His attitude towards the city's growing population of African Americans was made abundantly clear in late 1967, when he was only several months into his new job as police commissioner.

On November 17, 1967, some 3,500 black highschool students marched on the city's board of education, demanding a program in black studies. Rizzo had already prepared to meet them with a veritable army of police. As the students demonstrated peacefully outside the school board building, the police, initially under the command of then Lt. George Fencl, stood by observing them, but taking no action. Then Rizzo arrived on the scene and immediately put the officers into offensive mode. Although no riot was in progress, Rizzo implemented "riot plan number three." Rizzo had his officers surround the students. He ordered a brutal charge with a shout recorded by television news cameras: "Get their black asses!" The ensuing police riot led to dozens of injuries, as both high school and junior high school students were clubbed, kicked, stomped and beaten by Rizzo's finest.

For many police and young blacks in Philadelphia, it was a decisive moment. A point at which certain lines were drawn. To Rizzo's boys, it was a message: under Chief Rizzo, anything goes when dealing with the city's blacks. And if Philadelphia's young African Americans didn't know it already, the message was equally clear: the police are out to get you.

Not long afterwards, in early 1969, the Black Panther Party set up shop in Philadelphia. This new national organization of militant African-Americans was dedicated to defending urban blacks against what the Panthers saw as a quasi-military police occupation of their communities. The Philadelphia chapter of the Panthers became a special target for the wrath and harassment of then Police Chief and later Mayor Frank Rizzo and his men in blue.

Rizzo had a special unit in place and ready to use for harassing the Panthers—the so-called Civil Defense Squad, or CD Squad (headed at the time by Lt. Fencl). Established in 1964 by Howard Leary, the police commissioner who served as Rizzo's liberal predecessor, the CD Squad was originally designed to help reduce conflict by dealing in a proactive way with the urban protests and demonstrations which were beginning to grow in size and frequency in Philadelphia and other major cities. But under Rizzo, who took over as acting commissioner in 1966 and officially became top cop in 1967, the CD Squad was quickly converted into something entirely different: an organization with an MO that included eavesdropping, phone tapping, using undercover agents, trumped up arrests and nighttime raids. It would soon become a model for President Richard Nixon's notorious COINTELPRO—a nationally coordinated campaign of spying, dossier collection, and domestic psy-war operations, as well as deliberate disruption, harassment, break-ins and possibly even murder (as in the case of the killing of Panther leader Fred Hampton), targeting radical and progressive organizations of all kinds.

As Frank Donner writes in *Protectors of Privilege*, a groundbreaking study of the various "red squads" that operated in the nation's largest cities during the 1960s and 1970s:

The evidence is quite clear that as early as the summer of 1967, the CD had access to a supply of informers, sponsored and paid by the Federal Bureau of Investigation. More important, collaboration between the FBI and the Philadelphia police in destructive counterintelligence initiatives against the Philadelphia black activists was used as a model for the bureau's aggressive intelligence program (COINTELPRO) in this sector, begun in August 1967 and expanded in February of the next year.[5]

That the CD—and the FBI's COINTELPRO program—had their eye on the Panthers and on the young Wesley Cook (who later became Mumia Abu-Jamal) very early on is clear and indisputable. As early as mid-1969, a memo from the Philadelphia bureau of the FBI to FBI headquarters in Washington, D.C. stated that there were plans to "follow and report" on his activities with the Black Panthers. It added:

> In spite of the subject's age (15 years), Philadelphia feels that his continued participation in BPP activities in the Philadelphia Division, his position in the Philadelphia Branch of the BPP, and his past inclination to appear and speak at public gatherings, the subject be included on the Security Index.[6] *

Listed as sources for the information in the memo are "informants" in both the "Civil Disobedience Unit" (later to be called the Civil Affairs Unit) and the "Intelligence Division" of the Philadelphia Police Department. This makes it abundantly clear that spying and dossier collection was also going on at the local level. Other pages (most of them heavily censored) among the several hundred in FBI files relating to Wesley Cook (obtained by his defense through a Freedom of Information Act request for files) refer to undercover informants working for the local police within the Panther office.

The pressure from Rizzo on the Panthers was intense and unrelenting. As Donner writes:

> Raids on Black Panther centers climaxed a long train of harassment: vendors of the Panther newspapers were regularly abused, frequently arrested, and detained for hours without charges. Panther posters supporting political candidates were removed; members' cars were stopped and searched; Panthers were cursed and denounced if they merely looked tough; their cars were indiscriminately ticketed. On one occasion the owner of an inoperative, junked car received a ticket for "speeding."[7]

---

* The Security Index, also called the ADEX file, was a list of alleged dissidents developed by the agencies involved in COINTELPRO who were considered national security risks, to be constantly surveilled and to be rounded up in the event of a national emergency.

This targeting was done although in Philadelphia the Panther organization was never successfully linked with any violent actions or even with the display of weaponry. Though Panther members in Philadelphia did have weapons, and did advocate the concept of self defense of the black community, they were not given, as were some of their more ostentatious and, some might say, publicity-seeking comrades in San Francisco and other cities, to publicly flaunting their arms. That mattered little to Rizzo, however. For him, the mere existence of a Panther chapter in "his" city was an affront.

While it was deadly serious business, Rizzo and his cops also took a good deal of pleasure in their campaign against the Panthers, and seemed particularly delighted when they found an opportunity to humiliate them. In his biography of Abu-Jamal, author Terry Bisson writes that Abu-Jamal told him that every time George Fencl, head of the police department's CD unit, passed him, he would cock his thumb at him, as though firing a pistol—"the same thing he would do years later, when Mumia was a newsman reporting MOVE stories the cops didn't want to hear." [8]

On August 31, 1970, a notorious police raid on the Philadelphia Black Panthers took place at locations all across the city. At Chief Rizzo's direction, some 200 police officers conducted a coordinated 2 a.m. raid on Panther offices and apartments in Germantown and North Philadelphia., exchanging fire at the Wallace Street headquarters. There, Fencl had his troops order the captured Panthers to strip, and made them available in that condition to press photographers. The following morning, Rizzo gloated to the media, "Imagine. The big, black Panthers with their pants down!"[9]

In another comment made following the raids, Rizzo said:

> We're dealing with a group of fanatics, yellow dogs that they are. We are prepared for any eventuality. We are dealing with psychotics and must be in a position to take them on. These imbeciles and yellow dogs...we'd be glad to meet them on their own terms. Just let them tell us when and where.[10]

Rizzo and his men clearly nurtured a special antipathy towards the city's Panthers. From a political perspective, it made perfect sense. Rizzo's electoral appeal—and by 1970, he was laying the groundwork for his successful run for mayor in 1971—lay in the ethnic blue collar districts of the city. Here, white working-class "Nixon-Democrats," also known as the "silent majority" in those days, fretted about crime and joblessness and harbored ancient tribal fears and hatred of the city's burgeoning African-

American population. But it may have been an even more personal thing. As Minister of Information, Abu-Jamal was the mouthpiece for the local Panther chapter. They were outspoken, self-appointed defenders of the African American community, and proclaimed loudly in speeches and in their local and national broadsheets, the need to stand up to police abuse and repression in Black neighborhoods. "Pigs" was the common epithet used in the late '60s by Panther activists to refer to the men in blue, and there clearly was no love lost in either direction.

Writes Donner:

> The justification for the raids [the fatal shooting two days earlier of a 29-year-old policeman named Frank VonColln during a bungled attempt by five people, allegedly all black, but not Panthers, to blow up a police guardhouse in Fairmont Park] was questionable on its face. A more convincing explanation for them is Rizzo's ferocious hatred of the Panthers, intensified by the VonColln killing. Perhaps the clearest evidence that it was vengeful fury and not law enforcement that inspired the raids is the manner in which they were conducted and Rizzo's response to those who criticized them. The early hour at which the searches were made, the fact that the raiders were specially chosen for their marksmanship and wore bullet-proof vests, and Rizzo's taunting of a number of Panthers as "yellow" because they dropped their guns in response to a police order rather than engage in battle all suggest that the raids were planned as a pretext to provoke a shoot-out.[11]

It is against this history of intense surveillance, harassment, infiltration by undercover and uniformed Philadelphia Police, and even probable efforts—largely unsuccessful—by the department to goad Panthers into a fatal shoot-out with crack police sharpshooters, that the Abu-Jamal trial took place. It is inconceivable that the police, and particularly those who were connected with intelligence or CD operations, would not be readily able to identify Abu-Jamal. They, and the FBI (which reportedly obtained much of the information it holds in its files on Cook/Abu-Jamal courtesy of the Philadelphia Police), knew Abu-Jamal was the information officer for the Philadelphia Panthers. Indeed, Cook almost certainly played a special role in the aftermath of the raid that surely would have earned him the special enmity of the police. On September 1, the day following the raid, a widely distributed and quoted press release condemned the raid as a further demonstration of the vindictiveness of Rizzo and his men. Who wrote that release? Probably Cook. During the raid, he wasn't in any of the targeted buildings, and thus, unlike most of the rest of the Panther chapter in Philadelphia, was free the following day to come to the defense of his comrades.

In that release, he revealed damaging information about police tactics. Besides just removing weapons, for which they had a legal search warrant, the police had gutted all three raid sites of furniture, bedding, clothes, file cabinets and party records, and had taken typewriters, tape recorders, cameras, copying machines, kitchen appliances and some $1000-$1500 in cash. The release also said police had ripped out plumbing, smashed windows, and even knocked out cinderblock walls. [12]

In the years following the break-up and collapse of the Panthers in the early 1970s, the police could only have become more aware of Abu-Jamal. Over the course of that decade he had moved into mainstream journalism, becoming a prominent voice on the radio. Often his reporting, on stories such as the violent police assault on a house full of members of the MOVE organization in 1978, portrayed the police in a distinctly negative light. But colleague Linn Washington, a Philadelphia-based African-American journalist and Temple University journalism professor whose early career roughly paralleled Abu-Jamal's, had this to say:

> Mumia Abu-Jamal is not a super-journalist of near mythical proportion who was convicted in large part for his reportorial exposure of police brutality. At the time of his 1981 arrest, Abu-Jamal's journalism was not up to the award-winning form that had earned him the title of "voice of the voiceless" for his poignant reports on issues involving society's dispossessed.[13]

That said, Washington says by the time of his arrest, Abu-Jamal had already built a solid record of reporting critically on issues that concerned the police and the city power structure.

> He reported on police brutality, deprivation in housing projects, the push for black political empowerment in Philadelphia, the budding anti-apartheid movement and MOVE.
> ...He did not isolate MOVE from the context of the other brutal police misconduct that was occurring daily in the City of Brotherly Love with the seeming sanction of the political structure.[14]

On August 8, 1978 an army of 600 police assaulted the MOVE organization's home in Powelton Village. A press conference by Mayor Rizzo followed that same day. The mayor had developed a chummy relationship with many of the reporters covering him, but on that day, he was confronted with some probing questions about the police version of events by some members of the press, including a radio reporter—Mumia Abu-Jamal.

Thanks to his sympathetic coverage of the MOVE organization, Abu-Jamal became a special target of police—and mayoral—wrath. At that press conference, Rizzo blamed the death of a police officer during that action on "a new breed of journalism."* Seeming to look directly at Abu-Jamal, he said, "They believe what you write, what you say. And it's got to stop. And one day, and I hope it's in my career, that [sic] you're going to have to be held responsible and accountable for what you do."[15] Whether that remark was aimed at Abu-Jamal or not, coming from the former police chief and current mayor, it was a clear signal to Philadelphia's police that they wouldn't be taken to task if they got tough with him and other aggressive reporters like him.

In a tacit acknowledgement that the presence of such hatred could play a role in skewing a murder trial, some critics of Abu-Jamal, including the Fraternal Order of Police organization and Faulkner's widow, Maureen, have tried to prove that he was never a significant critic of the Philadelphia Police. As the organizers of a website dedicated to enforcing the execution of Abu-Jamal, known as "Justice for Daniel Faulkner," puts it:

> It is easy to find articles written after the murder of Officer Faulkner in which Jamal's friends and colleagues gush about his talent. It is equally difficult to find any record of his actual work. One would expect that if an individual reporter were consistently exposing rampant misconduct by the Police, the Mayor, and various other city officials, that person's name would regularly appear in the news. Yet, an internet search on Jamal prior to December 9, 1981, reveals that his name appeared in just one article that had nothing to do with exposing corruption and wrong-doing.[16]

Since the whole idea of Abu-Jamal as a leading police critic is overblown, his critics argue, it is thus absurd to suggest that the police would have had any particular grudge against him when they picked him up at 13th and Locust after the shooting on December 9, 1981. As Dan Flynn, the director of the conservative organization Accuracy in Academia, writes in a pamphlet titled *Cop Killer: How Mumia Abu-Jamal Conned Millions Into Believing He Was Framed*, puts it:

> A computer check of the *Philadelphia Inquirer* and the *Philadelphia Daily News* reveals that Mumia Abu-Jamal's name appears in only one article within the pages of the city's two major

---

* It never was proven conclusively that the officer who died in the assault on MOVE was shot by someone in the MOVE house. There are suspicions that in fact, he died from "friendly fire" coming from other police, who had laid down a withering barrage from all directions at the house.

daily newspapers in the six months prior to his arrest for murder. While it would be hard to ascertain if the local police did have a consuming interest in the journalistic work of Mumia Abu-Jamal, the public clearly did not.*

If the police really did frame Abu-Jamal in hopes of silencing him, they couldn't have partaken in a more ill advised venture. In 1981, Abu-Jamal was a cab-driver whose freelance journalism reached a tiny audience. Today, he is a newspaper columnist, writes books read by tens of thousands of people, airs commentaries on national radio, and is the subject of numerous videos, internet sites, rallies, and concerts.[17]

Others have also sought to downplay the idea that Abu-Jamal was a police target prior to Faulkner's shooting. In his largely negative article on Abu-Jamal, appearing in the August 1999 issue of *Vanity Fair* magazine, Buzz Bissinger dismissed the black journalist's police reporting credentials. He cited William Marimow, a Pulizer Prize winning reporter for the *Philadelphia Inquirer* who had covered police brutality issues for the city's leading daily: "I was very attuned to everyone who wrote about Philadelphia police violence," said Marimow. "This guy didn't register a blip on my radar screen."[18]

Such a statement has a certain disingenuous accuracy. Unmentioned by Bissinger is that by and large Abu-Jamal didn't "write" his journalism— he was a radio reporter, and his work went out on the airwaves and then vanished without a trace. Most stations did not, and still don't bother keeping archives (one reason there is so little record of his work). And most of the stations he worked for had a target audience—black people—and thus never reached Marimow, along with most of his colleagues at the *Inquirer*.

Supporting his claim that Abu-Jamal was a non-entity when it came to coverage of police brutality and corruption issues, Bissinger also cited George Parry, who was in charge of a unit in the district attorney's office that handled police brutality issues. Said Parry:

> Mumia Abu-Jamal was just not a factor. I don't have any recollection of having spoken to him. It appears to be a triumph of propaganda over truth. You have to give him credit for that. The notion that Jamal has been framed because he was a critic of the

---

* Aside from the fact that Abu-Jamal's career as a journalist went back considerably further than July, 1981, looking for evidence of his significance as a police critic in the *Inquirer* and the *Daily News* would not make much sense. Journalists rarely get mentioned in news stories by other media. It would have been fairer and more to the point to check the *Philadelphia Tribune*, a paper read by black readers, for articles by or references to Abu-Jamal. Moreover, since most of his work was on radio, there would be no record of it in print searches.

police is just a hideous lie.[19]

Strong words, but then how surprising is it that the head of the Philadelphia D.A.'s police brutality unit would claim Abu-Jamal was not an issue for the department? From its establishment in 1978, right on up to the present day under District Attorney Lynne Abraham, the Philadelphia D.A.'s police brutality unit has done little to address the Philadelphia Police Department's penchant for excessive use of force. If anything, the office has spent most of its time covering up and explaining away police abuse. Indeed, in 1979, Philadelphia became the first city in America where the U.S. Justice Department felt the need to step into the breach and file a lawsuit alleging that top city officials actively condoned police brutality. In 1978, police were actually video-taped brutally "gang-banging" Delbert Africa, a black man who had surrendered to them. The D.A.'s office made a halfhearted effort to prosecute them.* Seven years later, when the police fire-bombed a MOVE house killing 11 people, including five children, and burning 63 of the surrounding houses to the ground, the D.A. failed to bring a single charge against any police. Writes journalist Linn Washington in the manuscript of a soon-to-be published book on police brutality:

> Historically, Philadelphia prosecutors rarely pursue charges in police brutality incidents without public protest. Prosecutors certainly do not pursue police abuse charges with the same vigor as charges of comparable violence against civilians.[20]

No surprise then, that a man who headed an office that largely pretended that rampant police brutality didn't exist might not notice—or at least acknowledge—what a critic of police brutality was saying. (Bissinger and *Vanity Fair* also failed to disclose that Bissinger himself was hardly a neutral observer in this case. For years he had been an unabashed cheerleader for Philadelphia Mayor Ed Rendell. With an office situated next to the mayor's, Bissinger spent several years focused on writing what amounted to an authorized biography of the politically ambitious Rendell.[21] Mayor Rendell, meanwhile, had been deeply involved in the Faulkner shooting case. At the time of Abu-Jamal's trial, he was Philadelphia's politically ambitious district attorney. As supervisor of the lead prosecutor in the case, Assistant District Attorney Joseph McGill, Rendell was in ultimate charge

---

*The case was so poorly handled that the trial judge issued a directed verdict acquitting them, saying not enough evidence had been presented to prove they hadn't been acting in "self-defense".

of the prosecution, and as D.A. he would have had to make or at least approve the decision to pursue the death penalty against Abu-Jamal. None of this was mentioned in the biography of Bissinger provided by *Vanity Fair*, which failed to mention Bissinger's 1997 book on Rendell, or, curiously, even that he had been an *Inquirer* reporter.[22])

Whatever the biases of Bissinger and other critics, the effort to minimize Abu-Jamal's role as a police critic and as a police target fails to hold up to scrutiny. The FBI itself included clippings of Abu-Jamal's work in its files, as well as comments from agents on his abilities as a communicator of Panther ideology; those communications were, of course, largely critical of the police. His journalism prior to his arrest included critical coverage of the police and of city government policy in minority neighborhoods. Moreover, contrary to the claims of those same critics, it garnered awards and official recognition. (For example, he was jointly honored along with three other top African-American journalists, Joe Davidson, E. Steven Collins and Linn Washington, by a group of community groups; he was singled out by *Philadelphia Magazine* in 1981 as one of the key people to watch in the city.[23] He was also elected to head the Philadelphia Black Journalists Association—a position he held at the time of his arrest). In fact he was so well-known in Philadelphia that several of the potential African-Americans questioned during the jury selection process at the start of his trial admitted to recognizing his name—and his voice (an admission that earned them a peremptory dismissal by McGill).

It must be added that the counter claim, asserted by many in the movement to "Free Mumia," that he was a pillar of Philadelphia journalism and a leader in rooting out police corruption and brutality, also does not hold up under scrutiny. Police corruption and brutality was not the primary focus of Abu-Jamal's journalism prior to his arrest and trial, nor to the extent that he did write on these issues was he doing the most groundbreaking work in that area. Nonetheless, as Rizzo made clear, Abu-Jamal's journalism fueled police animus.

But his journalism wasn't the only reason behind the antagonism police clearly felt towards him. Abu-Jamal's increasing involvement with—some might even say his obsession with—the MOVE organization, included his adoption of their vegetarian dietary practices and their favored dreadlocked hairstyle. This inevitably made him all the more an object of special scorn and anger among rank-and-file police officers and the police brass. For by the late 1970s, MOVE, with its in-your-face anti-authoritarianism and its undisguised disdain for law enforcement, had become a major thorn in the side of the police and the mayor.

It does seem extremely probable that this combination of things—his earlier prominence as the spokesperson for and the publicist for the Black Panther Party, his later frequent presence on the city's airwaves and at police and City Hall press conferences, and finally his sympathetic, even advocacy-style journalistic coverage of the MOVE organization and its various confrontations with police—made him well known to the police and City Hall. Maybe, had he never been a Panther, had he never reported on MOVE, the police wouldn't have paid much attention to his journalistic efforts over the years prior to the shooting. But in the context of his other activities and political sympathies, many of which would have led to his being included in intelligence gathering efforts by the police, it strains belief to suggest he was not on their radar at the end of 1981.

Some passionate supporters of Abu-Jamal have alleged that this hatred of Abu-Jamal is evidence that the whole shooting of Faulkner was an elaborate conspiracy to "get" him. But it is hard to imagine anyone successfully organizing or even attempting to organize a situation that would have required luring him, his brother and a particular police officer to the same place at the same time.

Yet the question of whether Abu-Jamal was singled out as a Panther and as a journalist cannot be so easily dismissed. It is almost certain that within minutes of the fatal shooting of Officer Faulkner, at least some police, including some senior officials, on the scene knew exactly who they held in custody as a suspect. (They had in hand his wallet and his hack license). And it is not at all difficult to imagine that, from that moment forward, efforts to "get" Abu-Jamal would have commenced. Worse, these efforts would have tended to preclude other angles for investigation (for example the possibility of a third person fleeing the scene, as reported by a number of apparently credible and disinterested witnesses).

Consider these factors: a well-known black critic of the police; a dead white cop; a police division that was breaking records for corruption. If incriminating evidence of his guilt was being manufactured, it no doubt would have begun at this point.

(A personal note: I do not find it at all hard to imagine that police "target" journalists whom they consider to be "enemies." Back in the mid-1970s, when I had my own alternative newspaper in Los Angeles, my colleagues and I became the targets of a campaign of harassment by the Los

Angeles Police Department. Our paper, the *Los Angeles Vanguard*, was publishing articles about police spying and police shooting of unarmed individuals. Our office and members of our staff individually, myself included,
found ourselves tailed by police cars, stopped for non-existent traffic offenses, and even surveilled by helicopters. These sometimes hovered over our
office, and even followed us home at night with searchlights. Eventually, in
the course of a major class action lawsuit against the LAPD's "red squad,"
the Public Disorder Intelligence Division, we learned that our newspaper
had been penetrated by an undercover cop in PDID, whose stated goal had
been to discover our sources within the department. We also learned later
from someone who had worked as our ad sales representative that the
police may have intimidated our ad sales firm into ceasing efforts to find us
advertisers, effectively killing the publication. The City of Los Angeles settled a lawsuit filed by over 200 victims of LAPD spying out of court for a
damage payment of $1.8 million. I was allocated $2,000 of that settlement
for personal damages.)

Signs that evidence fabrication was practiced in the police department surfaced much later, during a second federal probe of police corruption in Philadelphia in 1995. It was discovered, as part of that scandal, that
Officer Thomas F. Ryan and four other officers in the 39th District (not
part of the Center City area), had regularly manufactured evidence and
bribed prostitutes to lie on the stand about suspects. And Ryan had been
involved in the Abu-Jamal case 14 years earlier. In the 1995 corruption
case, Ryan and his partner, John D. Baird, were both convicted of paying a
prostitute named Pamela Jenkins to lie on the stand and say she had bought
drugs from a Temple University student. The scandal dated back to 1991,
when Ryan and Baird falsely arrested an out-of-state African-American
Temple University student named Arthur Colbert. They had paid Jenkins
to say what they wanted—that she had bought drugs from Colbert. Her
false testimony had been enough to wrongfully convict him. The two cops,
who later were found guilty of a string of such deliberate false arrests and of
using their badges to rob people in the community, were subsequently fired
from the department for the Colbert arrest. Ryan pleaded guilty and turned
state's evidence, and eventually served a 10-month jail sentence for his
crimes. Baird was sentenced to several years in prison.

But this perjured testimony in the Colbert case turned out to have
been just one of many such examples of false testimony by Jenkins, who
went on to explain that she was paid $100 a week by Ryan and Baird to per-
form such services. Baird and Ryan, it turned out, had used Jenkins fre-

quently when they needed a ready witness. In the end, because of such lying and manufacturing of evidence by Ryan, Baird and three other officers in the so-called Five Squad, much of which involved Jenkins as a witness, the D.A.'s office had to dismiss drug convictions against several dozen people, including Colbert.

While the targeting of Abu-Jamal by the police and the mayor before Faulkner's shooting, and the amazing number of corrupt police involved in his case, heighten suspicions about the fairness and integrity of his trial, they don't prove it wasn't fair. But there's more: a direct link between the corruption in the 39th precinct and the Abu-Jamal case. In 1997, as part of Abu-Jamal's lengthy Post-Conviction Relief Act hearing, Jenkins testified that she had known the prosecution's star witness at the original trial, the prostitute Cynthia White. She said White had been a police informant at the time of the Faulkner shooting, and that she had "turned tricks" for police officers in the district.[24]

The hearing provided a rare window on the dynamics of police corruption in Philadelphia. At the time she testified at the hearing she was in jail for a violation of probation on a knife possession charge and thus was potentially vulnerable to law enforcement retaliation. Nonetheless, under questioning by Leonard Weinglass, Abu-Jamal's lead attorney at the time, Jenkins said that she had not been at the scene of the shooting. But within three days of the incident, the same Thomas Ryan had sought her out and brought her to the Central Police Station to be questioned by a Detective Richard Ryan (no relation). The two Ryans then labored mightily to get her to lie and testify against Abu-Jamal, she told the court. Under oath at the hearing, she described the scene as follows:

> Jenkins: They just told me—well, in other words, they were saying that it was shootin' and that Mumia had did it. And they was making slurs across me, trying to make me, you know, trying to pressure me into saying I was somewhere that I wasn't.
> Weinglass: Did they want to pressure you to say that you saw Mumia shoot the officer?
> Jenkins: Yes, they did...Because they kept asking, you know, was I there. They kept being persistent, pushing it. And Ryan knew I wasn't there, and they knew I wasn't there. So that's what I assume, it was pressure, if they are going to keep asking me the same question over and over again and I am telling them no, I wasn't there.
> Weinglass: Did you think you were being asked to lie for money?
> Jenkins: Yes.[25]

Thomas Ryan had good reason to believe that such pressure would work. At the time of the Faulkner shooting in December 1981, Jenkins told the court, she was "sleeping with" Officer Ryan, and being paid by him for information.

At the PCRA hearing, the District Attorney's office went to great efforts to discredit Jenkins. She had claimed that she had been a student at Simon Gratz High School at the time she had met Ryan. (He had been a truant officer before becoming a cop, only joining the police on August 17, 1981 after a brief stint as a correctional officer earlier in the year.) The D.A. brought a school board records officer into the court to testify that, at the time she had claimed to have met Ryan, Jenkins had not in fact been a student at the high school.

Offering another contradiction to her testimony, at the PCRA hearing, Ryan himself claimed that he had first met Jenkins on June 10, 1982, a full six months after the Faulkner shooting. But this claim fell apart when later, still under oath, he was forced to concede that on another occasion, he had testified under oath that he had known Jenkins for "five years" prior to September 1986. Had he perhaps merely been using the term "five years" loosely? The record in the federal prosecution of his corruption case settles the debate. It shows that he had himself told FBI investigators that he had had a relationship with Jenkins since she was 15 years old. This would have put their initial acquaintance well back in 1981. And, crucially, to a time before the Faulkner shooting.[26]

Having gotten Ryan, at the PCRA hearing, to admit that he had had a sexual relationship with the under-age Jenkins, defense attorney Dan Williams tried to delve further into his relationship with her. Williams sought to reveal how long he had used her as a source, and whether he had used other prostitutes as sources. But the judge overseeing the hearing, the same judge Sabo who presided at the original trial, upheld prosecutors' objections and blocked that crucial line of questioning.

Nonetheless, in demonstrating the lengths that police were willing to go in an effort to elicit false testimony aimed at incriminating Abu-Jamal, and in raising questions about the credibility of the government's star witness, the defense had clearly damaged the prosecution's case. One point is evident from the Jenkins testimony, a point the prosecution team at the PCRA hearing was unable to effectively disprove. Namely, at least some elements of the police department, including an officer and a homicide detective involved in the investigation of the Faulkner killing, were attempting to elicit false testimony in order to build a case against suspect Mumia Abu-Jamal. And it's also clear that such efforts began as early as three days after the shooting. How far-reaching that effort was, how coordinated it was within the police department, and between the police and the District Attorney's office, and most importantly, how successful it was, remains a major question.

Whatever the implications of Officer Ryan's actions are for Abu-Jamal's case, he was but one in a group of corrupt cops involved in that case. What they had in common was that all had been either hired under Rizzo's tenure as police chief or mayor, or had risen to elevated positions during that time.

Prosecutors had also questioned another young cop from the Rizzo era, police officer Gary Wakshul. He had claimed to police Internal Affairs Bureau investigators, more than two months after the shooting, that he had heard Abu-Jamal make the now-famous hospital confession in the entryway of the emergency room "I shot the motherfucker and I hope he dies." Wakshul's claim, and an identical claim made by another officer, Garry Bell, provided the basis for the pursuit of that evidence by the prosecution. Though Wakshul was an original source of the confession claim, he was never questioned in court by the defense. As recounted in Chapter 1, he was never put under oath at the trial. He did not have to explain his claim to have heard a confession, or to explain his contradictory report written right after he had spent time with Abu-Jamal in the police wagon and hospital that "The negro male made no comment." He never testified because he was allegedly "on vacation." It was later revealed in his testimony at the 1995 PCRA hearing that while on vacation he had in fact stayed home in Philadelphia during the course of the trial, as instructed, anticipating that he might be called as a witness. That he was in town was almost certainly known to, and indeed was probably arranged by the prosecution. Had Sabo not been so ready to support the prosecution in its attempt to prevent any questioning of Wakshul, the officer would almost surely have appeared and had to explain his initial written statement.

So who is this Gary Wakshul? On June 18, 1986, four years after the Abu-Jamal trial, the Philadelphia police commissioner served Wakshul with a notice of dismissal for "conduct unbecoming a police officer" and "neglect of duty." As the document reports:

> ...on or about Saturday, December 7, 1985 at approximately 9:15 A.M., while you were on duty, you struck Mr. Louis McDonald in the head several times with your blackjack while he was hand-cuffed and in your custody inside the Sixth Police district, 11th and Winter Streets. Mr. McDonald was transported to Hahnemann Hospital for treatment of a fractured cheekbone, a split lip and lacerations of the scalp. Inside Hahnemann Hospital you further abused

Mr. McDonald by choking him with your hands while his hands are [sic] cuffed behind his back and by dragging him by the handcuffs.

Although your dismissal is based on the above substantive acts, on Wednesday, May 28, 1986, you were also arrested inside IAB [Internal Affairs Bureau] headquarters and charged with Aggravated Assault, Simple Assault and Criminal Attempt.[27] [a reference to a separate incident of violent behavior]

Wakshul's propensity toward violence and the physical abuse of prisoners in his custody was unknown to Abu-Jamal's defense team during the original trial. Even at the 1995 PCRA hearing, some nine years after Wakshul's dismissal, the defense was unaware of it. On July 13, 1995, only days before Wakshul took the stand at the hearing, a bizarre incident took place. He was working as a court crier, a kind of security guard in the courtroom, who also has the job of announcing the arrival and departure of the judge. This was after his ouster from the police force. Right in open court, in the Common Pleas Courtroom and in the presence of a judge, undercover police savagely beat him. In connection with that incident, almost two years later Kenneth Fleming and Jean Langen, two active members of the police department's vice squad, were suspended without pay. Unfortunately, that disciplinary action came long after the PCRA hearing had concluded.[28] The reasons for this beating go unexplained to this day. Abu-Jamal's defense team knew he was injured in some way, because his testimony had to be scheduled around a course of physical therapy he was undergoing to help him heal from the attack. But no one volunteered, nor did the defense request information as to the cause of his injuries.

Wakshul's problem with violent behavior towards those in custody raises a number of interesting questions:

- Could Wakshul have made up the Abu-Jamal "confession" in an effort to curry favor with a department that may already have been displeased with his obvious problem with out-of-control behavior?

- Was Abu-Jamal, as he claims, subjected to abuse in the police wagon while being transported to the hospital from the shooting at Locust and 13th streets, during which time he was left in the van to Wakshul's tender mercies? Evidence supports this possibility: there was testimony, even from the government's star witness against him, that he was beaten at the time of his arrest. Police even confirm that the officers who were carrying him rammed his head into a lamppost. Hospital personnel have also testified that as Abu-Jamal lay on the hospital floor seriously injured, police kicked him. Pertinent to the question of Wakshul in the wagon, the *Philadelphia Inquirer* ran a series of stories in 2001 detailing how Philadelphia police physically abused arrest subjects while under transport. The practice was so common it had been given a name: the nickel ride. According to the *Inquirer* reports, beatings in police vans have been so severe that some suspects have actually died or been paralyzed.[29]

- What questions might the defense attorneys have asked at the PCRA hearing, had they known of Wakshul's record of violence and of the recent attack on him in open court? That attack certainly raises questions concerning the truthfulness of his testimony at the PCRA hearing days later. Could that attack have put him under some pressure to support the prosecution's case at a time when, as a fired cop, he might conceivably have been inclined to break ranks? Efforts to locate and interview Wakshul were unsuccessful.

Wakshul may have been a loose cannon on the force. And Ryan was having sex with an underage prostitute whom he and a homicide detective were trying to pressure into giving false testimony at Abu-Jamal's trial. But there is also evidence that during the 1980s, the entire Central Division, rather than being a genuine police department, was little more than a criminal enterprise. This became apparent on November 4, 1982, just months after the conclusion of Abu-Jamal's trial. On that date, the division commander, Inspector John DeBenedetto—the man who was Officer Faulkner's boss and who had ultimate authority for overseeing the entire investigation of the crime, resigned from the police department. So did the head of the division's vice squad, Lt. John Smith. Both men had been called before a federal grand jury investigating corruption in the district. On May 17, 1983, DeBenedetto was convicted in federal court on seven counts of extortion and one count of conspiracy. Smith was convicted of eight counts of extortion and one of conspiracy. Three other officers in the district's vice squad were also convicted. The total amount of extortion charged in the men's indictment was $120,000. DeBenedetto had also been charged with obstruction of justice, for allegedly secretly removing evidence of cash payments from records kept in filing cabinets at his Central Division office at 20th Street and Pennsylvania Avenue.[30]

The evidence against these officers serves as an important indication of the level of integrity of the men involved in Abu-Jamal's trial. Brought by federal prosecutors, the case hinged upon the testimony of FBI informant Donald Hersing, a Levittown man who ran a prostitution operation on Vine and 12th Street, one of the places that were being extorted by police. During several visits by police, Hersing had worn a wire for the FBI. At the corruption trial, the prosecution played a tape clearly showing DeBenedetto threatening to run Hersing out of town for missing several protection payments. Another tape showed Smith, the officer who later resigned the same day as DeBenedetto, taking $1,300 from Hersing and explaining to him how it would be divided. $500 would go to the citywide Morals Squad to keep them from raiding Hersing's operation, $500 to be divided between Smith himself, DeBenedetto, and their Central District vice squad for protection, and $300 to protect another club located on 14th and Vine, also owned by Hersing.

Abu-Jamal's defense team deposed Hersing about these matters on May 10, 1999. In his statement, he reveals that corruption in the Central District began right at the top of the department, and went down to the line officers. In a sworn statement, he says:

> Inspector John DeBenedetto took over as Commanding Officer of the Central Division of the Philadelphia Police Department on about June 1, 1981. I first met DeBenedetto in August 1981. At that meeting DeBenedetto personally told me that when he took over the Central Division in June he had gathered his officers together and informed them that from that point on all pay-off money was to be passed up to him.[31]

The man in charge of the FBI's Philadelphia office, Special Agent John L. Hogan, confirms Hersing's claim that corruption was widespread. Hogan said at the time of the convictions, that protection extortion was "inbred" in the Philadelphia police force, and that police officers were "routinely extorting money from vice operations in Center City."[32]

While officers might expect wrist slapping and discipline for periodic transgressions, this scandal was different. The rot within the Philadelphia Police Department was so pervasive and deep-rooted that Deputy Chief James Martin was convicted of extortion and sent to jail—for 18 years. Martin, who had headed the police department's major investigations division, was said by federal prosecutors to have turned the division into "a weapon for city-wide extortion schemes."[33] Martin was the highest-ranking police official in any major U.S. city to have been convicted. Martin had ultimate responsibility for all major investigations conducted by the department; a responsibility that included the case of Officer Faulkner and Abu-Jamal.

By May 14, 1984, another 15 Philadelphia police officers, including a captain, four lieutenants and eight officers, had been indicted on charges of extorting another $400,000 between 1980 and 1984. In these new indict-ments, DeBenedetto, Smith and two other former Central Division officers already convicted were listed as co-conspirators. Among those arrested and charged was Lt. Edward Quinn of the Central District, about whom we shall hear more later.[34]

Martin, like DeBenedetto earlier, was also accused of crimes extend-ing beyond extortion: trying to destroy records and of bribing lower rank-ing officers to keep silent about the extortion payments he had received.

On March 20, 1986, Inspector Alfonzo J. Giordano and another offi-cer, Charles K. Howlett, were indicted. Giordano eventually pleaded guilty to charges of tax evasion relating to some $55,000 in extortion money he had received from shakedowns during 1979 and 1980 of Center City book-ies and illegal poker machine operators.

Giordano is particularly important when it comes to Abu-Jamal's case. A veteran of the Police Department's CD Unit during its war on the Panthers, Giordano showed up at the scene of the crime only minutes after the shooting of Faulkner and went over to the van holding the wounded Abu-Jamal. As mentioned in the preceding chapter, Giordano claimed that, when left alone with the suspect, he purportedly inquired as to his health. Giordano claims he noticed the empty shoulder holster under Abu-Jamal's jacket. Asking where the gun was, Giordano elicited the response that it had been left in the street "after I shot him."

That "confession" by Abu-Jamal was quickly leaked to the local press days after the shooting in December 1981. But it never made it to the jury in his trial, because only days after reporting this confession, Giordano was outed in the press as being a prime focus of the FBI's investigation of Central Division corruption. Prosecutor Joe McGill was unwilling to put such tarnished goods as Giordano on the stand to try and support the claim of a blurt-out confession having been made by the accused. While the odds are good that a jury will believe the cop when it's a cop's word against a black defendant, it is a different equation when the cop has a cloud of cor-ruption hanging over him. It was a wise move on McGill's part. Had Giordano testified and later been indicted and convicted, as subsequently happened, it could have been grounds for a mistrial on appeal.

But is that all there is to this story? What if this high-ranking police officer's claim to have heard a "confession" to the shooting was really some-thing else: the first step in a concerted effort by police to manufacture evi-dence in an attempt to "get" Abu-Jamal?

And what about Edward Quinn, a detective in the Central Division at the time of the Faulkner shooting? As mentioned earlier, federal prose-cutors indicted him on March 8, 1984. He was one of a group of 13 cops in the division who were indicted for allegedly extorting payoffs from video poker vending businesses in the Center City area over a period ranging from January 1980 through the time of the indictment. Quinn played a rel-atively obscure yet potentially very significant role in the Abu-Jamal case, a role that did not come to light until the 1995 PCRA hearing during the questioning of a witness named William "Dales" Singletary. At the time of the shooting, Singletary had volunteered himself to police as a witness, and had been interviewed shortly thereafter about what he had seen. But curi-ously, though police had interviewed this black tow-truck driver as a wit-ness to the Faulkner shooting, during the trial, neither the prosecution or defense ever called him.

Singletary was a peculiar, but potentially crucial witness for the defense. He originally told police he had seen another person on the scene of the shooting besides Billy Cook, Mumia Abu-Jamal and Officer Daniel Faulkner. Moreover, at the PCRA hearing years later, he actually testified that the fourth person had been the shooter, not Abu-Jamal. A Vietnam veteran and family man, Singletary was an honest and straightforward looking witness. It is clear that he was on the scene at the time of the shooting, because police testified that on the morning of the incident, he had been brought down to the station for questioning as a witness. But some of the things he testified to during the PCRA hearing are hard to believe. In particular, he referred to a helicopter hovering over the scene and shining a spotlight down, when there was no other testimony about helicopters. He also claimed Faulkner had talked after having been shot in the head—something that medical experts have said would have been plainly impossible since he would have died instantly from the explosion of the bullet in his brain.

But Singletary's strangest tale was about what allegedly happened at the police station. Testifying at the post-conviction hearing, he stated a black policeman named Detective Green questioned him. He testified that he was asked to write an account of what he had witnessed. But when he wrote his account, which included saying that Abu-Jamal was not the shooter, and that the shooter had fled the scene, he says, the detective "ripped it up and threw it in the trash." When he wrote a second, similar account, he told the court the detective again "glanced at it, balled it up and threw it in the trash."[35]

After his third attempt was rejected by the detective, Singletary testified, he was told "to write what he wanted me to write," and, anxious to get out of the stationhouse in one piece, he said, "that's what I wrote."

Asked whether the detective had threatened him in any way, Singletary said, "Yes, he did… He told me I wouldn't leave, that they would take me to the elevator and beat me up and that my business would be destroyed."

Singletary was asked at the PCRA hearing whether his final written account of what he'd seen the night of the shooting—which didn't mention his later claim that a fourth person was the shooter—was accurate. Singletary replied simply, "No, it is not."

Enter Officer Quinn. Brought into court by the prosecution during the PCRA hearing to counter Singletary, Quinn, a Caucasian, testified that he, and not some mysterious "Detective Green," had been the one who interviewed Singletary. Quinn insisted that it was his practice to type statements given by witnesses, not to have them write statements down themselves, so Singletary's claim to have written statements, which were then thrown away, couldn't have been true. He stood by Singletary's written statement that Quinn alleged he himself had transcribed, saying it was the only statement he had been given.

What the defense apparently still didn't know in 1995 was that in 1984, Quinn was one of those thirteen Center City cops indicted by federal prosecutors for extortion, conspiracy and other corrupt activity. The timing of many of these crimes alleged by the indictment, coincided with the period of Faulkner's shooting and Singletary's statement.

Unlike most of the others who had pleaded guilty, Quinn had demanded a trial, was acquitted in 1985 by a jury and got his job back with the police department. But at his trial, where the jury deliberated for nine hours before acquitting him, there was enough damaging testimony regarding him that it is surprising his record didn't come up at Abu-Jamal's PCRA hearing. Dan Williams, attorney for Abu-Jamal at the time of the hearing, says neither he nor the rest of the defense team ever knew that Quinn had been indicted or faced trial. "All we knew was that he was a current officer in the department," Williams recalled later in an interview. He added, "If we had known about his indictment, it certainly would have helped impeach his testimony, and it would definitely have handed the defense a propaganda victory."

Without any knowledge of Quinn's dubious history, the seemingly convincing testimony of an apparently honest cop just doing his job crushed Singletary's allegations.

Since 1981, as a result of the two major federal investigations into police misconduct focussed on just two of Philadelphia's police districts, over a hundred felony convictions in Philadelphia have been overturned because the evidence or the testimony was tampered with. These cases included some involving charges as serious as murder. There have always been critical questions regarding the integrity and honesty of key prosecution witnesses such as the prostitute Cynthia White and taxi driver Robert Chobert, both of whom were extremely vulnerable to police and prosecutorial pressure. There has also been solid evidence in the Mumia Abu-Jamal case of:

- the deliberate withholding of evidence (the Arnold Howard license document);
- of the pressuring of witnesses (in the cases of Veronica Jones and Pamela Jenkins, as well as efforts made to pressure Dessie Hightower, William Singletary and others);
- possible false testimony by police officers;
- and in the case of the non-availability of Gary Wakshul, possible prosecutorial misconduct.

The prosecution has always been able to refute these claims to the satisfaction of appellate judges. But the evidence of rampant corruption in the department during this whole period, and of law enforcement's willingness to lie in order to win convictions—none of which was deemed relevant to Abu-Jamal's appeals claims—strengthens the suspicion that all was not right in his trial.

The investigation of this case, despite the massive allocation of police manpower to it, was unorthodox and, in certain suspicious ways, unbelievably perfunctory. For example, police at the scene failed to test the alleged murder weapon to see if it had been recently fired, and no tests of the suspect's hands were done to see if he had recently used a gun. No effort was made to protect the integrity of the scene of the crime, which was left curiously unguarded the very morning after the shooting, according to journalist Linn Washington. Right after learning of the incident just four hours after its occurrence, Washington was able to freely inspect the crime scene, the vehicles, etc., with no police in sight.[36]

In terms of whether the trial of Abu-Jamal was fair, perhaps the most alarming thing is simply this: one-third of the 35 cops involved with the case had compiled a record of deceitful behavior and even evidence tampering. But during the original trial, all of this corruption was completely unknown to the defense, and to the jury.

Chapter Three

Mumia Abu-Jamal
Targeting Cops, or Cops' Target?

Mumia Abu-Jamal, the man 12 Philadelphia jurors convicted of first degree murder and sentenced to death after only a few hours' deliberation in July 1982, was a vicious rogue. An opponent of all that is good in society, he was a man who opposed the very basic rules that protect society from chaos. And he felt it was his right and duty to disobey laws and rules he didn't like—even to kill policemen if they were doing something he didn't like. This was the only real image the jury that sealed his fate ever had of him, a picture of him painted by Assistant District Attorney Joseph McGill in his closing argument in the case, and later in his summation during the penalty phase of the hearing. They certainly didn't get much else in the way of alternative views of the man, because not much was presented to them by the defense which was offered up by Abu-Jamal and his attorney, Anthony Jackson. Indeed, if they saw anything, it was an angry and frustrated Abu-Jamal telling them that what America needed was a revolution, and talking back to and even cursing a judge who repeatedly removed him from the courtroom and denied him the right to handle his own case.

As McGill told jurors during his summation at the end of the trial:

> ... when you arrive at the hospital and with the action that was just done and you speak out and you proclaim almost in a boastful and defiant way you say, "I shot him and I hope he dies,"[sic] that has to be the supreme arrogance that can be associated with such a vicious act, because it would take somebody with that frame of mind to shoot down a man on the ground. To shoot him in the back and then straight on in the face. That same kind of arrogance that would carry on through to the hospital and would be stated.[1]

He then referred to the killing of Faulkner, described as a shot fired in the back, followed by a *coup de gras* fired at almost point blank range directly into the wounded and prone cop's face:

> This is one vicious act. This is one uncompromising vicious act. This is one act that the people of Philadelphia, all of them, all of you everywhere is outraged over.[2]

McGill then delivered his powerful conclusion:

> I plead to you consider the thrust of such arrogance and hos-
> tility and injustice. The action of a judging body, the actions of all
> of you must be filled with the courage and the responsibility of see-
> ing to it that that man as he looked up, as he watched in the last sec-
> onds of his life, the very instrument the defendant purchased and
> carried with him loaded with those bullets demands action.[3]

McGill's strategy of linking Abu-Jamal's courtroom behavior with the
killing of Faulkner worked beautifully. In a post-conviction interview, one
juror said that it had shaken him up to sentence a man to death. He then
added, "His behavior made it easier to believe he could be a killer."[4]
Another juror interviewed said, "The man is intelligent but he was acting
stupid."[5]

During the sentencing hearing, which takes place as a separate phase
of a death penalty trial and directly follows the phase where guilt is established, McGill took up the task of seeing to it that his convict would be
sent to the gallows:

> ...Ladies and gentlemen, what we're dealing with now and
> who we're dealing with now is a convicted murderer. This man is no
> longer presumed innocent.
> This man over here is a killer. You're looking and have heard
> a killer. That's who we're dealing with.[6]

Lest some member of the jury might still have been harboring some
latent sympathy for the defendant, he turned to the threat he claimed Abu-
Jamal allegedly posed to all of society:

> ...Law and order.... This is what this trial is all about more than
> any other trial I have ever seen, and certainly more than any other
> I have been [involved in], because you yourself have seen, you have
> heard things that are going on and you have heard testimony of
> things that are going on as to what is lawful and what is not lawful,
> and actions, arrogance, reactions against the law. Law and order....
> ...So ladies and gentlemen, we then will simply make the
> response, at least ask yourselves the question, are we going to live in
> a society with law and order, and are we going to enforce the laws
> consistent with the intention of law and order, or are we going to
> decide our own rules and then, act accordingly?[7]

The prosecutor then went on to raise the specter of Abu-Jamal as
essentially an animal bent on returning society to the laws of the jungle:

> ...Why is it so important? Because, once we have the opportu-
> nity presented that anybody can kill a cop and it doesn't matter, you

may as well forget about law and order, just throw it right out.

...And, if you can at will kill police, ladies and gentlemen, you then make that extra step towards the area which is without law enforcement, which is an outright jungle. We are one step from the jungle...[8]

He concluded his presentation by recalling for the jurors Abu-Jamal's confrontational behavior in the courtroom, which included cursing and swearing at several judges who ignored his completely legitimate requests to represent himself and to have an adviser of his choice (John Africa) sitting at the defense table with him. Despite the fact that this assertive behavior was in no way violent, it was easy for McGill to get jurors to link in their minds such outbursts to the killing of a policeman. This link that would also help convince the jury later, during their consideration of the penalty, of the basic aggressive personality of the man whose fate they were considering.

Order, ladies and gentlemen, that you may not have seen; order that this defendant has decided is not good enough for him. Order that he says, I don't care about standing, I have no respect for him (the judge). I don't care if Justice McDermott is going to walk away. I don't care if Judge Ribner [the jurist who handled the arraignment and pretrial hearings] says things, I'm just going to curse at him and say it because I don't have to agree with him. I don't agree with this. So I'm going to do this. Completely in violation of any law and order is what you have seen and what you have seen in this very courtroom.

The arrogance, the defiance, all present, the grandiose defiance, continuously present.[9]

Even today, McGill seems to believe firmly that Abu-Jamal was not just someone who shot and killed a policeman in a momentary paroxysm of anger and concern about his brother's safety—one possible scenario that has been suggested. Rather, he was a volatile, hate-filled young radical seeking to overturn the established order, and who was ready and willing to kill if necessary in order to accomplish that. In an interview in June 2000, McGill put it to me this way, saying, "He's been very consistent in saying revolution is his goal. And remember, the person who was ranting and raving in court is not the same person you see today. Remember, there is a history of Abu-Jamal in terms of who he is, what he was doing, and who he had reverence for. I believe he came out of the MOVE trial [over the 1978 battle with Philadelphia Police who evicted the group from their home in a military-style assault] experience as a very bitter person, and you can see where he would react as he did when he saw his brother interacting with a police officer."

Something, however, is badly wrong with this image McGill depicts of a person who was out to commit violent revolution, predisposed towards violence and confrontation, and who believed that he should be free to do whatever he wanted to do regardless of the law. Here was a black man living in a city where racial profiling could have been invented, where a virtually all-white police force historically harbored a collective grudge against young black men in general and this young black man in particular. Especially because he had been a member of an organization targeted for disruption, harassment and arrest by Philadelphia Police and the FBI precisely because it called on black people to stand up to police abuse. How, then, did he manage to maintain a squeaky-clean record up to the time of Faulkner's shooting, when Abu-Jamal was 27?

Wesley Cook was born April 24, 1954, along with twin brother Wayne, in Philadelphia. His mother Edith "Cookie" Cook, and his father William, known affectionately as "Mr. Bill," were both country folks. They had moved north as part of that great stream of African Americans from the rural South who had migrated to northern cities in search of jobs, an escape from Jim Crow, and a better future for their families. The Cook family settled in what were known as the PJs—the projects in north Philadelphia. Not entirely an escape from Jim Crow or poverty, but certainly a better life of sorts. There were three older half-siblings, brothers Keith and Ronald, and sister Lydia by his mother's previous husband. Later came his younger brother, Billy.

With such a large family living on a limited income, things could be tough, but they got by. Edith and William planted a vegetable garden in the summer months, which helped with the food bill. There were also the monthly welfare checks to Cook's "single" mother. By hiding evidence of a man in the house each time there was a visit due by the lady from the welfare office (a common deception among welfare families struggling to get by), the couple managed to keep the checks flowing.[10]

By all accounts his was a stable and happy family, with loving parents who kept their energetic and inquisitive children on a tight leash. It was "yes ma'am and no ma'am" in the Cook household, and reports of misbehavior outside the house were met with a prompt paddling or some other dire punishment back home.

In most ways a typical young boy, Wesley nonetheless reportedly stood out early from his peers in some ways. He loved to read and could do so before beginning first grade. When other neighborhood kids were out on the street playing, he would spend time in the local library. He also liked to visit local houses of worship to ask precocious questions of the local priests, ministers and rabbis. And he liked to explore. Not content to just hang in the PJs, young Wesley could regularly be found wandering around places as remote as Center City, trying to learn about the larger world around him. It was an activity that earned him the nickname "Scout" among his friends.[11]

Like his brothers, when Wesley was old enough for school, he attended Kearny Elementary School and Stoddard-Fleisher Junior High, and later Ben Franklin High School. In a flagrant flaunting of the laws of the land, all three institutions in North Philadelphia remained segregated with over 90 percent non-white student populations. Philadelphia was then, and remains today one of the most racially divided major urban centers in the country—a legacy that dates back a century or more. (While it was a Quaker city, a center of abolitionist sentiment and a main terminal on the Underground Railroad, there was never any sentiment in favor of integration where housing was concerned. As late as the 1970s, Rizzo was campaigning on a platform of opposing the introduction of federally-funded low-income housing in the city's ethnic white neighborhoods. Lynn Abraham, the director of his redevelopment authority—which did very little housing renovation in minority neighborhoods in those post War on Poverty, anti-integrationist days—was later to become the city's ardently pro-death-penalty D.A., particularly when it came to black murder suspects.) The schools may have been poor and overcrowded, but these stumbling blocks didn't prevent Wesley from standing out scholastically, both among his classmates, and in his own family.

Before Wesley even got to high school, his father died suddenly and unexpectedly of a heart attack—a tragic event that helped make him grow up fast. He soon began acting more like a big brother to his twin brother Wayne and his younger brother Billy, protecting both against the insults of the streets and schoolyard so common to boys of that age.

It was in junior high that Wesley got his first whiff of politics. One fall day in 1967, while listening to a teacher talk about the Pilgrims, he heard students chanting outside the classroom window. Thousands of students from Ben Franklin and Penn, the two sex and race-segregated local high schools, were all shouting out the words "Black Power" and marching towards the city's Board of Education. Wesley and hundreds of his schoolmates were drawn to the excitement like moths to a flame. Over their teachers' protestations, they headed out to join the throng. The occasion was an impromptu rally at the school board headquarters to demand a black studies program at the city's high schools. Wesley marched a few blocks, but then split and headed home, deciding to take the unexpected holiday to read his beloved Spiderman comics on the couch.

Spiderman saved the day. Or at least Wesley's day. While he was squirreled away reading, defenseless student demonstrators suffered a brutal, bloody assault by Philadelphia police, on orders from the city's race-baiting new police commissioner, Frank Rizzo.

It was the last such political action he would miss voluntarily.

While the police shattered the 1967 march on the school board, the issue was at least partly won as black studies did begin to enter the high school curriculum in the later years of that tumultuous decade. The period of the late 1960s and early '70s was a time of dramatic political change in Philadelphia as in most of America, and even many of the teachers, especially in Philadelphia's inner city schools, were moving with the times. One of those teachers, a Kenyan immigrant named Timone Ombima, was teaching Swahili, one of the main languages spoken in central Africa. It was he who gave Wesley his new name and identity in 1967: Mumia. Another teacher, Kenneth Hamilton, introduced him to the empowering ideas of Malcolm X and W.E.B. Dubois.

At 14, Wesley/Mumia was already steeped in the new concepts of black identity, freedom and equality, and in the history of African-American struggle. And it was that year that he first got a real lesson in repression and police violence to go along with his newfound political consciousness. In the 1968 election year, the racist governor of Alabama, George Wallace, was running as a third-party candidate for president. With three equally audacious friends, the young Mumia decided to go to white South Philadelphia and the Spectrum Arena to see Wallace first-hand at a campaign rally.

They somehow made their way from the subway station into the stadium uneventfully, amid a sea of Wallace supporters. Inside, though, as a band began playing "Dixie," the four youths began shouting "Black Power" and giving the raised-fist Black Power salute. As the enraged crowd began to spit on them and throw things at them, some helmeted police came and removed them from the stadium. Outside, Abu-Jamal, in an essay recalling the incident, says he and his friends, along with some other black and white protesters who had been ejected, went to the bus stop to return home. Before they could board, however, a group of white men attacked them:

I was grabbed by two of them, one kicking my skull while the other kicked me in the balls. Then I looked up and saw the two-toned, gold-trimmed pant leg of a Philly cop. Without thinking, and reacting from years of brainwashing, I yelled, "Help, police!" The cop saw me on the ground being beaten to a pulp, marched over briskly—and kicked me in the face.[12]

The boys were subsequently arrested, taken to the hospital for treatment on the way to the station, and then charged with assault. After hearing the arresting officer explain what happened and the reason for the charge, the judge at the arraignment said, "Assault? This kid's face assaulted your fist? Case dismissed."[13]

It was the last time Abu-Jamal would call the police for help. But he recalls being grateful for the lesson, saying, "I have been thankful to that faceless cop ever since, for he kicked me straight into the Black Panther Party."[14]

Indeed, only several months later, someone stuck a copy of the Panther newspaper in his hand. The intoxicating slogan, "Power to the People," hooked him right away. Within months, he was a founding member of the Philadelphia chapter of the fledgling radical organization. At the tender age of 15, his gift for writing led to his being made, "Lieutenant of Information" of the chapter, and a member of the staff of the national organization's newspaper, *The Black Panther*. He had found his political home and his calling in one fell swoop.

The Panther years were intense, action-packed—and short. By 1970, the organization was splitting apart and Abu-Jamal had left in frustration. But in the little time he had been a Panther, he was in the thick of things, spending time not just in Philadelphia but in two major Panther headquarters—New York and Oakland. He also had his first run-in with the FBI, whose agents halted and searched him when he tried to board the flight to Oakland. That incident is memorialized in a document found in the FBI file obtained by Abu-Jamal's defense team more than two decades later and excerpted here:

On three sixteen, seventy, Wesley Cook, [DELETED] and [DELETED] all BPP members in NYC, boarded American Airlines Flight Number Fifteen, departing JFK Airport, NYC, at eleven thirty PM, scheduled to arrive San Francisco at four seventeen AM, three seventeen, seventy.

In accordance with prior authorization by AUSA Tony Lombardio, EDNY. Wesley Cook was searched by bureau agents before boarding the plane [DELETED] no weapon was located. Both [DELETED] and [DELETED] were frisked also, with prior authority, with negative results. No incidents.

Cook described as six feet, one six five lbs., black jacket, striped bell bottoms, afro hair style, dark sun glasses.[15]

Busy with his Panther work, Abu-Jamal, who had temporarily reassumed his birth name Wesley in keeping with a BPP practice of avoiding the use of pseudonyms, let his high school work slide. He kept busy, though (to the dismay of school administrators), attempting to educate fellow students about the black power movement and the BPP. He also began his first romance, with a West Philadelphia woman named Fran Hart, later to be named Habiba, or "Biba" by Wesley.

Hart, who also joined the Panthers, was soon carrying Wesley's baby. When she bore a son, Jamal, on July 18, 1971, she also gave his father a new last name, Abu-Jamal, or "father of Jamal." It was an identity he bore quite literally. When he began reporting for some of the city's local news organizations, colleagues say he could often be seen at news events with his son Jamal seated on his shoulders.

Still officially enrolled in high school at Ben Franklin, the young father Abu-Jamal led a movement to try to change the school's name to Malcolm X High, which resulted in his being elected president of the student body. It also got him expelled. (The effort to change the school's name failed, and today it remains the namesake of the city's most famous Founding Father—and slave-owner.)

After a brief stint in New York City, where he tried to hook up with the remnants of the Panther organization still active there, Abu-Jamal returned to Philadelphia. At the suggestion of some sympathetic teachers, he applied to college, getting accepted at Vermont's Goddard College.

He was reportedly popular and a successful student at Goddard. Heavy politics were for the moment forgotten in the tranquil and frequently marijuana-scented environment of a rural college in the midst of the Age of Aquarius. But though he didn't know it at the time, even there in Vermont, the FBI was still keeping tabs on him. As a document from his FBI file reports:

> [DELETED] Vermont State Police, Montpelier, Vermont, advised on 2/23/72, that WESLEY COOK appears on a list of students in the Third World Studies Program at Goddard College, Plainfield, Vermont, and is residing on campus.
>
> Subject has not been physically observed by Albany Agents and Albany sources have been alerted in effort to identify him and determine his activities.[16]

At Goddard Abu-Jamal discovered radio, a medium that seemed ready-made for him, with his resonant, baritone voice, and his abiding interest in the human drama around him. It was here, while working at the campus station, that he began developing the skills that would later make him an in-demand figure on Philadelphia radio.

But while his professional life was getting in gear, his personal life was getting a little messier. He had brought Hart and his infant son Jamal up to Goddard and got her enrolled at the college (as a political science major). He also got her pregnant again. But between his school activities and his social activities (which included relationships with other women)[17] he didn't have much time for home and family. Though he and Fran got married up in Vermont, the relationship wasn't working, and so she returned to Philadelphia to her mother's house with little Jamal. There Abu-Jamal's daughter Latifah was born.

Abu-Jamal returned to Philly without graduating from Goddard—something he would only manage to do much later, from a cell on death row. While he lived with his mother and didn't try to get his family back together again, he became an active, involved father to his two kids, and remains close to their mother, who to this day is a fixture at rallies and fund-raising events to support his cause.

In 1974, he began working for real in radio, taking positions at and doing assignments for such stations as WKDU, WRTI, WUHY, WDAS and WHAT. For a while, he even adopted a new professional name, William Wellington Cole, after a station manager at a white station where he was working told him that the name Mumia Abu-Jamal was "too ethnic" for the station's target audience.

As his career was moving along, so was his love life, this time with a woman now known as Marilyn Cook, nicknamed Peachie, a teacher and a politically active person in her own right. They married in 1977, and moved into her mother's house in Germantown, a section of Philadelphia just north of North Philadelphia. It was there, in September, that Abu-Jamal's second son and third child, Mazi, was born. [Fig. 2 p. 176b]

By the late 1970s, Mumia Abu-Jamal (or depending on where he was broadcasting from, William Wellington Cole), was becoming a well-known radio personality and a recognizable voice on black, and even on some white mainstream radio stations across the city. As mentioned in Chapter 2, he and his voice were so recognizable that at least three of the blacks in the jury pool at his 1982 trial told the court that they recognized his name. His stories often reached out to cover people whom the media generally tended to ignore—poor tenants whose landlords were ignoring them, elderly project residents who couldn't get the city to fix their elevators, students in under-funded city schools and homeless people. For this he was dubbed "The Voice of the Voiceless." He also started to earn serious mainstream recognition. In January 1981 he was included on a list of "People to Watch" in *Philadelphia Magazine*, which wrote that Abu-Jamal brought "a unique dimension to radio reporting."[18] (By that time, Abu-Jamal had also moved on to a third wife, Mydiya Wadiya Jamal.)

There were other honors and awards too, including one from a coalition of community groups presented at the headquarters of the Universal Negro Improvement Association. Shared by Abu-Jamal with three other ace black reporters, Linn Washington, Joe Davidson and E. Steven Collins, it was for reporting on issues and problems in the black community, including police abuse. Collins recalls one such story by Abu-Jamal, saying, "He was doing some work for WKDU, the Drexel University station, and there was this story he did called 'Saturday Night Special.' It was a piece about a killing of a black man by another black man. But Mumia did it in a powerful way that really made it clear what was going on here. The perspective he took made you realize what was wrong. You see, 'Saturday Night Special' was the term that the city's white police used to describe a black-on-black killing. It meant you didn't have to break your neck driving to get there. You could take your time because it wasn't important. It was just a black guy. Mumia made that point clear in the story."

It was in the mid 1970s that Abu-Jamal first found out about MOVE, a back-to-nature group that revolved around the person and teachings of Vincent Leaphart, a black man, obsessive dog lover and charismatic if somewhat off-putting, self-styled street philosopher who went by the name John Africa. His followers—mostly African-Americans, but with a smattering of whites and Hispanics—kept their first names and adopted the surname Africa, too. Abu-Jamal's first brush with the group, which espoused veganism, kindness to all living things, and militant resistance to modern technology and the current political system and its agents, came in 1976. It was then that the Philadelphia Police started confronting this group, pressed by neighbors who were complaining about the stench of dog manure and the noise from amplified MOVE political harangues conducted from the MOVE commune's front porch. They began attacking the MOVE people at their house in the Powelton Village section of West Philadelphia, an integrated black and student residential area near Drexel and the University of Pennsylvania.

In classic Philadelphia Police fashion, particularly where black people were concerned, they were over-reacting. While at work, Abu-Jamal received a frantic call from his former wife Fran, who lived just a short distance away from the group. One of the police officers harassing the MOVE people had actually ridden his horse up on her front porch, almost trampling young Jamal.[19]

From the start, MOVE was a controversial group. While the organization was liked by some because MOVE members were generous with their time, helping repair people's houses, or doing errands for elderly neighbors, MOVE tended to annoy many other people, black and white. The main complaints were that members used obscene language freely, had developed an affection for amplified bullhorns, and kept so many stray dogs that their communal house had become a neighborhood nuisance. At the same time, they had a basic message—of peace and harmony with nature and one's fellow man—which appealed to many veterans of the 1960s. Indeed some of Africa's followers were former '60s radicals, like former Black Panther Delbert Africa.

Abu-Jamal was immediately attracted by the MOVE members' in-your-face attitude towards authority. There was something reminiscent of the old Panthers in their fearlessness and in their militant stance—right down to the guns they insisted they had the right to keep for their own protection. They were also an important local story, a story that was getting hotter all the time. The same aspects of MOVE that appealed to Abu-Jamal were a red flag to the police and to the city's mayor, Frank Rizzo, who considered their very existence, like the Panthers before them, to be an affront. MOVE, whose house was located in an area of prime real estate development because of its nearness to two of the city's important universities, began getting cited by Rizzo's building and sanitation inspectors. Arrests began in earnest as early as 1974. By 1975 they were becoming commonplace, and cases soon numbered in the hundreds.[20]

On March 28, 1976, as a group of MOVE people were gathered outside their home celebrating the release of seven jailed members, police on foot and horseback charged. A small three-week-old baby, ironically named Life Africa, was trampled to death. Since there was no birth certificate for the child, who had not been born in a hospital, the police tried to claim there was no baby. MOVE responded by inviting the media to come and view the little crushed body. Abu-Jamal ran a story a week or so later interviewing an eyewitness who told him, "I saw the baby fall. They were clubbing the mother."[21] Although several neighbors of the MOVE house said they had witnessed the trampling of the baby, no charges were ever filed by the district attorney's office in the infant's death.

From the outset, the mainstream media's coverage of MOVE was universally negative, focusing on their scruffy, dreadlocked "reggae" appearance and use of foul language in public. It was rare for reporters to spend much time interviewing MOVE members themselves, and stories on the group leaned heavily towards official sources in city government and the police.

As time went by, with police ceaselessly targeting MOVE members for harassment and arrest, Abu-Jamal's interest in the group and his coverage of their travails and struggles grew likewise. Eventually he would be dismissed from one job because the station manager felt his stories were too heavily focused on MOVE, and were too subjective. (It is interesting that Abu-Jamal's critics, who on the one hand claim that he didn't do any journalistic work on police brutality or corruption, are quick to cite his having been fired for doing too many pieces on MOVE. The whole MOVE story revolved around the group's constant conflict with and harassment by the police.) On March 16, 1978, police intent on starving out MOVE members encircled their house with a blockade that included sharpshooters and machine-gun nests. The blockade gained national and international attention and led to major protests within Philadelphia, even by neighbors who before had been complaining about the group. The siege lasted two months. But local residents effectively circumvented the effort, smuggling food and water to the MOVE residents. Finally, Rizzo backed off, ending the siege. But not for long. On August 8th, hundreds of Philadelphia police, heavily armed and wearing flak jackets, began a military-style assault on the MOVE house. In the ensuing one-sided battle, which included guns and water cannons, dozens of MOVE members were beaten and injured. A police officer also died, quite possibly from "friendly fire" by police, since witnesses, including reporters on the scene, said few if any shots came from the MOVE house.

Whatever the real story, nine MOVE members were charged with manslaughter in the death of Officer James Ramp. Their 1979 trial, covered by Abu-Jamal, was a major story for the city and for him personally, for whom it confirmed the bias and unjustness of the city's legal system. It turned into a media circus with the defendants refusing to be represented by their assigned counsel. In the end, the nine were convicted of third degree murder, conspiracy, attempted murder and aggravated assault and sentenced to 30-100 years each.

A second legal confrontation also played an important role in Abu-

Jamal's life and in his thinking. That was the 1981 trial of John Africa, who had been arrested in May along with eight other MOVE members by federal agents on a bomb-making charge that was based on the claims of a former MOVE member, Donald Glassey, who had turned state's evidence. Africa opted to handle his own defense without a lawyer, as did his co-defendant Alfonso Africa. Instead of rebutting the prosecution's case, the presentation of which he had largely slept through, seemingly unconcerned, John Africa simply made an impassioned statement to the jury condemning the courts as tools of corporations that were destroying the Earth. The jury, incredibly, found him innocent, acquitting him on all eight charges. Following the verdict, the jury forewoman explained that the jurors, who deliberated for 44 hours, felt the government case had "a lot of loopholes," and that the government's star witness, Glassey, had not been believable.[22]

That stunning performance by Africa was to have a profound influence on Abu-Jamal when his own turn came to confront the American legal system, convincing him that he too should handle his own defense, hopefully with John Africa by his side at the defense table as an adviser. But the two cases had crucial differences, which Abu-Jamal apparently didn't take into account. Africa had been in a federal court, and was on trial on a felony charge that didn't involve the death penalty, and given that there had been no violent act or injury, there was therefore not the same degree of passion involved in the case. Abu-Jamal was in a Pennsylvania state court, charged with the murder of a white cop, a situation where, in contrast, passions were inflamed. Replicating Africa's performance would not be easy. In fact, it proved to be impossible, for Judge Albert Sabo not only stripped him of his right to handle his own defense, ordering his attorney Anthony Jackson to be lead counsel over Jackson's own protests, but also denied him the right to have Africa at his side. (Oddly, John Africa never showed up as a spectator at Abu-Jamal's trial, even as Abu-Jamal was demanding the right to have him present at the defense table.)

It seems clear, in surveying Abu-Jamal's early and formative years, that whatever his behavior during his trial, his life before the events of the Faulkner shooting don't square with McGill's claim of his being "one step from the jungle." Clearly, ever since he was a teenager he has espoused political views that are radically anti-Establishment. Yet the undeniable truth is that whatever his politics and organizational affiliations, he had, until his confrontation on the night of December 9, 1981, maintained a remarkable record of obedience to, or at least observance of the law.

At his pretrial bail hearing, at the end of the trial, and at his PCRA hearing, character witnesses, including several prominent black elected officials, came forward claiming Abu-Jamal was not a violent man. It is sometimes difficult to evaluate the statements of such inherently biased witnesses. But perhaps the strongest endorsement of the veracity of their testimony comes—at least in a backhanded way—from the District Attorney's office and the police themselves. With all the investigative tools at their disposal, law enforcement officials surely would have found any incident, however small, had one existed, demonstrating violent or out-of-control behavior on Abu-Jamal's part. Both at the trial and later at the PCRA hearing, they showed up empty-handed.

So what did those witnesses who did testify have to say about the young Wesley Cook they had known, or the Abu-Jamal they had known in his young adult days?

Nellie Reynolds was executive director of a residence advisory board, a tenants' rights activist, and a former teacher at Temple University. She said she had known Abu-Jamal since 1974, a period of eight years prior to her testimony at his trial, and told the court that whenever he spoke at her classes or at meetings of her tenants' organization, he spoke about the need to be peaceful and law-abiding.

Falai Shionesu, a community activist and radio station employee who said she had known Abu-Jamal for five years, testified:

> His reputation is beyond anything I can possibly say at this point. He is upheld in our community. He has always been from the time I have known him. He is a type of person who if there is an incident occurring he is the type of person that would help cool it out, because people respect him. He is the type of person who has done just that.
>
> Brothers who are younger who may have seemed hostile on certain incidents he may have said words to them and they have removed themselves from whatever incident they may have thought they wanted to get into.[23]

While these testimonials certainly don't jibe with the description of Abu-Jamal offered by prosecutor Joe McGill, the character references introduced at the end of the trial, in a critical effort to sway the minds of the jurors regarding their general impression of the defendant, were decidedly poor choices. Not in terms of personal integrity, perhaps, but in terms of their probable impact on the jury. These were people for the most part of limited public stature, or who had only known the defendant for a relative brief period. Moreover, their relationship with the defendant was for the most part not intimate, and in many cases, was purely professional. Most were co-workers at various radio stations where Abu-Jamal had worked, or were community activists whose work he had covered as a reporter. Few had known him for more than a few years.

What was going on in the minds of the defendant and his attorney when they developed this witness list? Notably absent from the parade of character witnesses were members of Abu-Jamal's family, though his mother, sister and brothers had attended his trial daily. Also absent were people from his neighborhood and his school. Likewise missing were some of the respected community and political leaders who could have testified on his behalf. One example of such a person who was available but not called was State Representative David Richardson, Jr. He had testified in favor of a bail reduction after Abu-Jamal's arrest, and much later he testified at his Post-Conviction Relief Act hearing in 1995. But Richardson wasn't asked to testify at the actual trial, when such a credible, prominent and respected witness might have had a real influence on jurors. Why such a B-string list of references was brought to the stand at the most critical point in Abu-Jamal's life (the moment before a jury was to deliberate on whether to convict him of capital murder), and why no character witnesses were later called during the subsequent penalty phase of the trial remains one of the great puzzles in this case.

As Mumia's appellate attorney Dan Williams writes in *Executing Justice: An Inside Account of the Case of Mumia Abu-Jamal*, his controversial book on the case:

> Anthony Jackson never thought about how to advocate for Mumia's life in the event of a conviction. He never assembled evidence about Mumia's life; he never consulted with people who had known him at various stages of his life; he never even talked with Mumia about the subject. It was, therefore, inevitable that the penalty phase would be, at the least, a perfunctory affair, and at worst, a disaster.
>
> McGill had focused almost exclusively on Mumia's early association with the Black Panther Party, knowing that the jury probably held an image of that organization as destructive, ruthless, and threatening to all that white middle-class America holds dear.[24]

That shortcoming of the original trial was amply remedied at the PCRA hearing. Representative Richardson, the noted one-time chair of the Black Elected Officials of Philadelphia and a leading black elected official in the state of Pennsylvania, spoke about his character, as did Abu-Jamal's high school history teacher and his sister Lydia.

Here's what they had to say once they finally did have the opportunity to take the stand on his behalf.

Richardson, who said he had known Abu-Jamal as early as the late 1960s, said that he had spoken in favor of reducing the defendant's bail, which at his arraignment had been set at a prohibitive $250,000. Richardson went on to say of Abu-Jamal:

> You know, it's not often that you see someone who has come through the ranks of the struggle that grows [sic] you, and that Mr. Jamal was one of those persons that had an opportunity to really grasp the issues within the community and, notwithstanding his profession as a journalist, was also able to work with the community organizations and groups who would listen to his wisdom and knowledge. And we grew to know him—and I'm speaking now on behalf of many other people whom I know who know Mr. Jamal—we grew to know him as being a peaceful, law-abiding citizen and a person who had a lot of compassion for people and compassion for those issues that did impact directly on vital issues, such as housing, such as health care, such as feeding the homeless. And also at a time in starting a breakfast program for needy children within the community. So there were a lot of attributes that seemingly tied directly into this individual, Mr. Jamal, as being someone conscious and concerned about the community, and not a phony...[25]

Richardson, asked if in his personal experience with Abu-Jamal he had ever heard him talk of using violence, said simply, "Never." He added:

> I know he was a strong advocate to be a peacemaker in many situations that were involved in the black community, African-American community when there were struggling differences between various groups. Many times that the Church of the Advocate at 52nd Street, the Parish St. Thomas, St. Thomas Parish Church I think it was called, and also 50th and Baltimore Hickman Church AME, that there were several rallies that were called and many times there were struggles and fights that would erupt. And it was Mumia's voice that sort of like quelled and got order back to those settings to try to get people to realize the importance of why we must not be fighting against one another in a unity sense.
>
> And I can say that we had many situations where there have been toe-to-toe confrontations in the community and it has been Mumia that has stepped in to be the peacemaker.
>
> He, he was one of those that not only abhorred violence but he was for trying to make sure that all the time we saw peace and unity within our community and we would not use the divisiveness or the division of seeing the fights that erupted in our community has taken us away from the struggle and kept us on those points.[26]

Radio reporter E. Steven Collins, a colleague and competitor of Abu-Jamal's, also testified at the PCRA hearing in 1995. He told of having had Abu-Jamal over to his house for dinner, along with then state representative Milton Street (brother of the current mayor of Philadelphia, John Street), on December 8, 1981—just hours before the Faulkner shooting occurred. Asked if there was anything unusual about the defendant's demeanor that fateful night, he recalled:

> Mumia was, you know, consistently the same temperament. He always ended the conversation by saying "peace." And he meant it. He always seemed to have a pretty even-keeled personality. He had a way of holding his feelings until he sort of sorted it out and then he would tell you how he felt.[27]

Asked about any latent hostility towards police, Collins added:

> See, that's the whole, that is the whole question here. I knew, I've known Mumia for a long, long time. During that period prior to this incident we were very, very close. And in searching my mind, I can't remember one time where there was ever a discussion, any hostility, verbal or otherwise, towards any law enforcement, or even a philosophical view that would suggest that.[28]

Unfortunately, even at the PCRA hearing, Mumia's attorneys did not delve further into his state of mind at that last dinner. If they had, they and the court would have learned more about his emotional state only hours before the shooting of Faulkner occurred. Collins, who is now national sales manager for Clear Channel Communications, as well as a talk show host at Philadelphia radio station WDAS, said in an interview for the book, "That night Mumia was certainly not in any murderous frame of mind. He was lively, serious, funny—his usual self. He was Mumia. I remember we were having spaghetti and some wine at my apartment. It wasn't a planned evening. Milton Street [only recently elected to the state legislature] and his wife had stopped by unannounced, and later Mumia stopped by. He and Milton had a difference of opinion on some political issue—it was a spicy discussion—but that's what we were about at that time in the '70s. There was a lot happening and we were discussing and debating politics all the time. It wasn't anything bitter. Just a friendly debate. And that's the way he was. It was a regular evening with Mumia & Company."

He went on to describe Abu-Jamal, whom he had known at that point for perhaps a decade, saying, "People have created this image of Mumia as an angry young black man, but that was never Mumia. Even when he was a Panther, he wasn't into violence. You know, he grew up in an area of town where kids were hanging out with drug dealers or the guys who do the numbers. He had to have something to hang with too, but for him it was the Panthers. But when he was with the Panthers, he wasn't running around with a gun, he was writing. That's what he did. Mumia was a guy who loved life. He was smart, thoughtful, fun and caring."

Asked about Abu-Jamal's attitude towards police, Collins said, "You know, we were reporters. There were people in law enforcement who were our friends, and who helped us out with stories. There were good cops and there were also some cops who were SOBs. It was just like it is today. You had racial profiling, only we didn't call it that, we called it police brutality then, and we talked about that and did stories about that, but he didn't hate the police."

A picture of Abu-Jamal earlier, as a student, was provided at the PCRA hearing by Kenneth Hamilton, Jr., a history teacher who taught Wesley Cook at Benjamin Franklin High School in the late 1960s. Hamilton said the young Wesley stood out from the first day of class because of "his intelligence, his sincerity." Hamilton went on to paint a picture of someone who was the antithesis of a violence-prone criminal:

> We used to use Mumia, or it was Wesley then, as a student mediator. Because in those days at Ben Franklin High School we used to have a lot of mobs with gangs and gang war. And Mumia was very good with his peers. And as a matter of fact, when we heard that there might be a gang problem, because Mumia lived in the area where one of those gangs came from, we used to use Mumia to help keep calm, and he had a very calming effect on his peers.[29]

Hamilton's testimony stands out because it reveals Abu-Jamal's ability to defuse tense situations, and a willingness to try to accomplish that where possible.

The person who surely knew Abu-Jamal the best though, was his older sister Lydia Cook Wallace, a trained nurse and human services worker. In her testimony at the PCRA, she said:

> Mumia was very, very sensitive. If his brothers got into arguments among themselves, he would be the peacemaker. He was a real sensitive kind of kid.
>
> He wouldn't lie. He wouldn't lie. He used to get us in a lot of trouble. Sometimes we would be doing something we had no business as children to do. And we would all get in a corner and say well, we going, we going to tell mom that we did this, we did that. And

everybody said yeah, this is the lie, this is what we are going to tell.
Not Mumia. He'd get us beaten every time. He would not do
that, he just wouldn't hang with the crowd.[30]

Abu-Jamal's sister told how he had shown an interest in spiritual
things, even visiting local churches and synagogues as a child to ask ministers, priests and rabbis philosophical questions. As he got older, she said,
these interests intensified:

> Yes, his curiosity about spiritual things increased. And I guess
> when you say spiritual things we have to talk about love, you have
> to talk about being sensitive to other people and emotion. Like if we
> were watching a TV show or something, and something would hap-
> pen where someone was oppressed or something negative happened,
> he would be really outraged about that. He felt that even a roach had
> a right to live. He, he always expressed equal rights for people and
> fairness, fairness and justice and those kinds of things.[31]

These statements are no doubt going to be discounted by some on the
basis that all the character witnesses obviously wanted to do what they
could to spare Abu-Jamal's life. But further evidence that Abu-Jamal was
not violent by nature comes from a hostile and unexpected source: the FBI
files on Abu-Jamal's history with the Panthers. Compiled with the use of
spies and informants, these were documents which were being used at one
time in an effort to build a case against Abu-Jamal as a dangerous criminal.
They may have even been used by the prosecution (which came to court
armed with newspaper clips about Abu-Jamal that were over a decade old)
in its effort to gather damaging information about the defendant.

These files were part of a massive surveillance effort targeting the
Black Panther Party, an organization that began in the melding of educated young African-Americans who had cut their political teeth in the civil
rights movement and rough-hewn urban black men and women. People
like the young Wesley Cook—who saw a road to liberation from the ghet-
to in the inspiring and uncompromising words of Karl Marx, Mao Tse-tung,
Franz Fanon and Malcolm X. Founded in 1966 by Huey Newton and Bobby
Seale, the organization experienced a short but heady period of public
attention and political influence during the late 1960s, when it became
almost the iconic vanguard of the anti-war, anti-Establishment American
cultural revolution. The in-your-face toughness of the Panthers inspired a
whole generation of counter-culture rebels, black and white. They were
almost de rigeur fixtures at political rallies in those days, standing on podi-
ums with strong arms folded, legs spread akimbo in a consciously military-

style "at ease" stance, their eyes hidden behind dark shades, their heads covered with the trademark black beret. And they often flaunted the fact that they were armed. But the Panthers were riven by internal tensions dating back to the group's beginnings, and by an East-West factionalism between power centers in Oakland, Chicago and New York. The national, state and local police apparatus, at the instigation of COINTELPRO, launched a deliberate effort involving agents provocateur and dirty tricks, as well as overt pressure, to exacerbate those differences. Under this intensive governmental assault, the Panthers imploded. Government agents at all levels conducted bloody raids on Panther headquarters. Some leaders like Fred Hampton were killed. Others, like Geronimo Pratt, who had his murder conviction overturned and was freed in 1997 after having spent 27 years in prison, were arrested on various charges, including murder, many of them trumped up.[32]* Factions were lured into violent confrontations with other factions by the clever and insidious efforts of undercover police and their paid informants and provocateurs. It was a time of fear, frustration, loss of trust, confusion—and of bitterness and anger.

Yet Abu-Jamal, this supposed espouser of the Maoist philosophy of power flowing "from the barrel of a gun," didn't get sucked into the Panthers' orgy of self-destruction. Though he was and remains a holder of strong opinions, Abu-Jamal walked away sadly from the Panthers rather than participate in the fratricidal struggle. The source for word of his departure is none other than the FBI, where Abu-Jamal's file contains the following notation:

> Cook left the Black Panther Party in mid-October, 1970, having resigned. He was not the object of party discipline. He along with several other individuals long associated with the Party, ceased their BPP affiliation.[33]

Is this the likely behavior of a man whose actions are ruled by his passions?

Actually, Abu-Jamal's former appellate attorney Dan Williams says that in his years of working with Abu-Jamal, he learned that his client has, if anything, the opposite type of personality. "Mumia has a hard time with conflict," Williams says. "He doesn't like face-to-face confrontation. When he has a disagreement with someone, and they go to see him face-to-face, he will back away from it. He's very uncomfortable with personal confrontation."

---

*A federal judge freed Pratt after ruling that the government had failed to disclose that a key witness against him had been an infiltrator and paid informant.

Journalist and author Terry Bisson, in an authorized biography of Mumia Abu-Jamal based on interviews with Abu-Jamal and his friends and family, supports this view with an illustration of his subject's character from an earlier time. He recalls an occasion when Abu-Jamal's girlfriend Fran was pregnant with his first son, Jamal:

> Once, at the corner of Market and 7th, Detective Fencl [one-time head of the Philadelphia Police Department's notorious civil defense squad] slowed as he passed, and smiled (he always smiled) and spoke softly (he always spoke softly): "I should get out of this car and kick that baby out of her stomach."
>
> Not a threat of course.
>
> "C'mon Biba," Mumia said. "Let's just walk away. It's okay. It's going to be okay."[34]

If ever there were an occasion for a man to unthinkingly lash out at an abuser, this threat to assault his woman and kill his baby would have been it. Yet Bisson writes that Abu-Jamal kept his cool. He didn't lash out. He didn't even talk back. Instead he walked away.

The FBI itself lends further support to the argument that Abu-Jamal was not a violent man. Among the hundreds of pages of FBI files compiled on Cook/Abu-Jamal by the FBI during the COINTELPRO campaign against the Black Panthers, is a memo from 1974 stating unambiguously that he is not violent:

> In March 1973, per bureau instructions, captioned subject was deleted from ADEX [the list of people deemed subversive and slated as part of COINTELPRO to be rounded up and detained in the event of a national emergency] and no additional investigation conducted concerning his activities.
>
> Sources, however, have continued to report periodically on COOK and, although he has not displayed a propensity for violence, he has continued to associate himself with individuals and organizations engaged in Extremist activities.[35]

Of course, while it would appear that his nature was not that of a violent person, we don't know how Abu-Jamal would have reacted to seeing his brother being beaten by a much larger policeman. An officer who appears, according to the testimony of several witnesses, to have been using one of those heavy metal department-issue flashlights as a cudgel. McGill at the trial was, and even today remains, careful to avoid saying that Faulkner and Billy Cook were fighting, or that Faulkner was hitting Cook. He has always been careful to refer to what went on between the two men as an "interaction." But the testimony of witnesses is clear. Whether justified or not, whether Cook struck him first or not, Faulkner was hitting Cook around the head with an instrument that bloodied, and could have potentially done far more serious injury to him. The history of black suspects being seriously injured or even killed at the hands of abusive cops in Philadelphia is long and gruesome, and so for Abu-Jamal, under those circumstances to have come running across the street to his little brother's aid, prepared to do what he could to protect him from further assault—if that is what happened—ought to come under a different rubric than "vicious killer."

That, however, is not the storyline that was presented by McGill. As we will see, he carefully downplayed the "interaction" that left Billy Cook dazed and bloodied. Instead, he pulled together strands of testimony from his witnesses to suggest that Abu-Jamal had for no good reason sneaked up behind an officer conducting a routine arrest, shot him in the back, and then executed him point-blank while he lay on the ground.

This is not the point to examine the question of whether or not Abu-Jamal fired the first shot in an exchange of fire with Officer Faulkner. Leaving that important issue aside for a moment, would some members of the jury have reacted differently, in their decision as to punishment, if not in their guilty verdict, had they felt Abu-Jamal's younger brother was being brutally battered by a police flashlight, and that Abu-Jamal had been coming to his defense? Again, we can't know. Such reasoning would have been unlikely on the part of the jury for one simple reason. The forceful assertion that this was a violent, mentally unbalanced individual who ran across the street with a gun in his hand, hatred of the police in his heart, and with an intent to kill in his mind, went essentially unchallenged.

In trying to bolster that case, McGill also made much of the gun that Abu-Jamal owned, and of the Plus-P high-energy rounds that he had loaded into it. He claimed that the use of the Plus-P bullets in and of themselves showed that Abu-Jamal was a killer, not a man of peace. As McGill told jurors in his trial summation:

> Let me talk about the weapon. Is that all that this is? Ladies and gentlemen, consider the bullets. Consider those bullets. These very cartridges used, the projectiles that came from those cartridges, and since I do not have one of those, because none of those were in evidence, since they were all shot and other than the one that was taken from his brain, we use this which I borrowed from an officer. In borrowing that I tried to show you through the witness' testimony that various parts of the bullet represent. The projectile, the casing and so forth and fragments and whatever. This at the top is what is called a Plus P projectile. A Plus P is what was fired from this

weapon. A Plus P is what destroyed a life. A Plus P is what broke into pieces a brain. Plus P bullets. Highly powered bullets that officers by and large are not permitted to use.

Isn't it ironic that Daniel Faulkner after stopping someone in the normal course of his duties was killed by a bullet that he could not put in his own gun, because it was too highly powered?

Isn't it ironic that the shot he was able to get off, because it wasn't a Plus P, did not kill the individual? That is fortunate that that individual was not killed, but just isn't it ironic.

It is not the one bullet, ladies and gentlemen, that took his life, but several shots of Plus P highly powered projectiles, whether it be the back or the brain.

I would point out, ladies and gentlemen, to please consider when we go through all of the evidence that fact, because that is reality and that is what you are deciding on.

Ladies and gentlemen, in thinking of terms of intent to kill can there be any question of what was the intent of the Defendant when it was done? Because, ladies and gentlemen, as you heard this weapon being loaded as it was and the size that it was with those highly powered projectiles took eight to ten pounds of pressure, eight to ten pounds each time and it is fired five times.[36]

But is the case that clear cut? Abu-Jamal bought the gun—and registered it legally—after he had been robbed at gunpoint while driving his cab. It's a fair assumption that a lot of cab drivers—indeed millions of Americans in all walks of life, and including many district attorneys and even journalists (though not me)—own a pistol, and they own them not because they want to kill people but because they feel the need to carry some kind of protection. Like all those other Americans with a handgun, he bought that pistol not because he wanted to kill police, indeed not because he necessarily wanted to kill anyone, but because he felt the need to protect himself when he was driving a cab alone at night. As for the bullets he purchased, it doesn't seem particularly surprising that he might have asked the gunshop to give him something that would stop an assailant. (There is no evidence that Abu-Jamal bought either the gun or the ammunition with the intent of using them on a police officer, though McGill, in his summation to the jury, was clearly implying this.) If you're buying a weapon to protect yourself, you're already contemplating the eventuality of having to fight for your life, and at that point it makes little sense to go halfway and get something that might not do the job. Maybe it's not something that a pacifist would do, but in the context of America, where guns are next to motherhood, unless we want to call all the millions of men and women who buy guns to defend themselves and their families bloodthirsty wannabe killers, the mere fact of owning a weapon armed with high-velocity rounds shouldn't be equated with viciousness. To get there you have to also have a person with a demonstrably vicious personality.

And on this score, among others, McGill has failed to prove his case.

Mumia Abu-Jamal was and is, as his writings from prison clearly demonstrate, a militant, a radical, an advocate of black empowerment, and a critic of the current American political system. But the people who have known him since he was a child, who have known him as a young political activist, who have known him as a mature professional journalist, husband and father, all clearly state that he is not and never was a man prone to violence.

It should be added Abu-Jamal has spent over 20 years on death row, most of them spent in a supermaximum security prison designed to turn men into caged beasts. (And the record shows that violence in supermax prisons is epidemic, both among inmates and between inmates and guards.) Through it all, Abu-Jamal has maintained a record of good behavior that is nothing short of exemplary. This despite major provocations by prison authorities, which have included the illegal snooping through his privileged correspondence with attorneys, the denial of his request to attend his mother's funeral, and indignities too numerous to mention.

None of this is to suggest that such a man could not get angry, or even that such a man could not take a gun in his hand and shoot and kill a police officer. The question of whether or not he did such a thing will be examined later. What it does say is that any fair assessment of Mumia Abu-Jamal's life would have to lead to the conclusion that he was not a violent man by nature; not a man for whom violence was the first choice of action even in a crisis.

That is something that needs to be remembered as one considers and weighs the testimony of witnesses in this case, and in any reconsideration of the penalty for the crime in question. It is also something that it is safe to say was probably not considered by the jury in this trial, which had almost nothing to go on in trying to ascertain what kind of a person the defendant in the case really was.

Chapter Four

The Trial Part I:
Stacking the Deck for Conviction

"Your attorney and you goofed!"[1]

Uttered by presiding Judge Albert Sabo, that one line was blurted out in response to a desperate last-ditch effort by Abu-Jamal and his attorney, Anthony Jackson. It was the final day of testimony on capital murder charges in the summer of 1982. Abu-Jamal was attempting to get the court to compel the appearance of Police Officer Gary Wakshul, the officer who had accompanied him on his van ride to the hospital, and who stayed guarding him at the hospital until he was treated by doctors for his gunshot wound.

As mentioned earlier, what made Wakshul so crucial to the defense is a contradiction that drives at the heart of the case. The policeman's official report to a detective on that morning's tour of duty showed he had written that he had stayed with the suspect the whole time, and added that during that whole time, "the negro male made no comment." [Fig. 8 pp. 176f-g] Then, months later, he claimed to have heard a shouted-out confession: "Yes, I shot the motherfucker and I hope the motherfucker dies."

Admitting to Judge Sabo that he had failed to notice this remarkable notation tucked into a box near the bottom of the Wakshul interview (one of hundreds of documents supplied to him by the prosecution), Abu-Jamal's attorney, Anthony Jackson pleaded overwork:

> Mr. Jackson: I was forced to try and remember everything that everybody said and I couldn't do it.[2]

The exchange between the judge, the defense and the prosecution on whether to allow a key piece of evidence and to review the contradictory claim by a police officer, sheds a harsh light on how justice played out in Judge Sabo's courtroom.

Here was the interchange:

The Court: What is this officer that you want? What is he going to testify to?

Mr. Jackson: That he picked Mr. Jamal up at the scene.

The Court: So?

Mr. Jackson: During this time the negro male made no comment. He
was with him the entire time.

Mr. McGill: He is not around. I am going to object to bringing this guy
in. He is not around.

Mr. Jackson: That is what he says.

Mr. McGill: I am not bringing him in at the last minute.

The Court: You knew about this before. I am not going to hold up this
trial.

...

The Court: I don't know what he means by this. During this time the
negro male made no comments. That may be as far as he is concerned.

Mr. Jackson: He remained with him the entire time.

The Court: Look, there were a lot of police officers in that room. There
were other people that were there that may not have heard it.

Mr. Jackson: Judge, he didn't say "I didn't hear anything." He said he
made no comments.

The Court: Made no comments as far as he was concerned. There are
other police officers that were in that room and the only two that
heard anything was [sic] Durham and I forget who the officer was.
There was nobody else that made any statement that they heard
anything...

...

The Court: It is a fact he didn't hear it. It doesn't mean it wasn't said.

Mr. Jackson: It isn't a matter of him not hearing it. He is saying, in fact,
that he made no comment.

The Court: As far as he is concerned. He can't speak for everybody else
that is in that room. I am not going to delay the case any longer.

Mr. McGill: Judge, this Defendant has nothing else to do except this
case. It seems to be the strategy to delay it. We are getting closer to
the July 4th holiday and it would seem to be to get this jury disgruntled and upset.

The Court: It may hurt the defense, too.

...

Mr. Jackson: I think it is a matter that is crucial enough for us to do it.
How long is it going to take to get a police officer here?

The Court: How do I know? He could be on vacation.

(At this point there was a short recess.)

(The following is a discussion in chambers with both counsel present.)

Mr. McGill: Your Honor, I have made efforts to find out where Officer
    Wakshul is and am informed that he is on vacation until July 8th.
Mr. Jackson: Does that mean he is not in the city?
The Court: I am not going to go looking for anybody now. You had the
    opportunity to let us know in advance and we could have made the
    effort to bring him in.
Mr. McGill: It is not your fault, it is his. [Abu-Jamal's]
The Court: Who knows where he is?[3]

This exchange raises several issues. Was the testimony of a policeman
that contradicted the testimony of others relevant when others had said
they heard the confession? It's a critical question. But surely it was a critical question for the jury to ponder, not for a judge to prevent a jury from
considering by barring its presentation and exploration in court.

A second issue concerns how long a trial should drag on. Capital murder cases are notorious for being drawn out. But while no justice system can
permit endless delay, this trial had been in session only since June 17, a
mere 14 days. Apparently Sabo felt that waiting a few extra days would be
an undue burden on the jury and the court, even with a person's life hanging in the balance.

Lastly, the collection of arguments shows a judge attempting to
prevent evidence and testimony from being explored. First, he told
Jackson that he was not going to delay the trial to bring in Wakshul.
Then, perhaps realizing that this position on a matter of such significance to the defendant might look bad, he changed tack, suggesting that
Wakshul's written statement wasn't really that significant anyway.
Finally, he suggested to Jackson that delay might hurt the defense by
pushing the trial past the July 4 holiday, and upsetting the jury. At last,
in a curiously prescient moment, he suggested that in any case, Wakshul
might be on vacation. Sabo also pretends the issue is simply whether
Wakshul heard anything, and not that his changed report might point to
a conspiracy.

Shortly after this discussion at the bench, a defeated and deflated
Jackson announced to the court that the defense was ready to rest. This
critical decision was not arrived at in consultation with the defendant, but
simply announced. Abu-Jamal, who understood clearly that he was being
railroaded and that Jackson was giving up, immediately disagreed, saying
the defense did not rest. He demanded to have Wakshul brought in to
answer questions about the conflict between other witnesses' belated
claims that there had been a confession and his own contemporaneous
written statement that there had been none.

Denying the request yet again, Sabo's mocking response was blunt: "Your attorney and you goofed!"

Wakshul wasn't heard from again until 1995 at the Post-Conviction Relief Act hearing. As we will see in Chapter 8, it was revealed then that he had in fact been in the city during the exchange above on July 1, 1982, waiting and no doubt even expecting to be called to testify. That testimony will be explored further later. For now, suffice it to say that with that one line, Sabo insured this much: as the jury headed into deliberations on the fate of the defendant, it would be convinced "beyond a reasonable doubt" that he had heartlessly confessed to—and even bragged about—the murder within less than an hour of committing it.

The importance of Wakshul's testimony to the defense was amply demonstrated by the vehemence with which prosecutor McGill opposed having the officer called in. Did McGill actually know at the time that Wakshul was waiting at home? We have no way of knowing, because Sabo cut him off before he could respond to Jackson's question about Wakshul's whereabouts. Why didn't the defense pursue this? By that point in the trial, badgered by both Sabo and McGill, and berated by his unwilling client, Jackson seemed a beaten man, and didn't bother to press the matter. He didn't even ask for permission to appeal the decision as he had done on other issues.

That Sabo could have spoken so cruelly and cynically to a defendant whose life was on the line and who at that moment still had the presumption of innocence, and that he would have put courtroom efficiency ahead of getting all the evidence before the jury in this case, should come as no surprise. Prosecutors in the city had long considered having a homicide case assigned to Sabo to be the next best thing to having a defendant confess and enter a guilty plea. "Anyone will tell you that Sabo's reputation was that he was just another D.A. in the courtroom," says Jack McMahon, an attorney who worked as a prosecutor in the homicide division of the Philadelphia district attorney's office during the time of Abu-Jamal's trial. "The ethics of the prosecutor were the only limits on what went on in Sabo's courtroom."

Elected to the Philadelphia Court of Common Pleas in 1974, Sabo for the prior 16 years had been an undersheriff in the Sheriff's Department. Until his election to the bench, from 1958-1974, he had been a member of the law enforcement union and lobbying organization, the Fraternal Order of Police. An ardent conservative, on the day that murder defendants' cases went to the jury (including Abu-Jamal's), he routinely wore a tie plastered with the phrase "law and order."*

One of a group of Philadelphia judges who were routinely handed the city's murder cases, these were in fact the only types of trials Sabo sat for. According to a study by the *Philadelphia Inquirer*, Sabo presided over 31 murder cases in which defendants were sentenced to death—a national record. Of those cases, 29 were non-white, including 27 who were black— also a national record.[4]

In an editorial published during Abu-Jamal's PCRA hearing in 1995, the *Inquirer*, hardly a supporter of the black journalist's cause, nonetheless wrote of Sabo:

> The behavior of the judge in the case was disturbing the first time around—and in hearings last week he did not give the impression to those in the courtroom of fair-mindedness.
> Instead, he gave the impression, damaging in the extreme, of undue haste and hostility toward the defense's case.[5]

A month later, in a second editorial also focused on the PCRA hearing, the paper wrote:

> Over the last several days in a handsome City Hall courtroom, the search for justice in the case of death-row inmate Mumia Abu-Jamal might have been a serious, sober, national affair—a proceeding that enhanced respect for the law.
> That, unfortunately, has not been the case. And it has been, in large part, because of the injudicious conduct of presiding Commonwealth Court Judge Albert F. Sabo.
> Perhaps it is not relevant that he holds America's record for sending defendants to death row. Perhaps it is not relevant that he is reputed to see things the prosecutor's way.
> Those are not the facts that have led us to question his temperament and good sense. It has been seeing him in action in a highly charged case, in a volatile courtroom.
> He has allowed himself to be drawn into petty fights with defense lawyer Leonard Weinglass, an attorney with a long career of baiting judges in trials he has orchestrated into causes celebres. Mr. Weinglass has pushed far beyond the limits of what the law allows in

---

* While the phrase "law and order" might seem rather prosaic and natural in a courtroom, it should be noted that back in 1981 at the start of the Reagan Administration, and only six years after the Nixon Administration, the term still carried a far more loaded political meaning. It was used by both those presidents in their campaigns for office to signify a hard-nosed, anti-crime attitude that disdained and derided many constitutional protections such as Miranda warnings and due process which were deemed "liberal" and "soft on criminals."

such proceedings. He has had a heyday insulting the judge in the press, and sometimes to his face.

That Mr. Sabo was goaded though, is no matter. It is his job to remain above the fray, to deflect the needling, to set a tone of respect.

Instead, with his body language, baleful stares, barely concealed contempt, he has telegraphed an impression of hostility to the defendant, Abu-Jamal...[6]

Stuart Taylor, writing for the conservative-leaning *The American Lawyer*, attended the PCRA hearing in 1995 and put the case against Sabo more forcefully:

From July 26 to August 15, and the closing arguments on September 11, Judge Sabo flaunted his bias, oozing partiality toward the prosecution and crudely seeking to bully Weinglass, whose courtroom conduct was as correct as Sabo's was crass.[7]

His conclusion, looking back to the original 1982 trial:

The unfairness of Jamal's 1982 trial was almost guaranteed once it was assigned to Judge Albert Sabo.[8]

In addition to the original trial, Sabo later presided over the 1995 PCRA hearing, where he played the crucial role of "factfinder." As such, he largely established the limits within which the defendant could appeal to higher courts, and particularly to the federal courts. This is because, since 1996 and passage of the Effective Death Penalty Act, federal courts have been obliged to assume the facts as determined at the state court level to be true. The only exception is if a federal judge determines that a factfinder has been not just wrong, but *unreasonably* wrong. As we will see in Chapter 10, Federal District Judge William Yohn, despite finding a number of things wrong with Abu-Jamal's trial and appeals process, kept determining that the errors and improprieties he observed were "reasonable" or "not unreasonable," and thus not sufficient to require an overturning of the verdict.

Abu-Jamal's PCRA hearing would be presided over by a retired judge on call, since Sabo when he reached the mandatory retirement age of 70 in 1991 had ceased working as a regular judge. Two years after that hearing, Common Pleas Court Presiding Judge Alex Bonavitacola ousted Sabo from the bench entirely. No official reason for his removal was given. Age may have been a factor, but not necessarily: one retired judge was allowed to stay on the "senior judge" list until he was 91. A more likely reason comes from an official in the Supreme Court described by the *Philadelphia Inquirer* as "close to the decision." That unidentified source told the newspaper the decision concerning whom to cut was based on "productivity and temperament."[9] Since a hallmark of Sabo's trials was speed—Abu-Jamal's case being no exception—it's a safe bet that of the two possible reasons cited for his dismissals, productivity wasn't the problem in Sabo's case.

But even putting aside Judge Sabo, with his legendary bias toward the prosecution, Mumia Abu-Jamal had the deck stacked heavily against him from the moment police appeared on the scene of the shooting. As journalist and Temple University journalism professor Linn Washington puts it, "It didn't matter whether he was Mumia Abu-Jamal or not. You had a white cop shot dead on the street and a nigger with a gun sitting next to him. The cops in Philadelphia were going to nail his ass whoever he was."

Things went downhill from there fast. The first officer to respond to the scene, Robert Shoemaker, testified that he kicked the wounded Abu-Jamal in the head, knocking him over, because he thought the suspect was reaching for his gun. Then, according to the testimony of a number of witnesses—including some called by the prosecution to make its case—as more police arrived at the crime scene and several began attempting to handcuff Abu-Jamal, some began beating him with blackjacks or fists. After that, several police officers picked him up, carrying him face-downward, and rammed his head into a lamppost, then dropped him face down on the concrete. "An accident," they would later claim. Hemorrhaging internally from the bullet fired into his chest by Faulkner, Abu-Jamal was tossed into a police wagon. Jefferson Hospital's emergency room was just 3 blocks away. Yet he had to wait over half an hour before getting there. Along the way, it was his misfortune to be guarded by Police Officer Gary Wakshul, a man who years later was dismissed from the force because he had a record of battering suspects in his custody. There was evidence that this is exactly what happened to Abu-Jamal on the way to the hospital, in the form of bruises, cuts and lacerations on his body, though whether it was at Wakshul's and other officers' hands or simply because of rough driving by the van driver isn't known. Once at the hospital, police dropped him onto the floor of the ER entrance. One hospital doctor testified that Abu-Jamal was then viciously kicked by the crowd of police officers who surrounded him. Finally, he was tossed roughly onto a gurney by his captors for treatment by a hospital resident physician. Upon finally seeing Abu-Jamal, a hospital resident physician judged him to be near death from blood loss.

But that was only the beginning. If vengeful police on the scene hadn't managed to kill Abu-Jamal, the District Attorney's office, headed by future mayor Ed Rendell, was prepared to get the job done. Rendell, later a chair of the Democratic Party's National Committee who in 2002 also became the Democratic Party's Pennsylvania gubernatorial candidate, authorized seeking a death penalty in the case. He assigned the task to Assistant D.A. Joseph McGill in his office's homicide division. Now in private practice where he has been handling medical malpractice claims and defending police officers against various charges, McGill was a prosecutor's dream. A tough but soft-spoken Scottish-American with a flair for the dramatic, McGill is a master at playing to a jury. He had already prosecuted six death penalty cases successfully, making him one of the D.A.'s most experienced homicide prosecutors. When it came to convincing a jury to convict, he knew what he was doing.

Daniel Alva, the attorney for Abu-Jamal's brother Billy Cook, recalls going up against McGill as the defense attorney in a mob murder case. "It was a gruesome murder. The killer had taken the victim, who was a witness against him in another crime, to the river, tied him to a rock and threw him in alive," he recalls. "Well, McGill had a cop come into the court lugging that very rock. Then, when he got it in there in front of the judge and the jury, he dropped it onto the floor with this enormous thud. Dropping it was supposed to look like an accident, but I'm certain that McGill had him do it on purpose, because the impact on the jury of that heavy rock landing on the floor was enormous. I knew we'd lost the case the minute it happened!"

In an interview in 2001, McGill was asked about whether he had arranged for the cop to drop the rock. "I'm not going to comment on that," McGill said with a laugh. While he wouldn't confirm that aspect of the trial, McGill did say, "With or without that incident, I do often use drama in my trials. For example, I often use a witness to do a demonstration."

He also recalled how he had stunned the defense in a 1980 capital case concerning the slaying of a Philadelphia police officer, by agreeing to seat a nun as the first member of the jury. "She reminded me of the teachers I used to have back in parochial school," he said. "She seemed tough, but of course, being a good Catholic, she said she opposed the death penalty, saying it would be killing twice." Instead of summarily rejecting her, though, McGill questioned her further. "When I asked her if she could impose the death penalty, she said, 'I could follow the law.' So I said, 'Wait a minute, are you saying that if you found an aggravating circumstance that outweighed the mitigating circumstances, that you could vote for death, even though you're against the death penalty?' She looked at me with the kind of look I used to get in third grade when a sister said it, and told me,

'Sir, I could follow the law.' I told her, 'You know sister, I believe you.'"
When he agreed to seat her, McGill said he could hear sniggering from the
defense table.

"They thought I'd made a mistake. But sure enough," he said, "when
the jury went into deliberations, they sent back a message asking the judge
if they could include the phrase 'in accordance with the law' in the reading of their verdict. At that point, I knew we'd won. When they came out,
the jury foreman read out the verdict, saying, 'In accordance with the law,
we sentence the defendant to death.'"

So who did Abu-Jamal have working in his corner against the D.A.'s
ace?

From the start, his family had turned to an up-and-coming young
black attorney who had developed quite a reputation in the city's African-
American community for taking on the hot issue of police brutality.
Anthony E. Jackson, a Temple Law School graduate, had worked briefly in
the prosecutor's office under Arlen Specter, a liberal Republican who later
became the state's senior senator. But though Jackson had participated in
defending a capital case as an assisting attorney, he had never been the lead
counsel. In the process of getting his own private law practice set up,
Jackson knew this was a celebrity case. A case that, if he could win it,
would at least put his name on the map. He had a lot going for him—his
race, his politics, and a will to win. But he lacked experience in the arcana
of capital cases. Death penalty experts, from those at the National
Association of Defense Attorneys to those at the Philadelphia Public
Defenders Office, say that it is a disaster for anyone without capital case
training and experience to handle a death penalty case. The technical
issues are so great, with a raft of limitations on what can be appealed.
Beyond winning, a defense attorney's task in stepping through the mine-
field is two-fold. First, it is crucial to build a solid record as a basis for an
appeal to a higher court. Second, it is equally crucial not to make mistakes
at the original trial that would preclude an appeal.

Jackson's crucial lack of experience in death penalty cases might have
been overcome: Philadelphia's progressive legal community had begun
holding meetings to develop a crack team to handle the case of this well-
known progressive black journalist. But as several lawyers and local journalists recall, once Abu-Jamal and his family made it clear that they were
associated with the MOVE organization of John Africa, this effort collapsed. "Many local attorneys had felt burned by MOVE over the years.
Especially after the trial of the MOVE 9, which was a circus, and they sim-

ply didn't want to get involved," recalls Linn Washington, referring to the 1980 murder trial of MOVE activists charged in the death of a police officer following a 1978 police assault on a MOVE house. In their trial, the MOVE 9 defendants had refused to participate in the legal process, forcing their court-appointed attorneys to act in their defense without their cooperation. A lawyer active in the local chapter of the National Lawyers Guild confirms this account of the thinking among progressive attorneys in Philadelphia at the time. Whatever the reasons, no progressive or radical attorneys in the elite Philadelphia legal establishment came forward offering to serve as counsel for Abu-Jamal's defense, or even as co-counsel.

That meant the whole burden of handling the case fell on Jackson alone. And Jackson had some serious flaws. One was a lack of organization. His law partner at the time, Tim Crawford, recalls that his junior partner "had always had trouble keeping his papers organized." In a case as complicated and dependent on documents as this one, such a fault was no minor character flaw but a major train wreck waiting to happen. The police had interviewed well over 100 witnesses in the case, and to be prepared, a defense lawyer needed to meticulously review every single interview report for all those witnesses, many of whom had been interviewed multiple times by police investigators. One critical example of Jackson's failure to review those documents has already been mentioned: by his own admission Jackson failed to note the written comment in the Wakshul report to the effect that "The Negro male made no comment"—a point directly contradicting prosecution claims that Abu-Jamal had blurted out a confession—in time to include Wakshul on the defense witness list.

Jackson also apparently had a substance abuse problem. A number of journalists, prominent attorneys and black officials in Philadelphia unrelated to the Abu-Jamal case have said that it was well known among those circles that Jackson was "into the sauce" and a cocaine user. Circumstantial evidence of both problems can be found in his sometimes-odd behavior at trial, which ranged from overly emotional, even teary, to hyperactive and excited.

Billy Cook's attorney, Daniel Alva, spoke to the matter directly: "I wouldn't have hired that guy to fix a traffic ticket for me."

In fairness to Jackson, Crawford says he never saw any signs of drug abuse by his former junior partner. One would think that Abu-Jamal, who had certainly seen and known his share of cokeheads growing up in the projects, should have been able to spot the problem, too, yet he never made any such complaint. But in 1992, Jackson was officially disbarred for financial irregularities. One attorney familiar with the case suggests that these irregularities (technically co-mingling client funds) that led to his being disbarred actually had to do with supporting a drug habit.

Efforts to locate and discuss these issues with Jackson for this book, including messages left on his answering machine, were unsuccessful.

In any event, as the date for Abu-Jamal's murder trial approached, the line-up looked like this. On one side was a seasoned homicide prosecutor backed up by one of the largest prosecutors' offices in the country and supported by the investigatory machinery of the fourth largest police department in the nation. On the other side was a lone lawyer with a new practice, a man organizationally challenged who was without a secretary, who had virtually no death penalty experience, and who may have had substance abuse problems.

Mumia Abu-Jamal's trial before Judge Sabo began as scheduled on June 1, 1982, nearly six months after Faulkner was shot and killed. But during the intervening six months, a lot of things had happened—and didn't happen—that largely determined the way this case was going to go.

First, the judge who handled the pretrial proceedings involving the allocation of resources to the defense, defense motions to suppress evidence or witnesses, and other matters, Judge Paul J. Ribner, made a number of adverse rulings that seriously handicapped the defense. Efforts to have key prosecution witnesses, including Cynthia White, face a line-up, to prove whether they could actually recognize the suspect, were summarily rejected. (It turned out much later, however, that the police themselves had used photo line-ups to test at least two witnesses on their own). Requests for more than the state's standard paltry allowance of $150 per expert to hire an investigator, a ballistician and a medical examiner were likewise rejected. When defense attorney Jackson told the judge no one would work for the defense for that small amount of money, the judge replied, "Tell them to trust me." Given the Pennsylvania Courts' reputation for slow or even non-payment of such extra fees when billed, no one did.

While some states (but not Pennsylvania, even today) require the provision of two attorneys in any death penalty case, Judge Ribner refused the overworked Jackson's request to have a second one assigned to help him in the case. Perhaps most serious was the judge's response to the defense's request for the addresses of the dozens of witnesses interviewed by the prosecution and police. Agreeing with the prosecution's unsupported claim that providing such information to the defense could endanger the witnesses, the judge denied it. The lack of this critical information, combined with the lack of funds to hire a qualified investigator, made it almost impossible for the defense to contact witnesses without relying on the help of the prosecutor, who then had control over those witnesses. (Particularly in a case like this where many if not most of the witnesses were people from a notorious "red light" district who had criminal backgrounds or fears regarding law enforcement, having to rely on police to serve them with subpoenas was a major handicap for the defense.) The impact of this ruling by Ribner was devastating. In the short time the investigator hired was able to work on the limited fee provided, he was able to locate and interview only two potential witnesses. In both those cases, the discovery of the contact information resulted from the police inadvertently leaving address information on some of the documents handed over to the defense.

Judge Ribner, meanwhile, was perhaps not the unbiased magistrate he should have been in his pretrial role. Ribner had been similarly in charge of a February 1977 case involving a several MOVE members collectively charged with assaulting police officers. In that case, Ribner had shown a degree of vindictiveness towards the MOVE defendants that troubled many observers at the time. When MOVE defendant Robert Africa, in keeping with the group's custom, refused to stand when Ribner entered the chamber, instead of ignoring their protest as most jurists do when faced with similar behavior, he provocatively ordered sheriffs to force him to stand. In the case of two other co-defendants who hadn't shown up for the hearing, he ordered warrants for their arrest, despite being informed that they were out of town and would appear at the next scheduled hearing date. Ribner went on to try several members of the group in absentia, handing them unusually long sentences in state prison instead of giving them the usual short terms in the county lockup. In 1982, the judge's openly antagonistic attitude towards Abu-Jamal, who was publicly associated with MOVE and who wore his hair in the dreadlock style favored by MOVE members, was evident. For example, during early pre-trial hearings, he denied a reasonable defense request to have witness Cynthia White pick Abu-Jamal out of a line-up. (Ribner accepted prosecutor McGill's deliberate misrepresentation that White, actually his star witness, was not a key witness for the prosecution, but rather, just "a link in the chain of evidence.")[10]

In May, only weeks before the start of his trial, Abu-Jamal became increasingly concerned about the obvious shortcomings of his court-appointed attorney Jackson. He requested and received permission to act as his own attorney, with Judge Ribner assigning Jackson as his "back-up counsel." At that point, Jackson later related, a critical event happened.

Jackson stopped working on case preparation, assuming that his client would be handling that crucial work. Then, on the first day of the actual trial before the just-impaneled jury, on June 17, Judge Sabo revoked Abu-Jamal's permission to represent himself. Over both the lawyer's and the defendant's strenuous objections, Sabo required Jackson to assume the role of lead counsel, forcing the lawyer to play that role with absolutely no preparation.

Before the trial could even begin, there had been the matter of selecting a jury—an important step in any trial, but particularly critical in a capital case. In cases where prosecutors seek lesser punishments, it is not permissible for attorneys to ask prospective jurors about their willingness to impose penalties, on the theory that making them contemplate the penalty before hearing any evidence could prejudice them against the defendant. When prosecutors are seeking the death penalty, however, potential jurors are questioned rigorously about their willingness to choose the ultimate sanction in case of a defendant's conviction. Willingness to impose death is a pre-condition for becoming a juror and the prosecution has the right to remove all potential jurors who say they could not do so. Prosecutors can remove such jurors "for cause," meaning that there is no limitation on the number of candidates they can excuse. A corresponding right of the defense is supposed to even the score: the defense may likewise remove a juror who professes to believe all people found guilty of murder should die. But this hardly makes for balance. While many people will admit, and even take pride in declaring their opposition to the death penalty, almost no one holds, or at least admits to holding such an extremist view as wanting all murderers executed.

This weeding out of those opposed to the death penalty raises some troubling issues. Since juries are supposed to represent the local population, and since in most parts of the country a third to a half of the population opposes capital punishment, screening out those opposed to capital punishment is a radical departure from this principle. Yet if juries truly represented a cross-section of the population, then every jury in a death penalty case would contain at least a few jurors opposed to the penalty. Prosecutors, who in most states, including Pennsylvania, must attain a unanimous verdict to win the death penalty, would face an insurmountable obstacle. They would be forced to convince this representative sample of those opposing the penalty that, in the specific case they are judging, the crime is so heinous that jurors would put aside their beliefs and mete out the sentence. Should the principle of a jury of their peers be cast aside, as it is today, so that the hurdle is low enough that those found guilty of murder can more readily be sentenced to death? Or should that principle of the jury-as-representative-of-society be upheld, setting a high hurdle for this ultimate penalty?

Study after study has shown that this "death penalty qualifying" process in capital cases has an impact beyond the penalty phase of the trial. People who advocate the death penalty tend to be conservative politically, tend to believe authorities, particularly prosecutors and police, and are conviction-prone.[11] Thus death qualifying a jury produces a panel whose members tend to fit those categories. The job of the defense attorney in capital jury selection, then, is to try to "save" as many of those potential jurors as possible who seem both open-minded about the case and who have expressed reservations about or opposition to capital punishment. In this literally life-and-death game, the defense tries to get the potential juror to agree that, given some suitably horrible or grisly scenario, she might, under such circumstances, be able to condemn a defendant to death.*

Once the defense has accomplished this with a juror who is also generally opposed to the penalty, the prosecution is in a bind. If a prosecutor wants to remove the juror from consideration, she or he has to resort to one of a limited number of "peremptory challenges." The defense and the prosecutor each get an equal number of these challenges that allow them to remove jurors they don't like—20 each in the case of Pennsylvania. Jockeying for advantage, each side, then, can try to force the other side to use theirs up.

Abu-Jamal's trial took place in urban Philadelphia, where African Americans represented, in 1982, over 40 percent of the total population. This posed an additional problem for the defense. Since African Americans tend, on average, to be more likely to oppose the death penalty for historic reasons, the prosecution's removal of jurors who said they were anti-death penalty tended also to simultaneously remove many blacks from the jury pool. Indeed, the final jury selected to hear the case was overwhelmingly white.

But McGill took things even further. Of the 15 peremptory challenges that he exercised, challenges for reasons other than opinions opposed to the death penalty, 11 were used to remove black jurors—even those who said they supported the death penalty. In the end, this left a jury of nine

---

* The manifest unfairness of this whole process should be clear. Jurors are supposed to start with a presumption of innocence. When, during the trial, they are then forced to contemplate what they would do if the defendant were to be found guilty as charged, it may lead to at least some of them beginning to think of the defendant as already guilty.

white and only three African-American members, plus four white alternate jurors.[12] (Later, one of those seated blacks was removed, to be replaced by a white alternate.)

Was that racism? McGill insists it was not, as of course he must, since exclusion of jurors solely for reasons of race would lead a federal court to declare a mistrial. As he states, "I do not—do not—pick jurors because of race. What kind of fairness do they show. What kind of body language do they have in reference to the defendant. Sometimes it's a question of age or interest. Who would be more likely to listen to his radio show?"* he said in an interview. "It's the total package. Whatever the numbers were, it was how they reacted to me, what they said, whether they were the kind of person who'd be mesmerized by his persona. And I would not want to have people who would not like me. If they seemed antagonistic towards me, I would try to get rid of that person. What I wanted was a person who would not be swayed by the parties in the case. I don't remember a death penalty case in which I didn't have at least three, four, maybe five African Americans. It's absolutely incorrect to say that I didn't chose jurors because they were black."

Maybe so. But the objective result of McGill's deliberate removal of young blacks (he did accept a few older black jurors, but consistently rejected younger ones, often with peremptory challenges) from consideration was a jury composed largely of older middle-class whites. Just four years later, in 1986, in a key case known as *Batson v. Kentucky*, the Supreme Court ruled that trials where blacks were excluded from the jury disproportionately, were inherently unfair. (The ruling applies to Abu-Jamal's case because it was still on its initial state appeal at the time of the Supreme Court ruling.) In his case, the record shows that statistically blacks were sixteen times more likely to be struck from the jury by McGill than were whites.

From the first day of the jury selection process, on June 7, 1982, McGill showed what his true concerns were in his handling of the first potential juror. Under his lengthy questioning, Janet Coates, a 20-year-old black woman, explained that though she did not personally agree with cap-

---

* Here's an interesting philosophical and legal question: If McGill was, as he says, removing jurors because they were "more likely to listen to" Abu-Jamal on the radio, this would obviously be because, as blacks, they were more likely to listen to a radio station that had black demographics. Since the whole idea of marketing to and building a radio audience of a certain racial demographic is by definition race-conscious, isn't selecting a jury based on their likely preference for such racially-targeted radio stations in itself race-conscious jury selection?

ital punishment, she could impose the death penalty. She also stated that she would make her decision on guilt or innocence based upon the evidence, not upon her own feelings. On its face, she seemed a perfectly satisfactory juror.

It was the defense's turn to question her next. This was done by Abu-Jamal, who at the beginning of the jury selection process was acting as his own counsel. He focused on whether or not she understood the concept of a "presumption of innocence," to which she replied affirmatively.

At that point, McGill requested and received permission to ask a follow-up question. Here he homed in on an earlier statement Coates made to the effect that she liked to believe there are "two sides to every question." What would she do, McGill asked her, if Abu-Jamal chose to put on no defense.

Although the woman insisted several times that she could reach a decision based solely on the evidence put forward by the prosecution, McGill kept pressing, finally getting her to say:

> A: I wouldn't hold it against him, but I think that he should have some
>   kind of evidence on his behalf. Even if he did it or not, but if he did
>   it, he still should have some evidence to uphold his behalf, right. But
>   I can't judge if he's guilty or not just coming from you."
> Q: You can't judge that?
> A: No.
> Q: Challenge for cause, Your Honor.[13] [Meaning he sought to excuse her
>   without having to waste one of his 20 peremptory challenges.]

Abu-Jamal, who clearly wanted this woman on his jury, or at least, if he couldn't have her, wanted to force McGill to waste one of his peremptory challenges on her, sought to rescue her with a follow-up question. He asked whether she would hold it against him if the state presented what she felt was insufficient evidence of guilt but he presented no defense at all. She replied simply, "No." McGill had been trying to get Coates, whom he obviously didn't want on the jury, to say something which would imply that she would not be fair if the defendant were to decide to exercise his right not to present any defense at all. Abu-Jamal successfully defeated that attempt.

Judge Sabo in the end denied that challenge for cause by McGill, which had been a stretch in the first place, so McGill tried another tack. This time he put forward the argument that Coates had an "inability to grasp the issues or the law." This was clearly not the case, as the juror made it quite clear that she understood the principles of presumption of innocence, and the requirement of the prosecution to prove its case "beyond a reasonable doubt."

Abu-Jamal countered that the juror had made herself clear on the issues and said:

> Now Mr. McGill is saying that she's not the most articulate juror in the world, but we are not looking for articulation. We are looking for honesty and impartiality.[14]

He then added:

> I understand what Mr. McGill is saying, but the point, I guess, is she's answering based on some logical feelings that if she didn't hear anything from me she would think that wasn't fair.
>
> Now, obviously what Mr. McGill is not saying is that I will present a defense and she will hear from me.[15]

When McGill continued to suggest that the juror has an "inability to understand" the law, Sabo, in what was to be one of the few times during the trial that he sided with the defense, said:

> The challenge for cause is denied. I think she understands, Mr. McGill.[16]

Failing to convince the judge to accept his challenge for cause, McGill used his first peremptory challenge and Coates was dropped. One potential black juror out. What makes this episode significant is the tenacity with which McGill can be seen trying to exclude this potential juror from the panel, and the abruptness with which he uses his first peremptory challenge once it is clear that he cannot find a way to get her excluded "for cause."

While he didn't manage it in the case of Coates, McGill did successfully eliminate several dozen potential black jurors for cause, without having to waste precious peremptory challenges. Sometimes in that effort he had the able assistance of the judge. For example in the case of Dawn Williams, a young black woman, McGill discovered during his questioning that she was opposed to the death penalty. By that point, attorney Anthony Jackson was handling the *voir dire* for the defense after the judge, at the urging of McGill, had removed Abu-Jamal's right to represent himself. He managed to elicit a response from the woman that in the case of "something extreme," she might be able to vote for a death penalty.

McGill came back and had the following dialogue with Williams:

> Q: No matter what Mr. Jackson might say, the Judge or any-

one, isn't it really true that really you could never in any case impose
the death penalty?

A: Yeah, that's true.[17]

In an effort to see if he could get her to agree again that if a crime were
sufficiently dreadful she could agree to the death penalty, Jackson asked if
he might follow up with another question. Sabo cut him off, saying simply,
"I am satisfied. You are excused."[18]

One of those black jurors rejected summarily by McGill with the use
of a peremptory challenge was Beverly Green. A 29-year-old black woman
who had grown up in North Philadelphia, Green said she had no philosophical opposition to the death penalty. In response to McGill's questions,
Green said she had no bad feelings towards either the legal system and the
D.A. or the defendant. She said she could read her verdict in open court
and that she could hear all witnesses impartially, even those with criminal
records. She said, like most of those in the jury pool including those who
were chosen to sit for the trial, that she had heard publicity about the case,
but that she could still be fair. She was, in other words, at least based upon
the responses she gave, the perfect juror for the prosecution in a death
penalty case. Perfect, except that she fit a certain category which McGill—
judging from his record of peremptory challenges—seemed not to want on
the jury: black, young, female and from a low-income part of town.

McGill used another of his peremptory challenges to reject her.

Despite his protestation to the contrary in 2001, McGill was extremely conscious of race in the selection of a jury panel for this trial. That he
assumed that, at least in the case of blacks, race might be a determinant of
attitudes towards guilt or innocence, was suggested by an incident during
the trial. During cross-examination by Jackson of Cynthia White, the prosecution's star witness, McGill suddenly noticed Calvin Wilson, a black
judge (now deceased) who had entered the courtroom to sit in the spectators' gallery on the side where Abu-Jamal's family was seated. It might be
reasonable for a prosecutor to be concerned when a judge seats himself in
the courtroom near the family. But McGill's concern is clearly race, though
when Jackson brings this up, McGill quickly recovers. Here's the incident
in full:

Mr. Jackson: Well—

Mr. McGill: Excuse me? Is that Judge Wilson over there?

Mr. Jackson: [still trying to continue with his cross-examination] It may
   refresh her recollection.

Mr. McGill: If the court pleases, the two black jurors may know him.

Mr. Jackson: Just because they're black —

Mr. McGill: Or anybody.

The Court: [ignoring McGill's interruption] Let me say this. What is the
purpose of this mug shot?[19]

Claims of racism in the jury selection process are countered by a simple fact: McGill did approve four blacks for the panel (though he did play
an active role in helping to oust one of those later, and though one, a middle-aged black man, was peremptorily dismissed by Abu-Jamal). But there
is a good reason why McGill approved those four: while he no doubt could
have succeeded in choosing a completely white jury in this case, this would
have been a mistake because on later appeal, the ultimate verdict would
have been vulnerable and possibly overturned.*

But how can this rejection of blacks for the jury panel, strategic as it
may have been, be construed as an issue of race? In 1997, evidence came to
light that race was an important factor not just in Abu-Jamal's case but in
every capital case in Philadelphia. Evidence that describes McGill's selection behavior precisely, that the D.A.'s office had long operated on the theory that it was an advantage to have a few of the "right kind" of blacks on
a jury. It was revealed that year, 15 years after Abu-Jamal's trial, that a
training video on jury selection for young assistant prosecutors in the
Philadelphia D.A.'s office had been made 10 years earlier. Produced by veteran prosecutor Jack McMahon, who had been a leading prosecutor in the
D.A.'s homicide section at the time of Abu-Jamal's trial, this tape encouraged prosecutors to keep low-income blacks off of jury panels. "In my experience, black women, young black women, are very bad," McMahon says in
the video, adding that educated blacks aren't good either. "You don't want
the real educated ones."

McMahon's instructions to the department's new recruits on how to
avoid getting into trouble on appeal over race, while continuing to use it
as a factor in jury selection were explicit:

> In the future, we're going to have to be aware of *Batson*, [the
> Supreme Court's 1986 landmark ruling on race-based jury selection]
> and the best way to avoid any problems with it is to protect your-
> self.... And my advice would be in that situation is when you do have

---

*Even before *Batson*, courts frowned on the barring of blacks from juries. As early as 1935, in
Norris v.Alabama, the Supreme Court barred the systematic exclusion of blacks from juries.
But until *Batson*, proving a racial motive for such exclusion was terribly difficult. Defense
attorneys were required to show a pattern of discrimination by a prosecutor over a number
of trials.

a black juror, you question them at length. And on this little sheet that you have, mark something down so that you can articulate later if something happens.... So if—let's say you strike three blacks to start with, the first three people and then it's like the defense attorney makes an objection saying that you're striking blacks. Well, you're not going to be able to go back and say, oh—and make up something about why you did it. Write it down right then and there.... And then you can say, 'Well, the woman had a kid about the same age as the defendant and I thought she'd be sympathetic to him' or 'She's unemployed and I just don't like unemployed people.... ' So sometimes under that line you may want to ask more questions of those people so it gives you more ammunition to make an articulable [sic] reason as to why you are striking them, not for race.[20]

Now in private practice where he has been defending death penalty convicts, McMahon contritely apologizes for what was said on the training tape. He went on to reveal more about the tactic in an interview in 2001, explaining that getting a few black jurors—ideally three or four elderly women from the south—can be an advantage for the prosecution. He suggests that such people are generally in favor of law and order, and will support the death penalty, and they insulate the verdict against a later challenge that the jury was selected by race.

The training tape was made five years after McGill prosecuted Abu-Jamal. But McMahon in 2001 says that on the video, he was explaining the long-standing methods and policies of the D.A.'s office. "All I was doing was talking without notes off the cuff, " he says. "I was just talking about the things I'd experienced over the years and that I'd been taught in the department."

How racism such as this has been handled in Pennsylvania is revealing. At the time of the video, the Philadelphia D.A.'s office was headed by District Attorney Ron Castille, a Republican. Later, he became a member of the state's Supreme Court, where he is still a sitting justice. In that capacity, Castille ruled on Abu-Jamal's appeal to the state's high court, which he declined to recuse himself from hearing.

For their part, neither Abu-Jamal nor Jackson did a particularly skillful job of jury selection, and a number of bad mistakes were made. One example concerned potential juror Delores Coleman. The middle-aged black supermarket cashier told Judge Sabo, who handled her *voir dire* questioning, that she thought she'd have a hard time being fair if she thought there might be a death penalty. But she also said she'd never had to think about that issue before. It had caught her by surprise. That was an obvious opening for the defense to try and "salvage" her as a juror by asking whether there might be horrific crimes for which she could support a death penalty. But the defense didn't bother to pursue this tried and true line of questioning, giving McGill a free pass to reject her "for cause."

More seriously, Abu-Jamal, early in the process when he was handling the questioning himself, wasted several peremptory challenges instead of saving them by building a case for a challenge for cause. Take the case of Kenneth Warner, a printer whom McGill found acceptable after routine questioning by the judge, for example. Abu-Jamal might have asked questions about how Warner felt about Abu-Jamal's looks, his race, the nature of the crime, etc., in hopes of eliciting some response that would have justified a challenge for cause. Instead, to remove the potential juror, he simply used one of his precious peremptory challenges.[21]

With the next potential juror, James Burgess, he did the very same thing. An army veteran from North Philadelphia and a customer service representative for the Philadelphia transit authority, SEPTA, Burgess said he had formed no opinion about the case, and that he would be able to vote for a death penalty. McGill found him acceptable. For some reason, Abu-Jamal didn't want this man on his jury. But instead of trying to pursue some line of questioning that might demonstrate some unfitness that would allow him to dismiss him for cause, he simply made another peremptory challenge.

Possibly because of Abu-Jamal's (and to a lesser extent Jackson's) injudicious early use of peremptory challenges, and because of Sabo's sometimes blatant interference in the process, the defense exhausted their allotment of 20 peremptory challenges. Then the selection process reached Edward Courchain, a middle-aged white postal worker. With no means of removing him, the defense was forced to accept a man who had candidly told McGill that he was biased against the defendant and would find it "a little difficult" to follow the instructions of the court. He said he had been swayed in his opinion about the case by the media coverage he had already seen and read.

When it was Jackson's turn to question Courchain, he asked point-blank whether he could be fair:

> Mr. Jackson: ...The questions I am asking you—although I know you can't predict with any absolute certainty what you're going to do in the future—we need to know now in your best judgement, whether or not you could be objective in this matter, stay in the middle, don't lean towards the prosecution, don't lean towards the defense, whether or not you could objectively determine the facts of this case?

The Prospective Juror: Do you want an honest opinion?
Mr. Jackson: Yes, sir.
The Prospective Juror: No.[22]

In his book on the case, defense attorney Dan Williams writes:

> Jackson, who had already unearthed sufficient grounds at that point to move to dismiss for cause, for some reason continued with his questioning, asking, "Sir, if I were to tell you that the law requires that if you were to serve as a juror you are to set that aside, could you do that?"
>
> Courchain paused. "I would try, but I don't know. Consciously, I don't know.
>
> Pressed further, he elaborated, "I said unconsciously, I don't think I could be fair to both sides."
>
> At that point Jackson asked that Courchain be dismissed for cause.
>
> "Denied," said the judge.
>
> When an astonished Jackson challenged the judge's decision, Sabo questioned Courchain further. All the juror could say was that he "would try" to be fair. That satisfied Sabo and he stuck with his ruling, accepting Courchain onto the jury.[23]

None of this might have mattered; at that point, a 12-member jury had already been seated and Courchain was only an alternate. But a few days later, an incident occurred involving one of the three black jurors, Jennie B. Dawley, making Courchain a much more dangerous figure for Abu-Jamal.

A feisty, older, retired black woman, Dawley was accepted onto the jury by both Abu-Jamal and McGill during the first day of jury selection. She had told both sides she could be fair. But later, on June 17, there was a problem. Sequestered in a hotel for the duration of the trial, Dawley had learned that her cat was sick. She asked for permission from the court to bring the cat to the veterinarian but was denied permission by the judge. The juror had requested that the prosecution and defense give their opinions on the matter, but Sabo didn't bother to alert either side. In sharp contrast, when a white juror requested permission to leave sequestration to allow him to take a civil service exam, Sabo not only granted him permission but delayed the trial for half a day while the juror was away taking the test. In any event, Dawley, worried about her pet enough to risk a contempt of court charge, simply left her hotel room, took the cat to the vet and returned 90 minutes later.

Informed of this violation of his sequestration order, both McGill and the judge decided she should be removed from the panel. A meeting on

June 18 was held in the judge's chambers and recorded by the court stenographer. Abu-Jamal was excluded, having at that point been removed
from the courtroom by Sabo for allegedly being disruptive. At the meeting,
the judge, the prosecutor, and the defense attorney agreed to remove
Dawley—the only juror actually selected by Abu-Jamal himself acting as
his own counsel. Jackson initially objected to her removal, saying that
since Abu-Jamal personally had selected her, he should have a say in the
decision. The judge and the prosecutor, who clearly wanted her out, probably because of her demonstrated willfulness and feisty behavior, ganged up
on him, telling him that she would be bad for the defense:

> The Court: I thought you ought to know about it [her violation of
> sequestration]. Believe me, I was not going to keep her in the begin-
> ning.
> Mr. McGill: I thought she was good. She hates him, she hates Jamal,
> can't stand him.
> The Court: That's not the point, that she hates Jamal.
> Mr. McGill: Can't stand him.
> The Court: That's one point, but doing what she did worries me.
> Mr. McGill: That's a violation of the law. She says she won't follow the
> law.
> The Court: But the thing is when this case is finally over and she's out
> deliberating and they're taking too long, she's going to get up and
> walk out, just walk out, you know.
> Mr. McGill: That's true.
> Mr. Jackson: Unless she thought—well, I don't know if it's just the cat.
> ...
> The Court: I was surprised that you took her in the beginning. She had
> a very belligerent attitude.
> Mr. McGill: She was soft to me. She turned around and said, "Don't you
> ask me about my husband."
> Mr. Jackson: I thought it was a matter of whose side she ended up on but
> she was definitely belligerent.[24]

Her replacement was the openly-biased Courchain.

While the selection of the jury for Commonwealth of Pennsylvania v.
Mumia Abu-Jamal a/k/a Wesley Cook was a disaster for the defendant,
something else happened during that time which would further help seal
Abu-Jamal's fate. This was a process—some might say a conspiracy—
involving the judge and the prosecutor, aimed at preventing Abu-Jamal
from handling his own defense, and at driving a wedge between him and
his court-appointed attorney Jackson. The idea seems to have been to pro-

voke Abu-Jamal into becoming unruly and disrespectful in court in front of the jury. The process began during the early days of the trial, when Abu-Jamal sought permission to have John Africa sit as an adviser at his defense table. Ample precedents for having such non-lawyer advisers at a defendant's side included one case underway simultaneously in another courtroom of the same City Hall building involving a police officer as the defendant. Sabo, who consistently misstated Abu-Jamal's request as wanting Africa to be his lawyer, not just an adviser, absolutely refused. This led to repeated angry outbursts from Abu-Jamal. McGill was aware of Abu-Jamal's mounting frustration and soon saw a way to stoke it. Right at the end of the second day of the jury selection, he informed reporters covering the trial that he planned to ask the judge to take the responsibility for jury questioning away from Abu-Jamal.

McGill claimed that Abu-Jamal was frightening and intimidating jurors. Yet reports of the trial showed otherwise. One reporter covering the first two days of the *voir dire* stated that Abu-Jamal's "demeanor during the selection process has been subdued."[25] A day earlier, the *Inquirer* reporter Marc Kaufman, covering the first day's *voir dire*, had written:

> Although Abu-Jamal was disruptive and often demanding during last week's [pretrial] proceedings—frequently asking the judge, for instance, to allow MOVE founder John Africa to sit with him at the defense tale—he was intent and business-like yesterday.[26]

Was McGill really worried that the defendant was "frightening" jurors or making the process of jury selection too long? This seems unlikely. McGill's own questioning of jurors often dragged on longer than did Abu-Jamal's. More to the point, a defendant frightening jurors would tend, if anything, to work to the prosecution's advantage. Instead, suggests Abu-Jamal's former appellate attorney Dan Williams, McGill's concern might have been that Abu-Jamal was doing too good a job. As we saw, on the first day of the *voir dire* process, Abu-Jamal had even managed to convince the judge to reject McGill's challenge "for cause" of potential juror Janet Coates, forcing him to use a peremptory challenge to keep the young black woman off the jury. Writes Williams:

> The art of jury selection is simple, but few lawyers know how to do it, because the process of legal education actually throttles the ability to communicate spontaneously and authentically with real people. They inherit from law professors a liking for word games and rigid logic, and they develop a discomfort with the free-flowing give-and-take of genuine communication. Consequently, most lawyers ask mind-numbing questions, peppered with multisyllabic, sterile

words delivered stiffly—hardly an invitation to openness and honesty.[27]

In contrast, he writes:

> Mumia had always been a natural and fearless communicator, and he had honed that craft during his years as a radio commentator and journalist. But more importantly, he loved people and was unafraid to be vulnerable. As a result, he was open to hearing the good and the bad. He wanted to know if the prospective jurors didn't like his hair, if they were afraid of him, if they came into the city hall building already feeling that he was probably a cop killer. His own willingness to be open and vulnerable induced communicative reciprocity in many of those who he questioned.
>
> McGill didn't like that, so he wanted Judge Sabo to do something to put a stop to it.[28]

The veteran prosecutor knew how to get Sabo to agree to his request to remove Abu-Jamal from the *voir dire* process. This was, after all, a judge with a well-known predilection for moving cases along at high speed. Experienced prosecutors like McGill knew this judge didn't like his courtroom to get bogged down. So McGill would complain about delays. Accordingly, in asking Sabo to remove the defendant's right to handle the jury questioning, he offered the following reasons for his motion:

> The first is that I believe that the speed of the voir dire, or shall I say the pace...is extremely deliberate, very slow.
>
> The second reason is because of my own experience in past trials, I could say that in response to what I have observed during the course of this *voir dire* it appears to me and it will appear on the record certainly in the last two witnesses, it appears to me in that many cases throughout the *voir dire* there is an unsettling effect when the defendant, who is charged with such a heinous crime, if the facts are accepted by the jurors, particularly that of shooting a policeman in the back and then shooting him in the face at close range, it tends to create in the venireperson [prospective juror] an unsettling feeling, as a matter of fact in a few jurors outright fear.[29]

Though the defense failed to point it out, this second argument should have been laughed out of court. If jurors were "accepting as fact" that the man questioning them had actually committed those two "heinous" acts, they should have been automatically excluded from the jury; which is exactly what the defendant was attempting to discover. As to the matter of "pace," Jackson responded that a number of recent capital cases had taken as long as five weeks to select a jury; this objection from McGill came on only day three of the process.

Sabo, however, sided with McGill:

> Now, it is true I have not rebuked Mr. Jamal at any time, but the Court is not without cognizance of the fact that he has been very, very inexperienced in voir diring the venire panel and that he has been very, very slow in even getting started when it is his time to get started, and it has been a constant looking to you for phrasing of questions, which have taken a long time. I have been very patient about it and I haven't said anything, but that doesn't mean that I haven't noticed. I don't have to wait for the D.A. to tell me that.
>
> The fact is I have been very cognizant of the fact that these venire people [potential jurors] have been rather unnerved or upset when they have been questioned by Mr. Jamal. As a matter of fact, in some cases there has been outright dissension by these people, sort of like an antagonistic reaction.[30]

Again, if potential jurors were having such negative reactions to the defendant, it was arguably quite in his interest to see to it that they were removed from consideration for seating on the panel. But obviously those were people that the prosecutor was anxious to have included as jurors.

Sabo was going to help him. He instructed Jackson to take over the task of *voir dire* questioning, warning that if Abu-Jamal disagreed with that plan, the judge would take over the process for both sides.

Having already lost confidence in his court-appointed attorney, who had admitted he had not been preparing for trial, and who had asked repeatedly to be removed from the case, Abu-Jamal initially rejected the idea of having Jackson handle the jury questioning. He told the judge, "I object totally to that so-called compromise."

When Sabo said then that he would do the *voir dire* questioning, "in the interest of justice," Abu-Jamal said, "That's not in the interest of justice; it's in the interest of a conviction."[31]

So confident had McGill been of getting his way—and of getting the result that Sabo had proposed—that he had come to court already prepared with a list of questions for the judge to ask, which he said were designed "to cover the areas I believe that safeguard the defendant's rights." Sabo jumped at the offer and began going over the list.

At that point, Jackson told the judge he had been instructed by Abu-Jamal not to participate in the discussion.

McGill countered aggressively, saying that the judge had the authority to order Jackson to participate. He was clearly relishing the conflict it was causing between Jackson and his client.

When Jackson, who was trying to salvage relations with Abu-Jamal, said he felt "compelled to follow" his client's wishes, Sabo threatened the attorney with contempt of court and added, "I may very well sentence you to six months in prison."

Jackson stood his ground, saying:

> I appreciate that, Your Honor, but I think that under the circumstances my right to represent Mr. Jamal, even in this modified circumstance, I feel compelled to follow the wishes of my client. I appreciate and respect Your Honor's intention with respect to this issue, but I think under the circumstances my allegiance to my client is superior, quite frankly, Your Honor, than my abidance by the rules of the bar.[32]

Sabo responded immediately by citing Jackson for criminal contempt and sentencing him to state prison for six months—the maximum penalty permitted. Making what was perhaps a more serious threat, he added:

> I want to tell you I'm also going to send a transcript of this to the disciplinary board and I'm going to ask that you be suspended from the practice of law.[33]

Jackson was clearly being put under enormous pressure. It is to his enduring credit that he stood his ground, saying only "Very well, Your Honor. May I have the opportunity to secure counsel?" To which Sabo coolly responded "You will have the opportunity when you are up in the cell room."[34]

It is clear that Judge Sabo was quite sincere in being ready to pack Abu-Jamal's back-up attorney off to state prison for the "crime" of standing up for his client. It is equally clear that on a matter of principle, Jackson was ready to face the consequences. While Jackson made many mistakes in his handling of Abu-Jamal's case—mistakes that contributed mightily to his conviction and death sentence—he was sufficiently committed to his client's cause that he was ready to go to jail and even to risk losing his career over such an issue as this.

Some Abu-Jamal supporters, and his current attorneys, have charged that Jackson was part of a grand conspiracy to remove Abu-Jamal's right of self-defense. They base this claim on the undeniable fact that Jackson, on June 18, 1982, after Abu-Jamal had been removed from the courtroom for being "disruptive," consulted with Sabo and McGill on how to proceed. He told the two men that his client had instructed him "not to participate," not to ask questions at trial, in protest over the judge's denial of his *pro se* rights and his request to have John Africa as an advisor at his table. It is true, as was argued in a friend of the court brief filed by a California-based organization called the Chicana/Chicano Studies Foundation, and written by Abu-Jamal's current attorneys, Eliot Grossman and Marlene Kamish, that Jackson revealed defense strategy in his effort to learn how he should handle his new and unanticipated role as lead counsel. But it is also true he had been placed in a legal bind, not of his own making. His client, Abu-Jamal, had decided that if he couldn't handle his own defense, and if he couldn't have Africa at his side at the defense table, he would protest by offering no defense. Jackson felt obliged to go along with this instruction, but he had also been ordered by the state Supreme Court to act as lead attorney to the best of his ability, which he felt precluded him from just sitting silent. He may have made a legal or ethical error in discussing his dilemma with Sabo, but he was hardly engaged in a conspiracy. His gutsy stance when faced with jail and a threat to his license to practice law reveals that claim to be clearly false. Jackson may not have taken the proper steps to protect his client's rights—if indeed anyone could have succeeded in such an endeavor in Judge Sabo's courtroom. He may even have at critical points sloughed off on the pressing work of this trial in order to attend to other legal business he had, but it is going too far to try to allege that he was part of such a conspiracy. There may have been a conspiracy in practice, if not by intention, between the prosecutor and the judge to remove Abu-Jamal's *pro se* rights to self-representation and to have the obviously inadequate Jackson handle the case directly. But Jackson, who had made strenuous efforts to be removed from the case entirely, was not a willing party to it.

Having Abu-Jamal's attorney packed off to prison would have resulted in bad press for the case. Once McGill had gotten what he wanted from the judge—the removal of Abu-Jamal's *pro se* rights to handle his own defense—he immediately turned soft and conciliatory towards Jackson:

> Your honor, I'm quite sure that Mr. Jackson did not intentionally violate the Court's order.
>
> At this point, Your Honor, I would make the request at least to all conduct to date there has been no violations from Mr. Jackson's actions. I would ask that the Court consider withdrawing that order [of criminal contempt]. [35]

Nonetheless, the damage by this effort of the judge and the prosecutor to freeze Abu-Jamal out of the jury selection process was enormous. Immediately taking advantage of Abu-Jamal's unwillingness to let his attorney handle the process, Judge Sabo began handling the *voir dire*. The second juror he questioned, Patricia A. Vogel, a white woman, said two of her brothers were policemen in the Philadelphia Police Department, just as the slain officer had been. On those grounds, a fair judge would have right away disqualified her from the jury. Sabo did not.

Incredibly, rather than asking for dismissal for cause, Abu-Jamal made a peremptory challenge. Even the judge was surprised, asking "Peremptory?" Abu-Jamal, who appeared to be acting out of anger, stuck with his decision, thereby almost certainly wasting another in his allotment of 20 peremptory challenges. He went on to use three more peremptory challenges while Sabo conducted the questioning of jurors. During that time, when he was being barred from actually asking any questions himself, the prosecutor was able to dispatch a number of jurors "for cause" who might have proven more favorable to the defense. Had Abu-Jamal or Jackson been involved in the process, the defense might have been able to challenge and force the prosecutor to use at least some of his peremptories to keep jurors who might have shown favor toward defense arguments off the panel.

Though it lasted only a few hours, Sabo's handling of the *voir dire* was terribly damaging for Abu-Jamal's case. And Jackson knew it. Over the luncheon recess, he managed to convince the defendant of the risks of allowing Sabo to continue selecting his jury. Jackson came back after the recess and said that Abu-Jamal had agreed to allow him to continue the process "under protest."

By then, however, Abu-Jamal, with as many as five or six of his peremptories wasted, was at a distinct disadvantage to the prosecution, in terms of his ability to shape the jury. To make matters worse, Jackson's own skills in the *voir dire* were wanting. Juror Dominic Durso had a friend who was a police officer and who was wounded in the line of duty. Jackson, handling the questioning for the defense at the time, inexplicably failed to use any challenge, whether for cause or peremptory, to remove him. Meanwhile, by that point, even before the trial's opening arguments, Judge Sabo had managed to thoroughly alienate the defendant. Not just from the legal system, which with good reason he viewed as dead set on convicting him, but also from his own attorney, whom he now viewed as being inept and easily bullied. By the end of the *voir dire* process, Abu-Jamal was faced with a jury of three (soon to be reduced to two) blacks and nine whites, some of whom had close friends or relatives who were police officers.

With this unpromising background, presentation of the evidence to the jury began.

Chapter Five

The Trial Part II:

Shut Up and Shut Out:
With the Defendant Silenced,
The Prosecution Spins a Tale of Murder

This was one of the strongest cases I ever had to try. You had eyewitnesses, you had a gun, you had a motive, and you had a history of an individual who erupts instantly when he wants something, and who will do it aggressively. You have everything in this case," says retired Philadelphia assistant district attorney Joseph McGill, recalling the 15-day trial that single-handedly catapulted him to international status as celebrity—or villain, depending on your viewpoint. That's how McGill, now in private practice at a law firm in Philadelphia, views the case of Mumia Abu-Jamal today. And that's how he deftly managed to convince a jury to view it two decades years ago, right from his opening statement.

The opening statement is a crucial phase for both prosecution and defense, according to attorney Daniel Williams, who together with Leonard Weinglass and several other lawyers handled Abu-Jamal's initial post-conviction hearing, and who did much of the work of developing his federal court *habeas corpus* petition. The key to winning a jury trial in a case like Abu-Jamal's, he explains, is to develop a believable story line for the jury to follow. And the time to present that story line, he says, is during the opening statement to the jury. Explains Williams:

> An opening statement is no luxury, and it is certainly more than just a synopsis of the case. It is, perhaps, the most vital moment in trial advocacy—a moment that must be entwined with the jury selection process. This process, when done correctly, primes jurors for the theories and themes that will be communicated in the opening statement. Research powerfully suggests that jurors begin to develop their outlook on a case upon hearing the opening statements. What they hear at the beginning of the trial, if compelling, becomes the mental scaffolding upon which the case is constructed.

It guides the jury to construe the testimony in a way that is favorable to the advocate's side.[1]

The idea is that by telling a gripping and believable story of what happened at the start of a trial, a skilled attorney is able to keep jurors following along during the often tedious and boring process of presenting witnesses. These bits and pieces of evidence are then fit into that story. Even with internal contradictions or gaps in the attorney's case, and even if the other side presents counter-arguments, if a good story line is planted in the back of their collective mind, jurors will fill in the missing material and stay with the story as told by that attorney.

That is precisely what Assistant District Attorney McGill proceeded to do on June 19, 1982. The day before, Judge Albert Sabo made his task that much easier. On the second day of the trial, Sabo had yanked the right to represent himself from the defendant, and ordered his "back-up" attorney, Anthony Jackson, to take over as defense counsel. The move had been precipitated by Abu-Jamal's vociferous insistence that he be allowed to have the assistance of John Africa at his defense table, and that he be able to dismiss Jackson—both of which requests Judge Sabo adamantly rejected. Sabo's action set the stage for what was probably the most profound and far-reaching mistake of the trial. Jackson, prior to the order to take over as lead attorney in the case, had been doing nothing to prepare. As irresponsible as this might sound of Jackson, it was not entirely his fault. Earlier, when he was trying to get himself removed from the case, Judge Sabo advised him that his assignment a month earlier by Judge Ribner to the position of "back-up counsel" would require no preparation on his part. His role, he had been assured, was simply to be available to help Abu-Jamal negotiate the thicket of legal procedures during the trial.

Suddenly placed in charge of Abu-Jamal's case on June 18, and faced with a client who had no confidence in him, Jackson should at least have requested a delay—a month or even a few weeks—to allow him to prepare for trial. With Judge Sabo presiding, the delay might not have been granted. But had he at least requested it, it would have established the grounds for appealing to overturn a conviction later. However, Jackson made no request for delay, instead opting to try and wing it, even as the prosecution raced forward with its case.

The following day, McGill made his opening statement. Having never even discussed with his client what had happened that fateful morning when Faulkner was shot to death, and having no time to prepare, Jackson, having no alternative story to present to jurors, offered no opening statement to counter McGill's. This failure to provide an alternative may have irrevocably damaged the defense.

McGill, in contrast, was well prepared. "Mr. Jamal was observed on the night of December 9, 1981 shooting to death Officer Daniel Faulkner," began the energetic and animated prosecutor confidently, stating as fact to the jurors something that none of the several witnesses had actually seen quite so precisely. McGill, a stern, no-nonsense man who exudes an air of authority, went on with his description. Faulkner had earlier stopped Abu-Jamal's brother William's car; William had then hit the cop unprovoked, and at that point the defendant had run across the street from the parking lot, gun in hand, shooting the policeman "right in the back" at close range.

After advising the jury that they would hear testimony that, "as he fell down, Officer Faulkner was grabbing for something," McGill went on to say, "Then Mr. Jamal, the Defendant, takes a few steps over as Officer Faulkner was down and was shot himself during the course of this."

Left deliberately unclear was the reality that there was and would be no testimony at the trial regarding Faulkner's shooting of Abu-Jamal. The closest the prosecution would come to providing that would be White's belated claim that she saw the falling and wounded Faulkner "grabbing" for something.

Perhaps because he had no witness to explain how Abu-Jamal got shot by Faulkner, McGill hammered further on this point, on the old theory that through repetition, an assertion would become a fact. "After he had shot Daniel Faulkner and while Officer Faulkner was reaching and grabbing for something, then Mr. Jamal was shot himself during the course of this by Officer Faulkner." Again there was no mention of witness testimony because nobody ever did see how Abu-Jamal was shot. But, just as attorney Williams explained above, McGill was providing his story line, imprinting it in the jurors' minds before the first witness had ever taken the stand. And his story was that it was in this brief moment, between the shot in the back and the next shot which killed Faulkner, that the policeman shot and wounded his alleged assailant.

With the jurors, fresh in their roles as arbiters of justice, sitting in rapt attention, McGill then carried on with his version of events:

> ...then you will hear the testimony of various witnesses that this Defendant walks right over to Officer Faulkner, who at this point is on his back, and within twelve inches of his head he points the gun that he had that was loaded and unloads that gun. One [bullet] makes contact, and that was the fatal shot, right between the

eyes, literally blowing his brains out.[2]*

Seeking to anticipate and blunt what he knew would be later defense charges of police brutality, in his opening argument, McGill alleged that Abu-Jamal resisted arrest, and had tried to reach for his weapon as police approached him. Then the prosecutor embarked on the process, which he continued throughout the trial, of portraying the defendant as "a picture of extreme arrogance, defiance, and even a strange boastfulness," saying:

> Extreme arrogance, but that arrogance continues because we find again, ladies and gentlemen, a situation at the hospital which best symbolizes this entire episode, you may find, and that is this: when he goes into the hospital an individual...his former partner in there comforting Officer Faulkner as he is dying ladies and gentlemen, walks out to the Defendant who unloaded his gun in him and literally blew his brains out, and he looked right at him and this man, this Defendant, you will hear, looks up to him at the time when he's just dying and said, "I shot the MF'er and I hope he dies." Arrogance, defiance, you will see it.[3]

Jackson delivered no alternative story for the jury to consider. After he had passed up the opportunity to make an opening statement at the start of the trial, nine days more of damaging testimony would elapse before he would make his own statement at the start of the presentation of the defense witnesses on June 28. There is a good deal of confusion concerning Abu-Jamal's wishes and strategy during the course of the trial, and concerning Jackson's handling of the defense effort. While Jackson said he was trying to follow the wishes of his client, Judge Sabo was ordering him to be the lead attorney and to conduct the case as he himself wanted to. That lack of clarity about who was directing things pervades the entire trial, an issue meriting further discussion. But at this point, suffice it to say that the confusion of roles makes it unclear whose decision it was not to make an opening argument at the beginning of the trial. Jackson and Abu-Jamal both stated on the record that it was the defendant's strategy not to participate in questioning prosecution witnesses, but it was never stated on the record that Abu-Jamal had instructed Jackson not to make an opening statement. All Jackson said on the matter in court was, "Your Honor, I reserve making opening remarks till a later time."[4] This suggests that the decision to delay was his own, since he usually was extremely careful to inform the court when he was being instructed to do or not do something

---

*Actually, this description is factually incorrect. There were bullet holes in Faulkner's jacket, indicating that other shots fired at him had been taken from a good deal farther away than 12 inches, by a gun not pointed at his head.

by his client. Moreover at the time he made that statement, he was offi-cially in charge of the defense, upon orders of the court.

It seems probable that, as mentioned earlier, Jackson simply wasn't ready to present his opening statement, and with good reason. During the jury selection process, when Judge Sabo had first revoked Abu-Jamal's right to act as his own counsel and ordered Jackson to take over as lead attorney, the judge had promised Jackson that this arrangement would be temporary. Once a jury was impaneled, Sabo assured him, Abu-Jamal would again be his own counsel, with Jackson reverting to his back-up counsel role. Whatever the basis for Jackson's decision to hold off, it was clearly extremely damaging to the defense's case. For over a week, the jury had McGill's version of events fortified in their minds by the testimony of pros-ecution witnesses.

As Williams observes:

> No competent trial lawyer forgoes the opportunity to give an opening statement; and very very few skilled trial lawyers, if any at all, delay giving the opening statement. A skilled trial lawyer takes her case to the jury as soon as possible and as often as possible.[5]

Then finally Jackson's "opening statement" arrived, just ahead of bringing in the defense's witnesses, and only four days before the case went to the jury for deliberations. But there still was no alternative to McGill's version offered. Instead, he issued a simple plea for jurors to remember that there are two sides to every story:

> We are not going to stand up here and say we are going to prove this and the other, but what we would like you to do is now have an opportunity to see all of the facts that happened on that evening, on that early morning hour...not just some of the things that the prosecution wants you to hear, but of all the facts, because each and every one of the facts, each and every one of those persons who testified, their testimony is interrelated.
>
> ...
>
> The witnesses that you will hear are witnesses that have been available to the prosecution. You will see that the prosecution has interviewed these witnesses, that they have given statements to the prosecution. For one reason or another, the prosecution has decided not to present those witnesses to you.
>
> So what we are going to do is to present those witnesses to you so that you have an opportunity of making a decision. You recall you have the power exclusively to decide what the facts are, what the facts were, on December the 9th, 1981, at about 4:00 a.m.
>
> I ask you to do that in the name of justice.[6]

Coming after McGill's far more compelling, even gripping evocation of his version of events, and his string of witnesses, Jackson's statement was thin gruel indeed. There would be defense witnesses who undermined some of the key testimony of prosecution witnesses, and potentially McGill's version of events. But Jackson had given the jury no alternative plot line into which to fit the new information. Without a competing version into which to fit testimony of defense witnesses, these countervailing facts would have the impact of darts tossed into a river, making perhaps a small splash and some ripples, but leaving no trace. The river would continue its inexorable flow towards conviction.

Returning to the point where the prosecution's version of the events of December 9, 1981 became firmly lodged in the jurors' minds, the prosecution proceeded with its methodical presentation of the evidence in the case.

McGill's case against Mumia Abu-Jamal essentially rested on three sets of evidence. The first was circumstantial. The defendant's gun, empty of bullets, lay beside him at the scene of the crime, though it had never been tested to show whether it had been fired at all. There was the fatal bullet found lodged in the victim's skull that could have come from that gun, though that was never definitively proven. And there were five empty .38 casings from fired rounds. Added to these were bits and pieces of other evidence. These will be discussed at a later point.

The second set of evidence comprised the testimony of four eyewitnesses. And the third consisted of the accounts of several police officers and a hospital security guard concerning an alleged confession blurted out in the hospital. McGill needed all these elements because each had significant weaknesses.

The weakness with the eyewitnesses lay in the fact that none had seen the whole incident, only pieces of it, and each of them had her or his own problems of credibility. At least two were drunk at the time of the shooting, one was a prostitute currently in prison in Massachusetts, who had 38 arrests on her record and several pending cases. One was a cab driver currently on parole for tossing a firebomb for pay into a school and who was also driving his cab with a suspended driver's license in violation of probation in that case. One was the nephew of a former Homicide inspector and the cousin of a cop. And one, conceding he had had a few drinks, was driving a car and hadn't seen the whole incident. To make his case for first degree murder, McGill needed all four of them because none of them alone saw enough of what happened that early morning to make the case convincing "beyond a reasonable doubt."

And as for the confession testimony, because no one had reported any confession to investigators for over two months, that testimony was open to the suspicion that it had been manufactured to order after the fact.

On June 19, in order to establish who Faulkner and Abu-Jamal were and how they were found at the scene of the crime, McGill presented Faulkner's wife Maureen and the officers who first arrived on the scene of the shooting. It was routine stuff for a murder trial. But it also had the advantage of providing emotional impact. Putting on the young widow of the slain officer—a powerfully emotive victim of the crime—was a classic way to grab the jury's attention and sympathy.

Then he turned to his first key witness, Robert Chobert, a taxicab driver he claimed had happened on the scene just as it was taking place.

Chobert told McGill that he had just let out a fare and had parked at the curb directly behind Faulkner's patrol car to fill out his log when he heard a single shot. Looking up from his paperwork, he said he saw the police officer fall to the ground. Then he saw "Jamal" stand over him and fire "some more shots into him."[7]

McGill asked for more details:

Q: You looked up, and what did you see the officer do?
A: I saw the officer fall.
Q: And then what did you see happen? Just say what you saw happen then.
A: I saw him shoot him again several more times.
Q: Several more times?
A: Yes.
Q: Now, what then did you see that you referred to as the shooter do?
A: Then I saw him walking back about ten feet and he just fell by the curb.
Q: All right, and then what happened?
A: Then I got—I started getting out of my cab, I started walking to the cop to see if I could help him, and then all of a sudden Police Officers came and told me to get back into my cab.[8]

McGill also asked Chobert to describe exactly what he had seen when he reported seeing Abu-Jamal firing at the officer on the ground:

Q: Now, when the Defendant was standing over the officer, could you show me exactly what motion he was making or what you saw?
A: I saw him point down and fire some more shots into him.
Q: Now you're indicating, for the Record, a movement of his right arm with his finger pointed toward the direction of the ground and moving his wrist and hand up and down approximately three, four times;

is that right?

A: Yes.[9]

An interesting curiosity concerning this testimony was not addressed by either McGill or by Jackson. Chobert claimed to have seen Abu-Jamal shoot Faulkner to death and then walk a few feet away and sit down within clear sight of the injured officer. Would Chobert then, as he claimed, have gotten out of his cab and walked over to the scene to check on the fallen officer, knowing that the killer was sitting nearby, still armed? Chobert had no way of knowing the gun was empty, or if he guessed that it was, he couldn't have known that Abu-Jamal did not have bullets at the ready for reloading. As far as Chobert knew, he would have been putting himself at extraordinary risk.

That unanswered puzzle, which ought to raise questions about the veracity of the rest of Chobert's story, needs to be put in the context of what happened in the courtroom next. Following Chobert's testimony, the prosecutor walked over to the judge and informed him and defense counsel Jackson, that Chobert was currently on five year's probation for arson in a case involving the deliberate firebombing of a school. McGill asserted that this information about his witness's background and current status should not be mentioned to the jury because arson is not a so-called *crimen falsi*, or crime of falsehood. (Under court rules, if a witness has been previously convicted of a *crimen falsi*,* such as passing bad checks or some other form of deception, the jury must be notified so they can weigh the person's credibility accordingly.)

Jackson argued that while arson alone may not be a *crimen falsi*, arson for profit would be. Initially, Judge Sabo seemed to concur, saying that while arson alone wouldn't be a *crimen falsi*, "robbery would be, burglary would be."[10] When Jackson said that if the arson was done for personal gain or for profit then it would be *crimen falsi*, Sabo replied, "Well, we'll have to do that [discuss the arson] out of hearing of the jury."

When Chobert was questioned by the judge as to why he threw a bomb into a school, he readily admitted, "I got paid for doing it." Sabo promptly changed his tune and concluded, "That's not *crimen falsi*."* Therefore, the jury never heard about Chobert's being an arsonist for hire or about his probation record. Nor did they learn that he was in legal jeopardy at the time he was testifying, because of his driving a cab with a suspended driver's license (revoked because of a DWI conviction).

---

*Trial transcript, Commonwealth v. Mumia Abu-Jamal, July 19, 1982, p.222

Under cross-examination, Jackson did elicit testimony from Chobert that he was parked behind Faulkner's police car with its bright flashing dome lights when the shooting occurred. By all accounts, that shooting took place in front and to the right of Faulkner's vehicle. Therefore Chobert, seated in the driver's seat on the left side of his vehicle, would have been in a poor position to see what he claimed to witness because there was a police car situated between him and the incident. Moreover, a police vehicle on a dark night with its lights flashing brightly would have made visibility even more problematic. Chobert also told Jackson he never saw either Abu-Jamal's gun or a muzzle flash:

> A: I told you I saw him put his hand out and I heard shots, so he had to be shooting then.
> Q: He had to be shooting. The question is did you see him shoot; yes or no?
> A: Yes.
> Q: Okay, and you saw the flash from the gun?
> A: No, I didn't.
> Q: You saw what hand—what hand did he have extended?
> A: What hand?
> Q: What hand, his right hand or left hand?
> A: I can't tell you, I don't remember.
> Q: And you didn't see the gun either?
> A: No, I didn't.
> Q: You didn't see the gun, didn't see what hand, but you know he shot him?
> A: Yes.[11]

Based on forensic evidence of powder burns, McGill claimed that Faulkner was shot in the forehead at a range of 18 inches (not 12 inches as he said in his summation). If true, it is all the more reason to question Chobert's claim that he saw Abu-Jamal shooting the officer. To get the muzzle that close to the fallen officer, the shooter would have had to be bending over so far that his hand and entire arm would have been below the level of the body of the police sedan, well out of Chobert's range of vision. This point was never raised, and has still never been raised, by the defense.

The cross-examination of Chobert disclosed another significant fact. Immediately following the shooting, when Chobert said he left his vehicle and was standing on the sidewalk between the location of his cab and Faulkner's parked patrol car, he reported seeing no one else on the sidewalk. In contrast, McGill's star witness, the prostitute Cynthia White, about whom we will hear next, claimed to have been standing on the same sidewalk just a few feet to the rear of Faulkner's cruiser. Her testimony placed her only a short distance away from Chobert on the same sidewalk, where he surely ought to have seen her. As Jackson questioned Chobert:

Q: Now, the only people who were on that sidewalk was the police officer and Mr. Jamal; is that right?
A: No.
Q: Who else?
A: His brother, William Cook.
Q: William Cook. Anyone else?
A: No.
Q: You're certain of that?
A: Yes, I'm certain.
Q: You didn't see any woman on the sidewalk?
A: No.[12]

Jackson further observed that in Chobert's initial statement to police at the scene, provided on December 9, he had told them that the shooter was six feet tall and weighed 200 or 225 pounds. He then, in the courtroom, had Chobert look at the rather gaunt, six-foot-one-inch-tall, 185-pound vegan Abu-Jamal, who obligingly stood up at the defense table.

Q: Does he look like he's 225 pounds?
A: No, he don't.[13]

In his cross-examination of Chobert, Jackson uncovered another curiosity that will be of interest later when theories of what actually might have happened that morning are discussed, though nothing was made of it by the defense attorney at the trial. Chobert recalled seeing a policeman "running across the street" with a gun in his hand—the only gun that he claimed to have actually seen while he was on the scene. That officer, he said, ran across the road, shortly after the first few police had arrived in vehicles at the scene of the crime, at least raising the possibility that he may have been in the vicinity already, at the time of the shooting. Yet no police were interviewed as witnesses to the event—or at least no such records of interviews were ever provided to the defense.

Another angle, which Jackson didn't pursue—and that could explain his willingness to get so close to Abu-Jamal—was that at the time of the incident, Chobert might not have thought the man slumped on the curb was the shooter. As Jackson noted in his cross-examination, in his initial December 9 statement to police investigators, Chobert had said that he saw "another man" who "ran away" for about half a block towards 12th Street along the south side of Locust when he looked up after the first shot was fired. He claimed in his statement that police stopped that man, but that he didn't see him later. Jackson didn't pursue that matter any further, though if Chobert did think he saw the shooter run away, it might well explain why he would have felt safe walking up to the scene of the shooting as he said he did, before the arrival of police.

There were other problems with Chobert's testimony too. In a statement to police given an hour after the incident, he said that the shooter had run some 30-35 steps after shooting the officer, and he described that fleeing suspect as being "kind of heavyset" and wearing "a light tan shirt and jeans." (The thin Abu-Jamal had been wearing dark clothes that morning.)

Given all the problems with Chobert's testimony, it is surprising that neither Abu-Jamal nor Jackson, both of whom were suspicious about whether Chobert was even a real witness to the shooting, thought to ask him an obvious question. Why would a person with a suspended license have pulled up and parked his taxi cab directly behind a police officer's vehicle in order to fill out his log book? Most people with a suspended license tend to go out of their way to avoid being near police officers.

Turning to the prosecution's star witness, the one to provide the most damning account was Cynthia White, a prostitute with a long rap sheet of over 38 arrests. At the time of her testimony, she was in jail on a prostitution charge in Massachusetts. She had been brought down to Philadelphia by the district attorney's office under an interstate witness agreement. She was also facing three prostitution charges in Philadelphia, which McGill told the court she would go to trial on after her 18-month Massachusetts jail term was over. This thin, wasted-looking woman who probably had a drinking and drug-use problem was later found dead a decade later of a drug overdose, according to New Jersey State Police. She also had several outstanding bench warrants for non-appearance on various court dates at the time of her testimony.

McGill claimed there were no deals between the D.A.'s office and White. But he did report to the court and the defense that the district attorney's office had made a request to another court. It concerned a male friend of White's, a man he said was named Smith (but whom White later identified as Robert Small, nicknamed "Prince"), who had been arrested on a "theft" charge. The D.A. requested he be released on his own recognizance. Also at the D.A.'s request, no bail was required. McGill explained that "there was some concern over his safety in the prison because of his connection with her." The implication was that in jail, Prince, who was White's pimp, might be in danger from Abu-Jamal's supporters because of his relationship with a witness against the defendant. Jackson, who tried to show that the Prince deal was actually a kind of bribe to elicit favorable testimony from White, scoffed at this claim. He noted that since there had been no actual threat made against the man, and since no one would have known his connection to White except thanks to McGill's mention in court of the deal he had cut for him, the "security" issue was bogus.

White testified about the shooting as follows:

> The policeman got out of the car and walked—started walking over towards the Volkswagen. The driver of the Volkswagen got out of the car. A few words pass. They both walked between the police car and the Volkswagen up to the sidewalk. A few more words passed again between them. The driver of the Volkswagen then struck the police officer with a closed fist to his cheek, and the police turned the driver of the Volkswagen around in a position to handcuff him.
>
> ...
>
> I looked across the street in the parking lot and I noticed he was running out of the parking lot and he was practically on the curb when he shot two times at the police officer. It was the back. The police officer turned around and staggered and seemed like he was grabbing for something. Then he fell. Then he came over and he came on top of the police officer and shot some more times. After that he went over and he slouched down and he sat on the curb.[14]

The main obvious difference between White's testimony and that of Chobert is that White had Abu-Jamal shooting twice at Faulkner before the officer fell to the ground. Another difference is that White, unlike Chobert, said that the police surrounding Abu-Jamal were striking him with blackjacks (Chobert had not said anything about a beating). But what is perhaps most striking about White's testimony is not how different it was from Chobert's, but rather how different it was from earlier statements she had given to police at various times. Jackson made a strong effort to highlight those differences.

He noted that in her first statement to police—made on the morning of December 9, 1981, within half an hour of the shooting of Officer Faulkner—White had said of the shooter:

> He had a gun in his hand. He fired the gun at the police officer about four or five times. The police officer fell to the ground, started screaming.[15]

In the initial account, the gun had been fired several times before Faulkner hit the ground; in court, this had changed to be in line with the prosecution's account. White, pressed by Jackson to explain the two different accounts of what happened on December 9, tried to say that she hadn't been accurate in what she'd said right after the incident to police. "He got shot that many times, but it wasn't all at once and he didn't fall to the ground," she said.[16]

It should be pointed out here that some supporters of Abu-Jamal's cause have suggested Faulkner couldn't have screamed after having been shot in the back, since the bullet exited through his throat. In fact, Dr. Coletta, the physician who attempted to revive Faulkner at Jefferson Hospital, had to perform a tracheotomy on Faulkner to try and get him breathing again, and he said he noted at the time that the officer's larynx had not been damaged by the bullet. "He probably would have been able to talk and scream until the shot to the head," he says. Coletta adds that the shot to the back would also not have significantly disabled Faulkner "at least for a few minutes," as it had not struck any vital organs. This suggests that at least from a medical standpoint, the D.A.'s theory as to the sequence of shots, with Faulkner firing at his attacker after having been shot once in the back, would have been physically possible.

Jackson, who had been dealing with the Philadelphia police on brutality cases for several years, had from the beginning strongly suspected that White's testimony was manufactured by police detectives in order to support their case. This was in keeping with what was rumored (and later proved) to be a common practice at the time by the Philadelphia police and local prostitutes, particularly in the Center City Division. He moved on to a statement White gave to police three days after the shooting, on December 12. In it she had again referred to four or five shots being fired at Faulkner. Jackson also noted that it was on the 12th, not the 9th, that White first told police that William Cook had struck Officer Faulkner. Only on the 17th, he pointed out to the witness, did she mention "one or two" shots and the officer falling down. By January 8, White was saying just one shot had been fired before the officer fell down.

The importance of the number of shots fired, and the timing of the shots was that, first, the witnesses ought to have all heard or seen the same thing. Secondly, if there were two shots, perhaps one had been a shot fired at Abu-Jamal, which might have been *before* any shot was fired at Faulkner. Finally, the continuing shift in White's account, from a fusillade of shots all coming together, to two shots and then more shots, to finally just one shot and then several shots, seemed to suggest a too convenient adjusting of her account to fit the prosecution's theory of the crime.

It was at that point that Jackson made a dramatic and important discovery. Why, he asked, was White making so many statements to police in the days and weeks following the shooting, a total of five or six, including one on tape? She replied that she was being arrested repeatedly by police at that time; whenever she was brought down to the 6th District police station house, she would see a photo of herself posted on the wall with a note to her saying to "contact Homicide." Asked why her description of the events of December 9 changed from each statement to the next, White said, "They were asking me questions and they asked me in a different way to explain it."[17]

The police kept arresting White and bringing her in to Homicide, where the investigators on the case kept pressing White with questions. As they did so, her account of the incident shifted . Each adjustment was made not by a witness who was voluntarily at the station clarifying matters, but rather by a witness under arrest in police custody. Miraculously, each time she was brought into the station, her account of what she had allegedly seen increasingly came to better fit the mold of the prosecution's theory of how events had occurred. As Jackson pointed out, each time she was brought into the station, she faced bench warrants for failure to appear at court sessions, which should have required her incarceration. Just as miraculously, each time she made a statement, those warrants were lifted.

Yet McGill insisted, and continues to claim, that the prosecution had no deal with White.

It is particularly critical that the most important witness in a prosecution's case be an honest one. But with White, there are plenty of reasons to doubt the veracity of her testimony. Some of these would not be aired for 13 years until they surfaced at Abu-Jamal's post-conviction hearing, and others even later. But some should have been clear at the time of the original trial. First, as a prostitute with outstanding warrants and open charges against her, is it likely that seeing the shooting, she would have hung around until the police showed up, and that she would have then offered testimony voluntarily? Generally, prostitutes try to avoid the police. Veronica Jones, another prostitute who testified later at the trial, verified this when she explained why she left the scene as police arrived:

> It was too many police cars and hookers do not stand in the area
> where there is too many police cars.[18]

If White did approach police who arrived on the scene and volunteered herself as a witness, was she simply being a Good Samaritan? Or had she, a veteran, street-wise hooker, calculated that there could be potential benefits in it for her if she offered herself as a prosecution witness? Given her legal jeopardy, the former explanation seems quite a stretch.

There may have been even more to problems with White's veracity than the fact that her statement changed with each subsequent arrest by police. The fact that Chobert didn't see White at the corner where she says she was standing during the incident raises questions as to whether she was a witness at all to the shooting. In the confused intensity of a firefight, it might be possible that he didn't notice her, but he surely should have seen her after it was over. Several other witnesses also say she was not there. One who apparently had been talking with her at the time of the shooting (a man named William Singletary, who was not called as a witness until 1995) placed her well down the sidewalk south of the intersection with Locust Street, on the east side of 13th Street. If correct, that would have placed the corner of a building in the way of her view of the incident.

There is a further oddity about White that makes this key witness stand out from all the prosecution's purported eyewitnesses: White, alone among the eye-witnesses, was not brought over by police to the paddy wagon to view and identify Abu-Jamal. Instead, she was immediately hustled off to the Roundhouse, where she faced questioning by the Homicide unit. As we will see later, there are other reasons to doubt White's testimony, too. But even at this point in the trial, still more problems were evident.

One problem was with her view of Abu-Jamal even as she described it. White said she saw a gun in his hand as he ran across the street, or at least the barrel of his two-inch snub-nosed pistol. But this was at some distance—at least three or four car lengths away on a dark street, with flashing strobe lights running atop the parked patrol car, and with Chobert's and the officer's patrol cars at least partially blocking her view. Curiously, although she claimed to have been able to see a tiny two-inch barrel at that distance, she couldn't recall which hand had been holding the weapon. A second problem arises regarding her testimony that she saw Abu-Jamal shooting down into the face of the prone officer. White told McGill she couldn't see what Faulkner was doing because the shooter was standing in the way, with his back towards her. Here's the testimony from the transcript:

Q: Were you able to see the police officer do anything to the defendant?
A: No.
Q: Did you see the police officer once he was reaching and apparently

grabbing something and falling down? Were you able to see the police officer's arm?

A: No.

Q: Why not?

A: Because Jamal was standing over him. Jamal's back was like towards me. He was blocking my view from the police officer.[19]

If Abu-Jamal's back was turned towards White at the time he was allegedly shooting down at Faulkner, how could she have seen what he was actually doing with his hands? During cross-examination, Jackson didn't fully pursue this issue. Instead he focused on getting her to admit her willingness to lie. The lies were numerous: that she had given police investigators multiple versions of her account of what happened, that she had misled a judge about her legal status with regard to an outstanding bench warrant, and that she had repeatedly lied to police about her name and her address.

Another interesting aspect of White's testimony during Jackson's cross-examination is that it contradicts the testimony of other prosecution witnesses. She said that during the shooting and up until the police arrived on the scene, she did not see anyone else approach the curb where Faulkner and Abu-Jamal were. Nor did she say she remembered seeing Chobert's taxicab parked behind Faulkner's patrol car, where he testified he had parked and from which he claimed to have witnessed [Figs. 9, 10, p. 176h] the shooting. As she told Jackson during cross examination:

By Mr. Jackson:

Q: At what point did you see the cab there?

A: When the police were there that's when I noticed.

Q: You hadn't seen it before then, had you?

A: I wasn't looking at the cab, looking for a cab.

Q: I understand you weren't looking for a cab. My question is: you didn't see the cab before that time, did you?

A: No.[20]

According to their separate accounts, these two witnesses of McGill's had to have been only a few feet from each other. Curiously, their accounts shared one thing: neither had seen the other.

When McGill cross-examined White, he reminded her that in her December 17 statement to police—her third statement—White did refer to "a guy in a cab behind the police car." But, as Jackson correctly noted, this was a statement taken by homicide detectives investigating the Faulkner killing who had been repeatedly questioning the witness each time she was picked up by police and brought in on prostitution charges. In any event, White apparently forgot about what she had said on December 17 about seeing a taxi cab when she was testifying on June 22, 1982 at the trial. McGill was placed in the position of asking the jury to disregard prior statements to police investigators in some cases, such as her account of when and how many shots were fired, when doing so would help his case. But where those earlier statements supported his case better than her current testimony, he showed no hesitation in relying on them instead.

Jurors were left having to decide where the truth lay. In the context of Jackson's failure to provide the jury with an alternative scenario for what had happened, questions jurors might have had regarding White's conflicting testimony would have drifted off into a vacuum. It was a grave error by the defense.

White also gave different answers at different times regarding whether or not she had seen a gun in the shooter's hands when he was firing down on Faulkner on the sidewalk. Though she testified at trial to having seen the shooter holding a gun, Jackson noted that at a hearing before Judge Ribner on January 11, 1982, scarcely a month after the shooting, she had said the following:

> Question: Did you see him fire the gun?
> Answer: I knew he was firing. I didn't see the gun."
> Question: Isn't it a fact that you just heard the gun fire?
> Answer: Yes.[21]

The substantive and significant inconsistencies in White's testimony between her first statement to police investigators on December 9, 1981 and her trial testimony were one set of issues standing in the way of the prosecution's case being elevated "beyond reasonable doubt." Later testimony at the trial and especially at the PCRA hearing in 1995 would suggest something else: a motive for the gradual evolution of White's testimony towards more damning evidence for the defendant. This testimony would suggest that White was getting, or at least hoped to get, some kind of deal out of the prosecution in return for her cooperation. There would even be testimony later at the post-conviction hearing that White might not have ever actually seen the shooting, but only came on the scene after the shooting was over with. But we're getting ahead of ourselves.

White also testified at the separate trial of William Cook, who was charged with assaulting Officer Faulkner. This trial was also prosecuted by McGill. Jackson clearly had a copy of her March 29 testimony from that trial; he used a section of the transcript of her testimony in an effort to impeach her current testimony. At Abu-Jamal's trial, White was insisting she did not know one witness, William Singletary, who was standing with her at the time of the shooting. But at William Cook's trial, White said she knew the man.[22]

But there was a far more critical inconsistency between her testimonies at each of the brothers' trials. At William Cook's trial, both White and McGill give clear indications that there had been a passenger in the car with Cook. Yet a crucial element of the prosecution's case against Abu-Jamal was that there was no one else on the scene of the shooting besides the defendant, his brother William, and the police officer. Any evidence of a fourth person would have been important because it could have opened up the possibility in jurors' minds that someone else entirely could have shot the officer, or at least participated in the shooting. Surprisingly, Jackson made no use of this particular conflict in the testimony.

As White testified in the earlier trial of William Cook:

> A: I noticed a police car with the lights on and the spotlight on. The spotlight with the lights on the top of the police car, and it was pulling the Volkswagen over to the side of Locust Street. And the police got out of the police car and walked over to the Volkswagen. And he didn't get all the way to the Volkswagen, and the driver of the Volkswagen was passing some words. He had walked around between the two doors, walked up to the sidewalk.
> Q: Who walked?
> A: The passenger—the driver. The driver and the police officer.
> Q: When the officer went up to the car, which side of the car did the officer go up to.
> A: The driver side.
> Q: The driver side?
> A. Yes.
> Q: What did the passenger do?
> A: He had got out.
> Q: What did the driver do?
> A: He got out of the car.
> Q: He got out of the car?
> A: Yes.[23]

If Jackson had presented this testimony to the jury in Abu-Jamal's trial, McGill might have rebutted it through further questioning of White. Nonetheless, the testimony, with its clear references to a "passenger," might easily have raised doubt in the minds of some jurors about McGill's assertion at Abu-Jamal's trial that there was nobody else on the scene at the time of the shooting. But although this evidence was actually in Jackson's hands at the time he cross-examined White, he never introduced it, and never challenged White's trial testimony that there was no one else on the scene.

The reason why he didn't use it remains unknown. And when Abu-Jamal's appellate attorneys (Leonard Weinglass, Daniel Williams, Rachel Wolkenstein and Jonathan Piper) had Jackson on the stand testifying about his performance as Abu-Jamal's trial attorney, a second error was made. No one asked Jackson why he never used it the Cook trial testimony. "I'll concede that not asking about that was probably a mistake on our part," said Williams in an interview years after the hearing.

Turning to the third eyewitness for the prosecution, Michael Scanlan raised as many questions about the incident as he answered. Scanlan, a 25-year-old man who confessed to having had several cocktails shortly before witnessing the shooting, saw everything he witnessed from inside his car, which was stopped at a red light heading eastbound on Locust Street at 13th Street. This location had him looking straight through his front windshield across the intersection towards the rear of the parked police car and Cook's Volkswagen.

Since he was stopped across 13th Street facing the scene of the crime, the cab should have been the first thing in his line of sight, where Chobert had claimed he had parked behind Faulkner's cruiser. But Scanlan said he had no recollection of seeing a cab parked there. Since a taxicab is a hard thing to miss, this is rather strong evidence that Chobert was not where he said he was during the shooting.

Scanlan also said he recalled seeing nobody standing on the southeast corner of the intersection, where Cynthia White testified that she and a black male (William Singletary) had been standing while the shooting occurred. He did recall seeing someone further away from the incident, to the right of his car on the southwest corner of the intersection. Also according to Scanlan, the altercation between William Cook and Officer Faulkner took place in the space between the front of Faulkner's patrol car, on which he had Cook spread-eagled for a frisking, and the back of Cook's VW. Both Chobert and White had placed the two men on the sidewalk to the side of the two vehicles.

Scanlan also described a different sequence of shots: one as a man was running from a parking lot on the northeast corner of the intersection across the road towards William Cook and Officer Faulkner; one a few seconds later as the runner and the other two men were close together; and

then two "or possibly three" shots fired by the runner into the fallen officer. Here is the testimony he gave as he was examined by prosecutor
McGill:

> Q: What did you observe the officer and this man [the Volkswagen driv-
> er] do?
> A: They were talking. The black man spread-eagle in front of the car,
> and while he was spread-eagle he swung around and struck the offi-
> cer in the face with his fist.
> Q: All right. And at that time what then did you observe?
> A: At that point, the officer reacted, trying to subdue the gentleman,
> and during that time another man came running out from a parking
> lot across the street towards the officer and the gentleman in front
> of the police car.
> Q: And what happened?
> A: I saw a hand come up, like this, and I heard a gunshot. There was
> another gunshot when the man got to the policeman, and the gen-
> tleman he had been talking to, and then the officer fell down on the
> sidewalk and the man walked over and was standing at his feet and
> shot him twice. I saw two flashes.[24]

While Scanlan said he never saw a gun in the runner's hand, and saw
no muzzle flash coming from the area of the runner's hand, only a general
flash from somewhere in the area, he did see the runner raise his arm while
running across the street. It was Scanlan's belief that the runner fired at the
police officer first, but could that raised arm have been a reaction to the
runner's having been hit in the chest by the first shot? (Note that given
that a bullet travels faster than sound, Scanlan's sequence of events—the
arm being raised and then the sound of a shot—could have represented a
shot followed by the arm being raised, by which time the sound of the shot
would have reached Scanlan. The raised arm, then, could have been Abu-
Jamal's involuntary reaction to having been hit by a bullet in the chest.)

Whoever fired that first shot, if it was fired while the man was running across the street, it couldn't have been the shot that felled the officer.
Testimony from a witness for the prosecution from the police department
makes clear why: the shot into Faulkner's back had been fired from a range
of less than 18 inches.

Scanlan's testimony corroborates this. He says that it was after the
second shot, at which he did not recall seeing any accompanying muzzle
flash, that the officer fell onto the sidewalk.

Going with Scanlan's presumption that the runner fired the first shot,
the prosecution tried to suggest that the second shot that Scanlan heard
might have been the officer firing back at the shooter. But there is a prob-

lem with this theory: Scanlan was clear in stating that it was after the sound of the second shot, not after the first, that the patrolman fell.

The meaning of Scanlan's testimony is potentially the difference between a capital crime and a lesser offense: if Faulkner fell after the second shot, rather than the first, it would appear that Faulkner fired first. If indeed it was the second shot that hit Faulkner, as Scanlan's testimony indicates, then that shot could have been a response that was fired in self-defense.

One problem with Scanlan's testimony is that he also insisted that he at no time saw the officer with a gun in his hand. Then again, he was in a car stopped all the way back across the intersection from the incident, which was happening on a dark street, with flashing lights from a patrol car in between him and the action, so that may not be so surprising.

An additional difficulty with Scanlan's testimony is that he admitted to being confused as to who it was who actually fired the shots at Faulkner. When brought by police to the wagon containing the wounded Abu-Jamal, Scanlan incorrectly identified him as the driver of the VW, leading one police officer at the wagon to exclaim in disgust, "Fuck!" He also said that the man whom he saw running across the street had an Afro and was wearing a hat containing his hair. Yet it is undisputed that Abu-Jamal had dreadlocks at the time of the incident. (Other witnesses said Abu-Jamal did not have a hat on, and that William Cook was wearing a black beret.)

McGill's fourth eyewitness was actually more of an ear-witness, as he said he never actually saw the shooting, only heard it. Albert Magilton said he had been walking east along the south side of Locust Street, between 13th and Broad Street when he saw Faulkner's patrol car put on its lights and pull over Cook's VW. He had watched briefly and then turned to cross Locust at the intersection, on the west side of Locust. Here is his account as given to McGill at the trial:

> A: I observed the gentleman—well the police officer pulled over a blue Volkswagen at the corner of 13th and Locust.
>
> Q: And what did you then observe?
>
> A: Well, the officer was on the microphone, and then he pulled the car over. The driver got out and the officer got out, and they proceeded to the pavement. And then after that there, I proceeded to cross Locust Street, which I noticed the gentleman coming from the parking lot.
>
> Q: And what was this man doing, or this person doing, when he was coming from the parking lot?
>
> A: He was sort of like moving across the—across the street fast, and he had his hands back behind his back.[25]

At that point, Magilton (whose relatives included several police officers), says he turned away to continue crossing the street and lost sight of what was going on across the intersection. This at least suggests that the person he had seen going across the street towards Faulkner and Cook hadn't appeared particularly menacing to him.

Under further questioning, asked what happened next, Magilton said:

A: I heard some shots and I looked over and I didn't see the officer there no more.

Q: All right. And then what did you do?

A: Well, I proceeded back across the street to see what had happened to the officer. And then as I was moving across the street, you know, I was moving slowly across the street, I looked. When I got to the pavement, I had looked down and I had seen the officer laying there, and I didn't see the other gentleman until I—until I moved up closer and he was like sitting on the curb.[26]

Magilton said he too, like Chobert and Scanlan, was brought later by police over to the paddy wagon to view the suspect Abu-Jamal, whom he identified as "the gentleman I seen coming across the street."[27] This again raises the intriguing question: why were the police so diligent about bringing each witness they picked up at the scene over to the wagon to identify Abu-Jamal, yet never brought the person who had allegedly seen the most, Cynthia White, who would later become the prosecution's most important witness?

Magilton's account also differed in important ways from the other witnesses' versions of the event. Under cross-examination by Jackson, his testimony concerning the sequence of shots did not support the prosecution's theory of events:

Q: Now, you were just about to mount the sidewalk when you heard noise, shots?

A: Yes.

Q: Did you hear one shot, two shots, in rapid succession. As best as you can recall, what did you hear, sir?

A: Pow, pow, pow, and then pow, pow.

Q: Pow, pow, pow and then pow, pow?

A: Yes.

Q: Okay. So it's fair to say that you did not hear one shot and a pause, and then a few more shots?

A: Yes, I guess so.[28]

As with other witnesses, Magilton's testimony also contradicts the prosecution's version of events in other important ways. Like others, he did

not see White where she claimed she had been standing on sidewalk on the
southeast corner of the intersection of 13th and Locust Streets. Like
Scanlan, he testified that he did not recall seeing any taxicab parked
behind Faulkner's patrol car.

Was Cynthia White really right there? Even police testimony contradicts the claim. Officer Daniel Soboloski, the third officer to arrive at the
scene of the shooting, was asked on the stand directly if he saw Cynthia
White in the vicinity. "No," he answered. This is particularly surprising.
Those first police on the scene, still uncertain as to what had transpired,
must have been careful to scout out who was in the vicinity, and to have
viewed everyone in the area with a certain amount of careful suspicion, if
only out of concern for their personal safety. Unlike the other witnesses,
the arriving officers had training and experience; it seems highly probable
that they would have immediately taken note of everyone in the vicinity.
Questioned by Jackson, Soboloski is clear on this:

> Q: Other than police officers, were there any other civilians on that
> pavement of in that street in the immediate vicinity?
> A: At which time, when I pulled up?
> Q: Yes, sir.
> A: The only people I remember seeing were just two people, one police
> officer and one civilian—excuse me, I saw two police officers and
> one civilian.
> Q: Who was the civilian that you saw?
> A: Jamal.
> Q: You didn't see Cynthia White?
> A: I don't know Cynthia White.
> Q: Did you see a woman?
> A: No, I didn't.[29]

It would appear from that testimony that Officer Soboloski didn't see
cab driver Chobert at the scene either, though as we saw, Chobert testified
that he was standing outside his cab on the street at the time police arrived.

No review of the testimony and evidence would be complete without
an understanding of the atmosphere in the courtroom at the time. While
all this testimony and presenting of evidence was going on, the scene was
alternating between periods of tense calm with relative decorum, and short
periods of increasingly combative disputes between the defendant and the
judge. Abu-Jamal, who continued vehemently to demand the right—well
established by court precedent—to act as his own lawyer and to fire

Jackson, was repeatedly ousted from the courtroom by Judge Sabo. Tensions were high from the beginning in a courtroom filled to capacity every day. As viewed from the bench, the right side of the visitors' gallery was packed with largely black family and supporters of the defendant; on the left sat largely white police supporters and family of the slain officer. How the court functioned in this atmosphere can be seen through an incident towards the end of the day on June 18, as prosecutor McGill was preparing to give his opening statement. Abu-Jamal demanded again that Judge Sabo permit him to have John Africa as an adviser at his table. Sabo declined. When the defendant continued to insist, Sabo threatened to remove him from the courtroom. "That threat is meaningless," Abu-Jamal replied.

At that point, Sabo ordered the sheriff to remove Abu-Jamal. The gallery of supporters erupted:

> The Court: Please, sheriff, take him out.
> The Defendant: What I'm saying is, I want the defense of my choice so this case—get off of me.
> The Court: Sit down in this courtroom or you will be removed.
> The Defendant: They don't want to sit.
> The Court: You will be removed.
> A spectator: This is a fucking railroad, I say. What are you trying to do here?
> A spectator: What is this?
>
> (The defendant was removed from the courtroom.)
>
> The Court: Bring them back, bring those two men back. You are both in criminal contempt of this Court for your outbursts in this courtroom. I am summarily fining you to 60 days in the County Prison. That's it.
> A spectator: Take it easy, baby. It's all right. Say nothing. We in the right. Take it easy, baby. We right, we win. God is the Father.
>
> (The two spectators were removed from the courtroom.)
> (A short recess was taken.)
>
> The Court: I just want to state for the record that when the Court had ordered the sheriff to remove Mr. Jamal from the courtroom because he has been obstructing the court's orderly procedure in this courtroom, he became very abusive and some of his relatives or friends or followers, whoever they may have been, became very abusive, vile language, screaming in the courtroom. The Court was forced to order the sheriff to apprehend two of them. I don't know their names but now they're in custody. We'll ascertain what their names are later, I assume. Does anybody know who it is?

Mr. McGill: Yes. Mr. William Cook brother who was present at the
scene, the one that you will hear testimony concerning, and, I
believe, Mr. Wayne Cook, also brother.[30]

Such scenes would be repeated throughout the trial, as Abu-Jamal
continued to insist on his Constitutional right to represent himself in the
face of Sabo's adamant refusal to permit it. As a result, the jury was repeatedly witness to Abu-Jamal's frustrated outbursts. This worked beautifully to
McGill's advantage, who later cited them in his closing arguments as evidence of the defendant's lack of respect for "order" and of his purported
aggressiveness and temper.

The confrontations caused by the defendant's demands to represent
himself, to be rid of Jackson, and to have Africa as his advisor, and the judge's
refusal to grant those demands, had another important impact. Removed
repeatedly from the courtroom on orders of the judge, Abu-Jamal was absent
for roughly half of his trial. During that time, no effort was made to provide
him with a way to view or even hear what was going on at his own trial.
Incredibly, he was not provided with daily transcripts of the proceedings.

Sometimes the judge deliberately and repeatedly misconstrued Abu-
Jamal's request to have John Africa at his table as an adviser to be a request
to have Africa as his defense attorney (something any court would find
impermissible). And in his dealings with the defendant, he could be down-
right derisive. For example, during one expulsion from the courtroom, Sabo
told him to "take a walk."[31]

With this scene of continuing courtroom tension as a backdrop,
McGill presented his witnesses. In the middle of this, he shifted away from
the actual shooting to what happened when Abu-Jamal was finally brought
by police to Jefferson Hospital. His aim was to prove that the defendant
had blurted out a confession to the killing of Faulkner in front of several
witnesses. The importance of the claim that it was a "blurt out" is that normally police are required to have read a suspect his "Miranda" rights—
essentially a warning not to say anything before having an attorney present. An unprompted confession, however, is exempt from this requirement.

The emergence of the alleged confession has an interesting history. As
noted, no one had mentioned it to police investigators until more than two
months had elapsed after the shooting. In early January, in between the
shooting and the time that reports of the confession surfaced, defense attorney Jackson filed a complaint of police brutality in the arrest of his client.
Numerous witnesses, including Cynthia White, two physicians at the hospital, and others, as well as Abu-Jamal himself, provided ample evidence

that he was repeatedly beaten during the course of his arrest. Police Officer Robert Shoemaker admitted to kicking the defendant in the throat. It was also admitted—by prosecution witnesses—that officers carrying him to the paddy wagon rammed Abu-Jamal's head into a lamppost (the officers involved claimed it had been an accident). And a doctor at the hospital said she saw police officers kicking him while he was lying on the floor in the hospital entryway.

That brutality complaint filed by the defense triggered an automatic investigation of the incident by investigators from the police department's Internal Affairs Bureau. The initial investigation led to no action on the brutality charge, and the complaint was also deemed unjustified by the district attorney's office. But it did turn up something else: belated testimony from several police officers and a hospital security guard that Abu-Jamal had allegedly blurted out a confession in the hospital.

The evidence was first presented at the trial by Priscilla Durham. A young, black security guard at Jefferson Hospital, she said she was near the entryway when police brought in the injured Abu-Jamal. As Durham told McGill on the stand:

> A: Well, approximately the same time that Jamal was brought into the emergency area I was inside the emergency area behind the double doors. The double doors opened just as Jamal was placed on the mat leading into the Emergency Room treatment area. At this time I didn't know—all I did was hear him say, "I shot the motherfucker and I hope the motherfucker dies." And it was at this time that I realized who it was in reference to, what was going on.
>
> Q: And where was he when he said that?
>
> A: He was directly at my feet.
>
> Q: And what immediately happened after that?
>
> A: Well, in, you know, the scuffle with him and the police trying to contain him and the other policeman asking me where could they place him I just tried to think and, you know, proceed with the next business.
>
> Q: Okay. After the defendant said that what if anything or what were any other—did you hear any other responses from anybody?
>
> A: I heard a police officer respond, "If he dies you die."[32]

Durham went on to say that Abu-Jamal had made that statement twice while on the floor in the entryway surrounded by as many as 15 police officers. But she amended the quote to sound more like the response to a question: "Yeah, I shot the motherfucker and I hope the motherfucker dies." If there really was a confession shouted out, that single word "Yeah," at the front of the statement could be critical. If accurate, it would indicate that Abu-Jamal was responding to a question from one of the officers around him. If that was the case, it should have been inadmissible, since there was no indication he had been read his Miranda rights at that point.

McGill then had Durham identify Officer Garry Bell, a close friend of Officer Faulkner, as the officer who had allegedly made the "If he dies you die" comment. Bell later took the stand and reinforced Durham's testimony. Recalling that he had been standing near Faulkner's body as doctors worked over him when Abu-Jamal was brought in, his testimony went as follows under questioning by McGill:

> Q: ...Okay. At that time when they brought this man in what did you then do?
> A: I walked over to him. I wanted to see who did it, who shot him. And I looked at him and he looked up at me. He said, "I shot that motherfucker and I hope the motherfucker dies." Those were his exact words to me.
> Q: What did you do?
> A: I said something back to him. I said, "He shouldn't be the one that dies, you should."
> Q: Could it even have been something like—
> Mr. Jackson: Objection.
> By Mr. McGill:
> Q:—"If he dies you die?"
> Mr. Jackson: Objection. He's putting words in his own witness's mouth.
> Court: Yes, could you rephrase your question?
> By Mr. McGill:
> Q: Could it have been said in another way?
> A: It's possible. I was angry at the time.[33]

Under cross-examination of the two witnesses to the confession, Jackson questioned why both Durham and Bell had waited more than two months to mention it to investigators. Further, Jackson wanted to know, why was their initial report of it not to homicide detectives, but to investigators from Internal Affairs who were questioning them about the brutality charge issue? Bell claimed his lapse was a result of his having been so upset by Faulkner's death—an excuse that, coming from an experienced cop, raises questions. In contrast, Durham claimed—in a surprise revelation made for the first time on the stand that moment—that she had actually reported the confession to her supervisor the following day, on December 10th. Further, she stated that he had written it down. Incredibly, she had failed to mention this to several police investigators over a course of several months, even when being asked why she had taken two months to report the confession.

The existence of a written document from the supervisor was some-thing that McGill, along with everyone else, supposedly only just learned of, since it came up during cross-examination by Jackson. Nonetheless, McGill promptly—and with surprising confidence—offered to have a police officer obtain that document while Jackson was continuing with his cross-examination. Within less than an hour, while Jackson still had the hospital guard on the stand, an officer had returned, grinning, and handed McGill a typed sheet of paper. McGill dramatically announced that it came from James Bartelle, chief investigator in the hospital's security depart-ment. As McGill would naturally have known, standard evidentiary rules would require him to authenticate the authorship of such a document. But curiously, McGill did not bother to bring in Bartelle, or even offer to do so, though he must have realized that a plain sheet of white paper with typing on it, unsigned, would raise questions of authenticity, and Bartelle would be the obvious person to resolve those questions, if he indeed was the doc-ument's author as claimed. [Fig. 7, p. 176e]

Instead, in what would be one of the dramatic turning points in the trial, he and the judge allowed the unsuspecting Jackson to introduce the document as defense evidence. This was a colossal error on Jackson's part. Having done that, there was no longer any need for the prosecution to establish the authenticity of the document. It had become a defense docu-ment. McGill at that point had no interest in pressing the issue of its authenticity; it was highly suspect because it was typed, and Durham had insisted the statement had been hand-written, not typed. If Jackson had declined to use it and thereby forced McGill to be the one to introduce the document as evidence, Jackson could have then insisted that the prosecu-tion verify its authenticity.

Had Jackson followed this course, Sabo might have still refused to require McGill to provide authenticity. But such a refusal would have been solid grounds for an appeal.

Realizing the danger of introducing the document at all, Jackson tried to back out of using it, but the judge wouldn't let him:

Mr. Jackson: I don't think to bring that [the document] up in front of the jury is appropriate.

Mr. McGill: I said I would get it.

The Court: Wait after you [McGill] redirect then you can make it and give it to him, because I said that I would allow him [Jackson] to fur-ther cross-examine.

Mr. McGill: That's right. That's why I was going to let him have it now for recross-examination.

Mr. Jackson: Your Honor, rather, give me the statement and if there's
    something in the statement that I don't want to cross-examine...
The Court: You don't have to. You asked for it.
Mr. McGill : And I said I would get it.
The Court: And he said he would supply it.
Mr. McGill: What about now?
The Court: Do it now.[34]

The statement substantially conformed to what Durham had earlier
testified, though she insisted that Bartelle, her supervisor, had written, not
typed, her statement. In fact, she had looked positively surprised when presented with the typed document.

Jackson did notice a suspicious contradiction that should have raised
serious questions about the authenticity of the typed document, and thus
about the whole claim that Durham had reported a confession. The typed
statement referred to the fact that Abu-Jamal was bleeding, but Durham
testified that she hadn't known that to be true at the time she filed her
report.[35]

Jackson belatedly argued that the statement brought in by the officer,
although said by Durham to be substantially what she had allegedly told
her supervisor at the time, was not admissible evidence because it was not
authenticated by the witness. At this point, the judge made a claim that
was not really justified by the evidence at hand, asserting on his own
authority, with no testimony to support him, that it was simply a copy of
her handwritten statement which had been retyped in the supervisor's
office. In the end, he pointed out that in any event Jackson himself had
introduced the evidence, because (thanks to earlier being pushed into it by
McGill and Sabo) the defense lawyer had used it in his cross-examination
of the witness:

Mr. Jackson: She said it was handwritten, Judge. She said she never saw
    that.
The Court: She gave a handwritten statement and they took the hand-
    written statement and typed this.
Mr. Jackson: We don't know that. Judge, you can't assume that.
The Court: You can't assume that they didn't. Look, you cross-examined
    on that statement.[36]

Once presented to the jury as fact, the confession, with Durham's
statement on paper accepted as being authentic, was a devastating blow.
Juries in death penalty cases—even if they are supporters of the death
penalty in the abstract—are generally very reluctant to find defendants
guilty and to send them to the gallows for fear they might be making a mis-

take. But a confession can prove critical in helping to ease or eliminate those qualms.

It was only much later that Jackson found a way to undermine the evidence of the confession. As previously discussed, he had in his possession a detective's interview done early on December 9, 1981 of Police Officer Gary Wakshul. He was the officer who had accompanied the arrested Abu-Jamal all the way from the scene of the crime, on the ride in the paddy wagon and in the hospital, right through until he was treated for his gunshot injury. And in his observations on that period, Wakshul had told the interviewing detective: "The negro male made no comment."[37] A week later, he provided an investigator with a very detailed account of what he had observed at the shooting scene, which supported this evidence. He was asked again on that occasion if there was anything else he had to say about what happened that morning. His reply, "Nothing I can think of now."[38]

But because of the crush of daily business and his own disorganization, Jackson had failed to notice these comments or to realize their significance—until the last day of the trial.

As Jackson knew, if Wakshul had been with Abu-Jamal the entire time, including the period when the defendant had been on the floor in the hospital entryway, he would inevitably have heard the alleged confession, which both Durham and Bell insisted had been shouted out twice in a boastful and belligerent manner. And yet the officer had written that he had not heard any comment from the defendant. It all suggested a grand conspiracy to falsify evidence. After all, over a dozen police officers had been around Abu-Jamal at the time he had allegedly shouted out this obscene and vicious boast, and yet none reported a word about it until over two months after the "fact." Crucially, the jury was never to hear evidence that might lead to the suspicion that it was a fraud, or at least to doubts about the credibility of the reports of a confession. Judge Sabo refused to delay the trial in order to give the defense a chance to call Wakshul to the stand, and unless he was put on the stand, there was no way for the defense to introduce his written statement to investigators that "The negro male made no comment." As far as the jurors knew, the defendant had confessed to his crime and a written report of that confession had been made within a day's time by the hospital security guard.

Two decades after the trial, and in the wake of further evidence presented at the PCRA hearing that raised questions about the veracity of testimony about a "confession," McGill tried to downgrade the document's significance as a contributing factor in Abu-Jamal's conviction. "I don't even know if the jury saw that evidence," he said in an interview. "You'd have to check. I don't know if the court ever included that written statement of Durham's as evidence sent to the jury."

This is disingenuous. At the time of the trial, McGill was keenly aware that the lapse between the shooting and when the confession was first reported could sow reasonable doubt in jurors' minds. To counteract that possibility, in his summation to the jury at the end of the guilt phase of the trial, McGill took the document, identified ironically as defense evidence item D14, and waved it in the jurors' faces for emphasis, saying:

> This is D14. You recall that.
>
> That document, the interview that Miss Durham had given the very first day at 2:16 a.m., December 10th, 1981. Durham also stated that when Jamal was first brought in and lying on the floor Durham also stated that Jamal shouted, "Yes, I shot him and I hope he dies."
>
> D14 on December 10th. Not February, ladies and gentlemen, as was suggested to you.[39]

Efforts to locate jurors for this book and find out how they reacted to this presentation, and to ask them many other questions, did not succeed. Part of this failure may be for good reason: defense attorneys, who had that information, were unwilling to provide any assistance, perhaps for fear of damaging the value of potential witnesses in the case by having them talk to the press.

But McGill's case as presented to the jury must have been devastating. Not so much because it proved the case, as because there was so much of it. Jackson, who lacked sufficient experience with death penalty cases, but who was an experienced trial attorney, had managed to punch holes in the testimony of most of the witnesses. This despite the fact that his cross-examinations were often poorly organized and poorly researched, and were blocked or limited in crucial ways by Judge Sabo. But his efforts were simply overwhelmed by the tidal wave of evidence presented by the prosecution.

Jackson's lack of ability and resources were especially clear with respect to evidence presented from the police department's ballistician and the official medical examiner. Jackson had been unable to marshal any countervailing evidence because the courts had not provided him with adequate funds to hire his own experts in those crucial areas. A comment in the medical examiner's notes surmised that the bullet that killed Faulkner had been a .44 caliber, not a .38 caliber shell (which it would have had to be in order to come from Abu-Jamal's gun). Years later, at the PCRA hearing, the accuracy of this notation was denied even by an expert witness for the defense, who conceded that the slug was probably a .38. But in the meantime it became a celebrated piece of evidence by Abu-Jamal's supporters. A piece of evidence that was completely missed by Jackson at the time. Had the medical examiner's notation been noted during the trial by the defense, then correct or not, it might well have at least raised a reasonable doubt in jurors' minds as to whether the fatal bullet had come from Abu-Jamal's gun.

Jackson was also unable to offer expert testimony rebutting the prosecution's claim that, while falling to the ground after being shot by Abu-Jamal, Faulkner fired back up at his assailant. An expert witness would have been able to raise doubts, demonstrating that the bullet that hit Abu-Jamal had a downward, not upward course, meaning it would have been impossible for the shot to have come upwards from below, as the prosecution asserted.

Jackson had also been unable to hire an investigator to delve seriously into the case and to independently interview its dozens of witnesses. The reasons were two-fold. First, the court wouldn't provide adequate funds to hire one, and second, as discussed earlier, the prosecutor was permitted by the judge to keep the addresses and phone numbers of all the witnesses secret, making the job of investigation even more expensive than it had to be.

This imbalance in resources would have made Jackson's task daunting enough. But he also had an uncooperative, even antagonistic client who didn't trust him, didn't want him, and who often wasn't even talking with him or taking his advice. And he had a jury that in the end was comprised of working-class whites, with only two black members. Those jurors were far more in tune with McGill's law-and-order pitch than with Jackson's efforts to suggest that, in order to win a conviction, the police and the D.A. might be lying, and getting witnesses to lie.

With the conclusion of McGill's presentation of its case on June 26th, it became Jackson's turn to present the defense's witnesses. To turn it into a contest, Jackson would have to give the performance of his life.

Chapter Six

The Trial Part III:
Guilty Despite Reasonable Doubts

Anthony Jackson may never have offered the jury an alternative scenario in which to place his version of the evidence of the case, but he did offer up some witnesses who raised serious questions about the prosecution's version of events. However, his efforts to fully air their evidence were blocked for the most part by McGill's objections, which on almost every occasion were sustained by the judge. As we will see, Jackson's whole approach was reactive: to snipe and pick away at the prosecution's story, trying to demonstrate contradictions, altered testimony, credibility problems, etc. Even this reactive strategy was random and scattershot. This was partly because he was so woefully unprepared during cross-examinations, and because for the most part he didn't even bother to interview his own defense witnesses beforehand to determine what they would say on the stand.

Jackson had defended several homicide cases, but not many capital ones, in which the jury had been death-qualified before being seated as this one was. He was thus more accustomed to arguing before juries that represented a reasonable cross section of the city of Philadelphia, a racially mixed and ethnically diverse municipality with a fair percentage of political liberals. Some on these juries were likely predisposed to question authority—as represented by the judge, the prosecution and the police. Had he been dealing with such a mixed jury, his sloppy and haphazard approach might have worked. He was not, however. This was a capital trial where most, or all, of those potential skeptics had been removed at the outset for having objections to or qualms about the death penalty (or, as we have seen, simply for being black). Jackson was making his case to a largely blue-collar jury of politically conservative older white men and women. Their bored expressions during most of the periods when Jackson was questioning witnesses, and interviews with selected jurors after the trial had ended, suggest that this jury wasn't interested in what the panel members viewed as nit-picking by the defense. For them, the larger story—the only story they were given—was what mattered.

The three most important witnesses offered by the defense were Dessie Hightower, a young black college student in accounting, Dr. Anthony Coletta, the resident physician who treated both Faulkner and Abu-Jamal at Jefferson Hospital, and Veronica Jones, another prostitute who had been at the 12th and Locust, a little over half a block from the shooting.

Though he didn't actually see the shooting itself, Hightower was potentially the most compelling witness at the trial. With no criminal record, he had no apparent reason to give false testimony. He had been in the area with a friend, Robert Pigford (another young black man who later became a police officer), intending to go to a local after-hours bar called Whispers. Finding the doors there locked, they were heading back to their car in a lot on the north side of Locust west of 13th Street. Hightower recalled seeing Faulkner pulling Cook's blue VW over as he and Pigford were walking towards their car. But after watching Faulkner exit his cruiser and head towards the Volkswagen, and seeing nothing unusual about the stop, he paid no more attention to what was happening there. He and Pigford rounded the corner of a building on Locust to go into an adjacent parking lot. It was then, he said, that he heard the shooting. As he testified, under questioning by Jackson:

> A: ...We were in the parking lot, going into the car. I heard a series of three consecutive gunshots, then a pause, and one. Altogether I guess it was five bullets.
> Q: Five shots?
> A: Yes, three consecutive and a pause between the last two.[1]

After hearing the second set of shots, Hightower said he walked back and peeked cautiously around the corner of the building to see what was going on. At that point, in two separate statements to police and on the stand, he said he saw someone running away along the south side of Locust Street eastward towards 12th Street. Said Hightower:

> A: The person looked to be about the height of five nine, five ten, somewhere around there.
> Q: In which direction did the person run, when you say the person ran in the opposite direction?
> A: Then they ran—the car was parked here (indicating). They ran this way (indicating).
> Q: Towards 12th Street?
> A: Yes, towards 12th Street.[2]

What Jackson didn't know—in part because he didn't bother to interview Hightower himself in advance of putting him on the stand—was that the police, instead of pursuing Hightower's lead about a possible suspect running from the scene, went out of their way to try and ignore or even undermine his account. Only years later was it disclosed that Hightower, alone among the witnesses to the event, had been subjected to a polygraph machine test at the police station where he and Pigford had been taken for questioning shortly after the incident. No attempt was made to use a polygraph to test the veracity of the accounts given by White or Chobert, both of whom had criminal backgrounds and obvious credibility issues. Nor was one used on any of the other witnesses. Only Hightower, with no criminal record, was singled out for testing. On its face this might seem explainable: his account differed markedly from others who did not see anyone running from the scene. Yet the questions he was asked did not include any concerning the possible fleeing suspect he said he had observed.

Hightower later, at the PCRA hearing in 1995, claimed he was told by police that he had passed the polygraph exam. If true, the failure of the police and prosecutor to provide that information to the defense was a case of prosecutorial misconduct.

As Stuart Taylor, an attorney writing about the case in the conservative-leaning legal magazine *The American Lawyer*, commented later, "What kind of game were the police playing with this exculpatory witness?"[3] It was apparently presumed by police that Hightower, who had been with another man and who was visiting a bar frequented by homosexual men, was himself gay. Indeed, McGill even once suggested to a shocked reporter that Hightower was a transvestite, as though this, if true, would somehow weaken his credibility as a witness. Whatever the truth may be about Hightower's lifestyle, it looks suspiciously as though in subjecting this witness to a polygraph while he was in the intimidating environment of the police homicide unit, police investigators were trying to scare him off of the story he was telling. Moreover, if Hightower was gay, it would make the decision by this young black man to come out from behind a building and present himself as a witness (to police who were in the act of beating a young black man), all the more impressive; his testimony all the more credible.

A shy, soft-spoken, earnest man who works as a waiter, Hightower remains convinced to this day that the police simply weren't interested in pinning the crime on anyone but Abu-Jamal. "They never asked me about the guy who ran away," he said in a recent interview. "But I can still picture the scene as clear as day. He had on a red and black sweater and he was running as fast as hell."

Hightower says he was first held at the police station for about five hours, and questioned by two detectives. "Then they came to my workplace a week later and picked me up. That's the time they used the lie detector. They were nice. No strong-arm tactics, but they never asked me about the guy I saw running away."

The main reason he volunteered himself to police at the scene (an action which he says "pissed off" his friend Pigford, whom he says didn't want them to get involved), was that he saw police who arrived on the scene beating Abu-Jamal. "And," said Hightower, "I wanted them to know they were beating the wrong guy."

Hightower testified at the trial that police pulled the wounded Abu-Jamal by his dreadlocks, intentionally banging his head into a pole, and that three or four of the arresting officers kicked and beat him, some with billy clubs. Years later, during an interview, he looked gravely at the interviewer across the table and said, "I'll go to my grave saying Mumia didn't do it. I'm sure it was the guy I saw running."

Hightower insists today that he never saw a taxi cab parked behind Faulkner's patrol car, thus supporting prosecution witness Scanlan's testimony at the trial. Nor did he see Cynthia White at the scene where she claimed she had been. Jackson neglected to ask him about these issues, though, so the jury didn't hear about them.

There was one other curious element to Hightower's testimony. He insisted that he had seen a gun in Faulkner's holster as the officer was being carried to a vehicle to be driven to the hospital. Given the D.A.'s version of events, this is hard to imagine. Faulkner simply could not have been shot in the back, then unsnapped and pulled out his pistol, fired a shot at Abu-Jamal and then reholstered his gun as he fell to the ground. Yet it is not disputed that the bullet that critically wounded Abu-Jamal came from Faulkner's gun. (A gun described as being Faulkner's was picked up by police at the scene, along with Abu-Jamal's gun, and both were delivered to Homicide, according to police testimony.)

McGill tried to suggest—and indeed continues to suggest today—that the person Hightower saw running away was the prostitute Veronica Jones. But standing at only five foot three inches, Jones has a stature that would make her hard to confuse with a male. Moreover, her statements at the trial and to police conflict with McGill's suggestion: she claims that she had stayed back near the 12th Street intersection, more than half a block away from the shooting scene. Beyond that, Hightower's description of the person he saw running—hair in dreadlocks and wearing a sweater—doesn't match Jones. Jones had a large afro was wearing a light gray jacket.

Jones was a particularly important witness. Years later, she would become pivotal during the appeal of Abu-Jamal's conviction, when she recanted her original trial testimony and said she had been pressured and bribed into lying on the stand by police. She claimed to have been standing half a block from the shooting, over at the intersection of 12th Street and Locust. She had given a statement to police several days after the shooting where she reported having seen two men "jogging" away from the scene at the other end of the block. It was for this reason that Jackson called her as a defense witness. At the time of her testimony, Jones was in jail awaiting trial on an armed robbery charge. At first, she was a problem for the defense. Later, she evolved into one of the defense's most important witnesses. In an incredible example of inept lawyering that shows just what was passing for a defense in this capital case, Jackson neglected to interview Jones before questioning her. Not knowing what she was going to say, he simply assumed it would comport with the statement she had given to police which he had in his possession. He was then stunned when she denied under oath ever having seen two men jogging away after the shooting. As Jackson asks:

Q: Now, did you see anyone running away from the scene?
A: Running away?
Mr. McGill: Objection.
By Mr. Jackson:
Q: Jogging?
Mr. McGill: Objection.
By Mr. Jackson:
Q: Jogging?
Mr. McGill: Leading.
By Mr. Jackson:
Q: What, if anything, did you see anyone do when you turned around and looked up Locust Street? [following her hearing of shots being fired]
A: I didn't see anyone do nothing. No one moved.
Q: No one moved at all?
A: Not that I seen, no.[4]

Desperate to try and recover the situation, Jackson, who had been counting on her testimony to lend support to Hightower's claim to have seen someone running away, presented Jones with her earlier statement she had made to police. But Jones continued to doggedly deny that she had seen two men jogging away as the statement read. Jones denied that the five pages of the statement, each containing her signature, were actually what she had said. She claimed that the three detectives who had come to her house on December 15, about a week after the shooting, had handed her a blank sheet of paper, which she had signed (implying that what was written was put there after she had signed the paper, not before). Frustrated at his inability to get Jones to repeat on the stand what her statement to police had said regarding two men jogging from the scene, Jackson cast about wildly, like a drowning man searching for something that would rescue him. Almost as much to stall for time as anything else, he asked her if she had talked to police any other time.

It was then that Jackson stumbled onto something much more important: evidence that the police had attempted to get Jones to lie about what she had seen—and that they may have done the same thing with Cynthia White. The dramatic exchange began with Jackson still focusing on whether Jones might have evidence that White was not actually at the scene of the crime. At first, he seemed to have missed its significance:

Q: Now, other than this one day that the police came to your home in Jersey to interview you, had you talked to any other police at any other time?

A: I had got locked up I think it was in January. I am not sure. Not January. I think sometime after that incident. They were getting on me telling me I was in the area and I seen Mumia, you know, do it, you know, intentionally. They were trying to get me to say something that the other girl said. I couldn't do that.

Mr. McGill: Objection, your honor.

By Mr. Jackson:

Q: Did you give them an interview.

A: No. They had locked me up. No.

Q: Do you know Cynthia White?

A: Yes, I do.

Q: Did you see her that night?

A: No, I didn't.

Q: Now, you got a chance to look up Locust Street didn't you, on the 9th?

A: Just to be looking?

Q: Yes.

A: Did you see Cynthia?

A: No.[5]

Jackson continued to question Jones about White's whereabouts, and about a pimp named Prince, with McGill (who much more quickly than

Jackson, realized the danger to his case in what Jones had just said concerning "that other girl"), urgently objecting to many of his questions. Finally homing back in on the time Jones said she was picked up by police and brought in to the 6th District station, Jackson asked her whether she had given another statement. She said no, but then said the following:

> A: They were more so conversating [sic] among each other and I guess they expected me to say something in their behalf, you know, but I couldn't. I just saw what I saw.
>
> Q: And were they plainclothes officers or uniformed officers?
>
> A: Uniformed.
>
> Mr. McGill: Objection, your honor. It is his witness.
>
> The Court: Try not to lead, will you, please?
>
> By Mr. Jackson:
>
> Q: What, if anything, did you say in response to those questions?
>
> A: Nothing, really. I was just pissed off at the time.
>
> Q: You were just what?
>
> A: Pissed off.
>
> Q: Why?
>
> A: Because they picked me up for nothing.
>
> Q: And did they release you?
>
> A: Yes.
>
> Q: And you weren't sent down to the Roundhouse? [The place where the homicide unit is located]
>
> A: No. I was just held at 11th and Winter for about five hours. [The 6th District]
>
> Q: And how much time did they question you with regard to Cynthia White?
>
> Mr. McGill: Objection.
>
> The Court: Sustained.
>
> By Mr. Jackson:
>
> Q: How much did they question you with regard to what you had seen?
>
> Mr. McGill: Objection.
>
> The Court: Rephrase your question.
>
> By Mr. Jackson:
>
> Q: The police officers questioned you about December 9th, is that right?
>
> A: Yes.
>
> Q: I want to know when you were taken in for nothing how much time did they spend with you questioning you?
>
> Mr. McGill: Your honor, I object. He is talking about January.
>
> The Court: You better start over again.
>
> By Mr. Jackson:
>
> Q: Miss Jones, did you tell us that sometime after December 9th you were arrested by the police officers?
>
> A: I was picked up.
>
> Q: Do you know when?

A: No.

Q: Could it have been January or February?

A: It had to be the first week of January.

Q: You were taken where?

A: 11th and Winter.

Q: Which is the 6th District?

A: Yes.

Q: You were questioned by the police?

A: I wouldn't say questioned. Conversating [sic]. They had a couple of us. We had brought up—I call him [sic] Lucky. We had brought up —how come Lucky is not here?[6]

At this point, the normally composed prosecutor seemed clearly almost frantic in his efforts to stop Jackson's line of questioning, which was bringing out evidence of police tampering with a witness—his key witness at that. He needn't have been so worried, though. He had Sabo on his side:

Mr. McGill: Objection. Ask to strike.

The Court: Strike out that last thing.

Mr. McGill: This is January. Objection to the whole line, Your Honor. It is his witness.

[The point McGill is trying to make here is that an attorney is not ordinarily permitted to impeach his or her own witness, only the witnesses of the other side.]

By Mr. Jackson:

Q: I want to go back to your being questioned.

Mr. McGill: And I am objecting.

The Court: Rephrase the question.

Mr. Jackson: Certainly, Your Honor.

The Court: Don't say she was being questioned now. Come on. Rephrase your question. You are presupposing something.

Mr. Jackson: Your Honor, she did say that earlier.

By Mr. Jackson:

Q: Did the police ask you any questions about December the 9th when they picked you up in January?

Mr. McGill: I am objecting to that as being irrelevant.

The Court: I will overrule it. Go ahead.

By Mr. Jackson:

Q: In January did they question you about December the 9th?

A: It more so came about when we had brought up Cynthia's name and they told us we can work the area if we tell them.[7]

Jackson wanted to question Jones further about this evidence, to find out not only about how she was being extorted to give favorable testimony for the prosecution, but about whether Cynthia White may have gotten the same kind of a deal. Was she also given freedom to ply her prostitution trade in return for saying what the police wanted her to say about the shooting incident?

But as soon as Jones made the above statement, McGill objected. Since Jones was brought in as a defense witness, Jackson had no right to go outside of the area he had brought her to the stand for, which was to state what she had seen on December 9th.

Incredibly, Judge Sabo sustained McGill's objection. It is correct that ordinarily questioning of a witness can be limited to the area they were brought to the stand to testify about. However, the exception to this rule is when a witness gives genuinely unexpected testimony—which this clearly was. Jackson tried to argue just that, that the answer was a complete surprise to him, and that he should thus be able to pursue it. Any judge trying to seek justice and not a conviction would have seen that this was an avenue that had to be pursued in the interest of finding the truth. But Sabo would have nothing of it.

In a conference at the bench, out of hearing of the jury, Jackson argued that he should be able to question her about evidence that could show bias in her testimony. McGill fought strenuously against any return to that line of questioning, which quite clearly threatened to undermine his key witness—indeed his whole case. As McGill argued to the judge in the bench conference:

> Mr. McGill: I object to the whole area. As I have objected throughout. You are talking about not an individual that took a particular statement from her. This is supposed to be some police officers that at one time arrested her after the fact and you are supposed to say for whatever reasons they have, good, bad or indifferent, even if you take it as true they are supposed to have said, "All right. Tell us what you know about it and we will let you work the street." This particular individual is of no relevance. We have unknown people who happen to be police officers who tell them, "We will let you work the street like Lucky if you tell us what you know." Judge, it is absolutely irrelevant. I don't think one more question should be asked about that.[8]

Not surprisingly, Sabo agreed with McGill, addressing Jackson as follows:

> The Court: She is your witness. What she saw on Locust Street that night you can go into as thoroughly as you want to. All this other stuff is not relevant.[9]

At McGill's request, Sabo went on to strike from the record the earlier Jones testimony regarding Cynthia White and a police offer of freedom to walk the streets in return for testimony that Abu-Jamal shot Faulkner.

This meant it was no longer evidence to be considered by the jury even if they'd heard something. They were to disregard it. When Jackson tried to press further for his right to demonstrate bias on Jones' part, Sabo responded:

> The Court: We are getting too far afield in this case. We have got to stick to the issue. The issue is who shot the cop and who saw anything that night. That is what I am interested in.[10]

In the end, Jackson was left with no ability to pursue what clearly was strong evidence. Evidence that the police had pressured not just Jones, but White too, into giving testimony that was pro-prosecution, and most likely false. Jackson was clearly on to something big. But it would remain buried for more than a decade. It would not be until the post-conviction hearing in 1995 that Jones would come forward. As we will see, despite being threatened with jail, she very courageously told the court, in a hearing before the same Judge Sabo, that she had in fact been extorted by police into giving false testimony, and that she had in fact been induced to lie on the stand—specifically about not having seen two men running away from the scene. White, however, was never questioned again about the matter. By the time of the 1995 PCRA hearing where Jones recanted, she was dead, allegedly of a drug overdose. As we will see in Chapter 8, there would, however, be testimony—from a police officer—at that hearing that White had in fact been a paid informant of the police, and that, at least in the years immediately following the trial, she may have been getting put up in a fancy apartment across the river from Philadelphia in New Jersey.

Returning to the 1982 trial, Jackson had little to go on to defend his client. He had only Hightower, who hadn't seen the actual shooting, to counter McGill's four eyewitnesses. He was denied the opportunity to bring in and question police officer Wakshul as a way of challenging Bell and Durham's claim to having heard a confession. McGill and Judge Sabo had effectively blocked many other possible avenues for defense arguments. Jackson was consistently denied more than a few hundred dollars to hire an investigator and expert witnesses such as a medical examiner or ballistician. In fact, even with a few hundred dollars more from outside sources and from his own pocket, he was never able to hire either of the latter. His investigator only interviewed two witnesses for the small fee Jackson was able to guarantee him.

As mentioned, an enormous obstacle for the defense was that McGill had control over the contact numbers and addresses for all the witnesses. This meant that aside from the two witnesses Jackson's investigator was able to locate independently, any witness the defense wanted had to be located and brought in by police—a process that would be inherently intimidating to the witness and possibly bias-inducing. In one case, a white woman named Deborah Kordansky who had told police the morning of the shooting that she had seen a suspect running away from the crime scene, simply refused to come in. Not having her address, Jackson had been forced to try unsuccessfully to talk her into testifying on the phone. She never did testify at the trial, where her observation could have raised a reasonable doubt as to whether someone else might have been the shooter. Ironically, even Sabo himself at one point at least acknowledged the concern that Jackson's having to use the prosecution to obtain access to witnesses could be prejudicial.

> The Court: You don't object?
> Mr. Jackson: No. I don't object.
> The Court: You are not objecting to one of his detectives trying to induce her to come in?
> Mr. Jackson: No, I am not.
> The Court: You won't say there is some collusion here or something like that?
> Mr. Jackson: No, sir. I need that witness.[11]

McGill made things even harder for Jackson by telling him repeatedly that witnesses he wanted to contact did not want to speak with him, didn't want to testify, or that their testimony would be harmful to the defense. In fact, as it became apparent at the subsequent post-conviction hearing in 1995, some of those witnesses, including Kordansky, were not at all harmful to the defense, and would have testified if subpoenaed.

Jackson did bring in two Jefferson Hospital physicians in an attempt to rebut the prosecution's devastating evidence of a blurted-out confession. Dr. Regina Cudemo testified to having seen police kicking Abu-Jamal in the hospital entryway where he was alleged to have yelled out a confession, and to having been ordered to leave the area by police, who apparently didn't want any witnesses to their abusive behavior. Dr. Anthony Coletta, who had treated Abu-Jamal for his injuries after he was brought into the hospital by police, testified that the suspect had been weak from blood loss (at least one fifth of his total blood volume) and was about to go into shock at the time he was dragged in. In a recent interview, Dr. Coletta, now in private practice in Philadelphia's posh Main Line district, recalled that in his weakened condition, there was "no way" Abu-Jamal could have struggled violently with police as was testified. Coletta also added, "If he had been shouting out anything, I would have heard him. I heard nothing." In a subsequent interview, as reported in Chapter 1, he said that from the time Abu-Jamal was brought into the ER, he was with him, and he heard no confession, shouted or spoken. Jackson, however, was unable to elicit any statement that strong from Coletta at trial. This was thanks to repeated objections by McGill (all sustained by the judge), to any line of questions concerning the matter of how weak Abu-Jamal was at the time. What testimony there was from the stand by these two defense witnesses was clearly not adequate to undo the impact on the jury of the dramatic confession testimony offered up by McGill's two prosecution witnesses, Officer Bell and hospital guard Durham.

Crippled by Sabo's rulings limiting his line of questioning of various witnesses, and by his own failure to provide the jury with any alternative scenario for what might have happened on the morning of December 9, 1981, Jackson had little left to offer but a string of character witnesses. As mentioned earlier, that list of witnesses was curiously deficient in terms of people who knew the defendant intimately. Absent from the list were such people as Abu-Jamal's wife, his ex-wives, his mother or his children—any one of whom might have had a powerful influence on some jurors, had they spoken of his obviously caring nature as a sibling, child, spouse or parent. Likewise absent from the list were any prominent figures—for example legislators Milton Street and David Richardson, Jr., both of whom had willingly spoken on Abu-Jamal's behalf at his bail hearing six months earlier. There is no good explanation for this lack of powerful or emotionally gripping character witnesses. Most probably it had to do with the almost complete breakdown in relations between Abu-Jamal and his attorney, who by the end of the trial were barely speaking to one another. For days, Abu-Jamal had been referring in the courtroom to his attorney as a "bumbler," a "shyster," and as an agent of the court.

Meanwhile, the prosecution did an admirable job of demolishing some of those character witnesses the defense did call, who seemed completely unprepared for what they were likely to face. In the case of the first witness, the poet Sonia Sonches, McGill called attention to her having earlier written a forward to a book concerning the case of convicted police killer and fugitive from justice Joanne Chesimard. In the case of a number of other witnesses—mostly colleagues who had worked with Abu-Jamal at various radio stations—McGill was able to get them to talk about their own belief that it was sometimes okay to break laws that one felt were wrong. It was not the kind of thing likely to win over any jurors on that particular panel.

It became very clear as the trial neared its conclusion that, as with his defense witnesses, the overworked Jackson had done little or nothing to prepare his character witnesses. This made it easy for them to say too much and walk into traps set by McGill to get them to endorse the concept— popularized by activists in the civil rights movement but viewed negatively by the kinds of working-class whites who composed most of the jury—of civil disobedience in the face of what they might consider to be unjust laws. All of this worked to the advantage of the prosecutor's planned strategy of demonizing the defendant to the jury as someone who had no respect for law and order, who indeed was intent on subverting law and order. After all, these jurors were not steeped in the history of the civil rights movement. These were not people with any sympathy for the Thoreau/ Gandhi/ King concept of violating laws that one feels are unjust. On the contrary, they were the kinds of people who would view such civil disobedience as plain and simple lawlessness. McGill shrewdly played to those sentiments in his questioning of the witnesses.

If the trial was essentially a presentation of the prosecution's case and an example of a terrible imbalance of both talent and resources, its ending was even more so. Judge Sabo denied the defendant the right to make a closing argument to the jury. He told him if he wanted to present his version of the events that took place on the morning of December 9, he would have to take the stand as a witness. Of course, Abu-Jamal and his attorney knew this course of action would have been a disaster. It would have allowed the prosecutor, with the help of a judge who had already demonstrated his bias, to freely question him in front of the jury, where his words could be twisted and cut off at will. Abu-Jamal wisely declined that "opportunity." (Later, during the penalty phase of the trial, the prosecutor would find a way anyhow, with the help of the judge and the defendant himself, to question the defendant on the stand.)

Jackson's last hope was the closing argument.

Certainly no Clarence Darrow to begin with, what he offered was a peculiar and almost rambling monologue (much of which could have passed as a judge's instructions to a jury, rather than a defense statement). At times it seemed more helpful to the prosecution than to the defense, demonstrating a profound lack of understanding of the kind of jury that had sat through this trial. Beginning with an apology for the length of the trial, Jackson seemed to be criticizing his own client, since, at least from the perspective of the jury, most of the delays in the process had been caused by Abu-Jamal's incessant demands to have representation of his choice and the right to speak. He went on to praise the American judicial system, even saying that his client was "fortunate" to be having his trial in this country (somehow overlooking the fact that in most modern industrialized nations the death penalty had already been outlawed). All these oratorical efforts seem to have done was to convince the jurors that whatever seemingly biased behavior they might have witnessed on the judge's part during the course of the trial, it must have been okay if the defense lawyer was praising the system.

For some strange reason, Jackson falsely assured the jury that they had "heard all the evidence,"[12] when he knew this to be horribly untrue. They had been denied hearing Wakshul, had not heard crucial testimony from Veronica Jones, and had not heard from Kordansky—all witnesses who could have seriously undermined the prosecution's case. Nor had they heard from any ballistician or medical examiner on the defense side. And he had plenty of reason to suspect that much other evidence had been withheld from him and the defense.

Jackson then went on to offer an impassioned, and sometimes even compelling recitation of the weaknesses and contradictions in the stories of prosecution witnesses. He raised questions about why the police had done such a sloppy job of investigating the crime scene, for example failing to test the hands of Faulkner, Abu-Jamal and Cook to see who, if any, had fired a gun, failing to test the guns to see if they had recently been fired, etc. He raised questions about the testimony of Chobert and White—especially White—and pointed to the way their statements to police had changed over time, becoming increasingly well-fitted to the prosecution's theory of what had happened. And he stressed over and over that the jury did not have to be convinced of Abu-Jamal's innocence; only of some reasonable doubt about his guilt.

But in terms of offering the jury some alternative theory as to what happened, the closest he came was to suggest that possibly it was some additional person on the scene—the person several witnesses had said they saw running away—or perhaps William Cook—who had been the shooter. Instead of just attacking the credibility of the confession evidence, he even suggested that if Abu-Jamal had in fact confessed in the hospital, it could have been the noble act of a loyal brother who, thinking he was dying, decided to do something to definitively remove suspicion from his younger brother. Jackson also urged the jury not to chicken out by voting for a half measure, such as second-degree murder or manslaughter, which would have removed the threat of a death penalty. There was no evidence that Abu-Jamal opted for such a risky strategy. As he put it:

> I say to you now if you believe beyond a reasonable doubt that Mumia Abu-Jamal committed the crimes as the Commonwealth has suggested then you should find him guilty of murder in the first degree. I am his defense lawyer and I am telling you that. I don't want you to compromise this verdict. I don't want you to say well, I am not really sure if he is guilty of murder in the first degree. Maybe he is guilty of murder in the third degree, or maybe he is guilty of voluntary manslaughter. I am saying to you if you are not convinced that he is guilty of murder in the first degree then he is not guilty, because that is what the Commonwealth said they would prove, that he was guilty of murder in the first degree. Don't compromise your verdict in any way whatsoever. Face it head-on. He is either guilty or not guilty. That guilt must again be proven beyond a reasonable doubt.[13]

Jackson was followed to the floor by McGill. The contrast to the defense attorney's beseeching, rambling, and even at times tearful address, which had been delivered from a position well away from the jury box, could hardly have been greater. The veteran prosecutor strode up close to his key audience, pacing the floor and speaking forcefully—his craggy face framed by thick gray-flecked hair and mustache, and his resonant voice full of authority. At times he was stern and even angry.

Right from the outset, McGill tried to convince the jury that, far from following the dictum "innocent until proven guilty," and making sure that they didn't convict an innocent man, they should be careful not to free a suspect who might well be guilty. Such an argument risked providing grounds for a successful overturning of the verdict. Appellate courts, including the Supreme Court of Pennsylvania (in a case, ironically, involving McGill saying the same words), had already held that telling a jury in a summation that their verdict would not be final was grounds for a mistrial. In defiance of that ruling, McGill probably calculated that the politics of this case—a black radical convicted of killing a white police officer—would make such a reversal unlikely. The calculation would prove to be correct, as we will see later. He went ahead and tried the tactic again, telling them:

> ...If your decision of course were to acquit, to allow the Defendant to walk out, that is fine. There is nothing I can do and there is nothing that the judge or anyone could do that would affect

that in any way.

    If you find the Defendant guilty of course there would be appeal after appeal and perhaps there could be a reversal of the case, or whatever, so that may not be final.[14]

Nor was this the only place where McGill, with the judge's blessing, stepped over the line. At another point, he improperly encouraged the jury to draw a negative inference about the defendant's guilt by implying that Abu-Jamal's exercise of his constitutional right not to take the stand in his own defense somehow implied he was hiding something. As he put it:

> ...although they have no burden to do anything, of all that they had, all that was presented to them over that period of time you saw what the defense put on, and they don't have any burden, that is true, but...

Mr. Jackson: (interposing) Objection.

The Court: Your objection is noted.

Mr. McGill: Are they suggesting that there was a third man, a fourth man, or is he doing this all for his brother? I ask you to look through all of this, as well as any other strategy or tactics you have seen during the course of this whole particular trial and recognize it for what it is.[15]

During his review of the evidence, McGill also took other completely inappropriate actions. In order to bolster the credibility of hospital security guard Priscilla Durham, he cited a witness who had never been presented at trial—a second hospital security guard he called James LaGrand, whom he claimed had also witnessed an Abu-Jamal confession. Because this person never testified at the trial and was never tested by cross-examination, this was a major error that should have been stricken by the judge immediately. Jackson objected. But Judge Sabo said nothing, allowing it to go to the jury:

> Ladies and Gentlemen, the evidence is many fold. Whether it be photographs that we have shown, charts, statements made right after the fact by individuals that have nothing to gain and not even involved with the Police Department. Priscilla Durham. Present was also LaGrand as he comes in and makes that statement.

Mr. Jackson: Objection.[16]

Witness credibility is vital, especially when the death penalty is sought. Here, McGill also inappropriately vouched for the integrity of cab driver Chobert's testimony. He suggested to the jury that this white witness had absolutely no reason to lie. This was grossly misleading, to put it politely:

> ...The kernel of believability, the trust that you can have in an
> individual when he talks as he did I would not criticize that man one
> bit. Ladies and gentlemen, he knows what he saw and I don't care
> what you say or what anybody says, that is what he saw. Do you
> think anybody could get him to say anything that wasn't the truth?[17]

But while saying this, the prosecutor knew something the jurors did-
n't: that Chobert was testifying while on five-year's probation for felony
arson and that he was illegally driving his cab on a license that had been
suspended for drunken driving—a clear violation of the terms of his probation.

It is law journalist Stuart Taylor's view that, in vouching for Chobert's
veracity as a witness, McGill behaved improperly.[18] Indeed Taylor was evidently convinced that the confession claim was bogus, that Chobert was
offered a deal on his suspended license, and that White was either bribed
or pressured or both. In this light, he charges that McGill "also sponsored
possibly perjured testimony"[19] by Durham, Bell, Chobert and White during the trial. McGill vehemently denies the charges, citing the state
Supreme Court's upholding of the verdict. (The state's high court never
held any evidenciary hearing on that issue.)

McGill then, before going into his final summary of the prosecution's
case, appealed to the jury's emotions in a *tour-de-force* that stood in dramatic contrast to Jackson's lackluster performance. First he spoke of the
victim, a young, handsome white man who could have been the son of
many in the jury box:

> ...Constantly you have heard about the facts that this
> Defendant is on trial for his life. You have heard this all the time. Let
> me also add this. Will you understand that this Defendant is on trial
> for taking somebody's life, too. That is one thing we hadn't heard
> too much about. It may be true and indeed it is true that Daniel
> Faulkner on December 9th, at 3:51, as he looked up at the barrel of
> this gun did not have an opportunity to ask for any type of counsel,
> or to make any type of abusive remarks in relation to anybody, the
> system, the laws or anything. No one quickly ran down and said,
> "Do you want an attorney? Do you want something? Do you want
> this? Do you want that?" He was just shot in cold blood with this
> weapon.[20]

In truth of course, plenty had been said about the victim at the trial,
which had even heard testimony from Faulkner's wife, but accuracy wasn't
the issue here. Raw emotion was the object and McGill was playing it to
the hilt. Holding up a bullet for the jury to see, he explained that they were

Plus P cartridges designed to cause maximum damage. Then he turned art-
fully to focus on the victim. He reminded the jury of testimony that
Faulkner on another occasion had rescued the prostitute and defense witness Veronica Jones from a robbery and a beating, and that the night of the
shooting, he had arrested a rapist and brought into the same hospital in
which he later died the suspect's seven-year-old victim. He powerfully
evoked the dead officer's presence by once again, as he had done earlier
during the trial, picking up the victim's police hat as a prop, saying:

> What is there to remember? A hat without a badge. A hat that
> was found on the scene. This. The remnants of an individual. An
> individual that had done those things for so many people.
>   That is why this is such an outrage and what a way to go. What
> a way to go.[21]

McGill devoted remarkably little time to reviewing all the evidence
in the case. If anything, he glossed over it, knowing the jurors already had
his story line firmly in mind. Instead, he spent the bulk of his time trying
to bolster the credentials and credibility of his witnesses—particularly
Chobert and White with their unsavory criminal backgrounds. He was
careful to address the contradictions in testimony cited by Jackson, but
then knocked them down by setting up a straw man, implying that Jackson
was claiming a grand conspiracy to "get" the defendant—something
Jackson never came close to suggesting:

> ...If there was some kind of grand conspiracy for some God
> knows what reason to accuse that man of something he is supposed
> not to have done I am telling you it was made up pretty quickly,
> because twenty-five minutes after Mike Scanlan testified what he
> saw, he testified or gave a statement, and Robert Chobert forty-five
> minutes, forty-five minutes after it happened he gave his statement,
> and Cynthia White gave her statement within hours. The first hour.
> Albert Magilton within the same forty-five minutes. What a very
> fast moving conspiracy that was. All to get this man. Boy, that is the
> most fantastic conspiracy I ever heard.
>   ...One grand conspiracy, ladies and gentlemen? Really. Just to
> put it on this man.[22]

But a grand conspiracy was not at all what Jackson had tried to
demonstrate. Rather, he attempted to show, sometimes with considerable
skill, and often in the face of judicial obstruction, that at least in the case
of Chobert and White, their accounts of the events they claimed to have
seen changed over time. And he attempted to show further that there were
reasons why they may have been vulnerable to pressure from police and/or

from the district attorney's office. If it was a conspiracy Jackson was alleging, it was not one that happened, as McGill mockingly suggested, within the hour of the shooting. Rather, it was over the days and weeks following the shooting. Nothing McGill said during his summation challenged or even addressed that quite reasonable theory.

McGill's address wasn't really aimed at trying to convince the jury anyway, though. He was confident that he'd already done that during the course of the trial. What the prosecutor seems to have been doing was trying to make certain that the jurors would follow through with the conviction and the ultimate sanction. He didn't want just to convince them Abu-Jamal had shot Faulkner. He wanted them to hate him—indeed to hate him enough to want him dead. And he did his job well.

> Ladies and gentlemen, I would like to sort of conclude by asking you to remember again what I said what [sic] I first intended to prove at the beginning. I also mentioned, I don't know if you will recall, the ironies that exist in this case. The ironies that an individual who is killed and treated at the same hospital as the Defendant who killed him. The irony that the defendant who killed him would go to the hospital being brought there by the very police whose brother officer he killed. And the fact that if he had not been brought there by the police within a half hour or so and treated by Doctor Coletta he also may have died. While there at the hospital having been brought in by those policemen he then turns and looks at Gary Bell, the partner of Daniel Faulkner, straight in the eyes and says, "I shot him and I hope he dies."
>
> The irony of having both the killed individual and the doer shot by each other at the same time at the same scene. All of this and in particular the conduct of this Defendant. I plead to you consider the thrust of such arrogance and hostility and injustice.
>
> ...Ladies and gentlemen, I ask you, all of us, the Commonwealth, the people of this city, reach out to you and demand justice. Look at that intent to kill and that man who did it with that weapon and say, "The evidence is clear to us. You are guilty of first degree murder."[23]

Taken in its entirety, it was a compelling, if legally and ethically questionable, summation, powerfully delivered. The rest was anticlimax.

None of Jackson's attacks on the fabric of the prosecution's story worked—except perhaps his odd request to the jury that it not look for a compromise verdict. Abu-Jamal might even have been on the brink of being sentenced to manslaughter: at one point jurors did send in a note asking to be reinstructed on the definition of manslaughter—so that was obviously considered and then, for some reason, rejected. After deliberating for five and a half hours the following day, on July 2, the jury voted to convict Abu-Jamal of first degree murder.

The courtroom was surprisingly quiet after the verdict was read. Faulkner's widow Maureen wept quietly. While McGill looked obviously pleased, the police on her side of the room, some of them in uniform, looked stoic. Across the aisle in seats where Abu-Jamal's family, friends and supporters sat, there was also quiet. His mother sat ashen-faced, her hand gripped by Abu-Jamal's older sister Lydia. Jamal himself, however, looked defiant. The verdict didn't catch him by surprise. He had expected this outcome from a court and a legal system that he was convinced from the outset were out to kill him.

Now it was time to move to the second part of the trial: the penalty phase. It is a peculiarity of American jurisprudence that uniquely in the instance of death penalty cases, there are two distinct trials, before the same jury. The first is to establish guilt and then, if there is a conviction on the charge of murder in the first degree for which the sentence of death is one possible penalty, there is a second hearing. At this hearing, the convicted killer has the right to address the jury. (In a few of the 38 states with the death penalty, this penalty phase hearing is conducted in front of a judge, not a jury. In 2002, the U.S. Supreme Court ruled this approach unconstitutional. It is likely that in a short time, all penalty phase hearings will be heard by a jury in every state that has capital punishment.) He or she may also bring in a whole new set of character witnesses, and even, in some cases, witnesses to the actual crime. The goal of the hearing, from the perspective of the defendant, is to convince the jury that there are mitigating circumstances making the death penalty an inappropriate punishment. Examples of mitigating circumstances might be a clean record, a history of good deeds, a stable family life, etc. The goal of the prosecution, on the other hand, is to suggest to the jury certain aggravating circumstances that might help to convince them that a death penalty is appropriate. These might include evidence of particular viciousness on the part of the killer or, in Pennsylvania, by act of the state legislature, the very fact of killing a "peace officer" (which includes police) in the line of duty. Technically, the jury is supposed to weigh those aggravating and mitigating circumstances, and only those circumstances, thus arriving at some kind of a calculation that tilts either towards or away from death. In practice, of course, many jurors will have in mind all kinds of impressions that have come from their life experience, their days sitting through the trial, and the things that are said to them by the two sides' attorneys in their summations.

Since Abu-Jamal had an absolutely clean record before his arrest, and had strong family backing, McGill wisely focused on two areas: the killing of a police officer while he was on the job and in uniform, and evidence that Abu-Jamal was a vicious, aggressive individual.

What about Jackson? Astonishingly, he did nothing to defend his client's reputation. In what was clearly his major blunder in a trial already littered with defense mistakes and missed opportunities, Jackson failed to call a single character witness on Abu-Jamal's behalf during this penalty phase. Nor did he ask for a delay to give himself time to prepare a defense. Crushed and demoralized by the guilty verdict in the first phase, Jackson now seemed to be simply going through the motions. The day of the jury's deliberations had begun badly for him, too: he had been awakened at 6:30 a.m. by fire trucks which had been called to his house in a prank—not the first time this had happened. Then, when he'd gotten to his office at 8:50, he had received a frightened call from his 15-year-old son saying that some-one had made a threatening telephone call telling the boy: "You are the one we want. We will be over to get you." Before coming to court, he had driven home to get his son and bring him to his grandmother's house.

In a remarkable display of heartlessness, Sabo expressed no sympathy. He didn't show the basic courtesy of inquiring about the well-being of Jackson's son. Instead, he questioned the still-anxious attorney about his late arrival at court and asked suspiciously whether he might have gone to another courtroom to do some other business:

> Mr. Jackson: I didn't want to leave him alone. I don't know what is hap-pening to my house.
> The Court: He is back at home now. You weren't in any other court-room were you? You didn't go to any other courtroom?
> Mr. Jackson: I have no other trials. None.
> The Court: The next time I wish you would call here and let us know what you are doing.
> Mr. Jackson: I assure you that I wasn't thinking to call here. I was think-ing about getting home.
> The Court: Okay. The next time you call here and let us know. I mean it is terrible. It is 10:45.[24]

Faced with such judicial frostiness, it is perhaps no surprise that Jackson didn't bother to ask Judge Sabo for a delay of a few days to give him time to prepare for the penalty phase. Clearly if he had been over his head trying to conduct a defense during the trial, he had had no time to give any thought to defending against the death penalty. This is typical of many lawyers: even under better circumstances, defense lawyers don't generally waste time preparing for the penalty phase in a capital trial. First, they generally hope to win an acquittal. Even when they don't, once the verdict is handed down they are often given time to prepare for the penalty phase.

But this was Judge Sabo's courtroom, and prosecutor McGill, who knew this judge's fondness for express-lane justice, wasn't about to give the defense an inch. Sabo, in fact, seemed almost buoyant immediately following the guilty verdict. As he said to the two lawyers at the bench:

> The Court: It is practically 5:30. It is almost time for dinner for the jury. What is your pleasure? Do you want to do it [the penalty phase] tonight or do it the first thing tomorrow morning, or what?[25]

Before the still shell-shocked Jackson could even open his mouth to respond, McGill, pressing his advantage (though not to the absurd extreme of saying to go ahead into the evening), replied:

> Judge, I think the first thing tomorrow morning would be in order.[26]

Jackson said nothing, but Abu-Jamal, who had been busy preparing a response to the verdict he had anticipated receiving, asked boldly to have the jury brought back in for him to make a statement:

> The Defendant: Can the jury be called back in?
> The Court: They are going to dinner.
> The Defendant: Can they be called back in for my statement about their decision?
> The Court: I don't think that is proper at this time.
> The Defendant: Is it possible, Judge? They just left.
> The Court: It is not proper for you to give your opinion to the jury.
> The Defendant: I said my statement.
> The Court: Or your statement. They are not finished yet. The second phase they have to go into is the penalty phase.[27]

McGill, hearing that Abu-Jamal had prepared a statement, could hardly hide his gleeful anticipation:

> Mr. McGill: Mr. Jamal will have the opportunity to speak and say anything he wishes.[28]

The prosecutor was right to be enthusiastic about Abu-Jamal's plans to address the jury. That next morning, McGill introduced only one witness (someone from the police department's records office who testified to the fact that the slain officer had received commendations and had no disciplinary record in his file). He then turned the floor over to the militant and unbowed defendant. Abu-Jamal proceeded to excoriate the judge, the prosecutor, the police, his own lawyer and the jury itself for having convicted him.

> This jury is not composed of my peers, for those closest to my life experiences were intentionally and systematically excluded, peremptorily excused. Only those prosecution-prone, some who began with a fixed opinion of guilt, some related to city police, mostly white, mostly male remain. May they one day be so fairly judged.[29]

No one could argue that this was a speech designed to win friends on the jury panel! Based upon the evidence of his request to Judge Sabo the afternoon before, it appears it was really intended to be a response to the jury's guilty verdict, not an appeal to the jury considering the nature of his punishment. That was a grievous tactical error on Abu-Jamal's part, because at this point, having been found guilty of murder, what he needed to do was gain at least the sympathy of one juror during the penalty phase of the trial. Most of what Abu-Jamal eloquently stated about the nature of his trial—that the jury had been denied important evidence such as Wakshul's testimony, that the defendant had been denied the right to an adviser of his choice when other defendants in other trials were permitted such advisers at their table, that his own lawyer was "inadequate to the task," and that the judge had been a "black-robed conspirator"—was true or arguably true. But Abu-Jamal, who as a professional journalist obviously had a remarkable gift for connecting to his audience, was not talking in a way designed to positively influence his audience here.

As he had from the beginning, and as he continues to do to this day, Abu-Jamal asserted his innocence:

> I am innocent of these charges that I have been charged of and convicted of, and despite the connivance of Sabo, McGill and Jackson to deny me my so-called rights to represent myself, to assistance of my choice, to personally select a jury who's totally of my peers, to cross-examine witnesses, and to make both opening and closing arguments, I am still innocent of these charges.[30]

But he then cancelled out any sympathy he might have won himself with the jurors. First, he attacked their integrity, and then condemned "the system." But unlike him, these jurors didn't see the system as craven or oppressive. In making this argument, he played right into McGill's waiting hands, especially with his concluding remarks:

This decision today proves neither my guilt nor my innocence.
It proves merely that the system is finished. Babylon is falling! Long
live MOVE! Long live John Africa![31]

As McGill himself told me in an interview, referring to Abu-Jamal's speech to the jury, "Jamal made a major effort to use the tactics of the Panthers of 10 years earlier. But for all his so-called intelligence, he misjudged his public (the jury) and he misjudged the times."

McGill's point is an understatement. This trial was in the early 1980s, during the ascendant Reagan era. Had it been ten years earlier, at the height of the Vietnam War, Watergate and the domestic anti-war movement, there might have been some among the blue-collar types who were sitting on this jury who would have been ready to wonder whether the government was hiding something or in some way misbehaving. But by 1982, most Americans, particularly those who considered themselves part of the white middle class, were tired of that kind of contrarian, anti-Establishment thinking. Talking about "the System" as some kind of evil entity was passé. If he did anything with his attack on the "System" and every element of the court system, including the jury, it was to make a perfect segue to McGill's planned argument in favor of the death penalty: this defendant was an aggressive killer with no respect for the law. Moreover, Abu-Jamal never showed his statement to his attorney. Jackson didn't even have a copy of it when it was read in open court and was hearing it for the first time. This made Abu-Jamal incredibly vulnerable, opening all manner of areas up for the prosecution to cross-examine him on, particularly with Judge Sabo sitting as the arbiter as to what types of questions would be permissible. Expecting just such an opportunity, McGill came armed with newspaper clippings of the defendant's Panther days that he intended to use to send Abu-Jamal to the gallows—clippings he had tried to use before during Abu-Jamal's bail hearing, but which had been disallowed. When Abu-Jamal had had his say, McGill smoothly shifted into attack mode.

Anthony Jackson, for all of his shortcomings as a death penalty lawyer, saw what was coming better than his client. At this point, Abu-Jamal was looking on the whole trial as a sham—the very point he wanted to make in his statement to the jury. Jackson had already observed the prosecutor carrying around some newspaper and magazine clippings, and had seen him unsuccessfully trying to find a way to inject them into the January bail hearing. Before McGill could get started in his cross-examination of the defendant on the stand, Jackson sought to head him off:

Your Honor, I know, of course, I am anticipating, I believe Mr.

McGill has a number of newspaper articles and publications and perhaps other quotations. I would object to the authority purportedly attributed or if attributed to the defendant, if they are not authenticated or without authentification and without any acknowledgement or truth, but, simply, to the defendant himself. I would object to the questioning in that even if he asked the question, "Did you say so-and-so," whatever his answer is, or is going to be, it's already prejudiced the minds and inflamed the jury and I would object to the reading of anything that is purported to be from the defendant.[32]

McGill countered that this was a sentencing hearing, not a trial, and replied:

...I think he has opened up an extensive amount of doors. I can't begin to count them in the statement, including the inadmissible testimony or the inadmissible evidence, or documents and quoting of people, John Africa, among others. There are so many doors open, Judge, that really... [33]*

Overruling Jackson's objection, Judge Sabo said:

You knew that Mr. Abu-Jamal had the statement prepared and you knew that he was going to read it regardless whether the district attorney objected or not, so it seems in point that I will allow him to cross-examine him.
Go ahead.[34]

McGill proceeded to lead Abu-Jamal down a path in which he made or defended one radical statement after another. While the sentiments behind those statements were grounded in a long history of progressive, radical politics, and had nothing to do with a penchant for violence or for killing police, none of that mattered. As McGill knew, their effect on this jury of conservative older blue and white-collar workers, white and black, was decidedly not to Abu-Jamal's advantage.

The prosecutor began by asking Abu-Jamal why he wouldn't stand whenever the judge entered the courtroom. Abu-Jamal replied the he did not stand because the judge, in his view, ruled by force, not right. Then, warming to the battle, he added, standing up at the defense table:

Because he is an executioner. Because he is a hangman, that's why.[35]

McGill responded quickly and coolly, "You are not an executioner?"[36]

---

*It took some audacity for McGill to criticize Abu-Jamal for mentioning "inadmissible evidence" in his statement, since McGill in his closing argument had even cited an alleged witness who had never testified to support his case.

Then he got to the point he had been aiming for all along, saying:

> Mr. Jamal, let me ask you if you can recall saying something
> sometime ago, and perhaps it might ring a bell as to whether or not
> you are an executioner or endorse such actions.
>
> "Black brothers and sisters—and organizations—which would-
> n't commit themselves before are relating to us black people that
> they are facing—we are facing the reality that the Black Panther
> Party has been facing, which is..."
>
> Now, listen to this quote. You've often been quoted saying
> this:
>
> "Political power grows out of the barrel of a gun."
>
> Do you remember saying that sir?[37]

Abu-Jamal wasn't afraid of this line of questioning. He knew what he
meant when he made that statement, even though it had been made 12
years earlier when he was at the tender age of 15. It was a quote from Mao
Tse-tung, the leader of the Chinese revolution. As used by Abu-Jamal, it
was a clear reference to the fact that the Black Panther Party, of which he
was then a member, was under assault by the police, the FBI and other law
enforcement bodies. From the Panther perspective—and in fact in the
view of many observers, white and black—the entire black population of
urban America was under siege, with the police in the role more of an
occupying army in their neighborhoods than an agency of public safety.

The defendant objected to McGill's effort to sever the quote from its
context, as though it was simply a call to arms, an invitation to shoot cops.
He insisted on being allowed to read the entire newspaper article in which
the quote appeared. From the point of view of political argumentation, it
was a logical demand. But in a court of law, this was a trap. Abu-Jamal was
probably not aware of the dangers of saying too much. The opposing attorney can use anything someone says on a witness stand as a subject for further inquiry. McGill knew this well, and welcomed the opportunity to have
the entire article from the *Philadelphia Inquirer* read into the record by his
quarry. It meant he'd have more freedom to hang the man with his own
words. "Go right ahead," McGill invited.[38]

Abu-Jamal proceeded, in his mellifluous baritone, to read the article,
published on January 4, 1970, and written by Acel Moore, a colleague and
respected African-American journalist. Moore had been writing about the
local chapter of the Black Panther Party in the wake of the killings, by
police, of some Panther leaders in other parts of the country:

> The walls in the storefront headquarters at 1928 Columbia
> Ave. are painted black and plastered with revolutionary posters. The

faces are dark and determined. Black men and women bundled in coats and jackets against the cold of an unheated interior are busy with telephones, paperwork, or huddling in earnest conferences and barely take time to acknowledge new arrivals or departures. When they do, the standard salutation is a slogan, "All power to the people."

It was busy before at the Philadelphia Chapter Headquarters of the Black Panther Party. It's busier now.

Since the murders," says West [sic] Cook, Chapter communications Secretary, [referring to the killing of several Panther party members by police] "Black brothers and sisters and organizations which wouldn't commit themselves before are relating to us. Black people are facing the reality that the Black Panther Party has been facing. Political power grows out of the barrel of a gun.[39]

McGill tried to interrupt him there to focus attention on the quote. But Abu-Jamal and his attorney objected and the judge let him continue, allowing him to attempt to demonstrate that the quote referred to the guns being used not by, but *against* the Panthers and the black community, and to the reality of police power, not specifically to the Panthers using guns against the police:

Murders, a calculated design of genocide, and a national plot to destroy the party leadership is what the Panthers and their supporters call a bloody two-year history of police raids and shootouts. The Panthers say 28 party members have died in police gunfire during that period, two last month.

The article read into the record by Abu-Jamal went on to say that the Panthers saw themselves as defenders of a community under siege, and further described how the party ran a free breakfast program for needy children in the community, feeding an estimated 80 children a day.

McGill didn't care about the finer points of argument, however, and he was confident that those points were lost on the only audience he cared about anyway—the jury. What he wanted were juicy quotes that would scare them and convince them they were dealing with a crazed black revolutionary bent on killing police. He got more than he needed from the article. All he needed to do now was to get the Abu-Jamal on the stand to state that he still held the views that he had expressed—or seemed to have been expressing if taken out of context—in that 12-year-old article. But at that point, Abu-Jamal finally caught on to his plan and refused to play.

Q: Mr. Jamal, let me ask you again, sir, if I may—Was that or was that not a quote that you made to Acel Moore?

A: That was a quote from Mao Tse-tung.

Q: Is that one that you have adopted?

A: Say again?

Q: Have you adopted that as your philosophy theory?

A: No, I have not adopted that. I repeated that.[40]

Unable to get Abu-Jamal to adopt the Mao quote as his own, McGill took another tack, getting him to repeat angry statements and insults he had made in the course of his arraignment and trial.

Q: Let me ask you, Mr. Jamal, when you were before this court, I believe it was yesterday, you said: "The system is finished." Is that correct?

A: That's correct.

...

Q: Did you not continually question Judge Sabo and disagree with his rulings continually after he ordered you again and again and again and again? Is that correct?

A: (No answer)

Q: Or is it not?

A: Did I disagree? Most certainly I disagreed with his rulings.

Q: Do you recall in front of the Supreme Court Justice McDermott who had affirmed the order of this court that your counsel continue to represent you that you shouted to him as he walked out, "McDermott, get back here." Do you remember that?

A: No. (Shakes head negatively.) I said, "McDermott, where are you going?

...

Q: Mr. Jamal, on April the 29th, 1982, do you recall being in front of Judge Ribner?

A: Yes.

Q: And do you recall over about two or three actual pages of testimony saying such things as, and this was in court, open court:

"I don't give a damn what you think, go to hell. What the hell are you afraid of? What the hell are you afraid of, bastard?"

Do you recall saying that to Judge Ribner?

A: Sure do. (Nods head affirmatively.)[41]

McGill ended his questioning of the witness. He had what he wanted. He knew that the jury—his jury now that they had convicted Abu-Jamal—would see all this combativeness as simply further evidence of Abu-Jamal's aggressiveness and lack of contrition for what they had already decided he had done.

It remained only to lay it all out to them in a summation. And, as we have seen from his summation in the conviction phase, McGill would be adept at this.

But first it would be Anthony Jackson's turn. Faced with the damage done by Abu-Jamal's statement and his verbal bout with McGill, and with no character witnesses to demonstrate his finer and gentler qualities as a human being, everything hinged on Jackson's ability to sway the jury with a call for mercy. Yet it seemed the fight had gone completely out of him. His rambling narrative appeared totally unprepared—something he later admitted was true when he testified at the PCRA hearing about his performance at the trial. Depressed after the verdict, and with no time to marshal a defense, Jackson, amazingly, had not even talked to his client before coming in for one of the most crucial moments in the whole trial.

He began with an incredible claim that, when the legislature passed a law declaring that the killing of a peace officer in the line of duty would automatically constitute a so-called aggravating circumstance, which would argue in favor of death, they didn't mean to include police as "peace officers." It was a silly, futile idea that made a joke out of the rest of his presentation.

Rather than demonstrate that the youthful "power flows from the barrel of a gun" quote had been a reference to the power of the police, he tried to explain away the Mao quote by noting that the Panthers had done good things, and that in any event, America had indeed been built upon violence—the violence of the revolution, of battles against the Indians, and so on. It was an argument that, even if factually accurate, would be lost on this jury--that might have even hardened them against his client.

Jackson then went on to attack the death penalty itself. Since the jurors had been selected based upon their stated endorsement of that extreme form of punishment, this was another dead end.

No one could question Jackson's intentions or conviction. Midway through his summation, he was in tears. As he was pleading with the jury to consider life imprisonment instead of death, the court stenographer, whose job it is to dryly record the verbal record of a trial, noted:

> I ask you ladies and gentlemen...
> (whereupon there was an extended pause while counsel drinks
> water and composes his emotions.)[42]

But for all Jackson's emotion, the argument he presented against the ultimate sentence was unpersuasive. This despite ample evidence on which to build an argument for mitigating circumstances: there was in fact hardly any reference to the fact that this defendant had an absolutely clean record and was a dedicated father.

Where Jackson had been unorganized, ineffective and off-target, and emotionally distraught, McGill was organized, taut and focused on the jury. He didn't mince words:

> You've had an opportunity of seeing the person, the type of person he is, and how he is. That way, you again have an opportunity to reflect upon the incident, the events at the time.
>
> ...
>
> Because, ladies and gentlemen, what we're dealing with now and who we're dealing with now is a convicted murderer. This man is no longer presumed innocent. This man over here—(indicating by pointing)—is a killer. You're looking and have heard a killer. That's who we're dealing with. This is not a trial, this is a sentencing hearing.[43]

McGill then went to the issue of killing of a police officer in the line of duty. It would be the only aggravating circumstance he could pin on this defendant. But he nailed it on and drove it home with a spike by linking it to Abu-Jamal's assertive behavior in the courtroom. More importantly, he would convince the jury that in putting the defendant to death, they were standing between order and chaos.

Why is killing a police officer such an important aggravating circumstance, he asked:

> The fact of the matter is simply this. It's all called law and order. That is why that is so important, that aggravating circumstance. Law and order. And, ladies and gentlemen, this is what this trial is all about more than any other trial I have ever seen, and certainly more than any other I have been in, because you, yourself, have seen, you have heard things that are going on, and you have heard testimony of things that are going on as to what is lawful and what is not lawful, and actions, arrogance, reactions against the law. Law and order.
>
> So ladies and gentlemen, we then will simply make the response, at least ask yourselves the question, are we going to live in a society with law and order, and are we going to enforce the laws with the intention of law and order, or are we going to decide our own rules and then, act accordingly?[44]

To heighten the drama McGill again turned to a prop—a signature effect he proudly aims for in all his jury summations. He once more picked up Faulkner's hat, which by then he had transformed for the jury into an effective surrogate for the dead officer. McGill then made the case into a symbolic test of the jury's will to stand up against anarchy:

> Ladies and gentlemen, in plain view of everybody at 13th and Locust Streets, clearly with the simply—with the manifestation,

with the presence of law and order in that section of the city, from head to toe, that man was a police officer, able to be seen and maintaining order and not only walking over and maintaining order with his uniform, but also in a police car that was marked in plain view.

What does that mean? Ladies and gentlemen, this is our core, our unity of any kind of order, and that is, individuals that are trying to enforce it. Why is that so important? Because once we have the opportunity presented that anybody can kill a cop and it doesn't matter, you may as well forget about law and order, just throw it right out.[45]

McGill had the jury in his pocket. But he wasn't taking any chances. He went on to refer again to the defendant's behavior in the courtroom, to drag in the poet Sonia Sonches and her alleged support for a woman who had killed a state police officer in New Jersey. McGill even tarred him with the Mao quote. Never mind that he had failed to get Abu-Jamal to agree that this quote spoken twelve years ago as a teenager was something he believed in today. Never mind that Abu-Jamal had shown that he made the comment not in reference to the force the Black Panthers were using, but in reference to what police were using against them.

Again, this is what this is all about, law and order. How do we avoid it if we don't like it, we don't just accept it, and we don't try to change it from within, we just rebel against it. And maybe that was the siege all the way back then with political power, power growing out of the barrel of a gun. No matter who said it, when you do say it and when you feel it, and particularly in an area when you're talking about police or cops or shootings and so forth, even back then, this is not something that happened overnight.[46]

It was walking on the thin edge to appeal so blatantly to the jury's political emotions, as the appellate courts had already thrown out cases where such arguments had been made to inflame a jury, but McGill knew with Judge Sabo on the bench he was safe. He felt safe, too, going back onto the thin ice of telling jurors not to feel like they were really killing anyone by voting for death. In a statement, which would later form one of the arguments on appeal for the overturning of Abu-Jamal's death sentence, McGill said:

Ladies and gentlemen, you are not asked to kill anybody. You are asked to follow the law. The same law that I keep on throwing at you, saying those words, law and order. I should point out to you it's the same law that has for six months provided safeguards for this defendant. The same law, ladies and gentlemen, the same law that will provide him appeal after appeal after appeal.[47]

McGill's confidence in the trial judge and subsequent appeals courts was not misplaced. Although Jackson objected promptly to this effort to remove any sense of personal responsibility from the jurors for the decision they were about to make, Sabo allowed him to forge ahead. With Abu-Jamal's supporters in an uproar in the gallery, McGill did just that:

> The same law, ladies and gentlemen, that has made it so because of the constant appeals, that as Mr. Jackson said, nobody at all has died in Pennsylvania since 1962 for an incident that occurred in 1959.[48]

The judge gave his instructions to the jury and they were sent out a second time, this time to determine the fate of the defendant they had already determined had killed a police officer in cold blood. There was, the defense later claimed on appeal, a flaw in the forms that the jurors were required to use in establishing their verdict—a flaw that later would lead a federal judge to overturn the sentence. Those forms made it appear that the 12 jurors had to be unanimous in agreeing on a mitigating circumstance. In fact, unanimity was not required for mitigating circumstances; only for aggravating circumstances. (That is, if even one of the 12 jurors were to find a mitigating circumstance, it would have to be counted by the whole panel, but for an aggravating circumstance to count, all 12 jurors would have to agree to it.) The jury ultimately found one aggravating circumstance (the killing of an officer in the line of duty) and one mitigating (no prior record), but it may well be that some juror or jurors, though not all, felt there were other mitigating circumstances. It was clear that the mitigating factor they did find did not outweigh the aggravating one; the jury, in a decision that seemed to surprise no one on either side of the gallery, returned after a deliberation of just over three and a half hours to announce their decision: death.

The jury's announcement of their verdict was almost an anti-climax. It was followed by a strange quiet on both sides of the aisle separating the family and supporters of Mumia Abu-Jamal from the family and supporters of the dead officer, Daniel Faulkner. If there was any display of emotion, it was limited to police officers in the gallery who clenched their fists and smiled grimly.[49]

Turning to the seated defendant after the jury had been dismissed and left the room, an obviously pleased Judge Sabo said briskly, "All right, Mr. Abu-Jamal?"[50] Abu-Jamal sat stone-faced at the defense table. Sabo went on to confirm the sentence and explain to him his right of appeal. He added that there would be a psychiatric evaluation.

Abu-Jamal laughed wryly then at the absurdity of it all. As he was led from the room by sheriff's deputies, he walked briskly, punching his fist in the air and shouting his by then customary MOVE salute, "Ona Move! Long live John Africa!"

The court was dismissed, and thus began Mumia Abu-Jamal's two decades long battle from a tiny cell in death row to win a chance for a new, and fairer trial.

Fig. 1. The young Daniel Faulkner, shot and killed at the age of 25.

Fig. 2. Mumia Abu-Jamal with son Mazi. Early 1980s.

Fig. 3. (above) 1234 Locust, the scene of the shootings, showing the rear of an unidentified parked Ford sedan on the far left, William Cook's VW, and Officer Daniel Faulkner's police squad car. (police crime photo)

Fig 4. (right) Blood on the pavement where Officer Faulkner's body was found. (police crime photo)

Figure 5. (below) The view of Locust from the parking lot where Mumic Abu-Jamal had parked his taxi cab, and from which he emerged to cross the street. Cook's VW is still visible across the street, but Faulkner's squad car has already been removed. (police crime photo)

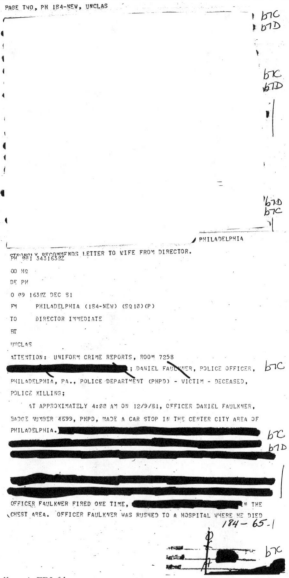

Fig. 6. Daniel Faulkner's FBI file

A Freedom of Information Act request for Daniel Faulkner's FBI file resulted in release of a heavily censored 10-page report. Explanations for the deletion of most of the missing material, which included the blanking out of several entire pages, were coded as b7C and b7D. The former refers to privacy concerns, which could mean family members were mentioned, or that other persons, still living, were mentioned. The latter means that release "could reasonably be expected to disclose the identity of a confidential source, including a State, local or foreign agency or authority or authority or any private institution which furnished information on a confidential basis, and, in the case of record or information compiled by a criminal law enforcement authority in the course of a criminal investigation..."

D-14

December 10, 1981

```
Interviewed - Priscilla Durham - Security Officer
Place       - Room 109, Main Building
Time        - 2:16 a.m.
Date        - December 10, 1981
```

Miss Priscilla Durham was interviewed by Investigators Bartelle and Begley and she stated that on December 9, 1981, she was outside the office of the Emergency Room clerk when Abu Jamal was brought in by the police. She stated he was on the floor with his body half out of the Emergency Room and half in the Emergency Room. She stated the police asked her where they can take him, meaning Jamal. Miss Durham stated she told the police that they can put him back in the Family Room. Miss Durham stated the police took him to the Family Room and about 10 minutes later, Mrs. Keating and two doctors went to the Family Room and said that Jamal needed treatment. She stated the police then took Jamal to the Cardiac Room.

Miss Durham also stated when Jamal was first brought in and was lying on the floor, she noticed he was bleeding. Miss Durham also stated that Jamal shouted "Yeh, I shot the mother fucker, and I hope he dies".

Fig. 7. The controversial alleged typed "confession" document

This typed document, unsigned and typed on a sheet of plain white paper with no identifying marks, was presented by the prosecution at the 1982 trial of Mumia Abu-Jamal as being the transcription by Jefferson Hospital security office supervisor James Bartelle of the account of Abu-Jamal's alleged confession to murder as overheard by hospital security guard Priscilla Durham. Durham had testified at the trial that Bartelle had written down her account by hand. The typed document was never authenticated by anyone. Bartelle is now deceased. D-14 is the number assigned to the document as a trial exhibit. The document was held up to the jury considering Abu-Jamal's fate by prosecutor Joseph McGill during his final argument, where he used it to validate the two-months-late report by a police officer of Abu-Jamal's alleged hospital confession.

03/06/2001 19:29 6094245144 YBF LBW PHL DA LAW DIV PAGE 02

07/14/1995 16:23 2156865725 PAGE 36

INVESTIGATION INTERVIEW RECORD

PHILADELPHIA POLICE DEPARTMENT HOMICIDE DIVISION

CASE NO.

INTERVIEWER: Kominsky 788

NAME: P/O GARY WAKSHUL #7363

AGE / RACE / DOB

ADDRESS: 6th District 3 Squad Group C-no van

APARTMENT NO. / PHONE

NAME OF EMPLOYMENT/SCHOOL

SOC. SEC. NO.

ADDRESS OF EMPLOYMENT/SCHOOL

PHONE

PLACE OF INTERVIEW: inside Homicide Division/PAB

DATE AND TIME: 12-9-81 5:50 am

BROUGHT IN BY

DATE AND TIME

WE ARE QUESTIONING YOU CONCERNING: the shooting of P/O Faulkner

WARNINGS GIVEN BY

DATE AND TIME

ANSWERS (1) (2) (3) (4) (5) (6) (7)

Q. Officer, would you tell me in your own words what you know regarding the shooting that occurred tonight?

A. I was assigned to EPW#601 with P/O Stevon Trombetta#7324 and at approximately 3:54a heard EPC#612 state he had a car stop at 1234 Locust Street. Radio dispatch was asking for a backup unit and I heard Officer Faulkner of EPC#612 asking for a wagon. We acknowledged the assignment and as we were heading to back him up, a civilian in a dark-colored auto, possibly a Ford, bearing New York license plates, stopped us at Juniper and Walnut and stated that a police officer was shot in the 1200 block of Locust Street and informed us that he would follow us to that location. The operator of this vehicle was a white male, approximately 42yrs of age, well dressed. I informed radio dispatch of this information and advised them that were enroute. When we arrived at the scene I observed Officer Faulkner lying on the ground and it appeared he had been shot in the head. He was lying on the south side of the street. My partner and myself got out of the EPW to assist Officer Faulkner and we carried him to the back of EPW#601. We then returned to the pavement where the officer had been lying because there was a negro male on the sidewalk, at the curb, near a dark-blue colored Volkswagen. This male appeared to be injured and was handcuffed behind his back. With the assistance

GOOD ☐ Yes ☐ No

VIEWED BY

Fig. 8.

Initial account of Police Officer Gary Wakshul of his time spent with Mumia Abu-Jamal. Wakshul had been assigned to stay with the suspect from the time he was placed in the paddy wagon to the time he was operated on in the hospital for removal of the bullet in his lower back. At the end of his detailed account, Wakshul states clearly: "We were informed to go to Jefferson Hospital and to have the male treated for any injuries. We stayed with the male at Jefferson until we were relieved. During this time, the negro male made no comments."

INVESTIGATION INTERVIEW RECORD CONTINUATION SHEET	CITY OF PHILADELPHIA POLICE DEPARTMENT	
NAME P/O WAKSHUL #7363	PAGE 2	CASE NO.

...other officers at the scene, we carried this negro male to the back of our EPW where I noticed the negro male had some type of white-colored strap running across his shoulder area. I brought this to the attention of an Inspector at the scene who proceeded, with my partner, pull the male's coat away from his left arm, revealing a shoulder holster under his left arm. I noted that the holster was empty. A wallet was also recovered from the negro male with a City of Philadelphia Press card bearing a muslim-type name which I could make out. As per orders from Inspector Giordano, we were to proceed, with the male, to the Homicide Unit, but enrout; these orders were amended via police radio and we were informed to go to Jefferson Hospital and to have the male treated for any injuries. We stayed with the male at Jefferson until we were relieved. During this time, the negro male made no comments.

> "During this time, the negro male made no comments."

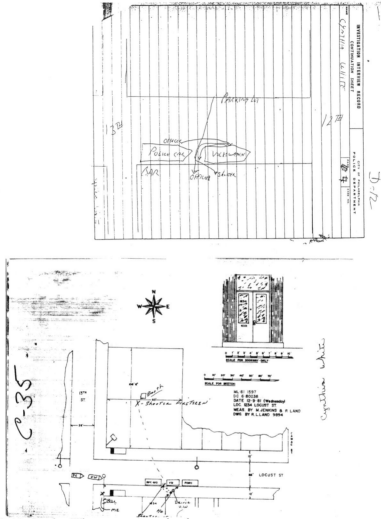

Figs. 9 & 10. Cynthia White crime scene sketches

The first illustration (identified as defense exhibit D-12) is a sketch made on the morning of the shooting by police investigators. It shows the crime scene and the crime as described by the prosecution's star witness, prostitute Cynthia White. Arrows show the paths of Officer Daniel Faulkner and the "shooter." Note that there is no drawing of a taxi cab in the drawing. According to the testimony of prosecution witness Robert Chobert, he had parked his taxi cab directly behind the police car.

Illustration two (identified as prosecution exhibit C-35), made later by a police artist, but signed by the witness, shows the vehicles placed more accurately on the street, but while this time it shows a third car, identified as a "Ford," which was undeniably parked in front of the police car and Cook's VW during the incident, there is still no taxi cab at the scene. (The two other vehicles in the drawing, hand-drawn with pointed fronts to indicate direction, are Officer Faulkner's squad car and Cook's VW shown earlier as they approached the scene of the shooting.)

IN THE COURT OF COMMON PLEAS
FIRST JUDICIAL DISTRICT OF PENNSYLVANIA

COMMONWEALTH OF PENNSYLVANIA : JAN. TERM, 19 82

vs. : No. 1358.

: TRIAL DIVISION
: CRIMINAL SECTION
: PHILADELPHIA

MUMIA ABU-JAMAL

FIRST DEGREE MURDER VERDICT
PENALTY DETERMINATION SHEET

We, the jury, having heretofore determined that the above-named defendant is guilty of murder of the first degree, do hereby further find that:

(1) We, the jury, unanimously sentence the defendant to

/X/ death

/ / life imprisonment.

(2) (To be used only if the aforesaid sentence is death)

We, the jury, have found unanimously

/ / at least one aggravating circumstance and no mitigating circumstance. The aggravating circumstance(s) is/are __________.

/X/ one or more aggravating circumstances which outweigh any mitigating circumstances. The aggravating circumstance(s) is/are A.

The mitigating circumstance(s) is/are A

AGGRAVATING AND MITIGATING CIRCUMSTANCES

AGGRAVATING CIRCUMSTANCE(S):

(a) The victim was a fireman, peace officer or public servant concerned in official detention who was killed in the performance of his duties (✓)

(b) The defendant paid or was paid by another person or had contracted to pay or be paid by another person or had conspired to pay or to be paid by another person for the killing of the victim ( )

(c) The victim was being held by the defendant for ransom or reward, or as a shield or hostage ( )

(d) The death of the victim occurred while defendant was engaged in the hijacking of an aircraft ( )

(e) The victim was a prosecution witness to a murder or other felony committed by the defendant and was killed for the purpose of preventing his testimony against the defendant in any grand jury or criminal proceeding involving such offenses ( )

(f) The defendant committed a killing while in the perpetration of a felony ( )

(g) In the commission of the offense the defendant knowingly created a grave risk of death to another person in addition to the victim of the offense ( )

(h) The offense was committed by means of torture ( )

(i) The defendant has a significant history of felony convictions involving the use or threat of violence to the person ( )

(j) The defendant has been convicted of another Federal or State offense, committed either before or at the time of the offense at issue, for which a sentence of life imprisonment or death was impossible or the defendant was undergoing a sentence of life imprisonment for any reason at the time of the commission of the offense ( )

MITIGATING CIRCUMSTANCE(S):

(a) The defendant has no significant history of prior criminal convictions (✓)

(b) The defendant was under the influence of extreme mental or emotional disturbance ( )

(c) The capacity of the defendant to appreciate the criminality of his conduct or to conform his conduct to the requirements of law was substantially impaired ( )

(d) The youth or advanced age of the defendant at the time of the crime ( )

(e) The defendant acted under extreme duress or acted under the substantial domination of another person ( )

(f) The victim was a participant in the defendant's homicidal conduct or consented to the homicidal acts ( )

(g) The defendant's participation in the homicidal act was relatively minor ( )

(h) Any other mitigating matter concerning the character or record of the defendant or the circumstances of his offense ( )

George W. Ewalt, Jr.
Foreperson

James T Mattare

Edward [illegible]

Joseph a Mangan

[illegible]

[illegible]

Domenic N. [illegible]

[illegible]

Miriam Adelman

[illegible]

[illegible]

Lois M [illegible]

DATED: July 3, 1982

Fig . 11. The jury sentencing form

This is the form used by the 1982 trial jury to sentence Abu-Jamal to death. Federal District Judge William Yohn overturned that sentence, ruling that the form was confusing, leading jurors to falsely conclude that to consider any mitigating circumstance, they had to all agree upon it, as is the case with aggravating circumstances. In fact, under Pennsylvania capital punishment law, if even one juror believes a mitigating circumstance exists, all the jurors must accept it in weighing their decision on death or life in prison without parole.

IN THE
Court of Common Pleas
of the County of Philadelphia

THE COMMONWEALTH OF PENNSYLVANIA

vs.

Mumia Abu-Jamal
aka Wesley Cook

_82_ Term _01_ No. _1358_

SUR CHARGE OF MURDER

1st degree Murder

And now, _May 25, 1983_ _____,

the sentence of the law is that you _Mumia Abu-Jamal aka Wesley Cook_, be taken hence by the Sheriff of Philadelphia County to the jail of that county from whence you came, and from thence in due course to the State Correctional Institution at Rockview in Centre County, Pennsylvania, and that you there suffer death during the week fixed by the Governor of the Commonwealth, in a building erected for the purpose on land owned by the Commonwealth, such punishment being inflicted by either the warden or deputy warden of the State Correctional Institution at Rockview, or by such person as the warden shall designate, by causing to pass through your body a current of electricity of intensity sufficient to cause death and the application of such current to be continued until you are dead. May God in His Infinite Goodness have mercy on your soul.

Albert F. Sabo
Judge

In Witness Whereof, I have hereunto set my hand and the seal of the said Court, this ___25__ day of _May_ A.D. _83_ .

_____
Clerk of Quarter Sessions

6-222 (Rev. 8/76)

Fig. 12. Judge Sabo's sentence of death.

This is the form, dated May 25, 1983, signed by Judge Albert Sabo, officially sentencing Abu-Jamal to death. His execution was initially to have been by electric chair, though the state later changed its mode of execution to lethal injection.

Chapter Seven

Return From the Dead
The Defense Fights Back

In the years immediately following Mumia Abu-Jamal's murder conviction, his case gradually faded from the news. Attorney Lesley Gelb, a public defender who may not have even fully read the transcript of his trial, made a more or less perfunctory appeal. On March 6, 1989, that appeal was rejected completely by the state Supreme Court. But the rejection came amidst some controversy: Chief Justice Robert N.C. Nix, Jr., an African-American jurist facing re-election who had raised serious questions about the trial's fairness during arguments, inexplicably absented himself from the court's ruling on the appeal. Two other members of the state's high court also recused themselves. Meanwhile, another justice, Ronald Castille, who had been D.A. in Philadelphia during Abu-Jamal's appeal, and who had signed prosecution arguments and briefs opposing that appeal, declined to recuse himself from the appeal. He voted against it, as did several other members of the court who, like Castille, had won election to their top court posts with the endorsement of the Fraternal Order of Police. At that point, the once-promising black radio journalist and political activist likely would have gone almost unnoticed to the execution chamber, had his case not been taken up by several groups. Each for their own reasons, felt he was more than just another death-row inmate.

The key group in this effort to rescue the case and the defendant from obscurity and death was MOVE. Abu-Jamal had shown considerable support for the organization, both in his journalism and by adopting some of the trappings of its members, such as wearing his hair in dreadlocks and adopting their slogan "Ona MOVE!" Initially, however, MOVE had kept a discrete distance from his case. Before the trial, at least one prominent African-African journalist in Philadelphia (who has asked not to be named for fear of damaging relations with the group) reports that he was told by a MOVE member that the group wasn't even sure of Abu-Jamal's innocence. Even during the trial, although Abu-Jamal repeatedly demanded that he be allowed to have MOVE leader John Africa at his side as an adviser, and although several MOVE members did relay communications between him and Africa, John Africa himself never showed up. Not even to provide moral support to the defendant as a spectator in the gallery.

The announcement of the verdict obliterated whatever reticence there may have been earlier. Not only had Abu-Jamal stuck doggedly to his demand that John Africa be allowed to assist him at the defense table. He later applied his journalistic skills from prison to blast the city government and the police for their deadly 1985 fire-bombing of the MOVE house—a domestic atrocity which burned to death five children and six adults and also destroyed over 63 other homes in the surrounding neighborhood. By that point, Abu-Jamal's case had become the major focus of MOVE activities. Pam and Ramona Africa, two acid-tongued, quick-witted and media-savvy MOVE activists, became the point persons in the struggle to elevate Abu-Jamal's case to national and international attention. They and other MOVE members, acting through an organization called International Concerned Family and Friends of Mumia Abu-Jamal, worked to raise money and obtain legal counsel for his appeal process.

MOVE helped line up Rachel Wolkenstein, a lawyer with the Partisan Defense Committee, an organization linked to a far-left Marxist/Trotskyite fringe group called the Spartacist League. The Spartacists saw and continue to see in Abu-Jamal an articulate political activist whose case illustrates the government's legal assault on people of color and anti-establishment political views. The PDC had provided legal assistance to MOVE members in an earlier trial in which several members were charged and later convicted in the killing of a policeman during a police siege of their house.

Wolkenstein, who helped Gelb with her appeal filing, began working for Abu-Jamal directly in 1992 on issues relating to his conditions of incarceration. She also helped to sign up a top legal gun: Leonard Weinglass. One of a handful of nationally-known progressive attorneys who have handled major political trials, Weinglass, along with William Kunstler, had defended the Chicago Seven political activists on charges relating to disruptions at the 1968 Democratic National Convention. He also had defended Angela Davis, Quentin Tarantino and Kathy Boudin on murder charges involving the killing of law enforcement officers. He had defended a number of others charged with murder, also, including two Native American activists in Los Angeles, Paul Durant Skyhorse and Richard Billings Mohawk, who were both found innocent in a jury trial.

Weinglass is a master tactician in the courtroom. But he also understood the importance in a political trial of maintaining the often fragile and tenuous connection between a political movement, which may be more interested in furthering its political agenda than in winning, and what goes on in court—where the goal is winning the case. After becoming Abu-Jamal's lead appellate attorney, he in turn assembled a crack defense team of death penalty experts, including a protege, Daniel Williams, and Steven Hawkins, a veteran of the NAACP Legal Defense Fund who now heads the National Coalition to Abolish the Death Penalty. Rounding out the defense team were two Partisan Defense Committee members, Wolkenstein and Jonathan Piper, the latter an attorney with the major Chicago corporate law firm Sonnenschein Nath & Rosenthal.

If Abu-Jamal was heavily outgunned by the district attorney's office at his original trial, this time the legal talent was first-class. Plus he now had the resources to hire experts and private investigators. All this was in no small part thanks to more than a decade of diligent efforts by MOVE.

Also working on Abu-Jamal's behalf was the Quixote Center and its affiliate, the Equal Justice Campaign. A Catholic liberation theology-based organization, which made his case a centerpiece of its ongoing campaign against the death penalty, it began a major publicity campaign and fundraising effort on his behalf. "Back in 1990, the Left didn't care about the death penalty," recalls Quixote Center Director Jane Henderson. "We decided that this was an important case in an important city for opposition to the death penalty. When we got involved in Mumia's case back in December 1990, our goal was to build a base of support for him, but it was never just about him. We said that his case was a microcosm of the death penalty, and the death penalty was a microcosm of the way the criminal justice system worked in the U.S." The center says it raised over $100,000 for Abu-Jamal's defense fund and spent over $250,000 more on a campaign of direct mailings, print ads and petitions about the case. It was later also instrumental in disseminating his radio commentaries and in their publication in two volumes, *Live From Death Row* and *All Things Censored*. In the late 1990s, however, there was a falling out between Abu-Jamal and the Quixote Center, with Abu-Jamal claiming the center was keeping 72 percent of funds raised for "administrative costs"[1]—something that Henderson flatly denies. Abu-Jamal also demanded that the Quixote Center provide its mailing list to MOVE—something Henderson said privacy considerations prevented her from agreeing to do. By 1998, the organization and Abu-Jamal had broken off relations. There were also conflicts between the Quixote Center and Weinglass, with Abu-Jamal's lead appellate lawyer wanting more of the Center's funds devoted to the defense fund (which paid his fee). Weinglass also was reportedly miffed that the Quixote Center chose to route its defense fund moneys through the Philadelphia Black United Fund, another tax-exempt organization, rather than send it directly to Weinglass, or to another tax-exempt organization, the Bill of Rights Foundation, with which Weinglass was affiliated.

Finally, there was the Bruderhof, a Christian communal religious group, some of whose members live right near the SCI-Greene super-max prison near Waynesboro in rural western Pennsylvania where Abu-Jamal has been incarcerated on death row. The Bruderhof, which helped with fundraising, also played a key role in helping to boost Abu-Jamal's name recognition and media profile. It provided a means for him to communicate with the outside world in the face of strenuous efforts by the state to cut him off and silence him. Efforts included intercepting his mail, limiting his visitors, barring recording equipment from being brought in by visitors, and blocking him from earning anything for his writing. By naming Bruderhof leader Steven Wiser as his "spiritual advisor," Abu-Jamal was able to have unlimited visits from at least one person, who was also able to bring him reading material, and to convey his own writings—mostly columns of political commentary—to the outside world. In 1997, the Bruderhof's publishing house, Plough Publishing, put out a book of Abu-Jamal's essays and personal vignettes titled *Death Blossoms: Reflections From a Prisoner of Conscience.*

All these efforts to bring Abu-Jamal's case to national attention would probably not have amounted to much had Abu-Jamal himself not been worthy of that attention. Like many others on death rows across the country, he claimed that he was innocent of the crime of murder and that he had not received a fair trial. But the former Panther publicist and polemicist, from his prison cell, would also destroy any notion employers and colleagues might have entertained back in 1981 that his journalism skills were lacking or on the decline. Over the course of his two decades in prison, he began writing as never before. Sometimes they were commentaries about current events, such as the police fire-bombing of MOVE's house and the burning of an entire community in West Philadelphia in 1985, and more often, exposés about the horrors of the U.S. prison system, and especially its scandalous and abusive death row purgatories. Those perceptive, well-crafted and often searing essays quickly gained Abu-Jamal a dedicated national and international following. As his critics in the Pennsylvania

Fraternal Order of Police and elsewhere derisively but accurately claimed, he had become "the poster child for the anti-death penalty movement."

As his fame—and notoriety—grew and spread, so did the government's determination to silence, and ultimately to kill him. The new Republican governor, Tom Ridge, had won the 1990 election in part on a campaign pledge to sign Abu-Jamal's death warrant. And FOP pressure had led to efforts by the state to prevent Abu-Jamal from earning any money from his writing of news articles and commentaries (and, as we shall see later, to cancellation of a planned series of his prison commentaries, "Live from Death Row," on National Public Radio).

It was at this point, in 1995, that Abu-Jamal's case burst back into the news, as he and his new legal team filed a request for a Post-Conviction Relief Act hearing. This legally mandated hearing before a state criminal court judge reviews the facts of a capital case, where old evidence can be expanded upon or challenged. New evidence and testimony may also be introduced with a view to establishing grounds for an additional appeal to the state's highest court. In Pennsylvania, a PCRA hearing is normally presided over by the original trial judge, on the theory that the judge who tried the case originally is the person most familiar with it. Of course, in a case where the judge has demonstrated a marked bias toward the prosecution, such a practice becomes an issue, as it did here.

Abu-Jamal's lawyers had hoped that in his case they wouldn't have to face Judge Sabo again, since he had already retired from the bench. In addition to his retirement, questions about his qualifications might also have served as ample reason not to call him back. A 1983 Philadelphia Bar survey—just one year after Abu-Jamal's trial—found that over one-third of those attorneys who responded felt Sabo was unqualified to serve on the bench. On September 13, 1992, *The Philadelphia Inquirer*, in an article investigating the record number of death sentences over which Sabo had presided, wrote that "through his comments, his rulings and his instructions to the jury," Sabo "favors prosecutors." Despite this record, the defense team's hopes of avoiding Sabo were dashed. The state's high court called the 74-year-old Sabo back specifically for this PCRA hearing, guaranteeing that Weinglass's defense team would have a battle on their hands just to get evidence admitted for consideration. The goal of the defense at the PCRA hearing was to raise all the issues that would demonstrate the unfairness of the original trial. These ranged from the excluding of blacks from the jury to the withholding of evidence and possible suborning of perjury by police "witnesses" concerning a purported hospital "confession," and by witnesses to the actual shooting, and finally to the failure of Abu-Jamal's attorney to present any mitigating witnesses at his sentencing hearing. But the goal was also to raise new issues—issues that would seriously challenge the prosecution's contention that Abu-Jamal was the killer and even the claim that he was the only person besides his brother Billy Cook at the scene of Faulkner's shooting. Doing this would require discovery—meaning court permission to question witnesses and to demand answers and documents from the police and the prosecution. It would also require using subpoenas (which can be quashed by a judge) so the defense could compel the appearance of unwilling witnesses. Having Sabo on the bench made it unlikely that the defense would be granted such powers. In fact, he denied all of the defense's discovery requests and quashed over 25 subpoenas, making it almost impossible for the defense to make its case. For Sabo, the issue was speed, and confirmation of the correctness of his handling of the original trial. He wanted the hearing to move at the pace of a forced march, and he didn't want a lot of new evidence, or undermining of old evidence.

The Governor handed him a way to do just that.

One of the strongest arguments against the government's case in Commonwealth v. Mumia Abu-Jamal is that, in the effort to convict him, the prosecution and the courts repeatedly resorted to such unprincipled and over-the-top tactics. Those efforts continued during his appeal of his sentence and conviction. By their very existence, the government's efforts belie prosecutor McGill's characterization of the case as "open-and-shut."

The almost certainly fabricated hospital "confession" claim, reported to detectives two months after the fact, of a few police officers and a hospital security guard is one example. Judge Sabo's refusal to let the defense call in police officer Wakshul to challenge that confession evidence on the last day of the trial was another. The barring of further questioning at trial of witness Veronica Jones concerning possible police pressure on her and on witness Cynthia White—on the absurd grounds that such questions were "irrelevant" to the case—was a third example.

It is standard operating procedure for the prosecution to respond to any death row inmate's appeal with a counter-argument in favor of denial. But here the desire on the part of law enforcement, the courts and the political establishment to execute Mumia Abu-Jamal became an obsession. Perhaps the starkest example of this was the secret campaign to intercept

his prison mail communications with his attorneys. The information discovered nearly cemented Abu-Jamal's execution.

Abu-Jamal's defense team only became aware of the state's interception of privileged mail communications between client and attorney four
months *after* his PCRA hearing. The information came out in the course
of a mail tampering lawsuit Abu-Jamal had filed in federal court, when the
defense learned that the assistant general counsel at the SCI-Green prison
where Abu-Jamal was incarcerated was routinely opening and photocopy-
ing all his mail. In the course of discovery it was learned that he was for-
warding those copies to the office of general counsel in the governor's
office. Confidential discussions about legal strategies and about his attorneys' evaluation of his possible appeals claims were being read. Worse yet,
these mail intercepts disclosed to the state his plans to file a request for a
hearing to review evidence from his original trial and to examine new evidence under the provisions of the state's Post-Conviction Relief Act, on
June 5, 1995. This information, forwarded to Harrisburg, apparently
enabled Governor Ridge to sign a death warrant just five days in advance
of the filing and to schedule an execution for 11 weeks later. Had the
PCRA hearing already been requested, it would have been unseemly and
improper for the governor to sign a death warrant.

Perhaps the one bright spot for Abu-Jamal in this near-death experience is that Ridge is no longer governor. In the wake of the September 11,
2001 terrorist bombing of the World Trade Center and the Pentagon, he
now heads the new Office of Homeland Security (where he, along with
others in the Bush Administration, has been developing ways to reduce the
rights of other defendants to fair trials).[2]*

The PCRA hearing began with the clock ticking on Abu-Jamal's execution, with the date set for August 17, 1995. Sabo refused to let Abu-
Jamal, who suspected the governor of having inside information concerning his defense strategy (the reason a mail-tampering suit was filed), subpoena Governor Ridge or his attorney, so what precisely was done with
those documents once they reached the governor's office remains a matter
for speculation. In a demonstration of unalloyed hypocrisy, the governor's
counsel argued against the subpoena based on a claim of the sanctity of
lawyer-client privilege—the very privilege the governor's office was violating in intercepting Abu-Jamal's private correspondence with his attorneys.

---

*It's interesting to note that seven years later, Governor Ridge, as President George W. Bush's
head of Homeland Security, along with U.S. Attorney General John Ashcroft, have crafted a
new set of federal laws—the USA Patriot Act—which, in the name of combating terrorism,
allow the government to legally monitor attorney-client conversations.

In 1996, Abu-Jamal's suspicions concerning this breach of attorney-client privilege would be verified. A federal court ruled that the interception of Abu-Jamal's communications by mail with his attorneys violated his Sixth and Fourteenth Amendment Constitutional rights, and declared that he had been "actually injured" by the action.[3] By then, however, the damage had been done. No steps were ordered to correct or remedy the "injury."

The injuries were clear though. Not only was he forced to cruelly and needlessly suffer through the process of his post-conviction hearing with a death date hanging over his head for most of the proceeding, Abu-Jamal and his legal team were also forced to rush through their presentation of witnesses at breakneck speed as the judge used the looming execution date as an excuse to reject the defense's requests for discovery and for more time to prepare. Whenever a defense witness would be late in appearing, the prosecution would offer, and the judge would express a willingness to put on a prosecution witness, thus interrupting the flow of the defense presentation of its case. On August 7, just 10 days before it was scheduled to happen, and with just a week left of the PCRA hearing, a stay of execution was finally—and only grudgingly—issued by Judge Sabo.

The looming execution date also added to mounting stresses within the defense team—stresses which quickly became debilitating, and which would grow to the point of rupture four years later. In 1999, two of Abu-Jamal's attorneys (Rachel Wolkenstein and Jon Piper), would quit, leaving only Weinglass and Williams.

During the course of the PCRA hearing, it was clear that there was growing bitterness and lack of trust among the attorneys defending Abu-Jamal. One immediate point of conflict was whether or not to challenge the execution date. Weinglass and Williams weren't worried about it, saying that there was no way it could be carried out since Abu-Jamal still hadn't even exercised his Constitutionally guaranteed federal appeal rights. But Wolkenstein and Piper were still concerned. Years later, in 2001, Wolkenstein would help Abu-Jamal attack his own lawyers after Williams published a book about ongoing efforts in the case. In an affidavit filed in conjunction with this effort, Wolkenstein says Weinglass and Williams, in the days following the filing of the PCRA petition, were expressing confidence that evidentiary hearings were months away and would follow a period of discovery (the seeking and interviewing of witnesses for the PCRA hearing). But she and Piper, she says, had been warned by Pennsylvania capital litigation experts that local judges were known to have rushed prisoners through the process right to execution in a matter of weeks, with the blessings of the Third Circuit Federal Court of Appeals. And if any judge liked to hurry things along, they figured—correctly it turns out—it was Judge Sabo.

Wolkenstein and Piper argued that the defense should ask to have the PCRA date, set for July 24, moved up to June 12, so as to give the defense more time to present its evidence. Williams and Weinglass worried that this would make it even harder for them to prepare witnesses in time for their questioning on the stand. Weinglass was aware of the fact that many of Abu-Jamal's supporters would not understand that the August execution date was not really a serious threat. Also being someone who by nature tries to avoid confrontation and personal conflict (at least outside of the court-room), Weinglass sided with Wolkenstein and Piper. He requested an ear-lier date.

Sabo granted that request, but then tried to order the defense to immediately begin putting its witnesses on the stand. This put Weinglass in the embarrassing position of having to ask for a delay again, because the team simply wasn't ready with its witnesses. Unable to get Sabo to agree, the defense appealed to the Pennsylvania Supreme Court, and the date was pushed back again to July 26, two days *later* than the original date.

In her 2001 affidavit aimed at demonstrating ineffectiveness of coun-sel by Weinglass and Williams, Wolkenstein writes of that period:

> The simple reality was that at this juncture Attorney Weinglass had made minimal preparations for an evidentiary hear-ing. Jonathan Piper and I urged Attorneys Weinglass and Williams, who were to handle the presentation of witnesses at the hearing, to begin preparing for the hearing in the event that Judge Sabo, based on his manifestly pro-prosecution bias, would deny any discovery or reasonable preparation time and instead would use the pending exe-cution date as an excuse to expedite the hearing. Ultimately Judge Sabo did precisely that. Attorney Weinglass's response to our urging was to say that "I can't deal with it," and that our proposals "give me a headache." He insisted that if there was an evidentiary hearing at all it would not come for six months. As a result of his complete fail-ure to prepare for the hearing, the defense team was caught off guard when the post-conviction court improperly insisted that the defense begin presenting evidence in July 1995. Attorneys Weinglass and Williams did not have a witness list, an order of proof, or even an outline for conducting an evidentiary hearing at the time we filed the post-conviction papers.
>
> ...
>
> When the post-conviction hearing began, the only issues on which Attorneys Weinglass and Williams had previously made any

real preparation efforts were ineffective assistance of counsel and the testimony of Dessie Hightower.[4]

Williams acknowledges that Sabo's decision to move ahead directly with the PCRA hearing, and to deny the defense any discovery or time to prepare, caused major problems. He writes:

> Rachel and Jon panicked and urged that we should request from the court an earlier date. Steve Hawkins and I, the most experienced in the area of appellate and postconviction death penalty litigation, disagreed, arguing that we needed the time to prepare for the hearing and that we would secure a stay of execution from a court—not necessarily from Judge Sabo, but from a court somewhere.
>
> ...
>
> Len, rarely one to openly offer an opinion on a legal issue, stayed silent while we debated the issue. He ultimately sided with Rachel and Jon, figuring that moving up the date to secure a stay of execution would not have a downside and would satisfy the clamor among some supporters for us to do something.[5]

But Williams goes further. He now claims that a prime reason the defense was unprepared to put on its witnesses early in the PCRA process—and why the defense appeared disorganized and poorly prepared during the course of much of the hearing—was that Wolkenstein and Piper kept insisting on adding a number of new witnesses to the case. These were witnesses whom Wolkenstein, a crack investigator and researcher, had dug up, but whom Williams and Weinglass found in many cases to be largely unconvincing or even potentially damaging to the case. "We were so busy having to deal with those new witnesses, and with Rachel's continuing pressure to do further discovery, that we simply weren't able to do the witness preparation we needed to do," says Williams. "That's why, when we finally began, we started with my questioning of the mitigation witnesses, instead of starting with a bang with the key witnesses."

Besides having to deal with these internal stresses, the defense found itself in a hearing and an environment that was much more contentious than even the original trial. By 1995, Abu-Jamal was a no longer just a reasonably well-known local journalist, but a celebrity death-row prisoner and prison journalist of international renown. Foreign governments were beginning to pass resolutions on his behalf, the Rev. Jesse Jackson and other celebrities made appearances at his courtroom hearing. And outside the courtroom on the streets, there were regular demonstrations—noisy, well-attended protest actions that featured not just MOVE members, but also large numbers of college students and activists of all stripes (and hair colors). The Free Mumia movement was in full swing. There was even a rowdy demonstration outside of Sabo's house at one point during the course of the PCRA hearing, at which several arrests were made. The shouts of "Free Mumia" by demonstrators on the streets around City Hall could be heard daily inside the courtroom as the hearing proceeded.

Both Abu-Jamal, the hero of that movement, and Sabo, its nemesis, seemed to thrive on the attention this hearing was getting. Abu-Jamal, from day one, would enter the courtroom from his holding cell with a brisk stride, his hair still defiantly worn in long dreadlocks. Ignoring courtroom decorum, he would turn to the left side of the gallery, where his supporters were seated, punch the air in a clenched-fisted salute reminiscent of his Panther days, and flash his winning smile to acknowledge the ensuing cheers before taking his seat at the defense table. From the other side of the courtroom, the police officers and members of the Faulkner family, including Daniel Faulkner's brothers and his long-suffering widow Maureen, would grimly watch this audacious display of bravado.

Sabo, retired but still cocky and trim at 74, had a bounce in his step too as he would enter his courtroom. He seemed to relish the challenge posed to his authority by the unruly and disrespectful spectators seated behind the defendant; he lost no time in expelling someone for allegedly being disruptive within minutes of arriving on the first day of the hearing— a power he exercised repeatedly through the course of the hearing. He exercised his power over the defense, too, threatening to bar Weinglass from the courtroom and later fining him $1,000 for contempt, and jailing co-counsel Wolkenstein for contempt on another occasion. (Both contempt charges were examples of judicial pique. In Weinglass's case, he had only been trying to verify that a witness on the stand, a Dr. Ian Hood, was referring to photos which were the same as those in the court record, and the judge demanded that he not examine them, but rather, hand them over to him. As Weinglass approached the bench—too slowly, apparently, for Sabo's liking—he was cited for contempt.[6] In Wolkenstein's case, the judge began at the start of the court session by cutting her off as she was trying to make a point regarding a subpoena he had quashed. This was a subpoena aimed at pursuing evidence that the jury pool had been rigged to reduce the number of blacks from the outset. When Wolkenstein tried to complete her sentence, saying simply, "Your Honor…," the judge ordered the sheriff to take her into custody. She spent several hours in a court holding cell.)[7]

The first order of business was Weinglass's motion for the judge to recuse himself. Weinglass offered a range of reasons why Sabo should not preside over the PCRA hearing. He mentioned that prior to his becoming a judge, Sabo had for sixteen years been a member of the FOP, which since 1982 has been actively lobbying for Abu-Jamal's execution. He went on to recite a long litany of reasons why the judge could not be fair, and submitted an affidavit from six former assistant district attorneys asserting that Sabo was "uniformly biased against criminal defendants."[8] Noting that he had resigned from the FOP upon becoming a judge, Sabo predictably rejected them all.

On the grounds that there was no way that the appeals process would be complete by August 17 (Abu-Jamal was entitled to a federal habeas appeal, which would take months or years following the PCRA decision), Weinglass then made a motion to stay the execution. He argued that an execution, if carried out before his appeals were resolved, would constitute an "irreparable harm." That effort, too, failed after the prosecution made the assertion that the defendant could not claim that an early execution date would lead to irreparable harm because "this argument assumes that death is an injury. That is improper."[9] But Sabo turned down the defense motion in a clever way that left the defense unable to challenge his decision. Instead of denying the request outright, he merely said he would "take it under advisement"—a move that left the date standing and the clock ticking—but without giving the defense anything concrete to appeal to a higher court. As Williams recalls:

> The fix was in. We now understood the real function of the August 17 execution. There would be no execution on August 17, 1995—of that I was certain. The governor established the August 17 date so that Judge Sabo could use it as artificial deadline by which the PCRA proceedings were to be completed; it thus provided a justification for him to create a climate of haste, which heightens the likelihood of mistakes and omissions. Mistakes and omissions would then be exploited in federal court, where the real fight would take place.[10]

Williams' point was that the prosecution (and apparently Judge Sabo), knew that if they rushed the defense, the defense inevitably would make mistakes. These mistakes—the failure to fully question witnesses, or failure to call certain witnesses—could then limit the defense's ability to appeal at the federal level. This is because federal courts are only permitted to consider issues that were properly brought first before a state court.

And mistakes were made. As became clear in Federal Judge William Yohn's opinion on Abu-Jamal's habeas petition, some of those mistakes would later contribute to Judge Yohn's decisions ruling against some of the petition's claims. These bad decisions included: examples of poor preparation such as failing to authenticate Abu-Jamal's FBI file; failure to question witness Chobert about why he would have gotten out of his cab and walked over to the crime scene if he really thought the shooter was sitting with his gun near the wounded officer; and failure to ask other witnesses whether they had seen Chobert's taxicab at the scene during the shooting incident. But even if the defense had been more successful in dealing with those things at the post-conviction hearing, it's not clear they would have gotten anywhere. For example, Judge Sabo denied the defense the right to call a witness to build a foundation for admitting the FBI surveillance files, saying it was not relevant to the case. Recalls Weinglass, "The time pressure put on us was tremendous. And we had to go to the hearing before we had even gotten an answer to our papers from the other side. I have never seen anything like this, before or since."

As it turned out, those time constraints under which the defense was working led to the PCRA hearing's being divided fairly neatly in two. In the first part, the defense laid out the errors of the 1982 trial. The failings of Abu-Jamal's court-appointed attorney, Anthony Jackson, were demonstrated. An effort was made to demonstrate that blacks were deliberately rejected during the jury selection process. And, by bringing in the character witnesses who were never introduced during the original trial's penalty phase, an effort was made to correct the record as much as possible. After that, in what might be called phase two of the hearing, the defense sought to introduce new evidence in the face of considerable resistance from the judge, evidence that served to undermine the "open-and-shut" case that the prosecution had presented at the trial. The defense brought in witnesses, some of whom had testified at the 1982 trial and some of whom had not previously been called.

In this first chapter on the PCRA hearing, we'll look it that first phase: the errors made at the 1982 trial. Here the defense presented witnesses who showed clearly that Abu-Jamal in 1981 was hardly the cop-hating killer the prosecution had made him out to be. Here the defense demonstrated that the jury which convicted and sentenced him to death had been systematically purged of blacks. Here too, Anthony Jackson, in a tearful session, explained how he had failed his client.

How the defense started their presentation was indicative of the different agendas in play. Neither the Free Mumia movement, nor perhaps Abu-Jamal himself, were fighting simply to alter the sentence from death to life in prison without parole—they were going for the whole enchilada: a new trial or an outright acquittal. Nonetheless, the defense presented character witnesses who, had they originally testified in the penalty phase of the 1982 trial (where none were presented), might have had a powerful mitigating effect on the sentence. Here, they provided dramatic evidence that murdering a police officer was completely out of character with this defendant's prior life.

As we saw earlier, E. Stephen Collins, a longtime colleague of Abu-Jamal's and a fellow radio journalist, spoke not just of his skills as a journalist, but of his basic humanity and sense of humor. State Representative David Richardson, Jr. had testified earlier at Abu-Jamal's bail reduction hearing in 1982. But, like the other witnesses at the PCRA hearing, there had inexplicably been no request for him to appear as a mitigating witness during the penalty phase hearing. Richardson also testified to Abu-Jamal's professionalism and his concern for peace in the community.

Kenneth Hamilton, Jr., Abu-Jamal's high school history teacher, told of how as a student, Abu-Jamal was the one he and school administrators turned to when they needed someone to calm incipient gang fights, and said he was "overwhelmingly elected" as president of the school's student body.[11] Hamilton added that Abu-Jamal played the role of father in his family after the death of his stepfather, particularly in his relationships with his two brothers, twin Wayne and baby brother Billy.

Finally, Lydia Wallace, Abu-Jamal's older sister, took the stand. A nurse and social worker, she said that from a very young age, Abu-Jamal had been a sensitive person, concerned about the suffering of others, and with a reverence for life.

These witnesses, all of whom knew Abu-Jamal well, had a powerful impact. So compelling were they that one of the four prosecution attorneys at the PCRA, Charles "Joey" Grant, virtually conceded the issue. A normally blunt-spoken and aggressive assistant D.A., Grant agreed that the defendant had "immense talents" as a journalist, adding:

> From all the descriptions of everybody that has come here—
> and they all are good people from what I can see, I believe—I don't
> think the shooting of Officer Faulkner is characteristic of this defen-
> dant.[12]

Would the jury at Abu-Jamal's original trial have sentenced him to death if they had heard that statement from the prosecution? One can only speculate. Just as one can only speculate on the impact of the character witnesses, none of whom testified at the penalty phase. Even the character witnesses the jury did hear from in the earlier guilt phase of the trial did not have the stature or familiarity with the defendant of these and several other witnesses now being presented at the PCRA hearing. And Grant's was certainly not the perspective they got from the original prosecutor, Joseph McGill—who told them Abu-Jamal was a vicious killer who had had it in for the police since he was a teenager.

Having definitively corrected the appalling lack of character witnesses at the trial's penalty phase (not to mention the B-list witnesses presented at the end of the guilt phase), the defense trained its firepower next on the issue of whether the jury had been unconstitutionally purged of African-Americans. A major point at issue was the number of blacks who had been peremptorily (without cause and at the discretion of the prosecution) rejected by Prosecutor McGill. At the state supreme court appeal, which was filed in 1986 and rejected in 1989, the district attorney's office, based upon an affidavit filed by McGill, had claimed that the number of peremptorily rejected black jurors was eight. The defense in its appeal had argued that the number was 11. But the state's high court had accepted the D.A.'s figures as correct, and then ruled that this number of peremptory challenges of blacks did not appear to be enough to have violated the U.S. Supreme Court's so-called *Batson* precedent. In fact, however, the state supreme court had ruled on the basis of incorrect evidence. A review of the *voir dire* process shows that the number of black jurors rejected by McGill on a peremptory basis was 11, as had been asserted by the defense. To prove the point, defense attorney Williams attempted to bring in three jurors who had not been included in the prosecution's tally of rejected black jurors— Alma Cranshow, Darlene Campbell and Beverly Green—to demonstrate their race to the court. Judge Sabo denied permission for this, saying:

> Counselor, the Supreme Court has already ruled on this. It's not proper. Okay. That's my position. You take it up with the Supreme Court later on.[13]

Weinglass countered that the court had ruled on an "incorrect and incomplete record," based upon a "false and misleading" affidavit containing only eight names of peremptorily excused black jurors which had been submitted by McGill. Weinglass told Sabo that, by preventing the defense from putting these other three black jurors on the stand who had been improperly excluded from the prosecution's tally of rejected black jurors, he was preventing the defense from establishing the correct record.

It should be pointed out that in addition to what the defense contested here, left uncontested—because it is accepted practice under Supreme Court precedent—was another set of rejections by McGill that also had a huge impact on the racial and political makeup of the jury. Aside from rejecting 11 potential black jurors peremptorily, McGill also rejected at least 20 other black jurors—a disproportionate number of potential jurors to be sure—because they had expressed opposition to the death penalty. As mentioned previously, this rejection for cause is something attorneys can do an unlimited number of times. It is widely accepted by scholars of the U.S. jury system that this process of excluding potential jurors from death penalty trials who oppose the death penalty changes the racial complexion of the jury. "Death-qualifying a jury basically eliminates half of the potential black jurors," says David Bruck, a South Carolina defense attorney who specializes in death penalty cases. "It's quite an ethnic cleansing that goes on and it is very disturbing."[14] Blacks, and women of all races as well, are more likely to oppose the death penalty than are whites, and particularly white males. The result is jury panels that are disproportionately white and male.* A number of academic studies have also demonstrated that this death-qualifying process results in jury panels that are more conviction prone, that don't understand or accept the concepts of innocent until proven guilty or of reasonable doubt, and that tend to believe the word of government witnesses over defense witnesses.[15] But Weinglass couldn't effectively contest that powerful skewing of Abu-Jamal's jury because it was all perfectly legal.

As Sabo stated, he adopted the prosecution's argument that the state supreme court had already litigated the issue, and that under the rules governing PCRA hearings, they were not to go into "previously litigated" issues. But there was an Alice-in-Wonderland nature to this argument. As Weinglass put it to the court:

> It was done on an inaccurate record and you know it. And that Court [the state supreme court] was misled and I object to this Court preventing us from presenting that record so the Supreme Court won't be misled again.[16]

How did the defense get put in the awkward position of having to prove how many blacks had been peremptorily dropped from jury consideration by the prosecution in the first place? Here again is a tale of incom-

---

*Published academic studies in 1982 and 1994 found that death-qualifying of juries led to a 50-percent higher disqualification rate of black jurors than for other criminal trials, and to a rate of disqualification of black jurors that was more than 2.5 times higher than of white jurors.

petence and unfairness far away from any minimal standard of justice. At the original trial, defense attorney Jackson, who initially had recognized the problem and the likelihood of such racial purging, failed to make public note in the court record each time a black was excused by McGill. Judge Sabo, on the other hand, made no such mistake. He was careful to try to protect the prosecution's case from challenge. The one time that the defense rejected a black juror with a peremptory challenge, Sabo recalled the juror after he had left the courtroom, and established on the record, with a question from the bench, that he was black. Sabo had neatly confirmed that the defense had excluded a black juror from the panel. That one defense peremptory challenge would later be cited by both the state supreme court and by the federal habeas judge in rejecting Abu-Jamal's claim of race-based jury selection. In contrast, the judge, in a clear demonstration of his bias against the defendant in the case, never asked the race of potential jurors excused by the prosecution. Neither did the defense.*

In retrospect, the issue of race-based jury selection may yet prove to have been the most important part of the PCRA hearing. Of the 20 claims for relief raised in Abu-Jamal's 1999 federal *habeas corpus* appeal of his conviction—all of which were rejected by Federal Judge William Yohn on December 18, 2001—only this one was certified by the judge for appeal. That certification is important. It means that Judge Yohn felt that even though he was rejecting the claim, the issue was worthy of further consideration on appeal by a Third Circuit three-judge appeals court, and that the appeals court should agree to hear arguments on the issue. Moreover, in rejecting Abu-Jamal's *Batson* claim, Yohn made what appear to have been some factual errors himself—errors which should compel the Third Circuit to order an evidentiary hearing on the issue.

At this point the claim of race-biased jury selection, therefore, is Abu-Jamal's best, and quite possibly his only hope for a reversal of his conviction.

Batson is legal shorthand for a 1986 U.S. Supreme Court decision in a case called *Batson v. Kentucky*. This court precedent expanded upon established rulings regarding the effort by prosecutors to keep blacks and minorities off of juries. Prior to *Batson*, in order to prove racial bias in jury selection, a defendant had to prove that a prosecutor had demonstrated a pattern of removing blacks over the course of several trials. *Batson* ended

---

*In fairness to Jackson, the whole issue of race bias in juries was much less important in 1982, four years before the Supreme Court's *Batson* decision. Still, a more alert attorney might have noted the race of jurors challenged peremptorily by the prosecution, even in 1982.

that burdensome requirement. Instead, the high court ruled that the simple fact that blacks were, on the basis of race, disproportionately removed from consideration as jurors in the trial in question could suffice to overturn a verdict. Although the ruling was made four years after Abu-Jamal's trial, the Supreme Court made it retroactive to all cases that were in the appeals process at the time of the ruling. Abu-Jamal's case thus fell into that category.

In an interview for this book concerning the *Batson* claim, McGill insisted, correctly, that he would have had a fourth black juror at the start of the trial. He said that this particular juror, whom he had already said was acceptable to the prosecution, was dismissed by Abu-Jamal, who used a peremptory challenge to have him excused. Claiming he has never in his career rejected a juror on racial grounds, McGill argues he lost a second black juror, ending up with only two on a panel of 12, because of the misbehavior of that juror. She, as we saw in Chapter 4, had ignored the court's sequestration order during the early days of the trial and left her hotel room to bring a sick pet to the veterinarian. Sabo, with the agreement of both McGill and Jackson, had her removed and replaced by an alternate juror, Edward Courchain, a white man. The prosecutor was well aware at the time that the defense had tried to have Courchain removed for cause after he said in the *voir dire* that he could not be fair in rendering a verdict!

It remains objectively the fact, however, that McGill used 10 or 11 of his 15 peremptory challenges to remove black jurors who would otherwise have been eligible to sit on the jury of a capital case. All had said they could support a death verdict, and were not removed "for cause."

The defense had subpoenaed McGill to testify at the PCRA hearing in 1995 on the *Batson* issue. Although the former prosecutor was in court ready to take the stand, he was never called, thanks to the prosecution's stipulation accepting two of the other three jurors as having been blacks who were rejected by McGill. It appears from the PCRA record that there was some confusion at the time as to whether it was necessary to have his testimony in order to make the defense's *Batson* case, though. At the hearing in 1995, the defense said they had subpoenaed McGill for several reasons: to obtain evidence concerning the Wakshul matter, to ask about any inducements offered to witnesses, and to question him about the *voir dire*. The prosecution objected to his being called on any subject but the *voir dire*. At that point, having won most of what they wanted regarding acceptance of the number of black jurors rejected by McGill, the defense apparently felt it no longer needed to call McGill. Williams says the defense was leery of calling McGill, knowing that he was such a skilled litigator. "You don't want to put someone on the stand when you don't know what they'll say," he says. "Especially when we felt we'd already met the basic requirement of *Batson*, which was to demonstrate *prima facie* evidence of race-based challenges."

That strategic decision not to call McGill in 1995—while it is supported by Philadelphia defense attorneys familiar with Judge Sabo—turns out to have been a mistake. In 1998, the state supreme court reaffirmed its 1989 decision claiming that even correcting for the D.A.'s misstatement of the number of black jurors peremptorily excused, the defense had not made a prima facie case of discrimination. And later, as we will see in Chapter 11, when Abu-Jamal's case was at the federal court, Judge Yohn also refused to accept evidence that McGill's peremptory challenges had been race-based, citing the state supreme court's decision. He also refused to accept defense assertions that McGill had a history of rejecting black jurors at six prior murder trials on two grounds. First, the defense hadn't called him and raised the issue at the state level. Second, that the data on the other trials was for a period after Abu-Jamal's trial. (Yohn was in error with his second reason.) While *Batson* doesn't require such evidence of a history of race-based jury selections, having such a history on the record might have tipped the scale in Yohn's mind regarding the reason behind the prosecution's 11 peremptory challenges of black jurors.

There was another bit of evidence Yohn declined to consider, because it was not presented at the state level (though in this case not for lack of trying on the defense's part). This was a scandal involving a training tape that had been made by another crack prosecutor in the D.A.s homicide office, Jack McMahon. That tape taught new assistant D.A.s the importance of removing blacks—especially educated young blacks—from jury panels, and how to do it in a way that would be hard to prove was discriminatory or in violation of *Batson*. It had been made in 1986, four years after Abu-Jamal's murder trial. (It had come to light during an election campaign when McMahon, now in private practice, was seeking, unsuccessfully, to be elected district attorney.) The tape also suggested that prosecutors should try to have some older blacks—especially older blacks who hailed from the South—on juries. Significantly, he said it was a bad idea to have an all-white jury, and suggested having a limited number of blacks, with the ideal being four (the exact number McGill seems to have been aiming for, and the number he told me he usually had.). McMahon, on the training tape, went on to detail how prosecutors should make notations every time they peremptorily excused a black juror, giving some racially neutral reason for the decision, so that later, if questioned, they could claim it was not a racially motivated challenge. Sabo rejected defense efforts to introduce evidence of the training tape, on the basis that it had been made after Abu-Jamal's trial. But McMahon, who says he is a former colleague of McGill's, and who expresses admiration for the retired prosecutor, insists today that he was only discussing on the tape strategies which had long been in effect in the D.A.'s office, including back well before 1982.

From the outset of the PCRA hearing, Judge Sabo made little effort to hide his evident bias against the defense in favor of the district attorney's office. Indeed, on the second day of the defense's presentation of its witnesses and evidence, Sabo went out of his way to act on behalf of the prosecution. Weinglass had moved to introduce into evidence the coroner's report on Daniel Faulkner's body. This report included the comment from the coroner that the bullet fragment recovered from the deceased officer's head appeared to be a .44 cal. projectile, raising questions since Abu-Jamal's gun was a .38 cal. pistol. Surprised that the prosecution didn't object to the introduction of this evidence, Sabo stepped in:

> The Court: Just a minute. Is there any objection to this?
> Mr. Grant: None, Your Honor.
> The Court: What's that?
> Mr. Grant: I have no objection.
> The Court: Okay. Go ahead, then.[17]

So one-sided was the judge's handling of the entire hearing that Stuart Taylor, a reporter covering the event for *The American Lawyer* magazine, wrote:

> Sabo denied all of Jamal's discovery requests and quashed over 25 subpoenas, many of which sought evidence that Sabo had barred the lawyers from exploring through discovery or other witnesses. He sharply restricted Jamal's lawyers in their questioning of witnesses, and blocked them from making offers of proof on the record to show the import of the precluded testimony.[18]

Prevented by the judge from introducing concrete evidence of race-based jury selection, the defense moved next to the issue of ineffective counsel, putting on the stand none other than Abu-Jamal's attorney at the trial, Anthony E. Jackson. While his testimony contained some revelations, what was perhaps the most startling fact was kept out of the trial by both prosecution and defense, for their own separate reasons: at the time he took the stand in this 1995 hearing, Jackson was no longer a licensed, practicing attorney. Neither Abu-Jamal's defense nor the District Attorney's prosecutors mentioned this fact (thus leaving the press and the public in the dark). The story? In February 1992, Jackson had been disbarred under an order from the state court, officially for "mishandling" over $57,000 in clients' funds held in his custody. People familiar with his case (who spoke on condition of anonymity), claim that the underlying reason for the mishandling of that money was substance abuse. Jackson was unavailable for comment on this and other issues, and did not return messages left on his answering machine.

The prosecution had no interest in raising the issue of Jackson's disbarment since it would have lent credence to the argument that Jackson's defense of Abu-Jamal had been inept, ineffectual and fraught with errors. This would have bolstered the defense's argument that resources, such as paltry funding by the court for such things as the hiring of legal assistance, a private investigator and expert witnesses, were inadequate to insure justice.

In *Executing Justice*, Williams mentions that Jackson had been disbarred for financial improprieties prior to his taking the stand at the PCRA hearing. Williams praises prosecutor Grant for refraining from "drilling in the knife" on that subject during his grilling of Jackson, saying that Grant chose not to "out of simple human decency."[19] Williams might have been too kind to Grant at that point. As a former friend of Jackson's, Grant may have taken no pleasure in embarrassing him. More importantly, though, it also would have done the prosecution's case no good to have exposed Jackson as having in any way been a "bad" lawyer. It also might have led inexorably into the area of substance abuse.

The defense didn't want to raise the issue of disbarment for other reasons. With Jackson ready and willing to fall on his own sword and take the stand to testify to his own mistakes and errors, Weinglass and Williams did not dare to risk Jackson's further cooperation by humiliating or embarrassing him. "Tony Jackson was courageously taking the stand and talking about his failure to adequately defend his client," recalls Williams. "We could not risk turning him against us by bringing up the issue of his disbarment." There would have been no point, Williams adds. Unless it can be shown to have demonstrably affected that attorney's conduct of the trial, evidence of substance abuse by a defense attorney has rarely led to the reversal of a conviction on appeal.

In any event, even without the issue of substance abuse, Jackson's testimony at the PCRA hearing showed clearly that he had not been up to the task of defending his client.

Attorney Weinglass began by focusing on Jackson's handling of Abu-Jamal's penalty phase hearing. It was here that Jackson seems to have made his most glaring and egregious error: the failure to put any witnesses on the stand to testify to the defendant's character, which could have mitigated the crime of murder for which he had just been convicted. (The jury had found one aggravating circumstance—the killing of an on-duty police officer—and one mitigating circumstance—his lack of a criminal record—and decided on balance that this favored execution. Had just one juror found another mitigating circumstance— for example his upstanding reputation in the community, or his record as a loving father to his children—he might well have been sentenced to life without parole instead.) Jackson said that he had no idea why he did not put any witnesses on the stand. His first explanation was surprise at the guilty verdict, which had left him unprepared for the hearing:

> ...Believe it or not, I didn't think that he would be convicted
> of murder in the first degree. That was the first reason. The other is
> because we had been I think working six days a week for a couple of
> weeks. And I first assumed that in the unlikely event that would
> have happened, we would have had at least an extra day to prepare
> whatever preparation would be available and necessary.[20]

Jackson's recollection that the 1982 trial had been rushed was correct. Sabo insisted on six-day weeks for courtroom testimony, leaving Jackson, a sole practitioner, with almost no time to prepare. Indeed, when the jury returned with its guilty verdict, Sabo had even indicated he was ready to move ahead directly that very evening with the sentencing hearing. Jackson could have requested some time to prepare. He did not. Instead he inexplicably accepted Sabo's decision to begin the penalty phase hearing the next morning, as proposed by McGill.

Trying to explain why there were no mitigating witnesses presented, Jackson said:

> Certainly the testimony on mitigating factors might have been,
> may have been more effectively presented with witnesses. If you recall,
> I am sure you know, there were limited funds in this case. There was
> limited time in this case. And unfortunately, as I said, the first thing
> that struck my mind after the Jury's verdict was to make sure that I was
> legally prepared to deal with the penalty phase. I didn't want to just
> helter-skelter go after witnesses without particularly knowing what I
> would do with the witnesses. But I, in retrospect, I don't know why I

did not call the witnesses. I don't know if there was a plan, I don't think so. I just don't know about it. I don't know.[21]

Over the course of three days at the PCRA hearing, Jackson explained in sometimes grippingly emotional terms (breaking down in tears at times), how he had failed as a defense attorney in Abu-Jamal's murder trial. He conceded that he had not gone over the testimony of crucial defense witnesses Dessie Hightower, Anthony Coletta, or Veronica Jones before he put them on the witness stand. Knowledgeable and experienced trial attorneys would immediately recognize this as a grievous error. In the case of Hightower, a defense witness, he offered no reason for the lapse, saying only, "I don't know what happened, why I never talked to him. I just don't recall."[23] In the case of Dr. Coletta, the physician who treated both Faulkner and Abu-Jamal, Jackson claimed that lawyers from Coletta's employer, Jefferson Hospital, had barred Coletta from talking to him. Further, Jackson was not provided by the prosecution with Coletta's medical report until the day the doctor was put on the stand. Then there was Veronica Jones, the prostitute who surprised Jackson on the stand by changing her testimony from what she had told police investigators concerning whether she had seen other people running from the scene of the shooting. Jackson said she had refused to talk with him.

A 1974 Temple University Law School graduate who had only been a practicing lawyer for seven years prior to taking on the Abu-Jamal case, most of Jackson's experience had been in civil cases. He claimed he had also made a major error in handling the testimony of prosecution witness Robert Chobert. Chobert was critical: he was one of four prosecution eyewitnesses to the shooting. As has been previously discussed, Judge Sabo barred Jackson from letting the jury know that the taxi driver was, at the time of the trial, on probation for felony arson-for-hire for the firebombing of a school. At that time, Jackson failed to cite a legal precedent that would have allowed him to reveal this. Jackson did argue at the time the principle of *crimen falsi*. Since Chobert had committed a crime of falsehood, the jury should know his testimony might be unreliable. Sabo disagreed, saying that arson would not fall into that category of crime. But whether or not Sabo's ruling on *crimen falsi* was correct, Jackson could have argued in addition that Chobert's probationary status by itself, and the fact that he had been driving his cab on a suspended license, introduced the potential for bias in the witness's testimony. Unfortunately for Abu-Jamal, he did not.

Asked why, and whether this was an oversight on his part, Jackson said:

I don't know if it was just an oversight as much as I don't think I knew at that time. I think, I knew that in some situations, just as the cases held that the record could be admitted for the purposes of showing bias. At the time, at the time the situation came up, quite frankly I don't think I knew, I knew that law.[23]

Weinglass had Jackson explain how he had been unable to hire a pathologist or ballistician for the defense because the court would only allow a few hundred dollars for each—an amount that no expert would work for. He said he was also limited in the amount of private investigation of witnesses he could pay for. The court awarded only a sum of about $150 for that purpose, later increased to about $600 with money out of Jackson's own pocket. Even this court sum was not awarded until six weeks after the incident, by which time many clues and witnesses had already vanished from the scene. Finally Jackson explained that, during the period before the trial, he had requested a second attorney to assist him. But Judge Ribner, the magistrate then in charge of the case, rejected this.

Expert assistance and a back-up attorney are both now common or even standard in publicly-funded capital defenses in many states, including Pennsylvania (today, Philadelphia courts will assign a second counsel on request in capital cases which are considered to be more complex, as this one certainly was). One direct result of Jackson's lack of either was that he missed the notation in the coroner's report that the bullet recovered from Faulkner's head appeared to be a .44 caliber projectile (Abu-Jamal's gun was a .38). Later testimony by a defense ballistics expert witness at this same PCRA hearing established that the bullet was in fact, probably a .38 caliber, not a .44 caliber. But the significance of Jackson's oversight was that the jury never got to hear that—on the basis of the evidence available at that time—the bullet might, in fact, not have been able to have come from Abu-Jamal's gun. That bit of ambiguity—neither the caliber of the shell nor the identity of the gun which fired it has ever been definitively established to this day—could have raised a "reasonable doubt" in the minds of some jurors. But because Jackson missed the coroner's notation, it never made it into the panel's deliberations. As Williams wrote in his book on the case:

When we realized that we could not, in fact, make out a case that the fatal bullet was a .44 caliber, we pursued a more limited point. Jackson's failure to notice the ".44 cal." reference on the first page of the autopsy report spoke volumes about his shoddy trial preparation. It would be one thing for him to decide, as a practical matter, that he would not use this reference in the report to undermine the reliability of the medical examiner's testimony; it's an entirely different matter to bypass its use completely because it simply wasn't noticed. It is difficult to fathom how any modestly prepared lawyer could have overlooked the ".44 cal." notation on the first page of the medical examiner's report. Jackson's failure to notice it illustrated just how ill prepared and overwhelmed he was.[24]

The four-member prosecution team wisely gave the job of cross-examining Jackson to Grant. Like Jackson, Grant was an African-American himself, thus avoiding the unseemly picture of Jackson being humiliated on the stand by a white prosecutor. Grant ripped into Jackson right from the start, trying to suggest that Jackson's affidavit submitted to the court listing efforts he had made in the original trial was written by Weinglass, not by Jackson. Jackson stood his ground, explaining that the affidavit, which he had signed, had been drafted by Weinglass based upon notes Weinglass had taken during a series of interview sessions with Jackson over the course of several years. It was a silly argument Grant was making. Attorneys—including prosecutors and police investigators—routinely draft statements for people based upon their notes of interviews with those witnesses, and then ask them to sign them as authentic.

Nonetheless, Judge Sabo, ever alert to the needs of the prosecution, tried to bolster Grant's accusation as follows:

Mr. Grant: May I have a copy of those notes, Mr. Weinglass?
Mr. Weinglass: Objection. Those notes are privileged. There is no basis for Counsel to ask to have them.
The Court: You have no privilege. There is no longer a privilege.
Mr. Grant: This is a statement of the witness, and he is taking notes as to the witness' statement. And I just want to see if the notes comport with the reality that I see typed here in front of me.
The Court: Well, if you have them turn it over to him.
Mr. Weinglass: I don't have such. I don't have the notes. And I believe the notes are privileged. I am Counsel to Mr. Jamal. That privilege still pertains.
The Court: This is not anything that Jamal said to you, it is what a witness said to you.
Mr. Weinglass: If it has anything to do with what I take down in terms of my representation of Mr. Jamal.
The Court: No, no.
...
The Court: If you have the notes turn them over. Otherwise the Court can conclude that you just manufactured this thing. If you have them give it to him.
Mr. Weinglass: Well, I appreciate the Court indicating the possibility

that it was manufactured.

The Court: Well, because he is going to argue that later on. And I am trying to help you now. Because if you have them give it to him.

Mr. Weinglass: Your Honor beat him to it. You are making the argument from the bench for the prosecutor. But I appreciate that observation. But I don't have the notes. There are no notes.[25]

In Chapter 5, the authenticity of another note was discussed: the typed statement purportedly of hospital guard Priscilla Durham. That written statement, in which the guard claimed to have overheard a confession, was extremely damaging to the defense. It was, in fact, the single most damaging piece of evidence at the trial. Although Durham said that the typed note was not the account she had given, as that had been hand-written, Judge Sabo's requirement for testing the authenticity of the typed document was only to ask her if the notes were an accurate version of what she had said. But at the PCRA hearing, the standard for proving authenticity, at least for the defense, had been raised. Just because the witness for the defense had signed a statement didn't mean it was authentic, Sabo decided.

Grant argued that Abu-Jamal's defense had more money available and spent more money on experts than had been alleged in their appeal. He did show that a few hundred dollars had been provided by outside organizations such as the Black Journalists Association. But at a later point, he conceded that, even including supplemental funds added to what the court provided, the amounts were minimal:

> [Jackson] ...And the record reflects that I spent seven hours with (ballistician) George Fassnacht, and what did he get? $350. And you said that was an exorbitant amount of money. I don't think that it was. This was a trial, as you know, that had 150 statements in it. There was a lot of work to be done. A lot of work. And we are talking about $150 for a pathologist?
>
> Q: No, I agree with you that seems like a relatively paltry sum.
>
> A: You are talking about, what's the amount for the ballistician? Mr. Grant, I am not going to even argue with these amounts of money. If you think that's enough money for these experts, so be it.
>
> Q: I am not saying that's enough money, I'm saying that your representations were untrue and–
>
> A: No, they weren't sir. I couldn't get another dime.[26]

A great deal of Grant's cross-examination of Jackson was aimed at showing that although he was officially the attorney during the 1982 trial, in fact it was the defendant who was running the show. Jackson gamely countered these efforts, insisting that the only time he was not "in control" of the defense was when Abu-Jamal was permitted by the court to act as his own counsel and Jackson was ordered to serve as back-up counsel. It was a role he repeatedly protested and objected to at the time. As Jackson explained:

> Well, let me just tell you this, Mr. Grant, and I am going to try to tell you for the last time. I have been practicing law for a long time. At no time, at no time that I know of I haven't been in control, when I was a lawyer. Those times that I wasn't, I went to the Supreme Court. I told them to let me out. Then they told me to be a backup Counsel. That's when I wasn't in control. I wouldn't do it because I wasn't in control. That's what this whole thing was about.
>
> But for some reason you seem to think Mr. Jamal was in control. Mr. Jamal was in control when he got the Commonwealth to respond to some political thing. When I was the lawyer I was the lawyer, I was doing what I wanted to do. When Mr. Jamal wanted me to do something I said Your Honor, Mr. Jamal wants me to do this. Mr. Jamal is ordering me to do this. If I didn't preface my remark that way, I was in control.[27]

Who held control was a critical issue. If Abu-Jamal was actually running his defense, and Jackson was only his assistant, it would not be possible for Abu-Jamal to then argue that he had ineffective counsel. One example concerned the case of Jackson's failure to put on the stand high-profile or emotionally powerful character witnesses, such as the defendant's mother and sister, or his colleagues, radio personality E. Stephen Collins or *Wall Street Journal* reporter Joe Davidson. If Grant could show that it had been Abu-Jamal's decision not to call such witnesses, and that Jackson had just gone along, the defendant would have no grounds to argue ineffectiveness of counsel.

A careful reading of the 1982 trial transcript clarifies the issue. Jackson was the trial lawyer for all but some of the pretrial hearings and part of the *voir dire* jury selection process. When Judge Sabo removed Abu-Jamal's *pro se* rights and ordered Jackson, against the defendant's wishes, to act as lead counsel in his defense, Jackson had no choice but to act as the lead counsel. Had he done any less, he would have been taken to task by Sabo—possibly even jailed for contempt, as was actually ordered at one point by Sabo. That is not to say that Abu-Jamal was always cooperative with Jackson. He most certainly was not, to the point of insulting him publicly, calling him a shyster and worse. Still the strategy of the trial, and many of the errors that were made by the defense, were quite obviously Jackson's. As he made clear in his testimony, for instance, the decision not to call Abu-Jamal's family members as character witnesses at the end of the trial was Jackson's, not Abu-Jamal's.

In his effort to get Jackson to concede that he was acting in accordance with Abu-Jamal's instructions in his conduct of the trial, Grant inadvertently elicited testimony from Jackson that demonstrated fairly convincingly Jackson's ineffectiveness. Grant tried to argue that the reason Jackson didn't seek to put mitigating character references on the stand during Abu-Jamal's penalty phase hearing was that he was intimidated by the defendant. He tried to suggest that because Abu-Jamal had cursed him for losing the trial, Jackson had been so afraid to face his client that he had not even dared to read the statement Abu-Jamal had prepared to read to the jury and the court. The statement, as we saw, was an ill-conceived political diatribe that opened the door for prosecutor McGill to question Abu-Jamal under oath, bringing into the record his militant statements as a Black Panther.

But Jackson stated clearly that he had no fear of Abu-Jamal, and that he hadn't read the statement because he felt the defendant had a right to make a statement—a decision which, while perhaps sounding admirable, was a huge disservice to his client:

Q: And did you see that before he delivered it?

A: No, sir.

Q: Did you ask him for it?

A: No, sir.

Q: And you knew you'd better not, didn't you?

A: I have never been–I mean if that's what he wanted to do what difference does it—yeah, that's right, why would I want to ask and see it? I don't know what it contained. He wanted to exercise his right. That's his right. I am not going to trample it. Who am I to do that?

Q: Well, who are you, you are the person that said basically because I didn't do those things I was totally ineffective as Counsel at the penalty phase. That's why I'm asking you these questions. Why didn't you look at it? Because you were afraid of the man, because you failed him in his mind and you didn't want to quarrel with his decisions thereafter; isn't that so?

A: At no time up until now have I ever been afraid of Mr. Jamal or any other man.

Q: Well, how about being apprehensive of contact physically or verbally.

A: What was he going to do? I have been called a lot worse names than Mr. Jamal has called me, believe me, a lot worse names. So that was it. I wasn't afraid of being called names. I wasn't afraid of him beating me up. I don't know what else I was supposed to be afraid of. I mean, what are you trying to say?[28]

It seems evident from the Jackson testimony and a reading of the transcript of the original trial that, if anything, the on-again-off-again nature of Abu-Jamal's self-representation seriously undermined Jackson's ability to function effectively as a lawyer. At Sabo's whim, Jackson was sometimes being shunted into a back-up counsel role and sometimes into the lead counsel role (always at that time over Abu-Jamal's strenuous objections). As back-up counsel, he felt obliged to take a back seat. When reassigned as lead counsel by Sabo, he was unprepared because he had not been actively working on the case for over a month. Furthermore, his acceptance of the lead counsel role (even though done under the threat of a contempt citation at trial), further alienated him from his client—something of which both Sabo and prosecutor McGill seemed to be clearly aware. Not insignificantly, the papers and documents that were being provided to the defense by the prosecution were sometimes going to Abu-Jamal, who was living confined in a cell remote from the courtroom, and sometimes to Jackson. This confusing and logistically awkward situation meant that at times Jackson didn't have all the relevant documents needed to try the case.

As Jackson testified during questioning by Weinglass:

> Q: And it is your testimony that between May 13th and June 18th, which is the date opening arguments were to be given, you were serving as backup Council?
>
> A: Yes, sir.
>
> Q: So for the five weeks preceding the giving of evidence in this case, you were backup Counsel from May 13th to June 18th?
>
> A: That is correct.
>
> Q: And it's in that period of time that you have told this Court you didn't know what your role ought to be?
>
> A: Didn't know what my role was, sir, didn't do anything.
>
> Q: And no one would tell you what your role was?
>
> A: Well, quite the contrary. Everybody told me what my role was.
>
> ...
>
> Q: Did you know yourself what your role was to be?
>
> A: No, sir, I sure did not.
>
> Q: Mr. Jackson, in your way of thinking back then, does backup counsel plan trial strategy?
>
> A: Certainly not.
>
> Q: In your way of thinking back then, does backup counsel plan trial tactics?
>
> A: No, sir.
>
> Q: To your way of thinking back then, does backup counsel prepare the case for trial?
>
> A: No, sir.
>
> Q: And in the last five weeks before evidence was taken in this case you

did none of those things?

A: No, sir. I did not.

Q: In your experience as a trial attorney, are the last five weeks prior to the taking of testimony a very critical time in terms of the preparation of your case?

A: Unquestionably.

Q: Would it be fair to say that it's the most critical time when an attorney begins to focus on his case?

A: I would say that's the most critical time, sir.

...

Q: And so would it be fair to say that you reacquired control of the case on the day that you had to give an opening statement?

A: That is correct, sir.[29]

Compounding, and underlying, many of Jackson's problems during the trial was his lack of experience as a capital litigator. There was, during his PCRA hearing testimony, and has been during the years this case has dragged on, some controversy, confusion and deliberate disinformation regarding that experience. The D.A.'s office and the FOP have for years claimed that Jackson was an experienced attorney with some 20 homicide cases under his belt. Years later, in January 2002, Judge Yohn, the federal judge ruling on Abu-Jamal's *habeas corpus* appeal, would accept that number as fact. In truth, however, most of those never were capital, or death-penalty cases. Many were also plea-bargained, and thus not actually tried before a jury. And in many, Jackson was not the lead attorney handling the case. Moreover, as Williams points out, any other capital cases Jackson tried had to have been *after* the Abu-Jamal case. Pennsylvania only reinstated the death penalty three years before Abu-Jamal's arrest, and during those three years, Jackson was a full-time attorney on the staff of Pilcop, handling civil litigation concerning police brutality.[30]

Jackson himself claimed under questioning by Weinglass in 1995, that at the time of the Abu-Jamal trial in 1982, he had actually only handled two death penalty cases that went to the point of the penalty phase. On one of those, he was only a co-counsel, and not involved in determining trial strategy. Moreover, in both those cases, the defendants had prior criminal records, and were not professionals with strong records of service and work in the community. This is a crucial distinction: until he had Abu-Jamal for a client, he had had no experience with a trial where it may have been important to bring in family and professional associates as character references during the trial and penalty phases of a trial. In many states today, with that minimal a background Jackson would have been considered too inexperienced to handle a death penalty case.

Overall, Jackson's testimony at the PCRA hearing gave the picture of a lawyer who had tried his best but who was clearly out of his depth in trying to defend a client who—with good reason—had no faith in him and wanted him off the case. Jackson won a couple of rounds at the trial—for example when he managed to elicit from the prostitute Veronica Jones the testimony (outside of the jury's hearing) that she had been pressured by police to give false evidence. But his errors, from the failure to notice the medical examiner's ".44 .cal" notation and his failure to put cab driver Chobert's probation status on the record before the jury, to his failure to put mitigating character witnesses on the stand in the penalty phase of the trial, vastly outweighed his successes. While Judge Sabo, acting as factfinder, would not agree, the defense had made a solid case that Jackson's actions fell below any reasonable minimal standards required for a fair trial.

Chapter Eight

Fighting Back
New Evidence and the Seeds of Distrust

On the morning of August 1 1995, former Philadelphia policeman Gary Wakshul maneuvered painfully into his seat on the witness stand during the Post-Conviction Relief Act hearing on the case of death-row inmate Mumia Abu-Jamal. It was clear that he had suffered an injury. But though the defense had to schedule his testimony around a program of physical therapy he was undergoing, Abu-Jamal and his lawyers were unaware of the reason for his obvious discomfort. They would have found it intriguing. On July 13, only days before the start of the PCRA hearing, Wakshul had been attacked and savagely beaten by two undercover police officers, Kenneth Fleming and Jean Langen, right in the courtroom where he was working as a court "tip," or crier.[1] This act of violence, still unexplained to this day, came at very sensitive moment on the eve of his testimony.

The defense did, however, know the reason Wakshul had become a court crier. On June 18, 1986 he had been fired from the police department for allegedly committing an act of brutality against an arrested suspect in his custody. The suspension notice, under the heading "Conduct Unbecoming a Police Officer," referred not only to the incident which led to his dismissal, but also to other violence:

> ...On or about Saturday, December 7, 1985 at approximately 9:15 a.m., while you were on duty, you struck Mr. Louis McDonald in the head several times with your blackjack while he was hand-cuffed and in your custody inside the Sixth Police District, 11th and Winter Streets. Mr. McDonald was transported to the Hannemann [sic] Hospital for treatment of a fractured cheekbone, a split lip and lacerations of the scalp. Inside Hahnemann Hospital, you further abused Mr. McDonald by choking him with your hands while his hands are cuffed behind his back and by dragging him by the hand-cuffs. Although your dismissal is based on the above substantive acts, on Wednesday, May 26, 1986 you were also arrested inside IAB [Internal Affairs Bureau] headquarters and charged with aggravated assault, simple assault and criminal attempt.[2]

Wakshul was a crucial witness for the defense because he was the officer who had been assigned to stay with Abu-Jamal from the moment the defendant was placed in the paddy wagon on the morning of December 9, until the operation to remove the bullet lodged near his spine. As we saw back in Chapters 4 and 6, it was also Wakshul who had told police investigators when first asked about his time spent with the suspect, "The negro male made no comment."[3] A week after his first interview by a detective, Wakshul was reinterviewed by the chief investigator on the case, Detective William Thomas from Homicide. He was asked if there was anything he wished to add to his statement concerning the incident and his time spent guarding the suspect. Wakshul had replied, "Nothing I can think of now."[4]

Jackson had attempted to have Wakshul brought in as a defense witness on the last day of the trial in 1982. His goal was to get Wakshul to explain under oath how he squared both those comments with testimony by another officer and a hospital security guard that the same man he had been guarding all that time had "shouted out" a confession. Wakshul would also claim to have heard it, but not until February 11, 1982 (more than two months after the Faulkner shooting), while being interviewed by Frank Goldberg, an investigator from the police department's Internal Affairs Bureau.[5] As we saw earlier, at the time of the trial, Judge Sabo had denied the defense's request to bring him in, saying that in not calling Wakshul earlier in the trial, Jackson and Abu-Jamal had "goofed." Sabo had further suggested (with curious prescience) that in any event Wakshul might be on vacation. He had prosecutor McGill—who had already been vociferously objecting to having Wakshul placed on the stand—phone to check on his whereabouts. McGill quickly returned to the courtroom to confirm that indeed the officer was "on vacation" and unavailable. The defense request to delay the trial for a few days so Wakshul could be located and brought in—a minor inconvenience and delay—was denied by Judge Sabo.

Now, 13 years later, the defense finally had the man on the stand and was able to question him about the original incident, about his written statements to investigators, and about his whereabouts during the 1982 trial. Wakshul was to be the first in a series of witnesses at the PCRA hearing whose testimony—sometimes dramatic and even unexpected by both the prosecution and the defense—would finally begin unraveling the web of arguments the prosecution had woven in its claim of a neat, "open-and-shut" case of first-degree murder.

Wakshul was not a friendly witness for the defense. A self-described personal friend of Daniel Faulkner's, he had refused to answer questions

posed by defense attorney Daniel Williams outside the courtroom. At the
time he was on the stand, he was appealing to get his dismissal overturned,
and moreover he had just been beaten by police officers under suspicious
circumstances. In this light, it is fair to ask just how candid Wakshul, who
appeared at the hearing wearing an FOP "Justice for Daniel Faulkner" pin,
was in his testimony. But even with that caveat, the story he told raises
questions not just about the veracity of the trial testimony concerning
Abu-Jamal's purported "confession" in the hospital, but about the integrity
of the prosecution and the police.

Early in his testimony, Wakshul told defense attorney Williams that
he had heard Abu-Jamal, on the floor of the hospital entryway, say, "I shot
him. I hope the motherfucker dies." The defense then confronted him with
the two interview statements taken from him by police investigators on
December 9 and December 12, 1981, neither of which mentioned such a
confession. Wakshul grew evasive, even denying recalling the interviews.
His main explanation for his failure to report a confession of murder for two
months was shock at Faulkner's death. As he put it:

> I was stunned at that point. I stumbled back into a little alcove
> and started to cry. Covered myself by going outside, closing up the
> wagon and getting myself together.
>
> I then went back into the hospital at some period after that.
> And I have…very little recollection of anything that happened after
> that point except for some snapshots in my mind of seeing Danny
> Faulkner's dead feet lying on a gurney, of, of standing next to some-
> place where I saw Mr. Jamal, and then leaving.
>
> I remember after that being in Homicide but I have no recol-
> lection of anything further that night until early in the morning of
> that morning, the following morning, when I was leaving work in
> my car, running into a cement pole with my car. And at that point
> I, I had more control over myself at that point.[6]

While extremely unlikely, a momentary memory lapse, even for a
trained police officer, might be believable under such traumatic conditions.
But Williams zeroed in on Wakshul's initial interview that same morning
on December 9. It had been conducted scarcely an hour after the confession had allegedly been blurted out. During that interview, Wakshul had
coolly and calmly recalled details about license plates of cars at the scene,
the color of cars, descriptions of witnesses, and the positions of Faulkner
and Abu-Jamal at the scene. He recalled details about the contents of Abu-
Jamal's wallet and other facts, and the time he had received his radio call
to go to the scene of the shooting. Despite this detailed series of recollec-

tions, somehow he had forgotten the confession. Citing all these details, Williams asked:

Q: Would the confession of a person saying I shot a police officer and I hope the mother-fucker dies, is that more important than noting the time that you received the radio call? [to go to the aid of a fallen officer]

A: I don't believe they are more important, no.

Q: You don't think that the confession is more important?

A: I said those items that you mentioned.

Q: Oh, okay. Pardon me. Right. The confession would obviously be more important than each one of those items, am I right, we agree on that?

A: I would say the confession is more important, yes.[7]

Interestingly, Wakshul did say, in his February 11, 1982 interview with the IAB investigator, that he saw no hospital personnel in the vicinity of Abu-Jamal when the then suspect was supposed to have blurted out a confession. Since the main evidence of that confession was the testimony of hospital security guard Priscilla Durham, who said she had been standing right near Abu-Jamal's head, and who claimed to have witnessed it (and to have reported it to her supervisor the next day), this observation by Wakshul raises further doubts about the whole confession story. One question is obvious: was Durham even there? Something else doesn't match, too: Wakshul said the confession was not shouted out (as Durham had claimed at the trial), but made in "a normal speaking voice."[8] Here is how IAB Investigator Goldberg's report of Wakshul's recalling the event read:

Q: When Jamal made the comment, "I shot him. I hope the mother-fucker dies," who else was in close proximity to him that may have heard him make this comment?

A: My partner [Stephen Trombetta] was near him. There were other officers in the emergency room but I just can't recall who they were.

Q: When he made this comment, were any hospital personnel in close proximity to him?

A: I didn't see them at all.[9]

An additional curiosity about Wakshul's testimony was that he placed his partner, Officer Trombetta, right at the scene of the alleged confession. But in interviews with police about the incident, Trombetta never mentioned hearing a confession, either shouted out or spoken, by Abu-Jamal. And to this day, Trombetta has never revised that claim.

But an even more explosive and revealing moment in Wakshul's testimony came a short time later. Williams was trying to discover when

Wakshul might first have heard word about a supposed confession. He asked the former cop at one point when he had first had dealings with the prosecutor in the case, Joseph McGill.

Q: ...Prior to the trial, did you meet with any persons from the District Attorney's Office?

A: I believe either in January or February of '82, having a prep meeting with Mr. McGill in reference to this case.

Q: What do you mean by prep meeting?

A: Umm, I believe he was the assigned prosecutor and he was going over different facets of the case with a large group of parties. Police officers I believe were the only ones, and detectives, who were present.

Q: So he was prepping several people at the same time?

A: It was, it was basically a large round-table discussion of events. I don't recall specifics of it. I believe that there were, there were some preliminary reports that he was going over, but I don't really recall in depth what happened.

...

Q: Did the subject of the confession come up in this meeting?

A: I believe it did.

Q: This, again, was a discussion with all the police officers present in this round-table meeting?

A: Yes. I believe they were all there, whoever was at the meeting.

Q: And was there any inquiry directed at you personally about the troubling fact that you had not mentioned the confession on December 9th or December 16th or thereafter until February 11th?

A: No.

Q: No?

A: No, I believe what happened was Mr. McGill said did anybody hear his statement. And I know I raised my hand but I don't recall any further discussion of it.[10]

The defense now believes it was at this so-called "round-table" meeting, disclosed by Wakshul, that a conspiracy was hatched to have police witnesses agree that a confession had been made by the defendant. Given the failure of any of the witnesses, trained officers (and a trained private security guard) that they were, to have come forward before the elapse of two months' time, this theory seems a strong possibility. McGill's role in such a scheme would be difficult to ascertain. If police officers were giving false testimony (a not uncommon practice among Philadelphia police officers in those days), they could have done it on their own. McGill may have just decided not to challenge them. (Skilled lawyers, besides being adept at posing questions that elicit desired testimony from witnesses, also know when *not* to ask too many questions of their witnesses or clients.)

Did McGill really think it possible that two trained police officers would for two months fail to tell him or police detectives that they had heard the suspect in a police slaying confess to the crime? "I certainly would have thought about it," he conceded when asked in May, 2002. "But I put him (Bell) on, so obviously I believed it. Any kind of witness I talk to, I consider the truthfulness, whether I believe it, whether it would sound credible, whether it would be acceptable, and whether I'd need it." McGill also argues that in any event, Bell's testimony was "not that important" in terms of the strength of his case. He says, "It was really Durham, with her written statement made shortly after the shooting, that was important."

Yet as we saw, Durham's purported statement is also suspicious; she says it was written down by her supervisor by hand and not typed, unlike the unverified document brought in and introduced as evidence by McGill, a "document" that was simply typing on a plain, unmarked piece of white typing paper. Moreover, while Durham claimed she had made that statement a short time after the alleged confession was made, she did not report the confession to police for two months. She then didn't say anything about a written report of the confession until the trial, another four months after her report of the confession, even though when she did first mention the confession, the police investigator actually asked her why it had taken her two months to come forward. Moreover, it seems odd that prosecutor McGill wouldn't have asked his witness, back in February, to explain to him her long delay in reporting such important evidence. Had there been a written report, why wouldn't Durham have told police about it then as a way of backing up her statement?

In any event, we are left to choose between two versions of events. The prosecution would have us believe that the two-month memory lapses of both Bell and Wakshul (not to mention Durham) are believable. The defense argues that these lapses point to a conspiracy.

But Wakshul wasn't through. He had still more dramatic testimony to offer. On the day back in 1982 that defense attorney Jackson and defendant Abu-Jamal had tried to have him brought in to testify, far from being away on vacation, Wakshul had actually been cooling his heels at home in Philadelphia, he testified. He had been ordered not to leave the city in case he was needed at the trial. This stunning revelation came as Williams asked Wakshul if he had ever been instructed to make himself available for trial.

Q: Were you ever instructed that you should keep yourself available for
   trial?
A: At that meeting?

Q: No, at any point.

A: I believe later on after our vacations were decided on, they were given out, and the trial date came out, being asked not to go away on vacations.

Q: Who asked you not to go away?

A: That I couldn't tell you. That could have come from, that could have come from Mr. McGill, it could have come from supervisors in the Police Department. I don't really recall where it came from. I recall that, you know, we were asked, or yeah, I believe it was more than one person at the time, we were asked if you are on vacation during that period, you know, try to stay available, something to that effect.[11]

Later, Wakshul stated that he had, in fact, been on vacation. But, he said, he was waiting at home during the last days of the 1982 trial—and in particular on July 1, when the defense sought to call him—in case he might be called to testify. Only in the latter part of his two-week vacation, which began on June 25, 1982, did he make several short outings outside of the city of Philadelphia. As he testified:

> My recollection is in compliance to a request to stay while cases were going on, I was here. And as I recall it, my own independent recollection was that I believed the testimony was over in the case and I was just, I had not been called and I figured I would not be needed and I was, I did take some time. I couldn't say if it was two or three days towards the end of the vacation. But I do recall that I was still on vacation when the information that I got was, or understood was that the trial had reached a conclusion.[12]

If, as Wakshul testified, he had been told to stay available while the trial was in session, how could the District Attorney's Office not know the whereabouts and availability on July 1, 1982 of this key witness to a confession? In strenuously objecting to defense efforts to call Wakshul on the last day of the trial, and also telling the court at the time that the officer was unavailable and on vacation, was McGill dissembling? Here is the way the conversation went at the bench in 1982:

The Court: What is this officer that you want? What is he going to testify to?

Mr. Jackson: That he picked Mr. Jamal up at the scene.

The Court: So?

Mr. Jackson: During this time the negro male made no comment. He was with him the entire time.

Mr. McGill: He is not around. I am going to object to bringing this guy in. He is not around.

Mr. Jackson: That is what he says.

Mr. McGill: I am not bringing him in at the last minute.

The Court: You knew about this before. I am not going to hold up this trial.

Mr. Jackson: I didn't.

The Court: What do you mean you didn't? Didn't you get statements from the detectives months and months ago?

Mr. Jackson: Absolutely right, Judge.

The Court: I am not going to delay the court.

Mr. Jackson: We can get the man by this afternoon. His testimony would be very limited. This is what he says, that he made no comment. You can understand with regard to at least the statements of Officer Garry Bell and—

The Court: (Interposing) Let me see his statement?

Mr. Jackson: I was forced to try and remember everything that everybody said and I couldn't do it.

Mr. McGill: I object to this. I think if Mr. Jamal the defendant in this case decides he is not going to give statements until the very last minute to his attorney that is on him. I don't see any reason why this trial should be delayed.

...

Mr. McGill: Judge, this Defendant has nothing else to do except this case. It seems to be the strategy to delay it. We are getting closer to the July 4th holiday and it would seem to be to get this jury disgruntled and upset.

...

The Court: You could have had this man long ago. I am not going to delay the case any more. There has been enough delay. It is a quarter after 11:00. I am not delaying this case any longer.

Mr. Jackson: I think it is a matter that is crucial enough for us to delay it. How long is it going to take to get a police officer in here?

The Court: How do I know? He could be on vacation.

...

(At this time there was a short recess.)

...

(The following is a discussion in chambers with both counsel present.)

Mr. McGill: Your Honor, I have made efforts to find out where Officer Wakshul is and I am informed that he is on vacation until July 8th.

Mr. Jackson: Does that mean he is not in the city?

The Court: I am not going to go looking for anybody now. You had the opportunity to let us know in advance and we could have made the

effort to bring him in.
Mr. McGill: It is not your fault, it is his [Abu-Jamal's].
The Court: Who knows where he is.[13]

At this point in the 1982 trial, Sabo and the prosecution were trying to have it both ways. On the one hand, Sabo had removed Abu-Jamal's right to handle his own defense, and forced Jackson to act as the defense attorney in the case. On the other, when Jackson said he had not seen the December 9 Wakshul statement because it was in a group of documents that were in Abu-Jamal's possession, McGill (who was already alert to preventing any future claim of ineffectiveness of counsel), argued that it was "on him" (the defendant), for not bringing it to his attorney's attention. Clearly, however, if there was a failure to notice the document and to recognize its significance as a way to impeach the testimony of a confession, it was Jackson's failure as the attorney in the case. This would support the claim of ineffective counsel. But mistake or no mistake, the judge, on the last day of the trial, had the ability to put it right by bringing Wakshul to the stand. Instead of making this simple effort to get at the truth in a case where a man's life was on the line, Sabo acted like a chess player telling an opponent he already lifted his fingers from a piece on a bad move and he can't take it back. Callously, he told the defense attorney and his client that they had "goofed."

Meanwhile, if one is to believe Wakshul's testimony at the 1995 PCRA hearing, McGill's assertion to the court in 1982 that the witness was not available was quite possibly a deliberate falsehood. In 1995, Wakshul testified that he had been instructed to stay in the city, and such trial-related instructions, while they might have been conveyed to Wakshul by a superior officer, would almost surely have originated in the D.A.'s office, not the police department. If so, the prosecutor's claim was a case of prosecutorial misconduct and perjury. Alternately, if the instructions had originated with Wakshul's supervisors, they should have so informed McGill when he allegedly called to inquire about the officer's whereabouts, again raising the question of prosecutorial misconduct in saying he was unavailable.

McGill, in an interview in May 2002, says an instruction to Wakshul to stay available during the trial could have come from the police or from the D.A.'s office. While he does not say definitively that he did not make such a request to the officer, he says he has "no recollection" of having done so. "Why would I have done that?" he asked. "I don't think I had any intention of calling him as a witness. Why would I?" He later added, "It could have been a blanket request to all [police] witnesses." Asked whether he was saying that he did not make the request for Wakshul to keep himself available, he responded, "I didn't say that. I said I have no recollection of doing it." McGill's surprising unwillingness to rule out the possibility that he might have been the source of the instruction Wakshul testified to regarding remaining available during the trial is revealing. It means the former prosecutor is at least conceding to the possibility that he might have lied about Wakshul's availability to the defense and to Judge Sabo on the last day of the trial when he said "he is not around."

Whatever McGill's role, it is clear from Wakshul's own testimony that he could have been brought in without even a significant delay in the trial. If he had been, jurors would then have heard testimony about his initial two interviews with police investigators, in which he not only said nothing about any confession, but actually asserted in writing that the defendant had said nothing during the entire hospital episode.

During his cross-examination of Wakshul, prosecutor Grant attempted to explain away this damaging testimony. In the February 11, 1982 interview by IAB investigator Goldberg, the first time Wakshul reported having heard a confession, Wakshul also recalled hearing something else. Wakshul claimed he heard officer Garry Bell respond to the purported confession, saying to Abu-Jamal, "If he dies, you die." Grant suggested to Wakshul that recalling that latter statement might have jogged him into remembering the confession itself. But even Wakshul seemed to realize that this was a silly argument, saying:

> I can't say 100 percent that that's what brought it to my recollection at this particular juncture. I do recall that the statement was made, and I do recall the response to that statement. And if I'm recalling correctly, I was at this point realizing that that statement was probably the complaint that was being investigated. And so both statements had to be made at this time.[14]

Wakshul's PCRA testimony undermined the credibility of the prosecution's confession story, raising the possibility that prosecution witnesses at the trial had fabricated the devastating testimony about a confession. But testimony from other witnesses the next day raised even bigger questions about the prosecution's case. George Fassnacht was a ballistics expert who had been paid to do some work for the defense during Abu-Jamal's original trial. But he had not testified because the defense did not have adequate funding to pay for him. Here, he questioned why on the morning of the shooting, police investigators had failed to conduct routine tests on Abu-Jamal's hands (the so-called wipe test), to see if he had recently fired a pistol. Further, they failed to conduct tests on either his or Faulkner's guns, to see if they had recently been fired. As Weinglass asked him:

Q: That just takes a few minutes?

A: Yes, sir.

Q: Now, if the police have a suspect who is suspected of shooting a police officer within minutes of the alleged shooting, is that a test that you would expect to see the police perform?

A: I would expect them to have performed that test.

Q: And there is no evidence that such a test was performed in this case?

A: Not that I have seen.[15]

Fassnacht, who had worked for the police in the 1970s as a witness in some brutality cases filed against officers, also called attention to a contradiction in the investigative report of prosecution firearms expert Anthony Paul. Paul, he explained, had written that the general rifling characteristics of the fatal bullet (referring to the markings on the projectile that would identify it as coming from a specific gun or type of gun) were "indeterminable." Then, on the same line of that report, Paul described those rifling characteristics as being right-hand direction of twist. Asked Weinglass:

Q: Did you find that to be a contradiction of terms, that on the one hand they say it is indeterminable and on the other they give one of the characteristics?

A: Yes, I do.

Q: Is there any explanation for that?

A: Umm, none that occurs to me at the moment.

Q: And you would have brought that out to a jury?

A: Certainly.[16]

In other words, Paul was probably inferring things that, because of the damage to the projectile, probably couldn't have been determined.

Fassnacht also said that Paul's testimony at the trial had an even worse contradiction—one that included a statement that went beyond what was supported by his report on the bullet. Paul, he said, after having written that the general rifling characteristics were "indeterminable," and as such could not have been traced to a particular gun, then claimed that they could be consistent with the specific Charter Arms revolver owned by Abu-Jamal. Paul, under cross examination by Jackson at the trial, had also later specified that the bullet showed eight lands and eight grooves with a right-hand direction of twist. Weinglass asked:

Q: But there was, according to the laboratory report, no eight lands and grooves that were found on this bullet; isn't that right?

A: That's correct.

Q: And yet it was made to the Jury that there was?

A: Yes.[17]

Prosecutor Grant sought to undermine Fassnacht's testimony by citing an old article on shooting evidence which claimed neither the smell test of a gun, nor a wipe test of the hands of a shooting suspect are reliable. But Fassnacht held his ground, noting that police (including the Philadelphia Police) continue to routinely do those tests in most gunshot cases precisely because they do render useable evidence. Grant claimed the wipe test might have proved nothing if Abu-Jamal's hands had been rubbed a lot against other hands and clothing during his arrest and transport to the hospital. That is correct, but while nobody pointed it out during the hearing, the wipe test doesn't produce false *positives*, only false *negatives*. That is, had the police conducted a routine wipe test of Abu-Jamal's hands, the worst that could have happened from their perspective is that they would have gotten no result. Under the circumstances, this would have then been inconclusive, but not particularly damaging to the prosecution's case. If they had picked up gunpowder residue, however, it would have been almost incontrovertible evidence that he had fired a gun, and as such useful in obtaining a conviction. This is the reason the police investigators' claim not to have done such a test in such an important case involving the death of a fellow officer (or to have reported having done one), remains so suspicious.

After Fassnacht, the defense put on Robert Harkins, a stocky, middle-aged man with a prior record of conviction for sexual abuses including corrupting a minor. At the time of the shooting in 1981, Harkins, then 41, had been working as a mechanic for the cab company that also employed Abu-Jamal. He was one of only four witnesses picked up by police the morning of the shooting who claimed to have actually seen Faulkner shot. But he was unique among those four. Though interviewed by police homicide investigators, he was never called by the prosecution—or by the defense. Harkins made it clear that he was no friend of the defense. He had refused to speak with defense investigators in the weeks leading up to the PCRA hearing, and said in court that he didn't like talking with anyone from the defense team.[18] He would only agree to answer their questions if it were in the presence of police detectives.

What makes Harkins important—and the likely reason he was not called as a prosecution witness in 1982—is that in his original interviews with police investigators he described a radically different shooting scenario than that depicted by the other witnesses. It was one that strongly suggested either that the shooter was not Abu-Jamal, or that Abu-Jamal was shot first by Faulkner, or possibly both. In interviews by police detectives shortly after the shooting, Harkins said that the man who shot Faulkner had grabbed the officer, spun him around, and knocked him to the ground on all fours. At that point, the shooter had fired a bullet into his back. This description of the initial shot at Faulkner comports with two crucial pieces of evidence that were not even raised during the trial. Firstly, there was a bruise on Faulkner's knee and a corresponding rip in the knee of his pants, both of which indicated that he had fallen hard in a face-forward direction, as described by Harkins, and not, as Cynthia White had claimed, onto his back. The second thing his story better fits with is the path of the first bullet, which went from the middle of Faulkner's back upward, exiting at his throat, where it blew off his clip-on tie. Harkins then told police detectives in his statement that as the wounded officer turned over on his back, the shooter stood over him and fired the fatal shot. Under oath at the PCRA hearing 13 years later, he stuck to that story.

Note too, that if Harkins' account of the shooting is correct, there was no point in the confrontation during which Faulkner could have shot his assailant in the way that Abu-Jamal was shot. That is, Faulkner would have had to have shot from a position of lying on his back on the pavement, which could never have resulted in a downward-coursing bullet from the nipple to the lower back, such as that which wounded Abu-Jamal. That kind of a shot would have had to be fired before the officer had been knocked down. This testimony fits neatly, then, with that of Scanlan, who saw a flash at the time Abu-Jamal was running across the street, well before he could have fired a shot himself.

Here is what Harkins said in his first interview with police done at 6 am on December 9, 1981, just hours after the shooting:

> On 12-9-81 between 3:30 am and 4 am while traveling east on Locust Street from Broad Street, I was approaching 13th Street when I observed a police car with its dome lights on. And then I looked over and observed a police officer grab a guy. The guy then spun around and the officer went to the ground. He had his hands on the ground and then rolled over. At this time the male who was standing over the officer pointed a gun at the officer and fired one shot and then he fired a second shot. At this time the officer moved a little and then went flat to the ground. I heard a total of three shots and saw what appeared to me to be three flashes from the gun of the man standing over the officer. When I saw the officer go flat to the

ground I drove down the street and at 12th and Locust Streets I saw a police wagon which was traveling south on 12th Street and I told them that a cop got shot back there, and one of the officers, the passenger, said "a cop?" and I said yes a cop.[19]

In a second interview by another homicide investigator on December 17, over a week later, Harkins explained what he had seen in more detail. He was right at the intersection of Locust and 13th Street, heading towards 12th Street, and then, after the shooting, continued to drive right past the scene along Locust to 12th Street, where he met police and reported the shooting. From where he was initially, he should, if the other witnesses were telling the truth, have easily seen cabby Robert Chobert and streetwalker Cynthia White. But he says he saw nobody else in front of him. As he told the second police investigator:

I was coming across the intersection of 13th Street on Locust when I saw the lights on the police car and I noticed the officer on the sidewalk. A guy grabbed him and spun him around. He grabbed him with this hand and spun him and he went down (indicating the male spun officer around with right hand. Then stood over the officer who was on his hands.) The man stood right over the officer and shot him three times. I could see the flashes and hear the pops. It was like hearing a cap pistol. The officer turned over on his back and his leg went out straight. I think his right leg.

Q: Can you tell me how this man was dressed, the man that shot the officer?

A: The clothing didn't appear too dark and it wasn't light.

Q: Can you tell me about how tall this male was?

A: He was a little taller than the officer, heavier than the officer and he may have had a beard.

Q: Did you see another man on the sidewalk besides the officer and the shooter?

A: No.

Q: Did you see anyone else on the street as you traveled east from the scene?

A: There was nobody in front of me.

Q: How many shots did you hear?

A: Three rapid like.[20]

In addition to issues that pertain to whether Chobert and White were telling the truth, the defense wanted to see if Harkins had been shown a photographic array at police homicide headquarters. Had this been the case, and had the prosecution not reported this to the defense, it would have been a clear case of prosecutorial misconduct.

But in putting Harkins on the stand at the post-conviction hearing, the defense knew it was taking a big gamble. Harkins had refused to talk with the defense team's investigator, and Williams says in his book that when he attempted to talk to Harkins himself in a surprise visit to his home, he was rebuffed. It was clearly dangerous to put such a hostile and unpredictable witness on the stand when he hadn't been questioned in advance as to what he would say. Williams had little success with regard to the photo array. Indeed, Harkins denied being shown a photo array. Prosecutor Grant, with the backing of Judge Sabo, made every effort through repeated objections to prevent Williams from asking other questions of the witness. Nonetheless, Harkins was quick to respond to Williams' repeated questions, and ended up supporting his earlier statements to investigators:

> Q: Do you remember telling that detective that the first thing you saw was Police Officer Faulkner grabbing a guy?
>
> A: They both had one another.
>
> Mr. Grant: Objection. Your Honor. This witness, according to their supporting affidavit and claims of error, the only relevance of this witness is because they say he was shown photographic arrays or in person line-ups and the Commonwealth did not alert them or tell them, therefore we suppressed the evidence. We are not here to try the case. And I would ask that they be restricted to their proofs.
>
> Mr. Williams: You Honor-
>
> The Court: You are restricted to your affidavit, okay?
>
> …
>
> Q: Let me ask you this, Mr. Harkins. There were discussions, were there not, on December 9th, 1981, about what happened, right?
>
> A: Yes.
>
> Q: And you told the police that you were very near where the shooting happened, right?
>
> A: Yes.
>
> Q: And that you saw the shooter, is that right?
>
> A: Yes.
>
> Q: You didn't see the shooter get shot, did you?
>
> A: No, I did not.
>
> Q: And how many people did you see there when you witnessed this shooting?
>
> A: Two.
>
> Q: You saw the shooter?
>
> A: Hmm-hmm, and the cop.
>
> Q: And the police officer?
>
> A: Yes.
>
> Q: You didn't see a third person, did you?
>
> A: I wasn't looking around.
>
> …

Q: Did you see a man running across the street?
A: No, I did not.

[At this point Grant objects to the line of questioning, and Sabo orders
    Williams to "get right to the issue" of the photo array. Williams
    moved on to ask about the second interview of Harkins by detec-
    tives.]

Q: Okay. Well, in any event, when you had to go down to the
    Roundhouse the second time, do you remember who was there?
A: No, I do not.
Q: Was there some law enforcement people there?
A: A couple of detectives and stuff and all were there, yes.
Q: And were they interested in asking you some questions about what
    you saw on December 9th?
A: They asked some questions and all but I couldn't tell you what. I
    don't remember.
Q: Did they ask you questions about who did the shooting?
A: No, I just, they just said, I just told them I seen the guy, he shot the
    thing, having the gun, the guy was laying there. They were spinning
    around the pavement.
Q: I'm sorry, who was spinning around on the pavement?
A: The cop and the–and they was like wrestling a little bit and the cop
    fell down.[21]

If Williams had stopped his line of questioning there, there would
have been enough conflicting material to seriously undermine the testimony of both Chobert and White, neither of whom mentioned any
kind of struggle between the shooter and the slain officer. A struggle
contradicts the prosecution claim that Abu-Jamal shot Faulkner in the
back first. Who shot first is pivotal. In Pennsylvania, intent to kill can
be something that occurs in the instant before an action is taken to slay
someone—for example firing a pistol point blank into a person's forehead. But this culpability changes if the victim had already shot the
assailant first. Such a shooting, even if done execution-style, could easily be construed then not as murder but as an act of self-defense. This
is particularly true if the person being killed was himself armed, as was
Faulkner, and could have posed a continued threat to the shooter.

But Williams continued his questioning of Harkins further, leading to testimony that suggested that the person Harkins saw struggling
with Faulkner was in fact Abu-Jamal.

Q: When they were talking to you, Mr. Harkins, did the detectives, were
    they trying to find out who the shooter was?

A: I guess so.
Q: And you told them that the person, the police officer fell down and
   that's when the shooting happened?
A: Well he leaned over and two, two to three flashes from the gun. But
   then he walked and sat down on the curb.
Q: The guy that done the shooting walked and sat down on the curb?
A: On the pavement.[22]

At that point, realizing that he had pushed the questioning too far,
Williams had a brief consultation off the record with Weinglass. He came
back and tried to establish that the last statement of Harkins' did not conform with what he had told police investigators—which it did not, as will
be discussed below. But Williams was blocked in that endeavor by Grant
and Sabo. Williams then moved to strike the earlier testimony, in the following interchange with the judge:

Mr. Williams: Then I move to strike that testimony. If I can't inquire
   into it I move to strike it.
The Court: You asked the question.
Mr. Williams: No, that was nonresponsive to my question.
The Court: Well, you should have objected then and asked to strike it.
Mr. Williams: I now move to strike it.
The Court: Too late, it's there.
Mr. Williams: Your Honor, I have never read any evidence code that
   puts a time frame on when I can move to strike.
The Court: Well, sorry about that, Counselor. I can't help what you
   read.[23]

Grant, obviously happy that Harkins in this last bit of testimony was
pinning the shooting on Abu-Jamal, wisely declined to cross-examine the
witness. This gave the defense no opportunity to come back and try to
question him further about the conflict between his latest testimony and
what he had told police investigators right after the shooting.

In his book, Williams ignores the problem posed by that last answer.
But he argues that Harkins' original account of the incident, as provided to
police investigators, matches up to other evidence much better than that
of Cynthia White, the only other witness who claimed to have seen the
entire shooting incident. His main point is that in Harkins' account, from
the time Faulkner was grabbed and spun around, there is no point at which
the officer could have shot his assailant. Therefore, Williams concludes,
Cynthia White's testimony and the prosecution's claim that Abu-Jamal was
shot by Faulkner *after* Abu-Jamal fired the first shot into his back is incor-

rect. By Harkins' account, Abu-Jamal must have been shot by Faulkner *before* Faulkner himself was shot. This scenario, if correct, would have at a minimum called for a charge other than first-degree murder.

As Williams writes:

> When did Mumia receive that gunshot wound to the chest, if not at the time suggested by Cynthia White? No doubt Mumia ran to the scene at a time when Officer Faulkner was having difficulty with Billy Cook. As Mumia approached, running, the officer may have panicked, fearing that this black man, with "MOVE-type hair"—and thus from Faulkner's probable point of view, with MOVE-type anger—was intent on interfering in his struggle with the driver. The trajectory of the bullet [that hit Abu-Jamal] is indisputably downward; the likely positioning of Mumia's torso as he is running toward the scene is slightly bent forward (typical for a runner). Faulkner fires from a slight elevation above the street by virtue of being on the curb. A bullet striking Mumia in the chest would thus enter and travel through his torso in a downward trajectory.[24]

Williams goes on to suggest that with Abu-Jamal felled by Faulkner's bullet, someone else—possibly a passenger in Cook's car—grabbed and shot the officer. He bases this theory on the testimony of witness Scanlan (one of the prosecution's eye-witnesses), who described the shooter as having had an "afro" hairstyle, while Abu-Jamal at the time had his trademark dreadlocks. Harkins too, as we saw above, described the shooter as being "heavier than the officer," while Abu-Jamal was, at the time of the shooting, quite thin.

As noted, Williams ignores the testimony of Harkins at the PCRA which placed the shooter as subsequently sitting down on the curb, thus suggesting Abu-Jamal was the shooter, and with good reason. This is an area that would have to be investigated further because it does not conform to Harkins' initial police interviews. Harkins had originally told police he was not sure he could identify the shooter. Indeed, in his first interview with a police detective, Harkins had said that once he saw the cop shot, he drove off down the street until he met a police wagon, where he reported the shooting. He did not say he waited to see what the shooter did after firing the fatal shot. Conceivably, by the time of the PCRA hearing, he had read about the case so often he knew the official story line and had adopted it, consciously or subconsciously. Also possible is that having been in the hands of police investigators a number of times, Harkins may have had that scenario suggested to him by police. In any event, the importance of the Harkins testimony for the defense is that it raises serious questions about the veracity of the other witnesses in the case, none of whom mentioned any altercation between the shooter and Faulkner. If Harkins is accurate, his testimony also makes it clear that Abu-Jamal must have been shot *before* Faulkner was.

If Harkins' testimony offered a new theory about the shooting, other witnesses at the PCRA hearing offered something else: strong evidence that the police and the prosecution weren't particularly concerned about finding out the truth of what had occurred. Rather it seems as if they were intent on pinning the crime on the man they obviously had decided was guilty, essentially from the moment they arrived at the scene.

Dessie Hightower, one of the few witnesses called by the defense in the original 1982 trial, had always been one of the most compelling of witnesses in the case. An accounting student and an upstanding citizen with no police record, he had volunteered himself to police as a witness right after the shooting, and told them he had seen someone he suspected was the shooter fleeing along the south side of Locust Street towards 12th Street. Significantly, as we saw earlier in Chapter 6, Hightower had come forward to police after the shooting because he saw police beating Abu-Jamal, and wanted to let them know that they were "beating the wrong guy."

Hightower wasn't the only witness to say police beat Abu-Jamal at the scene. Even Cynthia White, the prosecution's star witness, said she had seen police hitting him on the ground with their blackjacks. Physical damage on his body, including bruises and abrasions and a long cut on his head that required sutures, confirmed that testimony. The beating meted out to the gravely wounded Abu-Jamal by arriving police makes it obvious they thought they had the killer—or at least one of the killers—of a comrade in their hands. (Beating of suspects by arresting officers—especially police shooting suspects—is an established and continuing tradition in Philadelphia.) At the same time, though, it appears that police did at least initially pursue the idea that there may have been someone else involved in the shooting. As we will see later in this chapter, they even picked up several suspects, including Arnold Howard and possibly Kenneth Freeman. But despite the early statements of several witnesses concerning someone fleeing the scene of the crime, the police quickly dropped all investigations, except of Abu-Jamal. And once they settled on Abu-Jamal as the only suspect, they apparently went to work trying to alter the recollections of, or to undercut or intimidate those witnesses who claimed to have seen others at the scene of the crime. Thus Hightower, for his trouble in coming forward, instead of having his lead followed up, found himself repeatedly grilled by police, and singled out as the only witness to be subjected to a polygraph test at the police homicide unit. Hightower testified at the post-conviction hearing that during that exam, he was asked a lot of questions, but never was he asked about his statement concerning a fleeing suspect.

> By Mr. Weinglass:
> Q: When you read over these questions, they never even asked you that
>   when you were hooked up to the polygraph?
> A: That question's not down here.
> Q: Right, so you were telling them on the morning of the occurrence,
>   you were telling them a week later, you consistently said you saw the
>   man run away after the shooting, and when they hooked you up to
>   the polygraph they didn't even ask you that question?
> A: The question's not down here, Counselor.[25]

But the striking thing about the polygraph test administered to Hightower less than a week after the shooting, during a nearly six-hour session of grilling by police at a police station, was not just that police investigators never asked a question to test the veracity of his claim concerning a fleeing suspect. It was also that it was unique. There was no effort at all made by police or prosecutors to test the veracity of other eye witnesses who, unlike the upstanding Hightower, had criminal backgrounds. These witnesses had ample reason to be less than forthright or truthful in their accounts. No polygraph test was administered to eyewitness Cynthia White, though she was a prostitute whose arrest record would fill a good-sized notebook, and who thus had plenty of motivation to lie to make police happy. No polygraph test was administered to witness Robert Chobert, even though at the time of the shooting he was serving five years' probation for felony arson of a school, and was—in violation of that probation—driving a taxi cab. He was also drunk according to some accounts, with his driver's license already suspended for drunken driving. Clearly, again, this was a witness who had a motivation to say what he thought police wanted to hear. It doesn't take a rocket scientist, as the saying goes, to suggest the veracity of this witness might be scrutinized under polygraph. But police never conducted one on Chobert.

One has to wonder then what the police were trying to accomplish in hauling Hightower in to the station, keeping him there for over five hours, and then administering a polygraph test—especially a test that omitted asking him about a key element of his testimony concerning a fleeing suspect. The prosecution clearly had no interest in undermining the credibility of White and Chobert, the two witnesses who were most central to the prosecution's case, but was anxious to try and undermine the credibility of a witness whose testimony contradicted their stories.

As investigators at the time must have realized right away, Hightower's account of what happened on December 9, 1981 seriously discredits the prosecution's case. First there's his testimony about a fleeing suspect—an enormous problem because McGill's "open-and-shut case" was premised on the assumption that there was no one at the scene besides Faulkner, Abu-Jamal and Cook. Secondly, Hightower recalled hearing three shots in rapid succession—the same number of shots reported by Harkins—and then several more. According to the prosecution's story, there should have been one shot—Abu-Jamal firing into Faulkner's back— then another, as the wounded and falling Faulkner fired at Abu-Jamal, and then ultimately four more shots as Abu-Jamal stood over the prone officer and fired at him, emptying his gun. And there was a final discrepancy between Hightower's testimony and the prosecution's version. Though he was looking directly at the scene from across the intersection of 13th Street and Locust, Hightower says he never saw either White or Chobert, both of whom, by their own accounts, should have been clearly in the foreground of his line of vision.

At the PCRA hearing, Prosecutor Grant sought to undercut Hightower's testimony in several ways. First he tried to claim that Hightower had failed the lie-detector test when asked whether he had seen Abu-Jamal with a gun. Hightower, testifying under oath at the PCRA hearing, insisted that he had never seen Abu-Jamal with a gun. He also denied that he had ever been told he had failed the polygraph test. Second, Grant tried to show that Hightower knew Abu-Jamal prior to the shooting, suggesting that he therefore may have been trying to help the defendant by his testimony. Hightower conceded that he had once met Abu-Jamal years earlier; as a leader of the Philadelphia Student Union, he had been interviewed by Abu-Jamal, who was then a reporter for radio station WDAS. But Hightower pointed out that, at the time of his first interview with police, an hour after the shooting, he had no idea who the suspect was. Knowing Abu-Jamal would not have been pertinent at that point. Talking about the first time Hightower was interviewed by a police detective, at about 5 a.m. on December 9, Weinglass asked:

Q: At that time, did you know that Mr. Jamal was the person involved

    in this case?
A: No, I didn't.
Q: Did you know who was the suspect who was taken into custody?
A: You mean at that point in time?
Q: Yes.
A: No, I did not.
Q: And you were interviewed, were you not?
A: Yes.
Q: That night?
A: Yes, I was.
Q: Did you go down to the police station voluntarily?
A: Yes, I—yes, I did. I believe so.
Q: And you sat there and you were asked questions and you gave answers?
A: Yes.
Q: Do you remember telling the police that night, within one hour of the shooting, when you didn't know who was the suspect, you said, quoting Counsel [Grant], I seen a male run away wearing a red-and-black sweater. And then later you said I did see the guy who ran and he looked Jamaican too. And then later you said I just seen the back of him. He had on dark-colored pants and a red-and-black sweater, that's all I seen. He was about five-foot-eleven or six-foot.
A: I do remember, yes.[26]

Grant also tried to suggest that Hightower was not certain the person he saw running away from the scene was a man or a woman. It is true that on the stand at the 1982 murder trial, under cross-examination by Assistant D.A. McGill, Hightower had conceded that the person he saw might have been a woman. But at the PCRA hearing he stood solidly behind his two statements to police made the day of the shooting and a week later: that the fleeing person was a tall black male.

By Mr. Weinglass:
Q: Having read that [referring to the trial transcript when he was being cross-examined by prosecutor McGill on June 28, 1982], that question that was asked you in Court when you were testifying for the first time, do you remember saying anything to anyone that you were unsure if it was a man or a woman before you were in court?
A: I said it was a black male.
Q: Pardon?
A: I said it was a black male, five-eleven or six-foot.
Q: That's what you have always consistently said?
A: I said it was a black male, five-eleven, six-foot.
Q: Do you know if you've ever described the person you saw running as a female?
A: No, I don't.

Q: But the prosecutor in questioning you suggested that you were
   unsure. Is that right?
A: (witness shrugged shoulders.)
Q: Were you unsure?
A: I said it was a black male, five-eleven to six-foot.[27]

Why would police have backed away from pursuing leads regarding a possible second suspect or accomplice in the shooting of a fellow officer? Stuart Taylor, the lawyer and writer who followed this case for *The American Lawyer*, says, "The evidence at the scene pointed overwhelmingly to Abu-Jamal as the killer. The police may have been reluctant to develop evidence that someone else might have been involved because that would make it harder to pin the rap on him. I also imagine that if the police seriously entertained the thought that a third man had escaped, they probably had little confidence that they would ever catch him. Better the bird in the hand."

Further evidence that the police and prosecution were determined to confirm their assumption that the shooter was Abu-Jamal and were not interested in finding who—or who else—killed Officer Faulkner came just hours after the shooting. Police initially picked up a man as a suspect, but later dropped him—a man whose testimony pointed clearly to another possible suspect.

Arnold Howard, a childhood friend of the Cook brothers, was not a witness at Abu-Jamal's trial. But apparently he was an early suspect in the case. Unbeknownst to Abu-Jamal and his attorney Anthony Jackson, police had picked up Howard on the morning of December 9, 1981, in a pre-dawn visit to his home, and brought him to Homicide for questioning. Investigators had found a driver's license replacement application form bearing Howard's name and address in Faulkner's shirt pocket. The defense had been informed about the discovery of the license application form, but had been incorrectly advised by the prosecution that it had been found later on a seat of Cook's vehicle. The difference between where the item was actually found and where the defense was told it had been found is profound in its implications. If Faulkner had it in his possession, it means he had to have obtained it *before* the shooting occurred. How did it get there? Did he search the vehicle first? No one at the trial testified that Faulkner had done so (nor is it likely he would have done so without back-up and with Cook standing nearby). The only plausible alternative is that he must have obtained the license application from someone in the car. That would have had to be Billy Cook. But that doesn't make sense: Cook had a license of his own and therefore would have had no reason to give him Howard's document. If not Cook, was someone else in the car?

The possibility that there was someone else in the car besides Cook is corroborated by Faulkner's actions. The defense in this case has always wondered why Faulkner, an experienced cop, after announcing that he was making a traffic stop, quickly got back on the air and called for back-up. This seems an odd request for a routine traffic stop involving a single driver. What made Faulkner call for help? If he suddenly noticed that there were two people in the car, however, he might well have decided back-up was a wise idea. The presence of a passenger in the car might also explain two other things: why Faulkner reacted so aggressively to the alleged punch Cook took at him, and why he might have shot at Abu-Jamal as he was crossing the street, instead of just ordering him to halt. Faulkner may have been overwhelmed and gravely threatened.

Questioned at the PCRA hearing by defense counsel Weinglass, Howard recalled his trip to Homicide:

A: I had no choice.
Q: Why do you say that?
A: They came and got me.
Q: How many of them were there?
A: About five of them.
Q: Were they in uniform or out of uniform?
A: Cars outside in uniform and a couple detectives came to my home....
Q: Was it in the afternoon?
A: No, it was in the evening, at night. Before daybreak.
Q: Before daybreak. So would that be the early morning hours?
A: Yes, sir, the early morning hours.
Q: And how long did you remain at Homicide?
A: It was the thing that they were shifting me around for about 72 hours.[28]

Howard testified that he was asked to sign a statement, and he said that he was given a test "to see if I fired a gun or something."[29] (This makes clear that the police were cognizant of the importance of the wipe test. Yet they claim they never bothered to test Abu-Jamal's hands.)[*] He went on to say that he was told he was suspected of having been involved in the crime:

Q: Did the officers tell you why they were checking your hands?...
The Witness: Yes, they said by my license being found at the scene of a

---

[*] Interestingly too, at the PCRA hearing, the prosecution tried to argue that a wipe test hadn't been given to Abu-Jamal because in his alleged struggling against police arresting him, he could have rubbed off the trace chemicals. They also suggested that at the hospital, too much time had elapsed to get a reliable result. Yet according to Howard, they tested his hands more than an hour after the event, even though he'd been home and, had he been the shooter, could have washed his hands.

homicide, that I was somewhat involved in it.

Q: I'm sorry, that you were...?

A: Somewhat involved in it. They was thinking that I was some kind of fourth person that was supposed to be down there.[30]

Howard said police initially told him he was suspected of having been "the person who ran away" from the scene.[31] He went on to testify that he was later released after he explained to police investigators that he had loaned his application form to another mutual friend of his and Billy Cook's named Kenneth Freeman. He also claimed to have been far away from the scene at the time of the shooting, an alibi he backed up by a sales receipt from a Pathmark drugstore on Aramingo Avenue, a good distance away from the scene of the shooting. It was dated 4 a.m. on December 9, 1981—almost the exact time of the shooting.

That Howard was picked up in the first place makes it apparent that at least some police investigators, even after the arrest of Abu-Jamal as a suspect, were initially following up on witness testimony that someone else had fled the scene. They were seriously considering and pursuing the possibility of another suspect or an accomplice. Howard also said he was not alone at the station. Also brought in that morning, according to Howard, were two other black men: Kenneth Freeman, who was the co-owner, with Billy Cook, of a trinket stand located at 16th and Chestnut Streets, and a pimp known by the street name of Sweet Sam.

Howard attempted to state that Freeman was driving Cook's VW the morning of the shooting. If correct, this would certainly explain why Faulkner had the form in his pocket. If Freeman had been the driver when the car was pulled over, he might have handed Faulkner the only thing he had resembling a driver's license: Howard's application.

But Howard was blocked from that testimony by an objection of prosecutor Arlene Fisk. No one has been able to ask Freeman what he was doing that day, because he is dead—police claimed they found him, bound, naked and dead in a vacant lot on May 13, 1985, allegedly the victim of a drug overdose. But suspicion lingers: this is an unusual position for an overdose victim to be in. Oddly, his death occurred the same day that police fire-bombed the communal MOVE house on Osage Avenue, burning down a whole neighborhood, and killing 11 MOVE members, including five children. Moreover, despite the odd way his body was found, Freeman's death was officially listed as being from natural causes: a heart attack at the age of 31.

Police and prosecutors have never explained why they dropped efforts to prosecute Freeman, but there is reason to suspect that he was at the scene of the shooting. For one thing, Billy Cook's attorney, Daniel Alva (who also served as an attorney for Freeman), recalls being told by Cook, shortly after the shooting, that he had been driving around that early morning "with Ken Freeman." Freeman, who was stockier than Abu-Jamal, was known to own a gun, and also wore his hair at that time in an Afro, which fits with the description of the shooter given by Michael Scanlan.[32] It is also clear that after the Faulkner shooting the police had their eye on Freeman. In February 1982, only two months after Faulkner's shooting, Freeman was arrested in his home, where he was found hiding in his attic armed with a .22 caliber pistol, explosives and a supply of ammunition. At that time, he was not charged with anything.

According to a scenario long popular among some Abu-Jamal supporters, Abu-Jamal was shot by Faulkner as he was crossing the street, at which point the officer was shot by Freeman. This theory is supported by the testimony of several witnesses, most notably Robert Harkins, the eye witness to the shooting who was not called at the trial by either side, but who as we saw above testified at the post-conviction proceeding as an unfriendly defense witness under subpoena. Harkins' testimony explained the nature of Faulkner's back wound and also the otherwise unexplainable injury to Faulkner's knee and a tear in his pants leg. As explained earlier, his testimony also suggests that Abu-Jamal must have been shot *before* the Faulkner shooting, since Faulkner, on his hands and knees facing away from his assailant, was in no position to fire at that point.

Any shot fired later by Faulkner would have had to come while he was lying flat on his back on the ground. This would make Abu-Jamal's downward-coursing wound impossible to explain—even using prosecutor McGill's creative ballistics. The main difficulty with this theory is that the evidence of Freeman's having been present at the scene is sketchy. True, there is the mysterious license document bearing the name of Cook family friend Arnold Howard, which Howard later claimed he had loaned to Freeman, and which was recovered from Faulkner's pocket. And there is also testimony from several witnesses that the shooter had an Afro—the hairstyle worn by Freeman, but not by Abu-Jamal or his brother. But Freeman's own behavior following the shooting was odd for someone who had slain a cop, and who probably would have been seen doing it by Abu-Jamal's brother. Even after his and Cook's trinket stand had been burned down—by vengeful police, many at the time suspected—and after he himself had been arrested once at his home on a weapons charge,

Freeman never left town until he died in 1985.

What is certain is that the prosecution and the police, after a few initial efforts, suddenly and inexplicably lost interest in pursuing other possible suspects besides Abu-Jamal. There is evidence that, once having decided to make a case against him as the lone killer, they weren't beyond pressuring witnesses into supporting that scenario. As we saw in Chapter 2, pressuring witnesses into giving false testimony favorable to the prosecution, even in murder cases, was practically standard practice in the Philadelphia law enforcement community back in the 1980s—particularly in the Center City area where Faulkner was slain. And at the 1995 PCRA hearing, there was plenty of evidence brought forward by the defense to demonstrate that witnesses were pressured in this case. First, of course, there was Hightower, who though a voluntary witness who had come forward to help, was pressured— uniquely among those witnesses interviewed by police—to endure a tense grilling and a session with a polygraph machine.

Then there was Robert Chobert, the cab driver.

Chobert, at the 1982 trial, had testified that he saw Abu-Jamal pump several shots into the prone Faulkner. And it was his testimony, above all, that prosecutor McGill cited in trying to convince jurors that they were considering the case of a vicious killer. In his summation, he particularly vouched for the credibility of the white Chobert, saying:

> Ladies and gentlemen, he knows what he saw and I don't care
> what you say or what anybody says, that is what he saw. Do you
> think anybody could get him to say anything that wasn't the truth?[33]

But had Chobert traded his testimony in hopes of a favor regarding his suspended driver's license? Weinglass got to the heart of the issue quickly. At the PCRA hearing, he asked Chobert if he had had any conversation with McGill regarding this:

A: Yes I did.
Q: Do you recall what he said to you at the time?
A: Well, he said he'd look into it.
Q: And was that before the trial?
A: I don't know, probably during the trial, sometime during the trial. I don't know.
Q: All right. And when he said he'll look into it, that was in response to something that you had mentioned, was it not?
A: Yes, sir.
Q: And what had you told him?
A: I asked him if he could help me find out how I could get my license back.[34]

Chobert went on to say that he needed his license back because he was a taxicab driver and (remarkably, for a person who had been convicted of arson of a school for pay) a school bus driver. He needed his license in order to do either or both of those activities. Assistant district attorney Arlene Fisk initially attempted to get Chobert to back off of his claim that he spoke about the license problem with McGill before or during the trial, and he seemed unclear. But on redirect, when Weinglass asked him pointedly whether he had ever talked with McGill after his testimony at the trial, Chobert said, "No, I never talked to him after the trial."[35] The significance of this is clear. Whether or not the prosecutor was involved in trying to curry favor with a witness by offering to fix his legal problem, it seems clear that Chobert at least was hoping that he could get some help in high places. He couldn't have failed to consider that providing the testimony which the prosecution obviously was seeking could only work to his benefit. McGill (who claims to have only a vague recollection of any conversation with Chobert regarding his license problem), denies having offered any help to Chobert. But that dodges the issue. If McGill didn't offer any help with the license, then there is no prosecutorial misconduct. Yet it still leaves open the possibility—indeed even the likelihood—that this witness thought he could benefit himself by saying what he felt the prosecution wanted to hear.

Chobert's statements did indeed shift towards the prosecution. As we saw in Chapter 5, in his initial statement to police which had been made within an hour of the shooting, Chobert had claimed that the shooter had been "kind of heavy set," and that he'd been wearing "a light tan shirt and jeans." Abu-Jamal was lightly built at the time, and had been wearing dark clothes. Chobert had also claimed that the shooter had walked 30-35 steps away, and that another man had run half-way down the block after the first shot was fired. At trial, after having been interviewed several times by police and prepped by the prosecutor, he whittled away those 30-40 steps to a few steps. The runner, meanwhile, had simply vanished from his narrative.

More importantly, though, except for the equally suspect witness Cynthia White, who said she hadn't seen his cab until after police arrived on the scene, no other witnesses recalled even seeing Chobert's taxicab parked where he claimed it had been: directly behind Faulkner's police patrol car. This is nothing short of astonishing; a taxicab is a hard thing to miss. Since some witnesses reported seeing a cab some distance from the crime scene, it is possible that after police arrived, they waved Chobert

over to the spot behind Faulkner's cruiser. The defense claims that in fact
Chobert told their investigator, before his testimony at the PCRA, that he
had not been parked there, but was actually around the corner from the
incident.* But efforts by Weinglass to introduce that testimony were
blocked by the judge:

> By Mr. Weinglass:
> Q: Didn't you tell Mr. Newman on Sunday, August 6th, when he read
> you those statements [made initially to police investigators], that
> those statements are not accurate?
> Ms. Fisk: Objection, Your Honor.
> The Court: I will have to sustain that. He is admitted just for a limited
> purpose.
> Mr. Weinglass: Well, it is being limited on this side.
> The Court: No, it was limited to her too, only to identify them. Only
> that he identified his signature and he made them.
> Mr. Weinglass: They [the prosecution] brought in the statements, Your
> Honor, now I should be allowed to go into those statements.
> The Court: No, because you didn't allow her to go into the statements.
> Now you are on redirect.[36]

Meanwhile, there was more evidence of the pressuring of witnesses,
which came to light during the post-conviction hearing. Indeed, the press
and spectators at the hearing got an object lesson in the extent of that pressure when the defense put Veronica Jones on the stand. It wasn't easy for
the defense to get her there. Initially, though defense attorneys felt strongly that Jones, a former prostitute, had been pressured at the time of the original trial into giving false testimony concerning what she had seen the
night of the shooting, they were reluctant to call her to testify at the hearing. They didn't know how to locate her and needed the prosecution to
provide an address. But they had seen the police threatening to arrest
another of their witnesses, Dessie Hightower, in order to bring him to
court. The defense had also seen evidence that led them to believe police
had intimidated Harkins, who had refused to talk to defense attorneys
except in the presence of police detectives. Because the defense hadn't
called Jones during the hearing, the prosecution objected to a belated effort
to call her. In September, 1996, more than a year after the PCRA hearing

---

*George Michael Newman now claims that he was at the courthouse and available to testify
himself as to what Chobert had told him, but was never called by Weinglass. Newman's testimony, which would have been classed as hearsay, would not have counted for much, and probably would have been barred by Sabo in any case. Weinglass claims he couldn't get Newman to
testify, because he said he was working on a book on the case at the time and didn't want to get
questioned.

had concluded, Abu-Jamal and his defense team were back in court, arguing to Judge Sabo that they had located Jones on their own, that she was
ready to testify, and that they wanted the hearing reopened. As Weinglass
explained, in arguing for the additional hearing:

> That's why we wanted her address. We clearly indicated right
> at the outset we wanted Veronica Jones' address and we wanted all
> the other witnesses' addresses so we could bring them to Court, not
> have the police or detectives bring them. Particularly true with the
> case of Veronica Jones, who had previously been threatened and
> coerced into giving false testimony.[37]

In the end, the state supreme court agreed, and ordered an additional
day of testimony from Jones. But before she could take the stand, Judge
Sabo made it clear he was not happy with being overruled by a higher
court, and not happy with having her testify. When Jones' public defender
came in and said that Jones was willing to waive her Fifth Amendment
right (against self-incrimination) in testifying about prior false testimony,
Sabo threatened her, incorrectly. He said that she faced "seven to 14" years
for perjury "if you say something now which is different from what you said
at the trial." (The maximum sentence for perjury is seven years.)[38] This
was a clear case of intimidation by the judge, as demonstrated by one simple fact. If the witness was alleging she perjured herself because of police or
prosecutorial pressure, there is not much likelihood of her being successfully convicted of perjury, nor would a prosecutor be likely to ask for such
harsh retaliation for a witness who came forward. But, just to make Jones
nervous, and as an illustration of how far away the prosecution got from
searching for the truth, prosecutor Arlene Fisk hastened to add that the
seven-year maximum penalty could apply "for each incident of perjury,
your honor."[39]

Jones, who said that her own attorney had not mentioned the severi-
ty of the potential penalty for perjury to her, remained resolute. As a lay
person sitting on the stand she had no way of knowing it was probably an
empty threat. In the face of what she must have believed to be a potentially
heavy sentence, she displayed incredible courage, telling the judge that she
was still ready to go forward with her testimony.

And that testimony was to provide the high drama of the hearing—
not so much for what she said (which was dramatic enough), as for how she
was treated by the prosecutor and the judge.

Jones began by recalling that initially, on December 15, 1981, she had
told police investigators who came to her house that she had seen two men

run from the scene. Then she stated that, when actually put on the stand
by the defense in the 1982 trial, she had untruthfully claimed that she had-
n't in fact seen two men leaving the scene. Indeed, as has been discussed,
Jackson, who had not interviewed Jones before putting her on the stand,
had been caught by surprise by that testimony. He had expected her to
repeat what she had originally told the detectives.

Weinglass asked her how she had come to change her testimony back
then. Jones, who at the time in 1982 had been in jail awaiting trial on a
robbery and weapons possession charge, said she had been scared because
of the involvement of two police detectives. They had spoken with her
before she went on the stand to be questioned by attorney Jackson.

Meeting with her in her cell, she said these two detectives had offered
to help her if she cooperated with them. They had also threatened that, if
she didn't cooperate, she could lose her children:

Q: Did you have a conversation with them?
A: I did a little talking but I did a lot of listening.
Q: What did they tell you?
A: More so they was letting me know what I was facing as far as my
   weapons charges. And, umm–excuse me. That I could, you know,
   they could help me off those charges if I helped them. And it was a
   big decision to make but this is five or ten years away from my kids.
   And right then and there my kids was all I was thinking about.
Q: And it was because of that meeting that you changed your testimo-
   ny?
A: Yes, it is. Excuse me.[40]

According to Jones, the two detectives went so far as to stay in the
back of the courtroom during her testimony in 1982. She also said they had
made it clear to her that she would benefit if she testified against Abu-
Jamal:

Q: Now getting back to your meeting with the detectives prior to your
   testifying, do you recall what it was that they said to you about your
   testimony?
A: Well, when they came to see me at the jail?
Q: Yes.
A: It was just more so that, umm, I was to name Mr. Jamal (indicating)
   as the shooter, you know. And if I was to do that, I was supposed to
   do something like this girl named Lucky White. [Lucky was Cynthia
   White's street name.] They said we made a deal with her and it was
   going to work out for her so they could make it work out for me. All
   they kept expressing was don't forget five to ten years, that's a long
   time. They kept expressing that point. So flashback my kids, that's
   all I think about is my kids.

Q: And they told you what would happen to you if you did what they wanted you to do?

A: I don't recall, sir, I don't remember.

Q: Did they say anything about the charges against you?

A: The gun charges were supposed to be removed if I went with them.[41]

As Jones was making these damning claims, she observed that her children, now grown, were in court watching her. She explained her decision to lie in court in 1982, saying:

> But I did work the street and I don't regret that. Because I took care of them, good care of them. So I don't regret that. And if I had to do it again, not to be away from my kids for ten years, I don't know what I might do, I might do the same thing again because I loved them, I loved them a lot.[42]

Jones said that the pressure on her to testify favorably for the prosecution began as early as January, 1982, just a month after Faulkner's shooting and Abu-Jamal's arrest. She said she had been picked up off the street and brought in for the night—a common experience for prostitutes operating in the Center City 6th Police District. This time was different, though, she said. Instead of being left with the rest of the women to cool her heels for a while and then get fingerprinted, she says she was taken off and questioned by detectives. Jackson had stumbled on this same story at the trial but he had been unable to present it to the jury because of objections by the prosecution—objections that were sustained by Judge Sabo:

Q: Did they say anything to you about what you should testify to?

A: Asked me if my mind had been made up what I was going to do. And these were two policemen that were usually in that area. These were suits that I met. I'm sorry. They wear suits.

Q: By the way, who is, you mentioned a person named Lucky. Who is Lucky?

A: Cynthia White. She was, she was supposed to have been a friend of mine on the street but we, we just friends out there like that. But her name was Cynthia White, we just called her Lucky.

Q: Did her name come up with the conversation?

A: Yes; they said you don't see Lucky around here, do you? In other words, they didn't pick her up. See, a number of us got picked up but I didn't get processed, okay. And when we got picked up Cynthia was not in the bunch.

...

Q: I see. And when the police mentioned Lucky to you, did they say anything about your testimony as compared to what Lucky would do?

A: Just told me I would be able to work, I wouldn't have to worry about my charges, I could work. Basically, that was it.

Q: And did they say what you would have to do in order for you to be able to work?

A: Just name Mr. Jamal as the shooter.[43]

The D.A.'s office wisely chose Fisk, a woman, to cross-examine Jones, possibly for the same reason they selected Grant, a black, to cross-examine Anthony Jackson: it made the grilling she gave Jones seem less objectionable than it might have been had a man conducted it. Nonetheless, Fisk's attack was sharp. She observed that back on June 12, 1982, Jones had been arrested on both robbery and gun possession charges, which were pending when she was placed on the stand on July 28, 1982. She also established that on July 18, there had been a hearing before a magistrate. At that juncture, Jones' bail for the gun and robbery charges was dropped from $1,000 to $300. (This is a point that, one might argue, supports Jones' contention that she was getting treated favorably by the district attorney's office.)

Fisk went on to observe that while charges in the robbery case were dropped against Jones' alleged accomplices because a witness failed to appear, Jones' case remained active, and she failed to respond to a subpoena to appear to face trial on November 19, 1982. Jones confirmed that she had skipped her court date and fled to West Virginia with her children. In 1988, Fisk said, she had been arrested on a welfare fraud charge in New Jersey, and was then extradited to Philadelphia on the original charges, pleaded no contest, and was sentenced to five years' probation.

Fisk's goal was clear: damage Jones' credibility. She tried to show Jones had been untruthful on various minor occasions, for example noting that she had not, as she claimed, had her children with her the entire six years that she had been hiding in West Virginia.

But then Fisk dropped a bombshell: she announced that Jones had been arrested for attempting to pass a bad check in 1992:

Q: Well, do I take it, ma'am, that you're unaware that there is currently a bench warrant for your arrest in Woodbury, New Jersey?

A: I don't see how: I never got a court date, they never told me that.

Q: All right. Perhaps, Your Honor, Detective Sergeant Sheenan could be asked to enter the Courtroom. I believe he is out in the hallway. And just step up to the glass.

Mr. Weinglass: Your Honor, I object to this procedure. There is no reason for this. What is Counsel attempting to demonstrate here?

Fisk: That there is an active, open bench warrant for this witness and that she has to be taken into custody with regard to this.

Weinglass: Well, this is the usual form of intimidation. It is a continuation—

The witness: This is not going to change my testimony.[44]

Fisk and the Philadelphia District Attorney's Office had carefully arranged a piece of theater designed to punish Jones and embarrass the defense—and in the process certainly also intimidate any other potential defense witnesses, such as Abu-Jamal's brother, who might be considering testifying on his behalf. As established later by testimony from a police officer from Woodbury, NJ, who was called to the stand by the defense, Fisk had contacted Woodbury Police to alert them to the defense's plan to have Jones on the stand, and had invited them to come to the courtroom and pick her up on the minor charge. This being a case involving the appeal of a convicted cop-killer, the New Jersey police were no doubt happy to oblige. And so, with Jones in tears, Fisk, over Weinglass's objections, asked Judge Sabo to have Jones arrested right off the witness stand:

> Ms. Fisk: Your Honor, I would ask no more questions. Now, Your Honor, in light of the bench warrant in effect for this witness, I would ask that the Sheriffs take her into custody. There are detectives here from New Jersey with regard to that warrant. If this witness waives her right to an extradition hearing they can certainly return her immediately to New Jersey. If she does not, she'll be processed as a fugitive from justice.[45]

Amid the tumult in the courtroom, Judge Sabo made his own bias in the case clear:

> Mr. Weinglass: They [New Jersey Police officials] knew of her whereabouts. Now Your Honor has the power to allow this witness to return, her Counsel is here, to resolve the matter in Woodbury New Jersey. [Weinglass was referring to the public defender who was representing Jones during her testimony]
> The Court: Well he could go with them, too.
> Mr. Weinglass: Which is a check issue.
> The Court: He can go with them, too.
> Mr. Weinglass: No, Your Honor, she doesn't have to be taken into custody at all. The Court could arrange for her, the Court could give her one day, one day to appear in Woodbury with her Counsel to resolve this matter. She needn't be physically taken into custody.
> The Court: Well, that is not up to me, that is up to those detectives.
> Mr. Weinglass: No, Your Honor could order that.
> The Court: Counselor, I am not going to order anything. If they arrested her outside, I don't care. That's their problem.[46]

Even Fisk was forced to correct the judge. She stated that the detectives from New Jersey had no authority to arrest Jones because

Philadelphia, where the court was located, was outside of their jurisdiction. It was she who was in fact requesting that Philadelphia sheriffs arrest her. Weinglass again asked that the process of her arrest be stayed:

> Mr. Weinglass: And Your Honor has the right to inform the Sheriffs here that you are giving her one day to surrender.
> The Court: I am not giving her anything. That warrant has been out since 1994.[47]

Under questioning by Williams, Police Detective Sergeant Timothy Sheenan from Woodbury, NJ, made an important concession shortly after a sheriff's deputy had led Jones from the courtroom. His department had been aware of Jones' address in Camden, NJ for two years, but had never bothered to serve the warrant on her during that time. The decision to pick her up, he said, came after a call and invitation from Fisk. Attorney Williams had exposed the D.A.'s game. But Judge Sabo seemed untroubled by it:

> Williams: And now what we have is evidence of Miss Fisk's enforcing a bench warrant of a defense witness at this particular time. And I want to establish that it was intentional, intentional to intimidate thus witness,
> The Court: Maybe it was. Maybe it was. So what?
> Williams: Your honor isn't concerned about that issue?
> The Court: No, I don't see what it has to do with this PCRA matter. I don't.[48]

After participating in the abuse of witness Jones (and witnessing her courage in agreeing to testify in the face of threat of a lengthy contempt sentence), Judge Sabo, acting as the factfinder, determined that Jones' testimony at the PCRA recanting her earlier trial testimony was not credible. Three years later, the state supreme court agreed with Sabo. Two more years later, Judge William Yohn, in his *habeas* decision, would uphold that determination as being "not unreasonable."* Yet at least Judge Yohn felt compelled to add that to him, reading the hearing transcript, Jones sounded credible. As he put it:

> Although I do not say that the cold paper record compels the

---

*Note that under the terms of the 1996 Anti-Terrorism and Effective Death Penalty Act, federal judges may not overturn fact-finding decisions of state courts even if these are technically wrong, as long as they are not deemed to be "unreasonable." In this instance, Yohn seems clearly to believe that the fact-finding regarding the credibility of Jones' recantation is dubious, but he is unwilling to say that Judge Sabo and the state supreme court were "unreasonable" in so deciding. He could, however, have held a hearing and taken testimony in order to make his own judgement.

conclusion that Jones was incredible in recanting her testimony, I conclude that the state courts did not unreasonably determine that Jones was not credible in 1996.[49]

In fact, if the "cold paper record" looked convincing to him, Yohn might have been more gripped had he been sitting in the courtroom watching the events unfold. Jones refused to change her testimony, despite being moved to tears. She showed a remarkable attitude of defiance upon being told she was to be humiliated in front of her children and led from the courtroom in custody. Her motivations were clear and obvious to observers: at considerable cost of subjecting herself to such abuse at the hands of the state, and at the risk of years in jail, she was clearing her conscience. Fisk tried to suggest that because Jones had lied about prior arrests and her prior behavior as a young mother and a prostitute, she might well be lying in her recantation of her 1982 trial testimony. But common sense would suggest that she was telling the truth. After all, her motivation for the lying cited by Fisk was to try to protect herself and her children, who were in the courtroom, from embarrassment. But in voluntarily coming forward, she could have hoped for no possible gain. What she risked was great: years in jail for perjury in order to state under oath that she had given false testimony in 1982. (One has to ask, if the "cold paper record" left Yohn feeling uncertain about what Jones was really like on the stand, why he didn't at least order an evidentiary hearing on that one claim so he could see her on the stand in person. He did not do so.)

If Jones was telling the truth that she had lied on the stand at Abu-Jamal's trial—and her manner and bearing on the stand certainly strongly suggest that she was—the state of Pennsylvania has a lot to answer for. First, according to Jones' original statement to police and to her testimony at the PCRA hearing, there were other possible suspects who had fled the scene of the shooting. Second, it means the police were attempting to pressure prostitutes into giving false testimony against Abu-Jamal "like Lucky" in return for being allowed to walk the street untroubled by vice officers.

Was Lucky's (Cynthia White's) eye-witness testimony a lie like Jones said her own testimony was? There's nobody to ask, since White reportedly died in Camden, NJ on September 2, 1992, apparently of a drug overdose. (Attorney Len Weinglass, like many other supporters of Abu-Jamal, including his current defense team, remains skeptical about the report of White's death. He notes that she was listed as a "wanted felon" as late as 1997—five years after her reported death. In fact, the listing of deaths in New Jersey by Social Security Number for 1992 and later years does not include White's number. The speculation, for which there is no supporting evidence, is that she might be in some kind of perhaps informal witness protection program that is hiding her from Abu-Jamal.) In any case, as we have seen in Chapter 2, the Philadelphia Police Department's record—especially in the 6th Police District—is rife with eliciting false testimony from prostitutes during the late 1970s, early 1980s and on into the mid 1990s. The combined record of police corruption and Jones' willingness to risk jail for perjury might well have raised a "reasonable doubt" in some jurors' minds, had these been presented fairly and honestly at trial. Would this have influenced the jurors' decision? We'll never know.

There was further evidence to support Jones' claim that she had been pressured to give false testimony at the trial—evidence that she wasn't alone in facing such pressure. But as with much of the evidence in this case, it would not be a clear-cut win for either side. The conclusion of Abu-Jamal's post-conviction hearing had been delayed a year. Then, on orders of the supreme court, another several days of hearings were held to allow testimony from another witness: Pamela Jenkins. She was a prostitute who also claimed she had been pressured in an effort to get her to give false testimony in the case. Jenkins, who figured prominently in the conviction of corrupt police officers Thomas F. Ryan and John D. Baird, detailed in Chapter 2, had for a number of years accepted money from those officers in return for giving false testimony against people arrested by them. At the time of her PCRA hearing appearance she was awaiting trial on felony charges and was thus in a vulnerable position vis-à-vis the district attorney's office. Jenkins nonetheless stated at the hearing that within three days of the shooting of Officer Faulkner, Ryan was trying to convince her to lie and say she had been at the scene of the shooting, and that she had seen Abu-Jamal shoot Faulkner.

Jenkins, who claims she was "sleeping with" Ryan around the time of the shooting, says she refused to agree to give that false testimony. She also offered some information concerning the prosecution's star witness in that case: Cynthia "Lucky" White. She says that she knew White in 1981, and that White, like a number of prostitutes, was at the time a police inform-ant who provided information to the police in return for money and pro-tection. She additionally claimed to have seen White at a crack house five years after her reported "death"—in 1997.

Jenkins' credibility as a witness is supported by two key facts. One is that, at the time of her testimony she was facing felony charges. As Weinglass pointed out at the time of her testimony, these charges were lev-

eled at her within a week of the ruling from the state supreme court ordering her testimony.[50] These charges, if anything, would have served as an
incentive to cooperate with the prosecution. But it didn't work. In testifying against the prosecution's case, she was hardly acting in her own best
interests. The other factor buttressing her credibility is this: she had also
testified in other cases concerning Ryan and other corrupt police officers.
That testimony about having been paid to give false evidence was found
credible. It held up in court and contributed to the convictions of those
officers. Furthermore, her testimony was so credible that it also contributed
to the release from prison of a number of people who had been wrongly
convicted of felonies.

But the prosecution also had cards to play. They presented documentary evidence showing that Ryan had not been a police officer in December
1981 at the time Jenkins claimed she had been pressured by him. They also
proved that Jenkins had not been a student at the school where she says she
first met Ryan during a truancy arrest. It is still possible that Jenkins was
telling the truth. For one thing, Ryan himself, the officer she claims tried
to elicit perjured testimony from her concerning Abu-Jamal, first tried to
claim that he had known Jenkins starting in 1982—after the shooting. He
claimed that he had only slept with her briefly during 1984. But under further questioning, Ryan said that he had known Jenkins as far back as
1981—before the shooting. He also admitted that he had told FBI investigators in the corruption case that led to his imprisonment that he had been
sleeping with her when she was just 15. That also would have put the start
of their relationship well back into to 1981. Perhaps they began when Ryan
was in the police academy or working as a truant officer. Despite these possibilities, the documentary evidence provided by the prosecution left
Jenkins' credibility damaged.

During the additional PCRA hearing session held to question Jenkins,
the defense also put a police officer named Lawrence Boston on the stand.
Boston, who had been a foot patrol police officer in the 13th Street area
back in the 1981-82 period, supported Jenkin's testimony that Cynthia
White also went by the street name Lucky. He said that he had been told
by other prostitutes on the street in the period following the Faulkner
shooting that White was living in a condominium near a golf course outside of Camden, NJ.[51]

Despite continuous obstructions by the judge to lines of questioning,
and despite his quashing of most of their subpoenas, Abu-Jamal's defense
team at the post-conviction hearing was able to raise serious questions. The

team cast doubt on the credibility of the prosecution's main witnesses, on the integrity of the police investigation of the crime, and even cast doubt Abu-Jamal's guilt.

But there were problems, too. Some questioning of witnesses was not thorough enough, even putting Judge Sabo's clear obstructionism as a factor aside. For example, witnesses like Harkins and Hightower and other witnesses who had been at the scene were never specifically asked, "Did you see a taxi cab parked behind Faulkner's police cruiser?"

Another mistake was made concerning procedures set forth by Judge Sabo for calling as a witness Wakshul's partner, Officer Stephen Trombetta. When Sabo insisted on a filing explaining what the defense hoped to learn from his testimony, no effort was made to comply. As a result of this slip-up, Trombetta never testified at the PCRA hearing. Since Trombetta was with Abu-Jamal at the time he supposedly blurted out his confession, but never reported anything about a confession, his testimony could have been important. Trombetta, who had been in the paddy wagon with Abu-Jamal along with Wakshul, might also have been asked about the alleged confession in the wagon attributed to the defendant by Inspector Alfonse Giordano. As we saw in Chapter 2, this claim was made in Giordano's initial statement after the shooting but never introduced at trial because Giordano subsequently was indicted for and later convicted of corruption and would have made a disastrous witness for the prosecution. The point in asking Trombetta about Giordano's claim to hearing a confession, which Trombetta and his partner Wakshul never reported hearing, is that it would help demonstrate an early effort by Philadelphia Police to manufacture such evidence against Abu-Jamal. Giordano had been the officer in charge of the crime scene.

Neither did the defense call Anthony Coletta, the emergency room resident who treated both Faulkner and Abu-Jamal. He had been subpoenaed by the defense and was prepared to testify at the hearing. Coletta has repeatedly said, including in two interviews for this book, that Abu-Jamal never made a confession in the ER. Just as important, in Coletta's view, Abu-Jamal was so near to passing out from blood loss and could hardly speak at all that he would have had difficulty "shouting out" a confession as the hospital security guard, Durham, claimed.

Weinglass explained his decision not to call Coletta: he was concerned that the doctor, by not saying such a shouting out would have been medically impossible, might have done more harm than good.

Most critically, Billy Cook never testified, though he had at least at first reportedly indicated a willingness to do so. The prosecution, and now one of the prior defense lawyers, Rachel Wolkenstein, claim that Weinglass decided not to call him, despite his claim to the court that he simply couldn't locate him—something Weinglass strenuously denies. There is also a dispute as to whether the decision not to have Abu-Jamal himself testify was made by the defendant or by Weinglass. Significantly, under questioning by Judge Sabo, Abu-Jamal insisted that he was not going to testify "on advice of counsel."

Perhaps most importantly, as mentioned earlier, the defense had subpoenaed, yet never called to the stand, prosecutor McGill. Had he been called, he could have been asked to explain his peremptory rejection of 11 black potential jurors. Although the prosecution objected to McGill's being asked about anything but jury selection, and Sabo indicated he would support that limitation, the prosecution could at least have tried to inquire about what the circumstances were of the so-called "round table meeting" he led where word of a confession first surfaced and about the story behind his production of a typed report of a confession allegedly taken down from Durham by her boss at Jefferson Hospital. This at least would have provided a basis for raising those issues on appeal later. Despite his willingness to respond to a subpoena served upon him and his presence in the courtroom, he was never called to the stand. These and other problems made the hearing less convincing for the defense than it might have been. It must be added, however, that given Judge Sabo's tight control over the defense attorneys' ability to question witnesses, it's not clear that they could have gotten much more by attempting to question further witnesses, or to question existing witnesses further.

Added to the defense errors and omissions at the hearing, the prosecution scored some points of its own. Where Harkins had earlier told police that he couldn't identify the shooter, now at the PCRA hearing he had altered his testimony to say that Faulkner's assailant had walked a few feet and sat down on the curb. Prosecutors, with the support of Judge Sabo, were able to let that testimony stand by blocking defense efforts to question Harkins further concerning the conflict between his new testimony and his earlier statements to police. Prosecutors were able to undermine the credibility of Anthony Jackson by getting him to admit that he had received at least some outside funds to hire experts. They also managed to get Jones to admit that she had been untruthful in some of her PCRA testimony (concerning her whereabouts and a welfare fraud case), and to undermine some of the testimony of other witnesses.

But something else happened at the PCRA hearing that was to have far-reaching consequences. A rift developed within the defense team that would lead to a battle for Abu-Jamal's confidence, to a split in the team. And it would finally lead to the firing of Abu-Jamal's top legal experts, Weinglass and Williams—right at a critical juncture, in the midst of his *habeas corpus* appeal to the federal courts. The seasoned duo would be replaced by an untested pair of attorneys with very little death penalty law experience, Eliot Grossman and Marlene Kamish.

The basic issue leading to the shattering of Abu-Jamal's defense team appears to have been a dispute over the calling of certain witnesses at the PCRA hearing. Both Williams, in an interview, and Wolkenstein in an affidavit filed with the state court in 2001, have claimed that during the PCRA hearing, Wolkenstein, who was acting as an investigator for the defense team, dug up or checked out several people who claimed to have been witnesses to the shooting of Officer Faulkner. Each had a different story to tell, and each witness's story was significantly different from the others'. Williams claims that the witnesses were not credible, and that he opposed using them for fear that their testimony would weaken stronger evidence that was being brought out at the hearing. Wolkenstein, he argues, and her colleague Jon Piper, wanted to have some of these witnesses testify, despite some obvious problems with their testimony, because they claimed to have seen people other than Abu-Jamal murder Faulkner, and thus helped to support a claim of absolute innocence. Officially heading the defense team, Weinglass generally took a middle position.

For her part, Wolkenstein charges that Weinglass deliberately obstructed efforts to prove absolute innocence. In an affidavit dated August 7, 2001 and filed in the Philadelphia Court of Common Pleas as part of an attempt by Abu-Jamal and his new legal team to win a new PCRA hearing, Wolkenstein, who resigned from Abu-Jamal's defense team in 1999, says:

> The obstruction of the presentation of the exculpatory testimony of [Arnold] Beverly, [William] Singletary and [Billy] Cook as well as Jamal's own account was part and parcel of Attorneys Weinglass and Williams' refusal to present a defense that Mr. Jamal is an innocent man who is the victim of monumental police and prosecutorial misconduct including the fabrication of evidence. Attorneys Weinglass and Williams' suppression of evidence of their

client's innocence constituted disloyalty to and an effective aban-
donment of their client.[52]

The main point of dispute has become the claim of a self-described
African-American mob "hit-man" and career criminal named Arnold
Beverly. In a sworn affidavit taken by Wolkenstein in 1999, he asserted
that he and another unidentified man, and not Abu-Jamal, killed Faulkner.
Beverly claims in his declaration, and in a videotaped confession, that he
had been hired by corrupt police in the Philadelphia 6th District to kill
Faulkner, whom he claims was suspected by fellow officers of being an
informant against them working for the FBI. Beverly claims that after firing the fatal bullet into Faulkner's face (and being wounded himself by
another bullet), he fled into the subway tunnel, where, by prior arrangement, he was rescued and taken away to safety by another unidentified
police officer. In that same declaration, Beverly claims that Abu-Jamal,
who never fired a shot, was himself shot as he crossed the street, not by
Faulkner (who was already dead) but by "another cop."

Wolkenstein says she first met Beverly in 1989, when he was incarcerated at the Pennsylvania State Correctional Institute in Hunlock
Creek. At that time, she says, he told her about the hit on Faulkner, and
about Abu-Jamal's innocence, but not about his own alleged role in the
shooting. She claims that Weinglass showed little or no interest in
Beverly's story:

> Shortly after Attorney Weinglass was retained [in 1991], I
> advised him of what Arnold Beverly had told me. Attorney
> Weinglass bluntly told me he was not interested in pursuing this
> information—that it was too hot to handle—and did not want to
> discuss it further. Attorney Weinglass continued to refuse to discuss,
> let alone investigate, Beverly's account through the 1995 post-con-
> viction hearing, even though Jonathan Piper's background investi-
> gation confirmed that the Federal Bureau of Investigation had been
> investigating widespread and high-reaching police involvement in
> drug and vice rackets, including prostitution, in Philadelphia's
> Center City at the time of P.O. Faulkner's shooting.[53]*

When Beverly added the information that he was the murderer and
agreed in 1999 to sign an affidavit confessing to killing Faulkner,
Wolkenstein and Weinglass decided to test his story using a polygraph
machine. Two attempts were made, first by an expert selected by Weinglass.

---

* Piper didn't need to do an "investigation" to discover about the FBI investigation of the 6th
District during the early 1980s. That investigation was all over the newspapers all through the
1980s as dozens of police officers rounded up in the probe were tried for corruption.

The second attempt was made later by a polygrapher whom Weinglass had brought in as an expert during the PCRA hearing (to examine the police test administered to Hightower), but who this time was retained by Wolkenstein. Both testers found some elements of truth in Beverly's testimony, but both were also somewhat ambiguous in their conclusions. Weinglass and Williams argued against making use of Beverly's testimony, which they felt was bogus, and succeeded in convincing Abu-Jamal to agree with their analysis. At that point, Wolkenstein and Piper quit the case. Yet Beverly's testimony continued to haunt the case, ultimately leading, at least indirectly, to the firing of Weinglass and Williams, when Abu-Jamal changed his mind and decided to try to use it in his defense. But that was not the only issue that shattered the defense team.

Wolkenstein and Piper had also wanted Weinglass to make more of the testimony of another witness, William Singletary, who also claimed that Abu-Jamal had not shot Faulkner. Police had questioned this sturdy black Vietnam vet, who drove a tow-truck for a garage and had good relations with the police, at the scene on the morning of December 9. Unlike Beverly, Singletary was unquestionably a witness to the shooting. But he did not play a role in the trial in 1982, for either the defense or the prosecution.

According to Williams' recollection, there was a major debate within the defense team over whether to use Singletary's testimony. Williams, in his book, reveals that Wolkenstein and Piper were adamant about wanting to use him, while he adamantly opposed the idea. Weinglass was in the middle:

> We [Weinglass and Williams] agonized not so much because we suffered delusions that Singletary's account of the shooting, as opposed to the police misconduct, was plausible—we knew that it wasn't; we agonized because in a death penalty case, you discard an exculpatory witness only after thorough exploration of the pros and cons. Plus, Rachel and Jon insisted that we use him.... My argument was simple: I felt it was a mistake to commit ourselves to such a preposterous version of events. Why, I asked, should we allow ourselves to be attacked by the prosecution? It is far better to go on the attack and maintain the smallest possible target for the opponent. Rachel and Jon were nonetheless adamant. As far as they were concerned, Singletary's story exonerates Mumia—that was enough to merit calling him. As far as I was concerned, using Singletary was akin to putting up a billboard with a bull's-eye drawn on it.[54]

As a compromise, Weinglass decided to use Singletary, but sought to limit his testimony at the PCRA hearing to a narrow pair of issues. First was the question of whether, when being questioned by police at Homicide back on the morning of December 9, he had had his statements torn up until he finally wrote what the police investigators wanted him to say. Second was the question of whether he had been standing with Cynthia White when the shooting occurred. As Weinglass put it, in a rather strange introduction to a witness:

> Weinglass: If I may, there is one additional witness who is referred to in the Petition which Counsel has had now for two months. And this is a witness who is a person whose recollection of what happened on the night in question we believe to be not entirely accurate. We believe his recollection today is not entirely accurate. We believe his recollection which was given in a sworn statement in 1990 was not entirely accurate. However, this is a witness who advises us, and we have no reason to disbelieve this, that he was with Cynthia White on the night of the occurrence.[55]

It was, indeed, a strange witness to put on the stand—one for whom the defense attorney felt the need to begin by undermining his very credibility. But Weinglass felt he had to make that preface because Singletary's story was so incredible.

Things began well enough. Singletary, who spoke directly and with confidence, said that he had been brought to the Homicide division as a witness. Twice he had written a statement and twice, he said, a black police officer he identified as Detective Green balled it up and tossed in the trash. He claimed he was threatened with a beating and the destruction of his garage business unless he wrote what the police wanted him to write. After five hours, he finally signed a statement that had been typed by police. A statement he now claimed was actually not the truth. But by not asking Singletary what he had written in those first, rejected statements, or what was untrue about the statement he had signed, allegedly under duress, Weinglass avoided discussion of Singletary's incredible version of events. His intention was that by avoiding those questions, the prosecution would be barred on cross-examination from going into them. But with Judge Sabo on the bench, this was a vain hope.

Weinglass's excessive caution was a red flag to both the prosecution and the judge that alerted them that they should encourage Singletary to say more. Besides, thanks to what Williams calls a "blunder" by Wolkenstein and Abu-Jamal's first appellate attorney Leslie Gelb, Fisk already knew what Singletary was going to say. Back in 1990, Wolkenstein and Gelb, instead of just talking with Singletary, had made a transcript of his statement. Under the rules of evidence, the written document then had to be provided to the prosecution.[56] Sabo gave the prosecutor, Arlene Fisk, as much leeway as she

needed. Over Weinglass's objections, Fisk asked Singletary to state what he
had originally written, which he was alleging to have been tossed out by the
interviewing detective. Singletary put it this way:

> Well, I brought my car, parked my car at the southwest corner
> of 13th and Locust. I got out to go over to the club Whispers. The
> doors were locked. I came back across the street. There was a
> Volkswagen that was going south on 13th Street. He made a left turn
> onto Locust. Pulled to the curb immediately. There was a police car
> behind it. The police car pulled behind the Volkswagen. The driver
> of the Volkswagen got out. The police officer got out and immedi-
> ately started to walk to the wall. And immediately at that point the
> police officer was frisking the driver of the Volkswagen.
>
> There was an occupant in the Volkswagen on the passenger
> side started yelling and screaming, saying a lot of things. He had a
> long Army, umm, overcoat on. He came from the car, stuck his hand
> in his right pocket, pulled a gun.
>
> I immediately moved over to the highspeed line, the barrier
> there, and I ducked. I heard a pop. I ducked, I looked.
>
> …
>
> And the, uhh, when I looked over I saw the guy again point
> the gun in the direction of the police officer, firing into his face.
>
> …
>
> And as I saw the second shot the police officer fell backwards.
> This tall guy with dreadlocks looked at his right, looked to his left,
> placed the gun in the Volkswagen, started running. The guy who was
> driving the Volkswagen then started yelling a name or something
> and started chasing this guy.
>
> I peeped over to see, I peeped over to see if there was anything
> I could do for the officer. And I started backing up. There was a, the
> guy there said he was a cab driver and asked me what was that sound
> he heard. And I said the police officer was just shot, we need to get
> him help right away. And as I was talking to him he went towards
> the police car to make a call. Just to tell the police officer was down
> and we would need help right away.
>
> And I went back, started to see the officer, then another gen-
> tleman came across the street. He wasn't as tall as the first guy. He
> had dreadlocks and he said this is my brother's car, where is my
> brother. I said I don't know. I said there was two guys that took off
> running. I said the tall guy shot the police officer, took off running.
>
> And he said oh, my God, we don't need this, and he started to
> went over to the cop, is there anything I could do, anything I could
> do to help you. And he was laying forward, bending forward. And
> the police officer's gun, which was in his lap, discharged, striking
> him in the chest or someplace. And he screamed I'm shot, I'm shot.
> He staggered against the back of the Volkswagen.

> And then there was sirens and everything was becoming chaotic then. It was just like, you know. That's what I wrote down in the report.[57]

But Singletary didn't stop there. Under questioning by Fisk, he said that after police began arriving on the scene, a helicopter appeared and shined a bright light down. He also said that after Faulkner had been shot in the face, and after Abu-Jamal had walked over to try to help, Faulkner had said something. As he put it:

> He [Faulkner] was sitting on the ground and he was saying, the guy was asking could I get you some help, could I do anything for you. And he said get Maureen and he mumbled something else and I couldn't make out what it was. I thought it was something about some children or something, I don't know.[58]

There were two problems with this testimony. In 1981, the police did not own a helicopter in Philadelphia. Second, according to doctors' testimony at the trial, once Faulkner was shot in the face right between the eyes, he died instantly. Faulkner could not have been sitting up, much less talking. In this light, it is clear why Weinglass wanted to strictly limit Singletary's testimony. What isn't clear is why, after several weeks of dealing with Judge Sabo, Weinglass ever thought he'd be able to pull it off. In any case, Singletary's curious tale, while perhaps containing some elements of truth, collapsed under the weight of its own implausibility. Yet it left Wolkenstein, who had initially found Singletary, bitter. As she wrote in her declaration:

> In addition to his refusal to present the sworn confession of Arnold Beverly, Attorney Weinglass resisted and obstructed efforts to investigate, develop and present testimony of two other eyewitnesses, William Singletary and Mr. Jamal's brother William Cook, both of whom stated that Jamal did not shoot P.O. Faulkner.[59]

Since Singletary's testimony looked increasingly less credible the more he said, the question would seem to be not why Weinglass didn't make more of his testimony, but why he chose to introduce him as a witness at all. Weinglass has been steadfastly unwilling to comment on such matters. But Williams, in his book, claims that Wolkenstein had convinced Abu-Jamal of the merits of putting Singletary on the stand, and as Williams puts it: "Len would never veto Mumia."[60]

Williams, who professes admiration for Weinglass's skill as a lawyer, also says that the veteran political advocate is not as good in the role of lead attorney. "You need to be a firm leader," he says. "You have to be able to say 'This is what we're going to do.' And Len is not able to do that. He likes compromise and conciliation."

Weinglass agrees that the defense team at that point probably could have benefited from a more top-down authoritarian as lead counsel. "But I don't do tyrants," he says. "I'm a sixties person. I like to operate by consensus." He added, "Besides, Rachel had Mumia's confidence. She brought me into the case."

In her declaration, Wolkenstein doesn't mention another witness, William Harmon. His testimony was also a source of tension within the defense team. On the eve of the PCRA hearing, Harmon, a career criminal serving time on a drug charge at Mercer County Prison, had volunteered, through his attorney, that he was a witness to the Faulkner shooting, and that he could testify that Abu-Jamal was innocent. On August 3, 1995, with Weinglass and Williams in the midst of the PCRA hearing, and the clock still ticking toward his scheduled August 17 death date, Wolkenstein was dispatched to interview Harmon. After four hours spent debriefing him, Wolkenstein met with Weinglass and Williams at an IHOP Restaurant to decide what to do. Over pancakes, Williams says that he felt the story was absurd, and advised ignoring him. Wolkenstein felt it was important to have him as a witness. Weinglass went along with Wolkenstein, adding Harmon's name to the PCRA hearing witness list.

Later, Weinglass reportedly changed his mind. After Harmon had already been transported to the court from prison, Weinglass decided on August 10th not to call him. But by then, apparently sensing a chance to embarrass the defense, Judge Sabo wouldn't let the defense off the hook. He insisted on putting Harmon on the stand, over defense objections. The results were disastrous for the defense.

Harmon claimed that he had been with his girlfriend in a restaurant on 13th Street, between Walnut and Locust, when he saw Abu-Jamal standing on the sidewalk. He says he went out to meet the celebrity journalist so as to introduce him to his girlfriend. He says while they were talking, they heard loud voices coming from near the intersection of 13th and Locust. At that point, he says Abu-Jamal left and began walking across the street and through a parking lot on the north side of 13th Street towards the voices. Harmon said he followed. Then he says he heard a shot and saw Officer Faulkner fall. Abu-Jamal continued walking, he says, until there was another shot and Abu-Jamal fell, too. Harmon added that he had seen someone, who had been talking with the officer, run off towards 12th

Street after the first shot was fired.

At that point, Harmon's account got bizarre. He said:

> After I heard the second shot and I seen Mumia fall, a car came up beside him. And a guy got out of the car and pointed a gun at the cop and shot again, got in the car, backed the car up to 13th Street, and went down 13th Street the wrong way. They went, it went south on 13th.[61]

Harmon, it turned out, had a record of arrests and convictions that was extremely long. He had also worked as a police informant, and had been a pimp in the Center City area. By the time he was through being questioned, it was hard to take anything he said seriously, and the *Philadelphia Daily News*, in a column, began at that point referring to Abu-Jamal's defense as the "Scheme Team," a play on O.J. Simpson's "Dream Team" of attorneys. It was a sorry ending to a hearing which had, in fact, against great odds, produced considerable evidence demonstrating the unfairness of the original trial, and even Abu-Jamal's possible innocence.

Following the PCRA hearing, Judge Sabo predictably rejected every single piece of evidence, and every witness presented by the defense as being not credible. He upheld all of the facts and procedures of the original trial as being correct. Once they knew they were stuck with Sabo as the PCRA factfinder, this had been expected by the defense. The purpose of the PCRA hearing, for the defense, had been to establish a record upon which to appeal to the state supreme court and ultimately to the federal courts. And the PCRA hearing did successfully open up a number of avenues for appealing Abu-Jamal's conviction and his death sentence.

But the testimony of witnesses like Singletary and Harmon, combined with the lack of any testimony from Abu-Jamal and his brother Billy Cook, nonetheless left many observers with mixed feelings about the case. If the theory was that Abu-Jamal was innocent, which was what Singletary and Harmon were saying, and what Hightower's, Howard's, and possibly Harkins' and Scanlan's testimony suggested, why didn't he take the stand? Perhaps there were sound reasons for Abu-Jamal's attorneys to keep him from testifying under oath. But why didn't his brother—even if he did have legitimate fears for his own safety—come forward when his older brother's life was in the balance, as it was for most of the hearing? Alternatively, if what had happened was that Abu-Jamal had shot Faulkner in what he perceived to be an act of self-defense after having been shot first himself, as also suggested by the testimony of Harkins and possibly Scanlan and Hightower, why was he allowing his case to be weakened by the fantastic testimony of Singletary and Harmon? And again, why wasn't he or at least his brother taking the stand to explain what had actually happened on December 9?

With these questions on the minds of critics and even some supporters, Abu-Jamal's case moved to the state supreme court for final appeal.

Meanwhile, the conflicts within the defense team were reaching the boiling point.

Chapter Nine

A Life-and-Death Struggle Over "Life" or "Death"

In the spring of 2001, Mumia Abu-Jamal electrified many of his more zealous supporters around the world—and troubled others—with a series of stunning announcements. At the time, a federal judge was in the midst of evaluating a crucial federal *habeas corpus* appeal of his conviction. While that appeal was pending, Abu-Jamal filed a hand-written petition with the same court stating that he was firing his entire legal defense team—including lead attorney Leonard Weinglass—and replacing them with two largely untested attorneys who between them had no federal death penalty experience.* Second, Abu-Jamal announced he was filing a lawsuit to block the publication of a book about his case written by one of the key members of his own defense team, legal strategist Daniel Williams.

Finally, and perhaps most dramatically, at a poorly attended and hastily organized curb-side press conference in front of the Federal Courthouse in Philadelphia on May 4, 2001, his new attorneys, Eliot Grossman and Marlene Kamish, released affidavits from both Abu-Jamal and his brother William "Billy" Cook. For the first time, they gave what the lawyers said were the two brothers' accounts of what happened 20 years earlier on Locust Street. These affidavits were accompanied by an affidavit from Arnold Beverly, whose story was touched on in the preceding chapter. He is the career criminal and self-described mob-hit man who claims to have been the real killer of Philadelphia Police Officer Daniel Faulkner.

Abu-Jamal justified his firing of Weinglass, Williams and the rest of his defense team on the grounds that they had betrayed him. Williams, in

---

* Abu-Jamal also added two other defenders to his team: Nick Barnes and J. Michael Farrell (whose lawfirm coincidentally had been the public defender for PCRA defense witness Pamela Jenkins). But Farrell, a well-respected defense lawyer in Philadelphia, insisted that his role on the case was "minimal—basically acting simply as the required local counsel in the case because none of the other attorneys are members of the Pennsylvania Bar Assn." And Barnes, while perhaps an experienced attorney in his native U.K., is not even an American lawyer.

particular, was accused of abusing his privileged position as legal strategist to develop inside information for use in writing a book, titled *Executing Justice: An Inside Account of the Case of Mumia Abu-Jamal,* which was published in April, 2001 by St. Martin's Press. Williams received a modest $30,000 advance from the publisher, though at one point he had been willing to give the manuscript to a publisher offering him no advance. In the unsuccessful attempt in court to have distribution of the book blocked, Abu-Jamal claimed that Williams had violated legal ethics and breached attorney-client privilege in seeking personal gain from the publication of the book.

Williams says he did not reveal any secrets. He insists that he only used information that was already in the public domain. That depends upon what one is calling "public domain."

Certainly, where Williams is citing the court record, there is no question that he was not disclosing privileged information. But he also talks in his book about what he and other attorneys were thinking when they made decisions on strategy. Where he seems to be on the most controversial ground is in his revelations about the dispute within the legal team over what to do with the witness Arnold Beverly and Beverly's claim to have been the real killer of Faulkner. Here Williams asserts that the issue had already been mentioned in Buzz Bissinger's 1999 *Vanity Fair* article. He also claims that because more than just the lawyers were present at discussions of this issue, it was technically public information. Both these claims, while technically and probably legally correct, are a stretch ethically, it seems to me. In the *Vanity Fair* article, the only thing remotely approaching a reference to Beverly is a mention author Bissinger makes about Weinglass having referred to the possibility that the Faulkner killing was a police-sponsored "hit." There is no mention of a defense witness to support this, nor is there any mention of a conflict within the defense over whether to raise the issue on appeal. As for saying that there were others present at the defense strategy sessions on Beverly, Williams doesn't say who they were. If they were part of the Abu-Jamal support network, and if those people kept the matter quiet, it hardly would seem to justify saying the issue was already out in the public eye. In fact, the Beverly revelation did seem to come as a surprise to most of Abu-Jamal's supporters, suggesting that the dispute was kept quiet, even after Wolkenstein and Piper had quit the case over it, which was more than a year before the release of Williams' book.

It's true that, as Williams claims, Abu-Jamal knew that his attorney was writing a book. But Williams also readily concedes that his client never saw the actual contents of that book until it was already in galleys. It seems highly unlikely that Abu-Jamal was aware of William's astonishing equivocation on the matter of his own client's innocence, as for example when he refers repeatedly to the "ambiguities" of the case while at the same time insisting that he believed him to be innocent. Such a position is entirely appropriate for a writer striving for objectivity or seeking the truth. But it is a peculiar and would seem to be an ethically improper public stance for a defense lawyer to take regarding his or her client.

Weinglass says in his view Williams had revealed too much about the inner workings of the defense, in particular regarding the discussions concerning whether to use Beverly as a witness. Weinglass also criticizes Williams for criticizing Abu-Jamal's supporters, as he does in the book. "I don't think a lawyer should attack a support committee of someone who is on death row," he says. Williams argues it was not possible for him to provide a draft of the manuscript to his client while he was working on it because, having Abu-Jamal endorse what he wrote could have opened Abu-Jamal to a claim by prosecutors that he endorsed what the manuscript said. The truth is, Williams openly states that he wrote the book as an effort to "broaden the appeal" of Abu-Jamal's case to a wider audience. He says that in order to do that, he had to criticize "some of the nutty ideas being promoted by some of the more left-wing element of his supporters."

Williams says he also wanted to head off a potential attack from those same elements which he says he and Weinglass anticipated having to face if the *habeas* petition they had filed for Abu-Jamal in federal court were to fail. That attack, says Williams, would likely have come in the form of critics claiming that he and Weinglass had "deep sixed" a witness—Arnold Beverly—who could have proven Abu-Jamal's innocence.

In 1999, Abu-Jamal had agreed with Williams and Weinglass's advice to omit Beverly and Beverly's claim to have been Faulkner's real killer from the *habeas* petition. But in trying to anticipate a future political attack over this advice, Williams produced exactly the result he feared—only worse. His book led to the firing of both himself and Weinglass, and to a full-scale attempt by Abu-Jamal and his new attorneys to use Beverly as an argument for absolute innocence.

His book also had the perverse effect of producing exactly the opposite result he had been hoping for with the movement supporting his erstwhile client. He intended to drive away the "left" elements with their "nutty" claims about the case. Instead, by leading to the firing of Weinglass his replacement by Grossman and Kamish, the book led to the driving away of a significant part of Abu-Jamal's more mainstream support.

Weinglass insists Williams' book was the reason for the turn to Beverly and the once-rejected hit-man theory. "The Beverly strategy had been long dead," he says. "It was killed by Mumia himself in 1999 when he decided to let [Rachel] Wolkenstein and [Jonathan] Piper [who advocated for the strategy] quit. And it was not coming back—not as long as I was the lead attorney in the case. It was when I was fired that Mumia's new attorneys got all my files, and that's where they learned about Beverly."

In fact, at their May 4, 2001 press conference, Grossman and Kamish introduced reporters to the Beverly affidavit claiming they had "discovered it" in the files turned over to them by Abu-Jamal's former defense team Their choice of words suggested, incorrectly, that it was new information that had been buried. Clearly their client had known all about it for years.

Weinglass, who says he feared exactly this kind of thing happening, says that once he had read Williams' book in February of 2001, he tried to get his colleague to withdraw it from publication. Williams says that on learning of Weinglass's concerns, he wrote his publisher asking if the book could be held back from distribution. But, Williams was told, it was too late: the book was already printed and in warehouses waiting to be shipped to bookstores. Holding it back at that point was impossible. He says he decided then that he would make no further efforts to stop publication. But Weinglass claims stopping it might still have been possible: he had a lawyer—Martin Garbus—ready to take the publisher to court if Williams was willing to go that route. He wasn't.

The federal judge in New York hearing Abu-Jamal's case against Williams and his book threw it out and made no effort to criticize Williams or to recommend any investigation or sanction by the bar. In a technical sense, Williams can claim by virtue of this exoneration that there was no ethical violation. But considering the damage the book did by leading Abu-Jamal to fire his legal team in the midst of his *habeas* appeal, and by indirectly leading to the resurrection of the Beverly issue, one has to wonder about the wisdom of Williams' unorthodox project.

Clearly, if Williams felt the need to challenge elements of Abu-Jamal's support movement, and to write publicly about the defense and struggles within it, he should have resigned from the case to write his book. That, at least, would have avoided making Weinglass in any way responsible for what was written. "In retrospect," says Williams, "it does seem like the book produced a perverse result, but I have to say that at the time I was writing it, in 1999 and early 2000, I had no idea it would cause this kind of controversy." As to whether he should have resigned before writing the book, he says, "I always thought of this book as being helpful to the cause. I certainly wasn't trying to undermine my own position on the legal team by writing it."

Subsequent to his firing as Abu-Jamal's lead attorney, Weinglass has been accused by Abu-Jamal and his new attorneys and movement supporters (on the basis of little or no evidence) of everything from putting private gain over the interests of his client to failing to pursue a legal strategy of absolute innocence because of unsubstantiated fears of alleged death threats. He has even been accused of failing, because of an alleged fear of angering the Philadelphia Police, to pursue an argument that his client was framed. On their face, these accusations are ludicrous. Weinglass during his career, has defended convicted police killers and people, like Angela Davis, who were targets of the federal COINTELPRO program. He would hardly seem to be someone who would scare easily. Steven Hawkins, a black lawyer who as lead attorney with the Washington, D.C.-based National Coalition to Abolish the Death Penalty, is an expert on death penalty law, and worked as part of the defense team during Abu-Jamal's PCRA hearing and in the writing of his federal *habeas* appeal, does fault Williams for publishing his book. He says it improperly disclosed defense strategies, but Hawkins disputes the charge that Weinglass wasn't doing his best to free his client. "Len is an excellent attorney. In the years I've worked with him, I know he has had the highest integrity," he says.

If there is a reason to criticize Weinglass, it is for his apparent inattention to the book that he knew Williams was writing. As the lead attorney, if Weinglass didn't know what was going to be included in that book, and didn't insist in advance on ultimate editorial control over the contents, release time, etc., he was clearly remiss. He should have done a better job of monitoring what Williams was doing, and should have insisted on having final control over what could and could not be revealed. If he disagreed with some of the information that was being disclosed by Williams, he should have taken steps early on to prevent the work from being published. Weinglass, for his part, admits he didn't pay much attention while Williams was writing, explaining that "it was inconceivable to me that he would publish something like this before the case was over."

Whatever his thinking during the year that Williams was working on the project, once Weinglass had read a draft of the book and realized it would be published, and once he had failed in his effort to get Williams to stop publication, he attempted to convince Abu-Jamal that the book would be useful in building support for his case. In a letter to Abu-Jamal only a month and a half before publication of the book, Weinglass wrote:

> I must report to you on a troubling development. Both of us
> knew Dan was writing a book about the case. He has a publisher and
> the book is going into print, to be released on April 11th or there-
> abouts. Dan provided me with an early treatment of the opening
> chapter which I glanced at. There was nothing there that bothered
> me. On the contrary I liked his approach: He set up the prosecution's
> case as if it were clear cut and then slowly, methodically demolished
> it. But I was never given the opportunity to see any of his drafts as
> the book progressed and didn't really ask. However, Dan always reas-
> sured me that his treatment of the case would be favorable. I trusted
> that. Now that it's about to come out I was given a final galley copy
> which I read on my flying trips the last 10 days. The book is very
> favorable to the theme that you should have a new trial—not just on
> the penalty, but the guilt phase as well. It's well written and persua-
> sive. To the reading public it will be convincing of the fact that you
> have not received justice. There are, however, some aspects that are
> bothersome.

Among the things Weinglass says he found "bothersome":

> First, Dan strongly argues for a new trial, but takes a neutral,
> balanced position on the issue of innocence—distancing himself
> from segments of your support network who argue that you were
> framed as a former Panther and activist. He posits two extremes as
> equally off the mark—the FOP and those ardent supporters.... I
> believe Dan is thoroughly honest in arguing that the book is more
> credible with the reading public since he argues against those posi-
> tions and puts himself in the middle. Where I differ, and argued
> sharply with Dan, is that his role is that of an advocate and he
> should allow others to occupy the middle ground.
>
> ...
>
> Aside from this general, philosophical problem with the book,
> there are some specifics. Dan gives away Singletary and Pamela
> Jenkins as not worthy of belief. I don't think a lawyer should nega-
> tively comment in that fashion on witnesses that his side has put on.
> (Dan says this is nothing new—it's obvious in the record). He also,
> unbelievably, goes into the witness who we blocked from coming
> forward [Beverly] (I really objected to this since it has not surfaced;
> Dan thinks it will and this is a pre-emptive strike.)

Weinglass also criticizes the book for "revealing internal discussions and
debates," and for "dumping all over Rachel" [Wolkenstein]. But he concludes:

> Dan is convinced this book will save your life. And maybe it
> will. It's powerfully written. I just wanted you to know my own
> thinking on it.[1]

Weinglass says in the letter that on February 22, 2001, after having read the book, he met with Williams, and that in an "acrimonious meeting," was "told that it was too late to change the book to meet my objections. It's coming out."

Abu-Jamal, who after all has a right to know what his lawyers are doing with his case, had good reason to be angry at both Williams and Weinglass over the publication of *Executing Justice*. But his accusations that Weinglass and Williams didn't try to prove his innocence, and that they failed to argue that he was framed, are not supported by the record. They did try to show at the PCRA hearing that another person, most likely Freeman, had been at the scene and might have been the killer and the mysterious fleeing suspect. They did try to show, through the testimony of Veronica Jones and other witnesses, that the police and prosecution had tried to frame Abu-Jamal. In any event, it seems highly unlikely that either Weinglass—or Williams—would risk careers and reputation by deliberately sabotaging a case out of fear. Had fear interfered with their duties, a perfectly acceptable alternative existed: resigning and handing the case over to another attorney.

Whether true or baseless, the attacks on Weinglass were predictable, even necessary, given the new strategy. Once Abu-Jamal had decided, in the spring of 2001, to proceed with the once-rejected Beverly strategy, he and his defense team had to establish somehow that he had been misled by his attorneys in deciding in 1999 not to introduce evidence of Beverly's confession that he killed Faulkner. He really had no choice but to attack his attorneys, since under the terms of the 1996 Anti-Terrorism and Effective Death Penalty Act, and in accordance with Supreme Court precedent, convicted criminals are barred from using evidence if it had been available but unused for more than 60 days. His only hope to even attempt to introduce the Beverly evidence lay in convincing a court that he was the victim of an ineffective, or better yet, corrupt attorney. This was especially true since he himself made the decision in 1999 to stick with Weinglass and Williams, who felt Beverly was not credible, and to lose (through resignation from the case) attorneys Wolkenstein and Piper, who wanted him to use Beverly in his appeal.

What makes this effort so difficult, and what has no doubt thus far made it unsuccessful, is that Abu-Jamal did not reach his 1999 decision regarding Beverly in a vacuum. The pros and cons of using Beverly's confession were presented to Abu-Jamal by two sets of attorneys in both of whom he had a high degree of confidence—Weinglass and Williams on one side and Wolkenstein and Piper on the other. In deciding, back in 1999, to accept the strategy and views of Weinglass and Williams and to ignore Beverly, Abu-Jamal was consciously rejecting the advice offered by Wolkenstein and Piper, two attorneys with whom he had a relationship going back more a decade. That makes it hard to argue that he was simply misled or deceived by Weinglass and Williams. As Judge Pamela Dembe wrote in her decision rejecting Abu-Jamal's request for a new PCRA hearing on the Beverly confession and other evidence:

> The Beverly confession, which is the linchpin for all the arguments for reconsidering and reinterpreting the trial evidence, was not rejected behind the Petitioner's back. The debate among counsel was apparently so bitter that one of them [sic] removed herself from further participation in the case. Not only was Petitioner aware of the controversy, it is impossible not to infer that he chose to align himself with the lawyers who refused to call Beverly as a witness: he had a choice, and the fact that he continued to permit Weinglass and Williams to represent him refutes quite effectively any argument that he either did not know of or did not agree with their trial strategy.[2]

Whatever his reasons, Abu-Jamal's adoption in the spring of 2001 of Beverly's testimony, while energizing a narrow group of activist supporters, has dismayed others. A fall-off in financial support to his defense effort had become critical by 2002, as evidenced by a letter from his attorneys which was sent to a group attending a fundraising event at Riverside Church in New York City on May 23, 2002. In it, Grossman, Kamish, Farrell and Brown, the four attorneys of record in the case, say that there is "no money left" to pay for Abu-Jamal's defense.

> We will not dwell on the fact that since we took over Mumia's legal representation over a year ago we have not been paid one cent for the thousands of hours we have spent on his case—and have had to dig into our own pockets to pay thousands of dollars in litigation expenses.
>
> Instead, what we want to tell you about is the $30,000 that we need to restart and complete a stalled investigation which could blast another major hole in the prosecution's case and further expose how the frame-up of Mumia was put together. Our investigators are on the trail of a key witness. But we have no money to pay them to continue the investigation.[3]

Actually, it is not correct that the new legal team has gotten "not one cent" since taking on the case. Kamish and Grossman did submit bills to the Bill of Rights Foundation, which had been paying the prior defense team's bills, and they were paid for those invoices until the existing money—reportedly about $50,000—ran out, sources familiar with the fund say.

The letter goes on to admit that the attacks on Abu-Jamal's former lead counsel have hurt support for his cause.

> We understand that we have been criticized in certain quarters for exposing the truth about how Mumia's previous attorneys, Weinglass and Williams, suppressed the evidence which proves that he is innocent and otherwise sabotaged his defense. People need to understand that we have no alternative but to tell the truth both inside the courtroom and outside the courtroom about what happened because the courts will not consider this evidence without being given a proper explanation as to why it was not presented in June of 1999 when Mumia's previous lawyers had it in their hands.[4]

They also express "deep concern"[5] over the disbanding of the New York-based Committee to Save Mumia, which was chaired by actor/activists Ossie Davis and Mike Farrell, and which was folded by them in 2002. That committee was a major source of funds for the defense because of its high-profile leadership and connections to wealthy donors.

Farrell, an intensely committed activist in the anti-death penalty movement who is chair of the California-based organization Death Penalty Focus, expresses dismay at the turn in strategy in the case, which led him and Davis to decide to fold the committee.

"There's always been a kind of a tension—a sort of 'more Mumia than thou' attitude—where if you weren't willing to be an uncritical, absolute devotee, there was something wrong with you," he told me. "I was okay with that, in the sense that I was able to ignore it, because I have my own ideas. For some time I was hearing about political tussles within the self-styled hierarchy of control [in the Free Mumia movement]. I didn't care. But when it came to Len [Weinglass] being ousted, and the attempt by the new attorneys to say he had tried to sabotage the case, I found it highly offensive. I began to raise questions about who was running the show. I wasn't interested in raising funds for attorneys who were saying these things about Len and who were sabotaging all the work he had done."

Still, he says for a time, while he refused to send out any more letters to the committee's contributor list, he held off on disbanding it because of requests by members of the committee's advisory panel. "Even Len said 'Don't do anything that would be hurtful to the case,'" he recalls.

"But I did feel strongly that this attempt to control the process was being whipped into shape by forces I wasn't comfortable with. There were always representations that another attorney I would feel more confidence in would be taking the case on, but meanwhile the two people who had insinuated themselves in as the attorneys [Grossman and Kamish] seemed to be the ones who were running things. I finally said that I needed to separate myself from it. Ossie said the same thing. So we agreed to close it down."

There have also been other signs of flagging support following the adoption of the Beverly strategy. Supportive endorsements of Williams' book include a number of key long-time Abu-Jamal backers, such as Jesse Jackson, Farrell and Amnesty International Secretary Piers Bannister (all of whom contributed jacket blurbs for the book, and none of whom has so far come forward to condemn it or to retract his endorsement). Novelist E.L. Doctorow contributed a foreword. These endorsements of a book that denounces the Beverly strategy suggest that many of his celebrity supporters are troubled by the change in defense strategy, and by the Beverly claim. Indeed, in his foreword, Doctorow acknowledges his own doubts about the more extreme claims of innocence:* "At neither extreme can there be a legal certainty to match the righteousness."[6]

Since neither Abu-Jamal nor his attorneys are willing to discuss the reasoning behind his change of heart about using Beverly as a witness, or behind his decision to finally issue a statement giving his account of what happened on December 9, 1981, we are left to wonder.

There is an argument that if a court had agreed to a hearing on the Beverly claim, it might have opened the door to Abu-Jamal's bringing in other witnesses and evidence to bolster Beverly's testimony—evidence which on its own merits might have helped to overturn his conviction. This may explain why the D.A.'s office so strenuously fought to block a hearing on or even a formal deposing of Beverly. As Stuart Taylor, the lawyer/legal writer who covered Abu-Jamal's post-conviction hearing for *The American Lawyer*, observes, "I can only speculate that he knew that his chances of winning *habeas* were slim in any event, and that coming up with an alternative theory could not hurt much and might just help."

I have my own speculation. (And it is only that, since Abu-Jamal has chosen not to discuss his case with me, or with any journalists for that matter, though it is a speculation shared by a number of people who have for

---

*Doctorow says his position has not changed, noting that several years before the book's publication, he had already written an op-ed article in the *New York Times* making the same point: Innocent or not, Abu-Jamal did not get a fair trial.

years supported calls for a new trial.) Consider the context. A decision was fast approaching on his *habeas* appeal, which had been in the hands of Judge Yohn since late 1999. Following publication of Williams' book in early 2001, Abu-Jamal had lost confidence in his long-time defense team. Perhaps Abu-Jamal grew worried that he could end up spending the rest of his life in jail with no hope of release. This is, after all, a man who had already spent two decades languishing on death row, much of it spent in hellish conditions of near solitary confinement, and cut off from any physical contact with family, friends, even fellow prisoners. It is not hard to imagine why, particularly after feeling betrayed by his attorneys, he might grow concerned that the likely decision in his case would be exactly what it turned out to be—a kind of splitting of the difference that would leave him stuck in prison for the rest of his life, with no chance of parole and no right to appeal

Abu-Jamal is a very political person, and probably feels more at home taking a more aggressively political stand in his appeal. Indeed, he himself stated, in a letter read by Kamish to supporters at a demonstration in support of his case held outside Philadelphia's City Hall in May 2001, that it was his intention to move the case in a more overtly political direction. This direction would challenge the very legality of his arrest. In that message he acknowledged that he had been criticized by some supporters for adopting a new legal strategy, and for questioning the integrity of his former attorneys, Williams and Weinglass. But to those of his supporters who were unwilling to go along with his new strategy he said, "If you choose not to join me, one simple request: don't get in my way."

A savvy political observer and an incisive analyst of the workings of the American judicial system, Abu-Jamal must have realized at that point that for reasons both political and personal, it would take a very courageous judge to overturn the conviction of someone (especially a black radical) found guilty of murdering a police officer. Federal judges, like many people, likely harbor hopes of moving to higher office. Yohn, a Republican appointee to the bench, surely knew that if he were to overturn this particular conviction, his chances of ever being appointed to the appellate bench by a Republican president would be zero. Indeed, Judge Yohn was clearly well aware of what happened to a fellow Republican-appointed judge on the bench in the same Third Circuit. Judge Stewart Dalzell made an unpopular decision reversing a state court murder conviction in a much-less politically charged or well-known case. In 1997, Dalzell had found that the 1992 murder trial of a young woman, Lisa Michelle Lambert, in

Lancaster County, had been so blatantly unfair that he threw out her conviction and barred the state from retrying the case. His decision was
reversed on appeal on procedural grounds. But before that happened it led
to an impeachment campaign that garnered 37,000 signatures in Lancaster
County. It also led to calls by Lancaster-area congressmen for hearings, and
to several death threats against the judge.

Did such career motivations and potential for death threats influence
Judge Yohn's ruling? That isn't possible to discern. But it certainly was reasonable for Abu-Jamal to guess that these might be factors that would prevent Yohn from overturning the conviction, and for Abu-Jamal to craft his
strategy with that expectation in mind.

At the same time, it is clear from the record and from the arguments
made in Abu-Jamal's *habeas corpus* petition that he did not receive a fair
trial, or a fair appeal of his conviction and sentencing, in the court system
of the Commonwealth of Pennsylvania. Many fair-minded jurists—ranging
from the Cook County Bar Association, to the Illinois Association of
Criminal Defense Attorneys among many others—have agreed. In view of
this, what seemed likely to many observers was that Judge Yohn would split
the difference, as he ultimately did, finding fault with the way Abu-Jamal
was sentenced, but leaving his conviction standing. This would have a two-
pronged effect. First, preventing a gross and irreversible miscarriage of justice—the execution of a man for first-degree murder who had not received
a fair trial, and who may well not have committed a premeditated act of
murder. Second, it would not so infuriate the law-enforcement establishment and the Republican political establishment in Pennsylvania that the
judge's future prospects would be forever foreclosed.

In addition, there were external forces at work back in 1999 and 2000
that were pushing Abu-Jamal towards making a radical shift in his legal
strategy. Chief among these was the advice of Marlene Kamish. She had
taken up temporary residence in the vicinity of his prison. (She stayed for
some time with the nearby Bruderhof collective, which for years has actively backed Abu-Jamal. There was an apparent falling out with the group,
and she was asked to leave.) She reportedly became an unpaid advisor and
one of Abu-Jamal's most frequent visitors. Both Weinglass and Williams
say that Kamish soon became an almost constant irritant in their relations
with their client, calling their offices all the time and haranguing them
about their handling—or in her view, their mishandling—of the case each
step of the way.

It was not the first time Kamish, an attorney who only earned her law degree in 1990 from the Kent School of Law at the Illinois Institute of Technology, had taken an intense personal interest in a condemned man. Nor was it the first time she had helped to drive a wedge between a capital defendant and his attorneys.

Kamish was widely billed within the Free Mumia movement as the attorney who helped get death penalty prisoner Manuel Salazar off of Illinois' death row in 1995. But attorneys in Chicago familiar with her say that she actually played a primarily peripheral and outside-of-the-courtroom role in the Salazar case; a case which, in a manner eerily reminiscent of Abu-Jamal's, involved the fatal shooting of a Joliet police officer. In fact, Andrea Lyon, then Kamish's boss at the Capital Resource Center in Chicago, which was handling Salazar's post-conviction hearing, says she had Kamish removed from his PCRA hearing—the second stage of the appeal of his conviction—and from her full-time position as a unionized attorney with the center. Lyon had her transferred to a part-time position with the State Appellate Defender's office, where she remained for only a few months longer. Lyon, a highly regarded capital defense attorney who headed the Capital Resource Center and who is now a law professor at DePaul University Law School and director of the Center for Justice and Capital Cases, put it this way: "I took her off the case because I was unhappy with the quality of investigation that she did, and I had questions about the way she handled witnesses in the case."

"It's a close call whether you are preparing witnesses or whether you are putting words in their mouths," concurs Ron Hayes, another attorney in the Salazar case, "and I think she tried to push the envelope farther than she should have," in preparing witnesses for testimony in the PCRA hearing.

Kamish went on to serve as the third member of the legal team that handled Salazar's appeal to the state supreme court. But Charles Hoffman, the lead attorney in that appeal, says of her role, "Let me put it this way: I wrote the brief in that case. The biggest contribution Marlene made is that she got 500 people down to Springfield for oral arguments, and she also managed to get Salazar's paintings exhibited at a museum across the street from the state supreme court building during the hearing." Those two actions were surely important contributions to the public campaign to free Salazar, and both demonstrated organizing acumen, says Hoffman. But doing PR work and organizing supporters are not the same as arguing a case of life-or-death before state supreme court judges.

A number of the lawyers who worked on the Salazar case with Kamish claim that somewhere along the line she had become emotionally and personally attached to the client to the extent that it may have impaired her objectivity. (It's a claim echoed by some people in the Abu-Jamal movement, too.) Specifically, several, including Lyon, say that Kamish refused to go along with the legal argument developed by Salazar attorney Hayes, which ultimately led to Salazar's getting a new trial. This once again bears an eerie similarity to the Abu-Jamal case. Salazar got a new trial on a technicality: a guilt-phase jury instruction form that led to the vacating of his first-degree murder conviction. Hayes had noticed that at the time of Salazar's first state appeal, the state supreme court was considering another case that was challenging the jury instruction form used in capital cases. The argument was that the form didn't let jurors know they had the option of convicting someone of manslaughter, rather than just a choice between first-degree murder or nothing. In that case, the state's high court ultimately reversed the conviction it was considering. Hayes realized that because the appellate attorney working for Salazar at that time had neglected to have Salazar's case included in that state appeal, the court didn't extend its decision to include Salazar's case. By raising this issue again, and citing the new precedent, Hayes and the defense team were confident they could get the state's highest court to also order a new trial for Salazar. Once a new trial was ordered, even if he were not found innocent, they reasoned, he might well get a lesser conviction for manslaughter.

Kamish's position at the time was simple. "She didn't want that argument to be used because she said it would leave Salazar facing a manslaughter charge," recalls Lyon. In fact, in his retrial, Salazar *was* convicted of manslaughter. But as Hayes had anticipated, he was released on time served (11 years on death row).

Lyon's account of Kamish's tenure and of her dangerously divisive role in the Salazar case was supported by other lawyers involved in the case, including Karen Shields, now a state associate judge, who at the time of his post-conviction hearing was Salazar's lead appellate attorney. "She blocked our relationship with our own client," says Shields. "For some unknown reason, she didn't trust us and made sure that Salazar didn't trust us either. It was all very odd. I cannot understand why she'd want to cut him off from everyone else who wanted to help." Hayes agreed with Shields' account, saying, "It was very difficult to work with her. Some of her actions alienated the client from us, which is not a good idea in such a serious case. She spent an awful lot of time meeting with and talking with the defendant on the telephone, and she drove a wedge between him and us."

Kamish continued to have the confidence of Salazar, who later even named her as godmother of his son. She went on to assist with Salazar's subsequent retrial, and helped arrange to bring in as lead attorney in that case Milton Grimes, the prominent Los Angeles lawyer who had represented LAPD beating victim Rodney King. But even Grimes insists she played no courtroom role in the actual retrial of Salazar. Recalls Grimes, "She was obsessed with the case—I'll stay with that word—and she was helpful outside the courtroom in digging things up, but she didn't interview any of the witnesses." Meanwhile, he adds, "In the courtroom, she irritated and aggravated the hell out of the judge, so part of my job was just trying to bring him back down. She almost made herself more of a negative in the case."

Back in May 2001, Grimes issued what may in retrospect have been a prophetic warning, "She had better not start trying to be a trial lawyer in a death penalty case! If he [Abu-Jamal] traded Len [Weinglass] for Marlene [Kamish], he has made a big mistake."

A Lexis legal search of Kamish's name turned up only one record of her significant participation in a death penalty case prior to her becoming one of Abu-Jamal's lead attorneys. That was the Salazar Illinois State Supreme Court appeal, where she was listed as "of counsel," a much more minor role than "counsel of record." Her only other listing on Lexis was for a sexual assault and harassment case in 1992, in which she was one of two lead counsels.

Abu-Jamal's other new lead attorney, Eliot Lee Grossman, is a far more experienced trial litigator than Kamish. But, it turns out, he has even less courtroom experience than she has with legal issues surrounding the death penalty. A graduate of Swarthmore College who earned his law degree from the prestigious University of California Hastings Law School in San Francisco in 1977, Grossman in fact seems to have no practical background at all in this type of litigation. Attorneys familiar with his legal work say he has some expertise in international law and has handled some anti-discrimination cases, but they claim he has done little or no death penalty work in his home state of California, where he has offices in Alhambra and San Francisco. "I know people who are experts in all different areas of law," says one fellow National Lawyers Guild attorney in California, who asked to remain anonymous. "Eliot is not someone whose name would pop up on any of those lists." A Lexis legal search for Grossman turned up no death penalty cases at either the trial or appeals level. However, he is listed, along with Kamish, in a friend-of-the-court role in the Salazar state Supreme Court appeal, and in the retrial of that case, where both he and Kamish played distinctly minor roles.

As is the case with Kamish, there is not a lot of information available regarding Grossman's political background. He has been known to recommend the writings of Russian revolutionary leader Leon Trotsky to acquaintances, but also apparently once volunteered a ringing endorsement of the instruction offered by a right-wing southern California gun club based in Bakersfield, which used a quote from him in it's promotional literature.

Attorneys who know Grossman and Kamish describe these two members of the left-leaning National Lawyers Guild as dedicated and committed progressive attorneys. Kamish especially is said to be a passionate opponent of the death penalty, and someone who throws herself wholeheartedly into cases she's involved with. But she is also said to have a prickly personality that makes it difficult for her to work as part of a team. She is evidently an experienced organizer—and a good self-promoter—who has managed to get her name in the paper even on cases like Salazar's, where she was not the lead attorney.

Kamish and Grossman first came to public attention in the Abu-Jamal case when, on June 28, 2000, they attempted to file, with the federal court hearing Abu-Jamal's *habeas* petition, a friend-of-the-court brief on behalf of a little-known organization in California called the Chicana/Chicano Studies Foundation. In it they argued that Abu-Jamal had been improperly deprived of his right to be his own lawyer at his trial. The brief, fraught with errors and factually incorrect, was rejected by the court, but continued to generate a great deal of controversy within the Free Mumia movement. Abu-Jamal himself, in a message to his supporters, urged everyone to study it carefully.

It is not clear how familiar Abu-Jamal was with Kamish's and Grossman's limited experience with the death penalty at the time, almost a year after the amicus brief episode, that he hired them and sacked his prior attorneys. Efforts to find out what he knew, in the form of a Federal Express letter delivered to him at SCI-Greene, went unanswered. Marcus Redeker, a history professor at the University of Pittsburgh and a close friend of Abu-Jamal's, who checked out Kamish for him, says he was unaware of the criticism leveled against her by her former boss and colleagues in the Salazar case. The guidelines of the Illinois Supreme Court (where Salazar's case played out) for death penalty attorneys is that they ought to have participated in trying at least eight capital cases before they act as lead attorney in a death penalty case. For what it is worth, neither

Grossman nor Kamish would appear to even approach that standard.[7]

In Pennsylvania, the standards for court-appointed attorneys appealing death penalty cases is fairly low. There need to be two attorneys on the case, and they are supposed to have filed five legal briefs, and to have made oral arguments in criminal cases, as well as to have filed one appellate brief. They are also supposed to have demonstrated, through training *or* experience, a knowledge of the principles of constitutional law as they apply to death penalty cases. Grossman, and possibly also Kamish, would appear to meet these minimal standards.

There is, however, good reason to question the basic judgment of both attorneys. In terms of their handling of the media, they have been nothing short of amateurish. On the day Judge Yohn issued his ruling on the *habeas* petition, a pivotal moment in the case, reporters found that neither Grossman nor Kamish were returning phone calls. Most stories reporting on this major new development in the case consequently ended up reporting that efforts to reach them were unsuccessful. (When I called Grossman's office that day, his answering machine was so full it was no longer recording messages, yet he seemingly made no effort to clear it and answer his press calls.) On the crucial day the news broke, when most major national news media were giving play to the story for the first time in a long while, this absence by the defense gave Abu-Jamal's critics, from Philadelphia District Attorney Lynne Abraham to spokespeople for the Fraternal Order of Police and other critics, a largely free hand to spin the story their way. One example was Abraham's version. Widely quoted in the national media, she was able to peddle the false claim that Yohn had debunked all the "propaganda" of the defense's claims regarding the trial and earlier appeals. In fact, as the analysis in Chapter 10 of Yohn's ruling will show, this isn't true. The judge found a number of instances where the defense's witnesses seemed credible in challenging the prosecution's version of events, and instances where prosecution witnesses, including star witness Cynthia White, had seemed not credible. Though he felt constrained by Supreme Court precedent from overturning the verdict, this is far different from Abraham's claim that he debunked the defense's arguments.

I was involved in another example of media spin that day. On the evening after Yohn's decision was announced, CNN tried to line up a spokesperson from Abu-Jamal's camp for a lengthy report that also included a voice from the opposing side: Faulkner's widow Maureen. But instead of one of Abu-Jamal's attorneys, the network was offered rapper Chuckie

D, an ardent backer and friend of Abu-Jamal's who admitted he only had limited knowledge of the details of the case. At the last minute, an hour before the Aaron Brown News Night show was to air, the show's producer called on me. She sounded frustrated and desperate, and asked me to go on with Faulkner and Chuckie D as someone knowledgeable about the case. She said she was calling me largely because no one with a comparable or better knowledge of the details of the case was being made available from Abu-Jamal's defense team.

Grossman began talking to the press a day or two later. By that time, the story about Yohn's ruling was old and had ceased to be front-page material. A major opportunity to get Abu-Jamal's side of the story out to a national audience had been pointlessly wasted.

Several other important press events in Philadelphia were also badly organized and pulled together at the last minute. These included the release of the statements by Abu-Jamal and his brother concerning the events of December 9, 1981, in which notices to the media were sent out the day of the event. On a case where the local media has been ignoring the story anyway, the last thing the defense should be doing is giving editors an excuse not to send a reporter.

Abu-Jamal's attorneys also risked jeopardizing the viability of an important potential defense witness who is prepared to testify to Judge Sabo's racial bias and to his alleged judicial misconduct at Abu-Jamal's trial. This occurred when they asked the witness, who is a court stenographer by training, if she would attend a court proceeding before Court of Common Pleas Judge Dembe and record it for them. She declined, considering the request to do volunteer work for Abu-Jamal's case to be inappropriate. Had she gone along with their incredibly ill-conceived request, her usefulness as an unbiased witness would have been diminished.

On the legal side, Grossman and Kamish have also been sloppy, as for instance when, in their petition for a new PCRA hearing before Judge Dembe, they asserted incorrectly that alternate juror Courchain, who replaced one of the black jurors at Abu-Jamal's trial, became jury foreman. In fact Courchain was never jury foreman. That role went to George Ewalt.

Their biggest error, however, was in their original amicus brief for the Chicana/Chicano Studies Foundation. In it, they assert that Judge Sabo, in removing Abu-Jamal's self-representation rights at the start of his trial on June 18, 1982, had relied on a conference among judge and attorneys for which there was no record, and from which Abu-Jamal had been excluded. They go on to claim that there is "apparently no written record" of oral arguments before state Supreme Court Justice James T. McDermott concerning the same issue of Abu-Jamal's self-representation rights, and "apparently no written record" of the judge's ruling. In fact, those records of a morning meeting before McDermott do exist, and both Abu-Jamal and local reporters were present at that session (it was at the June 18 hearing before Judge McDermott that Abu-Jamal made his famous remark to the departing jurist, recalled by McGill during the sentencing phase of the trial: "Where are you going, motherfucker?").[8]

"Kamish and Grossman just didn't know how to use the court index," says Weinglass.

Grossman and Kamish are apparently getting some help with their appeal to the Third Circuit. Michael Yamamoto, immediate past-president of the California Attorneys for Criminal Justice, a specialized bar association of over 2,000 California criminal defense attorneys, is reportedly helping them with their appeal. He also filed an amicus brief calling for the panel to consider Abu-Jamal's Beverly-based claim of absolute innocence. It was subsequently rejected by the appeals court. Attorneys with the Philadelphia Federal Defender's Office are also reportedly offering informal advice on their own time. That office is also likely to file an amicus brief on the *Batson* claim, "to protect the interests of our clients," in the words of one office source.

But Grossman and Kamish are also being widely criticized in the Philadelphia defense attorney community for failing to seek help from local experts in what is an extremely technically difficult and crucial hearing for their client. In a June 2002 interview, David Zuckerman, the attorney who heads up the capital defense operation of the Philadelphia Public Defender's Office stated, "They have not been coming around looking for help in our office."

> I did not shoot Police Officer Daniel Faulkner. I had nothing
> to do with the killing of Officer Faulkner. I am innocent.[9]

So begins Abu-Jamal's brief statement about what happened December 9, 1981. The statement is then somewhat vague as to what had transpired. He claims to have been unconscious for most of the time—in particular during the period of time when Faulkner was allegedly shot. He explains that he did not come forward with his story before because, at trial he was "denied all my rights" and "would not be used to make it look like

I had a fair trial," and because, at his PCRA hearing, his attorney, Weinglass, "specifically told me not to testify." Explaining that, "Now, for the first time I have been given the opportunity to tell what happened," he finally tells his story. He recounts that he had just returned to the 13th and Locust Street area with his United Cab early on the morning of December 9, 1981, having just dropped off a fare in West Philadelphia. He says he was filling out his logbook, when he heard some shouting. He continues:

> I glanced in my rear view mirror and saw a flashing dome light of a police cruiser. This wasn't unusual.
> I continued to fill out my log/trip sheet when I heard what sounded like gun shots.
> I looked again into my rear view mirror and saw people running up and down Locust.
> As I scanned I recognized my brother standing in the street staggering and dizzy.
> I immediately exited the cab and ran to his scream.
> As I came across the street I saw a uniformed cop turn toward me, gun in hand, saw a flash, and went down on my knees.
> I closed my eyes and sat still trying to breathe.
> The next thing that I remember I felt myself being kicked, hit and being brought out of a stupor.
> When I opened my eyes, I saw cops all around me.
> They were hollering and cursing, grabbing and pulling on me. I felt faint finding it hard to talk.
> As I looked through this cop crowd all around me, I saw my brother, blood running down his neck and a cop lying on his back on the pavement.[10]

It had taken 20 years for Abu-Jamal to tell his story. He had long been unfairly criticized for not telling it at the time of his trial. But now that he had done it, the question arises: why did he come out with it now, after waiting for so long? There are solid reasons why a defendant should not testify at his own trial—and it has always been cynical in the extreme for Abu-Jamal's critics, detractors and enemies to use his failure to do so at his trial against him, as if his unwillingness to take the stand and tell his story were proof of his guilt. Once a defendant testifies, he is no longer able to avoid being questioned by the prosecution under oath. Skilled prosecutors (and McGill was certainly a skilled and experienced prosecutor) are adept at asking questions that can put the defendant in a bad light in front of a jury—for instance asking questions that compel the defendant to "take the Fifth," and refuse to answer. Even after the trial is over, it is rare for convicted defendants to take the stand in their own defense. Ken Rose is an experienced death penalty defender with the Center for Death Penalty Litigation in North Carolina. He says only some five to ten percent of defendants ever take the stand, even in a post-conviction legal forum, "and then only in limited areas where it is the only way to prove something—for example to testify as to what their trial attorney advised them to do." Rose says that even for a defendant to tell his story outside the courtroom, with the aim of building public support, can be dangerous because there are ways that the prosecution can bring such statements into the courtroom as evidence. Sean O'Brien is a death penalty specialist at the University of Missouri School of Law in Kansas City. He adds, "There is not much to be gained by a death penalty prisoner telling his story, because basically the courts and the press discount anything they say, knowing that they are desperate to get out of their predicament."

Weinglass and Williams deny that they advised Abu-Jamal not to testify at the PCRA hearing and not to go public with his story after the PCRA hearing in some public, non-legal forum. They say that he himself never wanted to do so. (But since he never expressly told them what had happened on December 9, it's also true that they were more comfortable not having him testify in a courtroom run by Judge Sabo. They knew the judge would give the prosecution a free hand cross-examining him, and they didn't know where his answers would go.)

It is quite possible, however, that Abu-Jamal is telling the truth that he was just following his attorneys' advice not to testify at his post-conviction hearing. Certainly when he was questioned by Judge Sabo about whether or not he wanted to address the court, Abu-Jamal was adamant that he did not, "on advice of counsel." It was a phrase he repeatedly insisted on using, to the consternation of the judge, who was trying to establish for the record whether or not it was the defendant's own decision. Indeed at that point in the hearing, Weinglass did specifically tell his client not to answer the judge.[11] Sabo eventually despaired of getting any different answer. On the record then, Abu-Jamal's decision not to testify, at least at the PCRA hearing, was indeed on his lawyer's advice. Williams and Weinglass, however, maintain that they had urged Abu-Jamal to tell his story *after* the PCRA hearing, to an appropriate media outlet. "I thought he should tell his story to someone who'd be sympathetic, like Ed Bradley of CBS's 'Sixty Minutes,' " says Williams. He suggests that such an account would only have helped with Abu-Jamal's public image, yet would not have been useable by the prosecution in court unless he later chose to testify.

In any event, it seems Abu-Jamal could have come out with his story at least a year earlier, and perhaps at a time and in a forum which would have contributed to a more detailed consideration of his *habeas* appeal. This was because back in 2000, Weinglass and Williams had included his name on the witness list sent to Federal Judge Yohn, who was then deciding whether to hold a hearing on his *habeas* appeal. Abu-Jamal, who for years has signed off on all legal documents in his case, asked to have his name removed from that list.

Whatever the truth of that matter, for better or worse he has told his story now. That story—while it has a gaping hole because he says he was unconscious for much of the time—has the merit of suggesting that Abu-Jamal was shot by a policeman, which comports with ballistics evidence that he was shot by Faulkner's revolver. It also suggests that Abu-Jamal, if he was unconscious or semi-conscious, could not have shot Faulkner. His claim to have been semi-conscious gets some support from the attending physician at Jefferson Hospital, who testified that he was close to passing out from shock and blood loss when police dumped him in the ER. Because of the undeniable trauma he had suffered, both from the loss of blood and from having his head pounded into a lamppost by police during his arrest, this account also would allow him a further plausible claim. Under any tough questioning from prosecutors (should it ever come to that), he could say his memory of events is unreliable.

Whatever the legal pros and cons of his putting his account on the record, whatever the truth as to whether it was Abu-Jamal or his lawyers who had him wait 20 years to tell it, it makes little difference in Abu-Jamal's current legal situation. The federal court refused to consider his statement or to admit it as an amendment to his *habeas* petition.

That doesn't mean we can't, or shouldn't, examine it, though.

The problem with Abu-Jamal's declaration is that it flies in the face of much of the testimony at the trial and at the PCRA hearing—testimony which, rightly or wrongly, has already been affirmed by state and federal courts as being credible and believable. The biggest difficulty is that Abu-Jamal's affidavit, taken at face value, has him crossing the street to go to the aid of his brother *after* shots had already been fired. This sequence of events conflicts with the accounts of all the major prosecution witnesses at the trial. But more importantly (given doubts we have already raised concerning the integrity of those witnesses' testimony), it also conflicts with the testimony of key defense witnesses. For example, it contradicts the testimony of trial defense witness Hightower, who, if he had looked around the corner after hearing a series of shots as he testified, should, by Abu-

Jamal's account, have seen him crossing the street. Instead, Hightower says he heard shots and then looked, by which time the incident was over, and there was no more shooting. It conflicts with Scanlan, who says he heard the first shot and saw an accompanying flash of light as a man, Abu-Jamal presumably, was crossing the street. It also conflicts with the testimony of PCRA hearing defense witness Robert Harkins. He had a clear view of all of 13th Street, and testified only that he saw someone struggle with, knock down, and eventually shoot Faulkner. But Harkins saw no one get shot in the street in front of him.

Billy Cook's affidavit makes things even more problematic. In it, he states that he was driving his battered VW with his vending-stand partner Ken "Poppi" Freeman (the man later found naked, bound and dead in 1985 on the day MOVE's house was bombed by police). He explains that he was stopped by Faulkner, and that outside the car, he got into a verbal dispute with the officer, who then beat him three times with a metal police flash-light, causing him to start bleeding from the head. Then he says that, with Faulkner remaining standing at the front of his car where Cook had been frisked, he was allowed to enter his vehicle to search the junk-strewn back-seat area for documents. This is a peculiar claim. It seems highly unlikely that any officer who was concerned enough to have frisked a driver, and who had already called for back-up, would allow a man he had just been in a fight with to rummage around, in the back seat of a car, hands unseen. It seems an even more unlikely version of events if, as Cook claims, there was another man in the vehicle also, who had not been frisked. In any event, Cook says that once he was inside his car looking around in the back, he heard gun shots.

> ...I saw flashes of a gun out of the side of my eye. He [Faulkner] was standing in front of the car but I didn't see him shot. I was fac-ing the back of the car.
>
> Out of my peripheral vision I knew, I could feel other people around but I can't say where they were. His car was behind mine and the policeman was standing on the street between my car and what-ever car was parked in front of me.
>
> When I first saw my brother, he was running. He was feet away from me. We hadn't made any plans to meet that night or anything like that and I didn't even realize that he came around that area there to pick up fares. He had nothing in his hands. I heard a shot and I saw him stumble. I didn't see who shot him. He was stumbling forward.[12]

Cook goes on to say that while he was looking in the back seat, his

partner Freeman was still sitting in the front passenger seat. But when he
looked up after hearing the shots, Freeman was gone:

> ...He had been in the passenger seat and I don't know which
> way he had gone. He left the area right after this happened.
>   Later, Poppi talked about a plan to kill Faulkner. He told me
> that he was armed on that night and participated in the shooting.
> He was connected and knew all kinds of people. I used to ask him
> about it but he talked but never said much. He wasn't a talker. I did-
> n't see Poppi for a while after that.[13]

This account, besides seeming improbable in its description of
Faulkner's wildly incautious actions, also appears to contradict Abu-Jamal's
account on one crucial matter: Billy Cook seems to be saying that he saw
his brother run across the street and get shot from his vantage point *inside*
the car. The first time he mentions getting out of the car is after he says he
saw his brother shot and after he notices that Freeman has left the car. (If
he were already outside the car by the time his brother ran across the street,
Cook would already have noticed that Freeman had exited the car, and he
also would have been in a position to see what Freeman was doing). As he
puts it at that point:

> I got out. I wanted to run maybe I could have gotten away. I
> even started to run. I did. But I couldn't run because of my brother.
> Not after I saw my brother down on the ground.[14]

Abu-Jamal, in his account, claims he was running towards his brother, who was "standing in the street staggering and dizzy." Yet Cook doesn't
describe himself as dizzy or staggering following his beating by Faulkner. In
fact, he claims he was permitted, and had the presence of mind, to go into
his car to search for documents after being struck violently by the officer.
But beyond this contradiction with his brother's account, the main problem with Cook's account is that it strains credulity. Is it conceivable that
this younger brother, knowing that Freeman had confessed to committing
the crime for which his brother was facing death, would have waited 20
years to tell his story? (Remember, in 1995, Abu-Jamal came within 10 days
of execution before having his execution date cancelled. Why not come
forward at that crucial moment?) Freeman, after all, has been dead since
1985, and so could not have been hurt by the truth. But even before then,
it's hard to believe that Cook wouldn't have come forward to say who the
real killer was, at least to his mother or his other brothers and sisters, or to
his brother's various attorneys, or to his own attorney. After all, his own
attorney, Alva, had an absolute right to keep the information to himself

because of lawyer-client confidentiality, yet he insists his client never told him what happened, either.

As it turns out, Abu-Jamal's belated account of the events of December 9, 1981, his brother's version of the story, Beverly's hard-to-swallow confession, and his replacement of his legal team, for all the upheaval these decisions have caused, have been largely irrelevant to the legal case. Irrelevant, that is, unless one accepts the notion that putting forward a claim of innocence based upon the claims of an unbelievable witness—and one whose story undermines the testimony of other defense witnesses—could sour a judge on the other more credible claims being made regarding the case.

This was precisely what had worried Abu-Jamal's former appellate lawyers, Weinglass and Williams. If that indeed happened, one might argue that by pushing the Beverly testimony on judges Dembe and Yohn, Abu-Jamal and his new attorneys Grossman and Kamish undermined his chances of winning a new trial on any of the 20 claims in his federal *habeas* appeal. Only Judge Yohn could say whether the attempt to use the Beverly, Cook and Abu-Jamal accounts in his *habeas* appeal did damage the other claims in the petition. But Weinglass and Williams both report that as recently as late 2000, when they were still handling the case, Judge Yohn was discussing with the defense a potential schedule for hearings. Once Williams and Weinglass were replaced, and the Beverly affidavit was filed, all such talk of hearings ceased, they say, and in the end there were none. Yohn made his ruling on the *habeas* appeal based solely on the record and the arguments filed by the two sides.

David Zuckerman, the most experienced homicide expert on the staff of the Philadelphia Public Defender's Office, thinks that the Beverly strategy sank Abu-Jamal's *habeas* appeal, particularly his effort to raise the issue of racial bias in the selection of his jury. "I think Judge Yohn might have ruled favorably at least on the *Batson* claim, before Abu-Jamal changed lawyers and tried to come in with Beverly," he says. Zuckerman also suggests that factual errors and obvious errors of interpretation made by Yohn in his ruling might well have been avoided had there been hearings on the claims where issues could have been clarified by the defense. Referring to errors of fact made by the judge in denying the *Batson* claim, Zuckerman, who participated in gathering the data used in one of the studies Yohn misidentified,[15] says, "Yohn was simply wrong. Unfortunately, if there had been a hearing held on it, the defense could have demonstrated that to him."

Neither the state court, in the person of Common Pleas Judge Dembe, nor the federal court, in the person of Judge Yohn, was willing to grant a hearing on the Beverly claim, or even to authorize the taking of a sworn deposition from Beverly, Cook or Abu-Jamal. Instead, Dembe denied the entire petition for a new or reopened post-conviction hearing on the case. Judge Yohn simply ignored it.

On December 18, 2001, as we noted earlier, Yohn split the difference, denying all claims for an overturning of the conviction, but supporting one claim that the sentencing hearing had been unfair and improper. Yohn found that the sentencing forms used by jury members, and Judge Sabo's instructions to the jury at the end of the sentencing phase of the trial, could have led jurors to a mistaken belief. Namely, that they had to unanimously agree on any mitigating circumstances for those to be considered as weighing against a death sentence. [Fig. 11, p. 176i]In fact, in Pennsylvania even one juror's finding of a mitigating circumstance means it must be included in the penalty deliberations of the entire jury. This is similar to the point that even one juror voting against guilt means a defendant is not guilty. And one juror voting against a death penalty means no death sentence. With that ruling, Abu-Jamal's death sentence was lifted, pending a decision by the Third Circuit Court of Appeals. His ruling is being appealed by both Abu-Jamal, who is challenging the rejection of the 20 constitutional claims concerning his conviction, and by the District Attorney's Office, which is challenging the overturning of his sentence.

Here things get a little complicated. Yohn, in overturning Abu-Jamal's sentence, mooted (or ignored) seven other claims of error regarding his sentence, on the grounds that he had already overturned it. Thus, if his order on the sentence were to be overturned on appeal, Judge Yohn would have to go back and reconsider those seven other claims on their own merits.

Ultimately, though, there will one day be a final decision on the sentence. If his death penalty is eventually upheld, it would be the end of the line for Abu-Jamal. Unless his sentence were commuted by the state's governor, he would be put to death. (This is a highly unlikely prospect given that both candidates for governor in the 2002 race, Republican Attorney General Mike Fisher and Democrat Ed Rendell, the former Philadelphia mayor and district attorney, are strong death penalty proponents and advocates of Abu-Jamal's execution.)

If Yohn's reversal of the sentence survives an appeal, then it will be up to the district attorney what happens next. If the D.A. decides to try and reimpose the death penalty, there would have to be a new sentencing hearing. This would mean impaneling a whole new jury, and essentially retrying the case before that jury so they could then decide between death or life in prison without parole. There would be no option regarding the conviction, which has been upheld. The D.A. could also decide not to do anything, and to simply let Yohn's decision stand. In that case, Abu-Jamal would have to spend the rest of his life in prison, with no chance of parole, and no further opportunity to appeal his sentence.

(There is, however, also the possibility that the U.S. Supreme Court or the Third Circuit Court of Appeals could undermine the *Mills* precedent on which Judge Yohn based his lifting of Abu-Jamal's death sentence. On June 16, 2002, the Supreme Court overturned and sent back to the Third Circuit a case, *Banks v. Horn*, involving a man, George Banks, who in 1982 killed 13 members of his own family. The Third Circuit, citing *Mills*, had lifted his death sentence, saying that there was juror confusion about whether they had to unanimously agree on mitigating circumstances. If the Third Circuit were to eliminate such a precedent, or if, on another review, the Supreme Court were to do so, Abu-Jamal would be back on death row, pending a reconsideration by Yohn of the other seven claims for relief on his death sentence which he earlier mooted.)

There is a tremendous irony in Yohn's *habeas* ruling. In the end, it was the work of Abu-Jamal's fired attorneys, Weinglass and Williams, which, only months after he had dismissed them, succeeded in lifting his death sentence. His new attorneys had not been allowed to amend or change the petition at all, and so had nothing to do with it. They are, of course, handling the appeal to the Third Circuit Court of Appeals.

The Beverly confession and the statements by Abu-Jamal and his brother Billy Cook, having been rejected by both state and federal courts, have little or no chance at this point of becoming part of his legal case—unless he gets a new trial. At that point, he could introduce any evidence and witnesses he wishes. That has not stopped him and his new legal team from continuing to push the issue of absolute innocence and the Beverly story, however. The risk is that by doing so at the Third Circuit Court of Appeals level, they may have the same effect on the three-judge appeals panel as they appear to have had on Judge Yohn. The judges might become soured on the other claims being made in Abu-Jamal's *habeas* petition, leading to a rejection of all claims.

The Beverly story should have no bearing on the *Batson* claim of race-based jury selection. But it does undercut many of the other claims of constitutional error in the *habeas* petition, all of which are being appealed. For example, both prosecution witness Chobert, in his early statement to police, and defense witness Dessie Hightower, in statements to police and testimony at the trial and PCRA hearing, spoke of a shooter fleeing, but not in the direction described by Beverly. The earlier defense theory had been that the fleeing suspect went down an alleyway located on the south side of Locust between 12th and 13th Streets, while Beverly says he ran down a subway entrance on 13th Street. (If it had been 12th Street, Veronica Jones, who was right there, should have seen him.) Though William Cook's claim that Freeman was in his car raises the possibility that Freeman might have been the suspect witnesses saw fleeing east, without a stronger case that Freeman was there, by pressing ahead with Beverly, the defense risks undermining the earlier fleeing suspect theory.

But whatever the effect of the Beverly strategy on the Third Circuit appeal, the new direction taken by Abu-Jamal and his new legal team, focusing on a claim of absolute innocence and on the alleged framing of Abu-Jamal because of his politics and his writing, is bound to remain a divisive issue among those concerned about his fate.

Chapter Ten

A Sentence is Lifted...
At Least for Now

For Abu-Jamal, who has reportedly told his attorneys and supporters over the years that he would rather die than spend the rest of his life behind bars, Federal District Court Judge William Yohn's ruling on his *habeas* appeal was the second worst of all possible worlds. It has removed, at least for the present, his death sentence. But at the same time, even if he can avoid being resentenced to death by a new jury, it makes it extremely unlikely that he will ever get out of prison. The strictures of the Anti-Terrorism and Effective Death Penalty Act and of U.S. Supreme Court precedent mandate that, absent convincing new evidence of innocence or of prosecutorial misconduct, a criminal defendant only gets one federal appeal of his or her trial. If Yohn's decision were to be upheld on appeal, the best Abu-Jamal could hope for would be to spend the rest of his life behind bars with no possibility of parole, and with no chance to further appeal his case.

His alleged desire to avoid just that outcome may well have convinced Abu-Jamal to attempt what fired attorney Daniel Williams has called "a legal Hail Mary pass"—a reference to the football term for a last-ditch long bomb fired off by a desperate quarterback as the clock is ticking down to zero. The hope is that a teammate will catch it in the end zone and win the game. It seems clear now that the long bomb failed.

That, however, should in no way diminish concerns about a central reality. Abu-Jamal, still in prison, and still at risk of facing a reinstated death penalty, did not receive anything approaching a fair trial, and did not receive a fair appeal of his conviction. He stands convicted of a crime—first-degree murder—which an enormous amount of evidence would suggest he may not have committed.

From day one, Abu-Jamal's many attorneys have all been convinced of the impossibility of his getting a fair trial either in Philadelphia's heavily politicized courts or in the equally politicized state supreme court. They all have pinned their hopes instead on his finally getting at least a measure of justice at the federal court level. In that light, it is stunning how little was won in Judge Yohn's ruling. It had taken over two decades for this case to finally reach the federal court. It had then taken Judge Yohn over two years of deliberations to reach a decision on Abu-Jamal's appeal. And what did he do? He rejected 20 carefully reasoned challenges to the constitutionality and fairness of the trial and state appeals process, certifying only one of these—the claim of racial bias in jury selection—for appeal. Then, turning to the penalty phase of the trial, he chose the most technical and seemingly mundane of reasons—the wording of the juror decision forms—to overturn the verdict of death. An appointee to the bench during the term of George Bush the elder, the judge didn't even bother to analyze the rest of the *habeas* petition's challenges of the penalty phase of the trial, saying that these issues were irrelevant since he had already overturned the penalty verdict.

In fairness, Yohn, like all federal judges handling *habeas* petitions these days, was operating within tight legal constraints. Conservatives in Congress, with the blessing of pro-death penalty President Bill Clinton, took advantage of the anti-terrorist hysteria that followed the 1995 bombing of the Murrah Federal Building in Oklahoma City, where 165 people had died, to pass into law the Anti-Terrorism and Effective Death Penalty Act. That law strictly limits the ability of federal judges to overrule decisions by state courts. Under the terms of the act, a state court's decision must be deemed not just technically or factually wrong but "unreasonably" wrong. Only then can a federal judge reverse the decision. Similarly, even if a state court decision is deemed wrong, it must pass a further test. In order for the federal court to overturn a trial result, the error must seem to have been serious enough that, if it hadn't been made, the jury would have come to a different verdict.

Moreover, there is no provision for the tallying up of such errors and considering their potentially cumulative impact on the jury. Even if there may have been 20 or 30 errors at a trial, to qualify as evidence that a trial was unfair, each error must stand alone in being deemed sufficient to have swayed the jury. A juror at the end of a trial might well conclude that 10 or 20 small doubts about prosecution's evidence add up to a reasonable doubt. But a federal judge in a *habeas* appeal may not combine the impact of all the errors to conclude that a trial was unfair.

Perhaps most seriously, the act requires federal judges to accept as true the facts of a case as determined by the state court judge. This last restriction on the actions of a federal *habeas* judge was particularly damaging in

Abu-Jamal's case. It meant that even when Abu-Jamal and his attorneys were claiming in his *habeas* appeal that Judge Albert Sabo was biased and unfair, Yohn was required to assume that all the facts, as determined by that same Judge Sabo at the trial and the post-conviction hearing, are true—even in reaching a decision concerning the fairness of the judge and his decisions.

It is incredibly tough for a defendant to overcome these hurdles.

That said, Yohn at times seemed to be bending over backwards to avoid ruling that Judge Sabo and the state supreme court had been unreasonable in any of their decisions. For example, Yohn ignored the astonishing, even unprecedented, extent of corruption within the Philadelphia Police Department, and the Center City division in particular, at the time of Abu-Jamal's arrest and trial. He ignored the large number of corrupt cops who were involved in the investigation of his case, and the fact that a large number of police personnel, including many who were involved in Abu-Jamal's case, were later convicted on charges of lying and manufacturing evidence to win convictions. Despite this horrific record Yohn dismissed out of hand the notion that there might have been a conspiracy among police to manufacture an Abu-Jamal confession.

Yohn also claimed that, because Abu-Jamal compiled the list of people he wanted as character witnesses in the guilt phase of the trial, this proved that he was also in control over the decision as to what other witnesses to put on the stand, and thus over the entire direction of his trial. Yet clearly, the naming of character witnesses, unlike regular crime witnesses, is uniquely something that only a defendant can properly do, and it is therefore an unreasonable litmus test of who is in control. He repeatedly cited errors that Jackson had made at the trial, such as failing to use Jones' testimony to impeach White. Yet he never took the logical next step of questioning Jackson's competence or effectiveness as an attorney.

Even a cursory read of Yohn's 272-page ruling on Abu-Jamal's *habeas* petition shows how heavily the Effective Death Penalty Act (EDPA) influenced the judge's rulings. Over and over again—indeed at least 70 times in the course of his lengthy ruling—Yohn cites errors and improprieties at the trial and during the case's various appeals, concluding each time that the mistakes and errors were "reasonable," or "not unreasonable."

A more careful review of the ruling, however, further shows that Yohn made a number of significant mistakes of his own, both of interpretation and fact. Some of these would suggest that he didn't even read the transcripts of the case very carefully.

Let's look at that decision.

1. On the first claim, that the state had induced false testimony from witnesses, Yohn concludes as follows regarding Cynthia White, the government's star witness:

> Although each line of impeachment [of her testimony by the defense] could permit an inference that White was being untruthful, I cannot say that the jury or the judge at the PCRA hearing—each of whom was able to observe White's demeanor on the witness stand for over two days—was *unreasonable* [emphasis added] in crediting her trial testimony...[1]

Yohn notes that Dr. John Hayes, the medical examiner who testified as a defense expert witness at the PCRA hearing, had said that the physical evidence suggested that Abu-Jamal could not have been shot from below. Then, using a double negative as linguistically tortured as his reasoning, Yohn adds that Hayes:

> ...also could not conclude that a bent petitioner could not have been shot by a falling Faulkner.[2]

He concludes:

> The state court therefore did not *unreasonably* [emphasis added] determine as a fact that Faulkner could have shot petitioner as described by White.[3]

Actually, Hayes had been quite definite and unambiguous in his testimony, saying that the bullet which hit Abu-Jamal had traveled in a straight line, without striking any bone, passing "from the right side of the chest, backwards, downwards, toward the left." This, he had said:

> ...would be consistent with a shooter above Mr. Jamal, possibly with Mr. Jamal slightly bent and a standing shooter firing horizontally.[4]

When it comes to Chobert, the cab driver, Yohn again gets stuck on the matter of reasonableness. But here he seems to get confused. The defense had suggested that Chobert offered testimony that was untruthful on the basis that it was at odds with that of other witnesses. For example he had failed to observe White at the scene, did not see a gun in the hand of the defendant, and did not see either an altercation between Billy Cook and Faulkner, or later, the police beating Abu-Jamal—both reported by witness White and others. Yet Yohn, curiously, cited these very inconsistencies as evidence that Chobert had no deal with prosecutors to provide false testimony. As the judge puts it:

> These elements of Chobert's testimony strongly indicate that
> the PCRA court's finding that he had no cooperation agreement
> with the prosecution was not *unreasonable*.[5] [emphasis added]

Yohn also makes a serious error, both logical and factual, in discounting the issue raised by the defense concerning Chobert's strange lack of fear in approaching the shooting scene before the arrival of police. The issue: why wasn't he afraid of being shot? The defense's explanation is simple: Chobert had initially told police that the shooter had fled the scene, and thus had nothing to fear. The defense has always argued that Chobert clearly felt Abu-Jamal wasn't the shooter; otherwise he would not have so casually walked right up to the fallen officer before police arrived, while Abu-Jamal, the man he only later pointed to as the killer, was sitting nearby on the curb. Yohn rejects this reasoning, saying the state court was:

> "...not *unreasonable*" [emphasis added] in "failing to account
> for Chobert's lack of fear in approaching Faulkner," because "other
> witnesses approached or remained at the scene of the shooting
> despite knowing what had transpired: Cynthia White, Veronica
> Jones, William Cook.[6]

But as the judge should have realized, there is a critical difference here between Chobert and those other witnesses. Putting aside whether White really was a genuine eyewitness, according to her own testimony, she didn't actually approach the shooting scene until after police had arrived. She stated that she stayed at the corner of the intersection, which was more than two and a half car lengths away from Faulkner and Abu-Jamal, until then, at which time it would have been safe to go closer. Billy Cook, meanwhile, didn't approach the scene at all; he was on the scene the whole time. Besides, Faulkner was dead and Cook certainly had no reason to fear his own brother! As for Jones, she was all the way at the far end of the block, at 12th Street and Locust and far from approaching the scene, actually left as police arrived. Yohn was simply incorrect in saying that she had been "at the scene of the shooting." It's hard to understand how Yohn could have compared the behavior of any of these three witnesses to Chobert, unless he hadn't really read the court transcripts carefully.

Two other peculiarities about Chobert's testimony should be mentioned, though the defense failed to raise either one, either at the trial, the PCRA hearing, or in the *habeas* petition. First, why would Chobert, reportedly inebriated and driving on a suspended license at the time, and therefore also in violation of parole, pull up behind a parked police cruiser with flashing lights? Several witnesses stated they saw no taxi where Chobert claimed to be parked. Only White recalled seeing his taxi there, where he claimed it was. Yet on the stand, even she said she didn't recall seeing it there until after the shooting was over and police had arrived on the scene.[7] This raises doubts about whether Chobert was actually that close to the scene of the shooting. Second, how likely is it that White, a prostitute with 38 arrests and outstanding warrants at the time, would have hung around the area of a police killing as police cars flooded into the scene? Judge Yohn can be excused for not considering these two issues, since the defense for some reason overlooked them in their *habeas* petition.

2. Regarding the claim of suppressed evidence that the real killer had fled the scene, Yohn dismisses assertions that Chobert altered his testimony, from first telling police on the scene that he had seen the shooter flee, to insisting on the stand that Abu-Jamal had been the shooter. He says Judge Sabo's determination of the facts are "not unreasonable." Here again the judge is falling back on the restrictions of the Effective Death Penalty Act. He goes on to rule on the matter of another witness, Deborah Kordansky. She had initially told police she had seen someone running from the shooting scene. But she had not been called as a defense witness at trial because the defense had been unable to obtain her address from the prosecution and was thus unable to serve her with a subpoena to appear. According to Yohn, this didn't matter. He determines that the state court's decision that her testimony wouldn't have likely changed the outcome of the trial was "not contrary to or an *unreasonable* [emphasis added] application of clearly established federal law."

But Yohn makes another major factual error here, when he rules that the state court found no evidence that polygraphs were only administered to defense witness Dessie Hightower. This issue is extremely important, for what the defense is attempting to demonstrate is that police investigators and prosecutors, from the outset of the case, had focused on pinning the crime on Abu-Jamal. They want to show that police investigators were deliberately ignoring witnesses who said there had been another shooter. And Yohn, in supporting the state court finding here, is dead wrong. In fact, at the post-conviction hearing, prosecutor Charles Grant conceded the point to the defense, stipulating that no polygraphs had been administered, except to Hightower. As he said during attorney Dan Williams' questioning of Detective William Thomas, the lead detective in the Abu-Jamal investigation, referring to whether any of the prosecution's witnesses in the case were tested:

> Mr. Grant: I will make it easy for them [the defense], Judge: Nobody was
>   given a polygraph. [8]

It doesn't get any clearer than that. Here is a case where the state court was wrong on the facts, and Yohn missed it. Again, however, this could be blamed in large part on the defense, which failed in its *habeas* filing, to counter the state court's incorrect fact-finding that no evidence existed as to whether prosecution witnesses might have been polygraphed. The defense could easily have cited Grant's stipulation that no tests had been administered to prosecution witnesses. It didn't. It is also Yohn's fault. In a complicated case, he opted, for some reason, to hold no evidentiary hearings, which meant he had no benefit of counsel for the two sides being able to explain its complexities to him.

Yohn, meanwhile, compounds his error of fact regarding this particular claim about the use of polygraphs by illogically supporting Sabo's unjustifiable determination that Hightower had not been coerced by police. Yohn's reasoning is that the polygraph administered to Hightower was voluntary. In a strictly legal sense, it was: Hightower was not under arrest, and he signed a statement in the police homicide office, saying he was taking the test "voluntarily." But in concluding that he wasn't coerced, Yohn conveniently ignores that this was a young black man who had been called in by the police and questioned (the term "interrogated" might be more appropriate) in the station for six hours. It is an ordeal most ordinary people would surely consider to be coercion in and of itself, even if one was a white, law-abiding citizen. Though Judge Yohn might be excused for not knowing it , since the defense was polite enough not to mention it, perhaps it would be appropriate to recall a few facts about Hightower. He was "outed" as an alleged transvestite by prosecutor McGill in the Philadelphia media. Besides being black, he was reputed to live what is euphemistically called an "alternative lifestyle." If true, he would have been all the more vulnerable—especially in police investigators' eyes—to intimidation through the use of a polygraph machine.

Then there is the matter of the prosecution's failure to tell Abu-Jamal during his trial that the license or license replacement application of Arnold Howard had been found, not in Cook's VW as the prosecution had told the defense originally, but in Faulkner's shirt pocket. As noted earlier, this goes to whether there had been more to the "interaction" between Faulkner and the person(s) he stopped in the car than McGill was telling the jury. That the document was in his pocket suggests there was considerably more to the scene than McGill's assertion that only Cook and

Faulkner were "interacting," with Abu-Jamal arriving later.

On this point, Yohn's reasoning is also strained. He argues that Howard had changed his own account, first telling investigators that he had left it in the car, and later at the PCRA hearing, saying he had given it to Kenneth Freeman. He then concludes:

> This additional information, considered in light of all the evidence presented, would not have given rise to a *reasonable* [emphasis added] probability of a different outcome. [9]

This is a very dubious conclusion. First, it should be perfectly understandable why Howard, when first picked up by police and told he was under suspicion in the killing of Faulkner, might have lied about the license application document. Such a document is legally acceptable in lieu of a license while someone is waiting for a new license to be issued. But loaning it to someone else is a crime, and he certainly didn't want to give police another excuse to hold him in custody at that point. In any case, there was no testimony that Faulkner had searched Cook's vehicle between the time he pulled the car over and the time he was shot, so he couldn't have found it in the car anyway.

That said, who knows what a jury would have done if confronted with information that Faulkner had had that license document in his possession at the time he was shot? When would he have obtained it, since there was no testimony that he had personally searched the car, and since Billy Cook had a valid license to show him? It certainly could have led jurors to contemplate the presence of another person at the scene. What Howard had to say about it was not really that relevant. The key point was two-fold: the prosecution had clearly misinformed the defense about where police found that document; just as important, the location of the document—in Faulkner's pocket—directly contradicts the prosecution's version of events.

But while the Effective Death Penalty Act's limitations may have had an effect on all these issues, it did its greatest harm to Abu-Jamal's appeal in the matter concerning witness Veronica Jones. As we saw earlier, Jones, on the stand at the PCRA hearing, had tearfully recanted her trial testimony, saying police had coerced her into saying she had not seen another shooter fleeing the scene. Recalling that testimony, Yohn says:

> Although I do not say that the cold paper record compels the conclusion that Jones was incredible in recanting her testimony, I conclude that the state courts did not *unreasonably* [emphasis added] determine that Jones was not credible in 1996. [10]

Coming from a federal judge, this is actually quite an astonishing comment. Here, he refers to the "cold paper record" that is, in fact, the basis of any appeals argument, and indeed is the whole reason courts pay to have court stenographers. He is saying here that the court record does not lead one to believe Jones was lying when she recanted her trial testimony and claimed she'd been pressured by police to lie about what she'd seen. That is, the paper record supports the truthfulness of her recantation. Indeed, the truthfulness of Jones' claim is further supported by the fact that outstanding charges were dropped against her following her 1982 trial testimony.[11]

Despite this, Yohn says that, whether right or wrong in their decisions, the state courts (that's Judge Sabo and the higher court), can still be considered not *unreasonable* in determining that her recantation was unbelievable. One would think that if Yohn believes that the paper record (which as we saw in Chapter 8 was actually quite dramatic) suggests Jones might be credible, it would have been appropriate for him to have ordered an evidentiary hearing. This would have allowed him to witness Jones' behavior and attitude on the stand first hand. Instead, despite his evident misgivings, he simply accepts Sabo's fact-finding as trumping the "cold paper record."

3. On the issue of Abu-Jamal's purported confession in the hospital, and the related issue of Judge Sabo's refusal to delay the trial in order to allow the defense to call Officer Gary Wakshul, Yohn again offers some extremely tendentious logic. Discounting the whole notion of a conspiracy, he suggests that if any two people say the same thing, then it must be true. As he puts it, the prosecution:

> ...could not have created or deliberately permitted witnesses to create a false impression that petitioner had confessed, given that two witnesses testified to the confession.

It is difficult to fathom the judge's thinking here. If we accept this rationale—that two people testifying similarly equals the truth—then the federal government's entire conspiracy statute ought to be trashed, along with the convictions of countless mobsters, racketeers and terrorists, who frequently end up being put away on conspiracy counts. Apparently, in Judge Yohn's worldview, conspiracies are only entered into by the bad guys, not by the good guys. The judge must not have been reading the local papers during the last two years while he was studying Abu-Jamal's appeal. During that time there have been a number of stories about Philadelphia police engaging in conspiracies, all of which involved two or more people saying the same untrue things. To cite only the most recent example, (which occurred while Yohn was still mulling the Abu-Jamal appeal), an early morning drunk driving crash by Captain James J. Brady, head of the Homicide Division, who hit several cars and a lamppost, went unreported. Then the fact that it went unreported was covered up, all with the help of a number of police officers who all offered up the same lies concerning the incident.[12]

Returning to Yohn's handling of the belatedly-reported alleged confession, these two witnesses were not exactly disinterested parties. One, Police Officer Garry Bell, was Faulkner's partner and close friend. The other, hospital guard Priscilla Durham, was friendly with Faulkner too, and admitted to having coffee with him on occasion. Like most people who work in the private security business, she perhaps harbored hopes of becoming a police officer herself. Furthermore, Yohn ignores the fact that at least a dozen other police officers and hospital personnel were around Abu-Jamal at the time of the allegedly "shouted" confession (including Wakshul's partner, Trombetta, who Wakshul said was right next to Abu-Jamal and him), yet none reported hearing it.

One thing Yohn didn't have in front of him in considering the issue of the reported confession was any testimony from Dr. Coletta, the physician who was in the ER when Abu-Jamal was brought in by police, and who told me in two interviews that he had heard no confession. As mentioned in Chapter 1 and elsewhere, Coletta went further. He told me in an interview that at the time Abu-Jamal was brought into the hospital he was so weak from blood loss (and short of breath because of the blood pooling in his lungs) that he probably would have had difficulty shouting anything. Coletta was not called by the defense to testify at the PCRA hearing, according to Weinglass because he was concerned that the doctor, on the stand, would not support the defense contention that Abu-Jamal was too weak to shout out a confession.

Yohn also accepts as not "unreasonable" Judge Sabo's fact-finding that Wakshul and Bell had satisfactorily explained their two-month delay in reporting the confession by noting that they had been "stunned" at Faulkner's death. But he ignores a far more unbelievable assertion by Wakshul, made when he finally reported the confession to a police Internal Affairs investigator on February 11, 1982. He claimed at that time that he had not mentioned a confession for over two months not because he had been stunned but because, "I didn't realize it had any importance until today."[13] This excuse, coming from a veteran cop, is so ludicrous on its face that taken all by itself it makes a strong case that the confession testimony was manufactured after the fact.

Judge Yohn goes on to say that the defense "has failed to prove that the unavailability of Wakshul was attributable to the prosecution."[14] This might be technically correct. Though it stretches the limits of believability, it is conceivable that the prosecution was unaware of Wakshul's availability. But even giving this enormous benefit of the doubt to the prosecution, something else is crystal clear. With the access to witnesses—particularly police officers—being entirely in the hands of the prosecution (which kept all contact information to itself), the defense was effectively prevented from learning directly whether Wakshul was available to testify. As it was later revealed by his post-conviction testimony, he was.

Finally, in a truly astounding ruling, Yohn says the petitioner (Abu-Jamal) failed to demonstrate that Wakshul's testimony would have established the lack of a confession "rather than merely creating a credibility issue at best."[15] This, of course, isn't the point. Even if Wakshul's initial three police interviews, in which he doesn't report any confession, don't *prove conclusively* that there was none, isn't the *credibility* of testimony regarding a confession still of crucial importance, especially in a death penalty case? Studies of jurors in capital cases have repeatedly shown that a confession is perhaps the single most critical factor in convincing jurors to convict, because it eases concerns that they might have about inadvertently killing an innocent person. Says Craig Haney, professor of psychology at the University of California, Santa Cruz and a nationally known expert on jury behavior in death penalty cases:

> Jurors certainly tend to believe confessions. Here, of course, there is some reason to doubt whether the confession actually happened. But if jurors believed that it did, it is hard to imagine a more damning piece of evidence to be introduced at trial. As the officers reported it, it not only seemed to establish guilt, but also evidence of a lack of remorse. A truly damning combination.

Might jurors have questioned the whole notion that Abu-Jamal had "shouted out" a confession, had they been informed that the officer who had stayed with the suspect from the time he was placed in the paddy wagon to the time he went into the operating room at the hospital had told investigators that Abu-Jamal "made no comment" during that whole period? Could this have changed the outcome of the trial?

4. Another issue raised by the appeal was the claim that the prosecution during the trial had withheld surveillance files on Abu-Jamal that were in the hands of the Philadelphia Police at the time of his arrest. In his ruling against that claim, Judge Yohn shows a complete naivete or a willful ignorance of the pervasiveness (as described in Chapter 2) of police spying in Philadelphia. There is no question that such files existed. The FBI, in the early 1990s, in response to a Freedom of Information request by the defense, provided some 600 pages of surveillance files specifically documenting FBI and Philadelphia Police monitoring and harassment of Abu-Jamal over a period of a decade. Because of an absence of a state open records law, the Philadelphia Police Department did not provide any of its files.

At the PCRA hearing, these files were not admitted into the court record because Judge Sabo upheld an objection by the prosecution that the documents were not "substantiated" as genuine. Here, Sabo was holding the defense to a much higher standard than the prosecution. As discussed elsewhere, his standard for substantiation of documents provided by the prosecution was entirely lax: with regard to the typewritten statement of hospital guard Priscilla Durham, Sabo made no requirement.

Yet Yohn has a point. Although those records from the FBI could only have been obtained through the official channel of a Freedom of Information Act request, it is fair to ask, as Judge Yohn does, why the defense never bothered to call an FBI official to testify to their authenticity—a major failing. Williams in an interview admitted that "it would have been easy" to have brought in a witness from the FBI to verify the authenticity of the documents. He lays that shortcoming on Wolkenstein, who he says was handling the FBI dossier issue.

Yohn also upholds the state courts in ruling that there was no basis for the admission of the files; that the defense had shown "no foundation" for their introduction into evidence. But in fact, the defense did make that foundation clear at the PCRA hearing by presenting the argument that the existence of the files demonstrated that the government had targeted Abu-Jamal and that the initial decision to charge him with Faulkner's shooting could have been influenced by police antipathy towards him. The defense at the PCRA hearing tried to strengthen its argument that there is a link between police surveillance and malicious prosecutions by presenting an expert witness, researcher and Native American activist Ward Churchill. Though he is an acknowledged expert on COINTELPRO and government spying, Sabo refused to permit Churchill to take the stand, saying his testimony was not relevant to the case.

This is a basic dilemma political defendants have always run up against in American courts. Judges simply won't admit that if law enforcement authorities have been targeting a person who has committed no crime, following him or her around, tapping phones and monitoring mail, it raises questions about the integrity of their prosecution when that person is later arrested. Clearly, the fact that the Philadelphia Police were watching Abu-Jamal for years, assembling files on him, and sharing them with the FBI, should have been made known to jurors at his trial. If nothing else, it raises the question of whether that was why police investigators, within hours of identifying Abu-Jamal as the suspect at the scene of Faulkner's shooting, seemed to lose all interest in witnesses' claims to have seen another man run from the scene. Nonetheless, despite these obvious questions, Yohn concludes:

> Indeed, it was not *unreasonable* [emphasis added] for the state court to conclude that police surveillance in general did not relate to specific police bias against the petitioner...[16]

5. Yohn shows no concern about the poor quality of legal representation Abu-Jamal received at his trial. He concludes that Jackson, contrary to his testimony as a witness at the PCRA hearing, was prepared for trial, and attributes Jackson's errors to Abu-Jamal's failure to cooperate with his court-appointed attorney. One basis for his decision is his uncritical acceptance of the state courts' determination that Jackson had "tried 20 cases in which his clients were charged with murder in the first degree, resulting in six convictions and no death sentences."

As discussed previously, these numbers, supplied by the district attorney's office and accepted at face value by Judge Sabo as the factfinder, and subsequently by Judge Yohn, are highly suspect. Jackson had never been the lead attorney in trying a death penalty case before a jury until he assumed the role of Abu-Jamal's defense attorney. Jackson, in fact, only opened his own law office in 1982, the same year that he started defending Abu-Jamal. Prior to that, he had been the director of Pilcop, a civic organization that was handling police brutality cases. A critical difference here was that these were civil, not criminal actions. Moreover, as a fulltime attorney for Pilcop, he would not have had time to handle a murder case. The death penalty was only restored in Pennsylvania in 1976. At best, Jackson acted as an assisting attorney in several cases, and many of his cases were settled through plea bargains. This was hardly the type of experience to prepare him for going up against one of the D.A.'s star prosecutors in a politically charged case as high profile as this one.

Recall in contrast the current standards in Illinois, where a lead attorney in a death penalty case must have participated in at least eight capital cases before assuming that role. It's not that Illinois' standards are so sterling, for even with that standard, twelve people have been freed from death row in that state after having been found to have been wrongly convicted. The outcry was so intense, in fact, that the pro-death penalty Republican Governor of Illinois, George Ryan, decided, on January 31, 2000, to declare a moratorium on carrying out the death penalty. As he put it:

> I now favor a moratorium because I have grave concerns about our state's shameful record of convicting innocent people and putting them on Death Row.... I cannot support a system which, in its administration, has proven so fraught with error and has come so close to the ultimate nightmare, the state's taking of innocent life.... Until I can be sure that everyone sentenced to death in Illinois is truly guilty, until I can be sure with moral certainty that no innocent man or woman is facing a lethal injection, no one will meet that fate.... [17]

But that was Illinois. This is Pennsylvania. Those Illinois minimums of experience in order to qualify as a lead attorney in a capital case did not, and still don't apply. Needless to say, they also held no sway with Judge Yohn either. (Philadelphia courts in recent years have finally established minimum standards for court-appointed attorneys handling homicide cases. But these only require that the attorney being appointed to a case have five years of trial experience, and a history of having been lead counsel in 10 criminal cases and associate counsel in at least two homicides. Jackson might have met this standard. One difference now, however, is that the rules say a judge should consider appointing an associate counsel in cases where there are a lot of issues [as in this case]. Jackson's request before the start of Abu-Jamal's trial for an assistant counsel was rejected by Judge Ribner.)

Yohn does cite a number of examples in Abu-Jamal's trial where Jackson's performance as a defense attorney was sub par—for example his failure to attempt to impeach Chobert's testimony based upon his probationary status, which Jackson completely ignored. But in the end he resorts to the reasonableness standard, saying that the state courts' denial of the ineffectiveness claim was "not unreasonable."

Judge Yohn does identify several crucial errors made by the state court on this representation issue. He finds that Judge Sabo's determination that

Abu-Jamal was belligerent during the *voir dire*, or jury selection process (the main reason Sabo gave for taking away Abu-Jamal's right to defend himself), was not true. Indeed he says:

> In fact, the record reflects the opposite. Therefore I find that portion of (PCRA) finding 65 concluding that petitioner had been "belligerent" is *unreasonable*.[18] [emphasis added]

But having said that, Yohn then denies relief on this claim, arguing that the state court's decision to remove the defendant's *pro se* right to defend himself was not based solely on that matter. Whether or not Yohn is right in this decision, there is a problem with his analysis of the situation. Judge Sabo as factfinder grossly misrepresented Abu-Jamal's conduct during jury selection, which after all was the primary reason he had cited as trial judge in removing his *pro se* right to represent himself (along with the ridiculous claim that he was intimidating prospective jurors). Given this, why didn't Yohn question the overall fairness of the judge, and perhaps also understand the reason for Abu-Jamal's anger at being represented by Jackson during the trial? There is no suggestion that he considered this.

On related claims, that Abu-Jamal had been denied his right to defend himself, and that he had been improperly ejected from his own trial five days in a row (for protesting the removal of those *pro se* rights), Yohn completely ignored his own finding that Judge Sabo had improperly characterized Abu-Jamal's courtroom behavior during the *voir dire* process as "belligerent." This false charge against the defendant was the obvious explanation for his angry outbursts and sometimes unruly arguments with the court on those days he was ejected from the courtroom. But Yohn concludes that the state court's determination that removal of his *pro se* rights and his repeated ejection from the courtroom were both proper was "not unreasonable."

6. In an example of circular illogic worthy of Lewis Carroll, Yohn denies a claim that the court impermissibly restricted the defense from obtaining favorable evidence. Yohn blames this on Abu-Jamal's lawyer. Be that as it may, at the same time, elsewhere in his ruling, he denies that the lawyer was ineffective. In this claim, Abu-Jamal had argued that the court had blocked his attorney from using the testimony of Veronica Jones to impeach the testimony of Cynthia White. This would have been accomplished with Jones' claim that police offered her the same deal as they had allegedly offered to White in return for her testifying against Abu-Jamal. Yohn says that Jackson erred in not asking White about Jones' claim even

after he called her back to the stand following Jones' testimony. Yet if this is true, shouldn't Yohn have considered this grievous error in passing up an opportunity to impeach the prosecution's key witness—particularly when placed in the context of his other errors at trial—to have been a failure on Jackson's part to provide an effective legal defense?

Yohn, in backing up his decision that the defense had not been barred from using Jones to impeach White at the original trial, also makes a truly astounding error in observing that neither Jones nor White was called by the petitioner at the original PCRA hearing in 1995. As Yohn writes in his ruling:

> The state court determined that petitioner [Abu-Jamal] had presented no evidence of any "deals" made by the Commonwealth with White or Jones in exchange for favorable testimony even after the Pennsylvania Supreme Court remanded the issue for a supplemental hearing, as neither White nor Jones was called as a witness by petitioner at the original hearing.[19]

In fact, Jones, it will be recalled, did appear in a reopened session of the PCRA hearing held in 1996. The defense made quite clear at the hearing and in the record of that hearing the reason Jones was called late. It was not because they had not wanted to call her earlier, but because it had taken them and their paid professional investigators more than a year to locate her. They cited previous examples of intimidation of their witnesses when the police were sent to deliver court summonses, and understandably said that they did not want to request such "help" from the prosecution in obtaining the address for such a critical witness. (Moreover, it wasn't even proper for Yohn to make this criticism that the witness had been called late. The state supreme court had specifically authorized a continuation of the PRCA hearing to accommodate Jones' testimony, meaning the state court had no problem with extending the PCRA hearing order to facilitate her appearance.)

As to the criticism that White was late in testifying, that is correct only if one is applying the other meaning for the word "late." The defense could hardly be criticized for not calling her as a witness: White had officially been dead since 1992! One really has to wonder at this point how carefully Yohn actually read the transcript of the PCRA hearing. The topic of White's death is covered at length in the PCRA hearing transcript. Almost a whole day's worth of that proceeding is devoted to proving whether White was in fact really dead. As mentioned, the defense, which has been trying for years to locate her, remains skeptical about reports of her demise, particularly as the fingerprints of the body identified as White's didn't match an earlier set of her fingerprints on file. Nonetheless, based in part on his erroneous claim that the defense had been derelict in not calling White and Jones as witnesses at the PCRA hearing, Yohn concluded on this count that the state courts' decision that no defense evidence had been restricted at the trial was "not unreasonable."

7. One of the more shocking aspects of Abu-Jamal's trial, which has raised an outcry around the world, from the parliaments of Germany and France to the Diet in Japan, was prosecutor McGill's comment to the jury, during his summation at the end of the guilt phase of the trial. Namely, that jurors needn't fear that they were condemning a man to death in convicting him of murder, since there would be "appeal after appeal and perhaps there could be a reversal of the case, or whatever, so that may not be final." As mentioned, McGill himself had had an earlier capital case he prosecuted overturned by the state supreme court for making almost the identical claim to a jury. The remark was clearly designed to remove the sense of gravity about the decision jurors were about to make. But Judge Yohn discounted the statement's impact on the jury's verdict. He wrote in his decision on this claim that even if in error, the statement was not the kind of:

> ...egregious misconduct...[that would] amount to a denial of constitutional due process.[20]

So, error or not, misconduct or not, he ruled that the state supreme court had not been "unreasonable." The court had based its rejection of the claim on a determination that McGill's comment, taken in the "context of the entire trial," had probably not prejudiced the jury.

What Yohn didn't know, because it wasn't specifically pointed out to him in the defense's *habeas* appeal, is that the State Supreme Court had actually made a special exception on this issue of a prosecutor's removing the gravity of the situation from the jurors just for Abu-Jamal's case. Only three years prior to ruling on his case, back in 1986, it had ruled (in a case prosecuted by McGill called *Commonwealth v. Baker*), that telling a jury in a capital trial that their verdict shouldn't be considered final because there would be appeals was not permissible. In Abu-Jamal's case, the supreme court justices reversed themselves. Only a year later, in the next case involving the same issue, called *Commonwealth v. Beasley*, the state's high court restored the precedent, ordering the "precluding of all remarks about the appellate process *in all future trials* [emphasis added]."[21] Since the court had already barred such prosecutorial statements back in 1986, only allowing one exception—the Abu-Jamal case—this decision not to make the 1990 ruling retroactive was clearly aimed specifically at ensuring it would not apply to his case alone.

Yohn also took some issue with another inflammatory statement McGill made in his summation. McGill's effort to evoke a general fear of crime among jurors by referring to a "war in the street" was "perhaps ill-advised," he writes. But despite this, he then concludes that this overstepping of the bounds was:

> ...insufficiently prejudicial to undermine the court's confidence in the fairness of petitioner's conviction.[22]

In other words, in Yohn's view, although McGill should not have made the comment, he feels that it did not in itself likely alter the jury's final decision.

In the end, Yohn's final word on the matter should surely dismay the thousands of trial lawyers (and prosecutors) who put such effort into and stock in their final arguments, and who pride themselves on their ability to win over a jury. Calling McGill's error-laden and over-the-top summation to Abu-Jamal's jury just "one minor phrase in the context of the entire trial,"[23] he concludes that the state court decision discounting claims that the summation was improper was "not unreasonable."

Note a double standard here in the appeals process. Each argument by the defense must be strong enough by itself to stand alone as a reason for ordering a new trial. The separate effects of these arguments cannot be combined to justify a new trial. Yet even a grave misstep by the prosecution, *which in another trial had been enough to throw out a verdict,* can be placed in the "context of the entire trial," and therefore dismissed as somehow of negligible significance. Defense arguments must stand alone; prosecution errors are seen in the context of the whole trial.

8. There was one claim that Judge Yohn did find had at least sufficient merit and constitutional importance for him to certify it for appeal. This certification means that he vouched to the Third Circuit Court of Appeals that there were good grounds for them to hear legal arguments on it. This was the defense's so-called *Batson* claim that blacks had been improperly removed from consideration as jurors. Certification means that even though Yohn rejected the claim, he apparently felt that there was enough merit to the defense's claims, or enough constitutional importance to the issue, that the full three-judge appeals court should accept arguments from both sides on it. There are several possibilities as to what this all means.

Some attorneys who are familiar with Yohn say he may be simply saying that this is an important issue that the appeals court judges need to consider on their own. Others suggest that Yohn may be subtly inviting the appeals court to overrule him and order him to hold an evidentiary hearing on the issue. According to this theory, Yohn may not want to take on himself the political heat for overturning Abu-Jamal's conviction based upon evidence of racism in the jury selection process. He may, this theory goes, be seeking the cover of having a higher court order him to hold hearings. Then, if the evidence of race-based jury selection is overwhelming, he would have no alternative but to overturn the verdict and order a new trial.

Whatever Yohn's reasons for certifying only this particular claim for appeal, alone among the 20 claims concerning the guilt phase of his trial, it now represents Abu-Jamal's best hope for gaining a new trial. (That's not to say that the defense cannot appeal the other 19 rejected claims. It can and has said it will. But unlike in the case of the certified claim, the appeals court is free to reject those other appeals without argument and simply leave Yohn's decisions standing without comment.)

There was some dispute at Abu-Jamal's initial appeal to the state supreme court as to the number of blacks who were peremptorily excused from jury duty by the prosecution. As we saw in Chapter 7, in responding to Abu-Jamal's original state appeal of his conviction, the District Attorney's office had submitted an affidavit from McGill which improperly and inaccurately claimed that only eight of the 15 jurors he excused with peremptory challenges were black. The defense, meanwhile, submitted an affidavit correctly listing the number of such black jurors as being 11. The state Supreme Court had accepted the D.A.'s fraudulent numbers.

When the defense came to the PCRA hearing prepared to put the other three excused blacks on the stand, and to call McGill to explain his actions, the prosecution agreed to accept that there had been more black jurors than the D.A.'s office had originally claimed. They stipulated to 10, which the defense accepted, though they had another affidavit from Jackson confirming that an eleventh juror was black also—a point made in the defense's *habeas* appeal. (The stipulation was agreed to, Weinglass recalls years later, because one of the three rejected jurors the defense had brought in to testify that she was, indeed, black, turned out to be the wrong juror. She had been counted already. But he says there was another black juror who should have been brought in.) But that stipulation, and the defense's acceptance of it, may in the end have hurt Abu-Jamal's appeals chances, since it led the defense to drop plans it had to call McGill to the stand.

The trouble is that in rejecting the defense's *Batson* claim, Yohn did not question the number of black jurors peremptorily dismissed by McGill. Rather, he refused to permit the defense to introduce evidence it had developed to support the argument that the excusing of those jurors was based solely upon their race—evidence that would have been introduced at the PCRA hearing had McGill been put on the stand as a witness. Instead, he accepted, as "not unreasonable," the state supreme court's 1998 decision that the defense had not made a prima facie case of discrimination in jury selection. In other words, he accepted that court's determination that the defense had not demonstrated that the excluding of 10 blacks by the prosecutor had been done because of those potential jurors' race. In his decision, Yohn criticizes the defense for not having put McGill on the stand at the PCRA hearing where he could have been asked about his peremptory challenges. Yohn says this was an error that precluded him from hearing McGill's testimony. He also denies a request by the defense for an opportunity, at an evidentiary hearing, to submit evidence of a pattern of peremptory dismissals of black jurors by McGill over the course of six other trials. Again he says that the defense, by not calling McGill at the PCRA hearing, had passed up its opportunity to do so at the federal level. The evidence of McGill's record, he says, was available in 1995.

He goes on to reject, on the basis that its data only goes back to 1983, the relevance of a study of Philadelphia juries by two academic researchers, David Baldus and Gary Woodworth, at the University of Iowa School of Law.

As was reported at the front of this volume, however, the judge was wrong on both of these points. McGill's record was not made available to the defense until after the state Supreme Court had already ruled on Abu-Jamal's appeal. *It should therefore have been considered by Judge Yohn as new evidence.*

Meanwhile, the judge's rejection of the defense's data on the Philadelphia district attorney's record of peremptorily rejecting black jurors was the result of his confusing that data with data in a study of race-based jury sentencing by the D.A. That latter study did indeed cover the 1983-1993 period. But the data on jury selection was for the period when Ed Rendell was district attorney. The data submitted in evidence not only covered the period of Abu-Jamal's trial; it included Abu-Jamal's trial. Moreover, the rejected data in question, which had been developed by Prof. Baldus and was used in another appeal known as *Hardcastle v. Horn,* had not become public knowledge until the appeals court had ruled on that case, which was after Abu-Jamal's state supreme court appeal had already been rejected. In other words, as with the McGill data, the *Hardcastle* jury data was new evidence available to the defense for the first time in 1999, when the federal *habeas* petition was filed.

Weinglass argues that Judge Yohn's biggest error, however, was in accepting the state supreme court's opinion that Abu-Jamal had not made a prima facie case of race-based peremptory challenges by the prosecution. "The state court applied the wrong standard," he says, explaining that under the U.S. supreme court's *Batson* decision precedent, the defense only needed to show evidence of race-based jury selection. It didn't need to prove its case. An attorney who specializes in federal appeals of indigent cases in Philadelphia, and who is familiar with the Abu-Jamal case, agrees, saying, "The state supreme court conflated the first two steps of the *Batson* claim, by speculating on race-neutral reasons for the prosecution's peremptory challenges."

In fact, Weinglass notes, the state's high court had no sworn evidence submitted by the prosecution to explain McGill's peremptory challenges of blacks in the case. The district attorney's office did offer explanations, but only in the form of a legal brief, not as sworn evidence (Judge Yohn included those explanations in a footnote in his opinion). Moreover, some of those explanations for striking black jurors are not as race-neutral as they might first appear. For example, in the case of at least five of the blacks peremptorily struck by McGill, a reason given was that the potential juror had "listened to" or "heard" Abu-Jamal on the radio. But a check of the transcripts of the jury selection show that was a question McGill only asked of prospective black jurors, not white jurors. Meanwhile, other reasons given for the striking of black jurors, such as "hesitated before answering," should have led to a lot of *disqualifying of white jurors too*.

In denying the *Batson* claim, Yohn also makes the argument that Abu-Jamal at no point made an allegation that McGill said anything improper regarding race during the *voir dire* process. As he puts it:

> Furthermore, petitioner points to no improper statement or
> question by the prosecutor during jury selection.[24]

In fact, while Yohn can be excused for not knowing it, because the defense apparently never noticed it either, McGill did make a clearly racially motivated comment during the trial itself, which was recorded in the transcript. As recounted earlier in Chapter 4, this occurred on June 21, 1982. During Jackson's questioning of Cynthia White, a black municipal judge came into the courtroom as a spectator and sat on the side of the courtroom where Abu-Jamal's family and supporters were sitting. As we saw, McGill openly expressed concern that the black judge's very appearance in the courtroom might sway the opinions of "the black jurors." Only after Jackson questioned his focus on just the two black jurors, did McGill quickly add, "or anybody." This brief conversation at the bench makes it crystal clear that McGill, despite his protestations to the contrary, actually viewed black jurors as distinctly different in their thinking than whites. This ought to cast his peremptory challenges in a different light. Unfortunately for Abu-Jamal, his defense attorneys overlooked that seemingly innocuous courtroom aside, and it was never brought to any court's attention, including Yohn's.

I should add here that it would be very appropriate if Abu-Jamal's original conviction were eventually to be overturned on the issue of jury selection bias, for race has been the big underlying issue in this case from the start. It was a hot issue originally in large part because it was about a prominent black man who was charged with killing a white cop. The white judge had a long history of sending black convicts to death row. The jury, thanks to court procedures which give the prosecution an unlimited right to reject potential jurors who express qualms about the death penalty, was largely white, male, and politically and socially conservative. This was true even aside from McGill's peremptory rejection of 11 black jurors who did say they could support a death penalty verdict.

(One point rarely gets mentioned in the debate over capital punishment. The concept of a defendant's being tried by a jury of his peers is never adhered to in a death penalty case. Every community includes large numbers of people who oppose capital punishment. Yet every one of those people may be legally barred from serving on a capital jury.)[25]

For whatever reason, Judge Yohn, who has an excellent reputation in the district as an intelligent and fair jurist, chose to rule that the state supreme court's decision that the defense had failed to make a prima facie *Batson* case was *not unreasonable.* Experienced defense attorneys familiar with Yohn, however, say it may well be this particular aspect of his decision that he is unsure of, and that this may be the reason he *certified* the *Batson* claim for appeal.

Judge Yohn's ruling on Abu-Jamal's *habeas corpus* petition has left nobody happy. Maureen Faulkner has, without any evidence to support her

charge, condemned it as a cave-in by the judge, whom she accuses of buck-
ling under pressure from Abu-Jamal's "celebrity" supporters.

District Attorney Lynne Abraham has already appealed the overturning of Abu-Jamal's sentence. She also requested and succeeded in having
the judge stay the order lifting the sentence. Instead of being transferred to
a regular prison during the course of his and the D.A.'s appeals, Abu-Jamal
must remain in the hellish environs of death row. This is a deliberately
punitive measure. This is particularly true if it later turns out that the
Appeals Court upholds Yohn's decision and the D.A. chooses not to retry
the case to restore the death sentence.

Abu-Jamal and his supporters are also disappointed. His conviction
for first-degree murder was upheld by the judge, all of his 20 claims for an
overturning of that conviction having been rejected.

Now, perhaps more than ever before, this case will move ahead on two
distinct tracks.

On the legal track, Abu-Jamal's new defense team will certainly try to
get the Appeals Court to reverse Yohn on all 20 of the rejected *habeas*
claims. But they will be focusing efforts on the certified appeal of Yohn's
rejection of Abu-Jamal's *Batson* claim concerning the removal of blacks
from the jury. That, without doubt, is now Abu-Jamal's best hope for overturning his conviction and winning a new trial.

The defense could also cite one of the errors made by Yohn—for
example his assumption that Cynthia White was alive and should have
been called as a witness at the PCRA hearing—and convince the Appeals
Court to reverse Yohn on another of the *habeas* claims, though this is less
likely to succeed.

Meanwhile, on the other track—the public relations battle—the Free
Mumia movement faces a dilemma. Having someone willing to say that he
is the real killer, and that an innocent man is now sitting on death row for
a crime he didn't commit, is certainly a compelling organizing tool, particularly for energizing existing supporters. But as we have seen already, in this
case it is a double-edged sword. The claim no longer has any realistic
chance of making it into the courts. And because Beverly's story is so far-
fetched, focusing on it runs the risk of turning away many potential supporters of Abu-Jamal's cause. That hasn't stopped the defense team from
promoting the hit-man execution theory at every public opportunity. They
even seem to be trying to get it considered again at this next level of the
appeals process, with an amicus brief filed by Michael Yamamoto, a

California attorney, raising the issue of absolute innocence based on Beverly's affidavit.

As his court battle moves to the next stage in the Third Circuit Court of Appeals, the battle for public support and media attention also enters a new stage. A major challenge will be to keep activists and supporters involved and energized now that the focus of their concern, Abu-Jamal, is no longer, at least for the time being, facing imminent death. Moreover, by appearing to take the pressure off the case, the Yohn decision also puts added pressure on the defense's ability to raise funds. How the defense and the movement handle this legal and political battle, given the new circumstances in which Abu-Jamal finds himself, will be crucial and remains to be seen.

Chapter Eleven

Media Bias
and the
Struggle for Truth

Throughout the course of this case, there have been two distinct lines of struggle for both sides. One, as we have just seen, has been in the courtroom, with Abu-Jamal and his various attorneys battling against a string of Philadelphia district attorneys and their staffs, the investigators of the Philadelphia Police, and the governor and his attorney general. The other struggle, certainly of equal and, some might argue even greater importance, has been in the court of public opinion. In this arena, Abu-Jamal, his family, his friends and a wide network of supporters now stretch across the globe. They are battling against the same Philadelphia district attorney, the same Pennsylvania governor, the Fraternal Order of Police and their supporters, and against Maureen Faulkner, the widow of Officer Faulkner, a compelling victim who engenders great sympathy. She has made the execution of Abu-Jamal a focus of her life for two decades.

The epic struggle of *The Commonwealth of Pennsylvania v. Mumia Abu Jamal* is unlike any other case involving a death row inmate for two interrelated reasons.

Though he would perhaps deny it on political grounds, Mumia Abu-Jamal is no ordinary prisoner. Blessed with a fine intellect, he is college educated, a gifted writer, handsome and even charismatic, with journalistic experience. He has a resonant voice that can snap a listener to attention immediately. These not only serve him well as his own spokesperson. They have helped him use his dire predicament to publicize to the outside world the inhumanity and suffering on the inside of America's vast prison-industrial complex, and especially inside its own maximum-security killing fields where over 3,700 people, overwhelmingly black and poor, await their date with death. For that reason alone his case has become much more than just the struggle of one man to prove his innocence. For those who support him, and even many who only hear about his case sporadically, he is in a sense everyman inside the prison system. This has assured Abu-Jamal of automatic support among liberal and leftist groups that oppose the death penalty, or that seek to reform the U.S. justice system. His celebrity and potential martyr status in Europe and Asia have made his story emblematic of what many see as the barbarity of America's capital punishment obsession and the racism and fundamental unfairness of its justice system.

At the same time, he is also a political person, standing far to the left of the American mainstream. In speaking out and writing against a system that condemns millions of its citizens to spending their lives being shuttled in and out of prisons—especially citizens with black or brown skin, but also those of any race without the money to hire top-flight lawyers when they get arrested—he is confronting a powerful system, a system that fights back. Once charged with the killing of a policeman (and a white policeman at that), this former active member of the radical, militant Black Panther Party was bound to be viewed as more than just a garden-variety felon. For those who want to see him executed, he instantly became public enemy number one.

There are plenty of people in jail and on death row who have killed police officers. But none has aroused the organized antipathy of law-enforcement organizations, right-wingers who focus on the issue of law and order, and conservative politicians who troll for support in those circles, as has Mumia Abu-Jamal. In contrast, few Americans outside of Illinois, and probably not that many inside the state would know who Manuel Salazar is, even though he killed a Joliet police officer in the course of being arrested. Convicted first of capital murder, his case was overturned, and he was then convicted of manslaughter in a retrial and freed for time served. Yet if Salazar were to give an address at a college graduation today, few would object. When Abu-Jamal gave a taped graduation speech to Antioch College in May 2000, however, hordes of burly off-duty police descended on the bucolic campus to protest. The event drew national press attention (though the focus was almost exclusively on the police, not on the certainly newsworthy phenomenon of a death-row prisoner addressing a graduating class or on what he had to tell them).

Articles and pamphlets have been written on both sides, condemning Abu-Jamal's trial, his incarceration and his death sentence, and condemning him and the movement to free him. Hyperbole has been rampant on both sides. Some of his more earnest supporters claimed, in a case of serious résumé inflation, that he was a leading critic of police corruption before his arrest. For their part, some of his critics, including Maureen Faulkner, have claimed, falsely, that Abu-Jamal has "made millions" from prison through his writing.

The challenge for Abu-Jamal has been to get his message out of a prison where he is so restricted and confined that reporters and supporters cannot bring a tape recorder, much less a camera or video recorder when they visit him. His written communications are monitored and restricted, and visits from outsiders are extremely limited.

For his opponents, the challenge has been to silence a man who is extremely resourceful, and who has access at least to the more progressive media—certain publishing houses, the Pacifica radio network, and alternative newspapers.

The controversy reached the level of a pitched battle in 1994 when National Public Radio planned to have Abu-Jamal do an ongoing series of reports on life inside a maximum-security prison. When the National Fraternal Order of Police found out about this plan, they pulled out the stops to get it taken off the air. Just as the first installment of the series was about to air in May, the NFOP turned to Senator Bob Dole, then a conservative Republican from Kansas with presidential aspirations, getting him to condemn the planned programming on the Senate floor. Dole threatened to cut the funding for the Corporation for Public Broadcasting, a mainstay of NPR. The network caved, and then impounded all the tapes that had already been produced, preventing them from being aired elsewhere.

Explaining the cancellation of the program, NPR Vice President Bill Buzenberg suddenly argued that the network didn't think it was appropriate for someone who was a party in such a "highly polarized and political controversy" to be presenting commentaries. Oddly, though, after dropping the program, NPR aired not a word about this "highly polarized and political" case for over a year. It entirely ignored the dramatic PCRA hearing that ran from June through August 1995, not airing a story until August 19, four days after hearings had ended and two days after Abu-Jamal's August 17 planned execution date had passed.[1]

When it did finally run a story on the case, NPR's coverage was hardly balanced. Reporter Scott Simon, usually perceived as having a left-of-center perspective in his work, performed a hatchet job on Abu-Jamal. He began by misstating the facts, saying that there had been three eyewitnesses to the shooting, when as we know there were only two. (A third witness, who saw the shooting, couldn't say who he had seen do it.) Simon failed to note that both these witnesses were badly compromised because of their legal problems at the time of their trial testimony.

Turning to the matter of the purported hospital confession, Simon interviewed Officer Garry Bell. He did ask Bell why he had waited two months to tell his story to investigators, but then without challenge let Bell attribute his delay to the need to take care of Faulkner's widow. Simon didn't mention that Wakshul, the cop who had stayed with Abu-Jamal the whole time he was in the hospital, had written that the suspect had made "no comment" during that entire time. Simon told listeners that Abu-Jamal's emptied gun was found near him, but he failed to tell them that police never tested it to see if it had been fired recently, or that they had also failed to test his hands to see if he'd even fired a gun. He didn't say that the bullets that were recovered from Faulkner' body were never definitively linked to Abu-Jamal's gun. He concluded his piece by letting Maureen Faulkner challenge Abu-Jamal's silence on the events of the night of that fateful shooting. Yet Simon was surely aware that it is both normal practice and a constitutional right for defendants not to testify.

Although NPR impounded the tapes that Abu-Jamal had already produced, in 1995 the nation's most well-known death-row denizen published his essays as a book titled *Live from Death Row*. Then beginning in 1997, he began airing a version of the same program idea on Pacifica Radio. It went out to a far smaller audience than NPR would have afforded, but this at least got his stories and musings about prison life on death row and a broad range of other political issues, domestic and international, out.

Stiff resistance to his efforts continued. On publication of his book prison authorities, acting on pressure from the state FOP and reportedly from the governor's office as well, barred him from having any contact with reporters. Only in 1996 did he succeed in having a federal court overturn that punitive restriction. When Pacifica began carrying Abu-Jamal's commentaries on the program "Democracy Now," the network saw over half of its affiliate stations drop the show. At Temple University in Philadelphia, which owns WRTI, a public radio station that was airing "Democracy Now," the university's president ordered the program off the air. Since the station is at least nominally a student-run entity, and the station's editors wanted to air the program, this caused a major furor among faculty and students over the issues of academic and press freedom.

The biggest problem confronting Abu-Jamal in this bitter public relations war has been a distinct bias in the mainstream press against him and his advocates. This has been particularly evident in his native Philadelphia. The city's leading newspaper, the *Philadelphia Inquirer*—long noted for its hard-hitting investigative reports—has never assigned a team of crack reporters to look into this controversial and problematic case. The *Inquirer* and the *Daily News* did do a solid job of covering both Abu-Jamal's original trial and his PCRA hearing, and the *Inquirer* editorialized forcefully against the biased and unprofessional behavior of Judge Sabo. But after the PCRA hearing ended in 1997, the two papers' coverage of his case seemed to shift dramatically.

One example occurred in December 1997. Abu-Jamal's supporters organized an "International Tribunal" to air the facts of the case before an international panel of distinguished intellectuals and jurists, including South African writer and political prisoner Dennis Brutus, retired New York State Supreme Court Justice Bruce Wright, Ulf Panzer, a judge in Hamburg Germany, and Gilma Camargo, coordinator of the American Association of Jurists. Seven hundred people attended the event. Journalists from Canada and Europe covered the event. Yet the *Inquirer* and the *Daily News* (both owned by the same publisher, Knight-Ridder), completely ignored it. Responding to a phone call query from me about the news blackout, the *Inquirer's* ombudsman explained that the city editor on duty had decided to ignore it and not send a reporter, since it was "just a publicity stunt." The newspaper may have a point: it was, after all, not an event organized by an impartial panel. Yet if a newspaper applied this standard across the board of refusing to cover events organized by partisan forces, it might have interesting results. Every politician's press conference, every "photo op" by the president, every corporate unveiling of a new product, is a publicity stunt, as are most other press conferences in which only those on one side of an issue hold court. If newspapers didn't run articles on events that by this standard were publicity stunts, they would be devoid of almost everything but ads.

But it has clearly been bias, not standards, that have governed local coverage. On June 14, 1998, the FOP placed an ad in *The New York Times* arguing against Abu-Jamal's cause.[2] Such paid advertising is undeniably nothing but a publicity stunt, yet the *Inquirer* actually ran a piece about the ad. When supporters subsequently placed a counter-ad, however, the *Inquirer* ignored it.[3]

In any event, while the tribunal may have qualified as a publicity stunt, Amnesty International's release of a lengthy legal analysis and critique of Abu-Jamal's case on February 17, 2000, was surely not. This report—a genuine piece of important breaking news by a respected international human rights organization—claimed that Abu-Jamal's trial and his appeals process had been "deeply flawed" and had "clearly failed to meet minimum international standards safeguarding the fairness of legal proceedings."[4] This report was unarguably a major development in the case of Philadelphia's most famous convict. Yet the *Inquirer* relegated this major indictment of Pennsylvania's justice system to a short and uninformative single paragraph as the fifth item in its "News Briefs" column on the inside page of the paper's second section.[5] It would have been impossible to bury the story any further and still run it.

At the same time that the *Inquirer* has underplayed news stories favorable to Abu-Jamal, such as the Amnesty report, it has not hesitated to give front-page play to stories that are critical of him or his supporters. The paper ran a series of front-page articles on efforts by the Pennsylvania Secretary of State's Office to shut down fundraising by Abu-Jamal's main fundraising organization, the International Concerned Family and Friends of Mumia Abu-Jamal. The effort was almost certainly politically motivated: the state was demanding accounting records from the organization dating back 10 years—something that was almost impossible for the organization to do (especially after a suspicious break-in during which only files and computer data were allegedly stolen). Those newspaper stories, and the Secretary of State's harassment, led the city government to remove the ICFFMAJ organization from the official list of eligible charities of the Black United Fund, an organization to which city employees can allocate automatic charitable contributions from their paychecks. For Abu-Jamal's defense, it was a major loss of access to easy fundraising.

The *Daily News* showed its true colors the day after Judge Yohn's decision overturning Abu-Jamal's death sentence. In an editorial headlined "Let Mumia Rot in Darkness," the paper wrote:

> In practical terms, the best possible outcome in the case of convicted cop-killer Mumia Abu-Jamal would be to relocate the world's most famous death row inmate from the center of attention to the general prison population...for life.
>
> So we applaud the decision yesterday by U.S. District Judge William Yohn to refuse a new murder trial for Abu-Jamal—but to overturn Mumia's death penalty and order a new sentencing hearing....
>
> If he were rotting in a jail, the inflation of Abu-Jamal's resume from a small-time radio reporter to an "award-winning" journalist might have been limited....
>
> Without the death penalty, Mumia might have turned into just another prison poet, not the center of a surreal campaign of distortion by Internet.[6]

The evident bias in coverage of this case by the *Philadelphia Inquirer* and its sister paper, the *Daily News*, probably has several causes. An editor at the *Inquirer* confided confidentially that "most of the paper's staff," relatively young and from out of town since the paper's several rounds of cutbacks and buyouts of seasoned journalists, "don't know the background of this story and of the Philadelphia Police's history of corruption." They have "decided that he's guilty." In addition, there's the matter of the paper's ongoing problem with declining circulation. As the city's population has plummeted, the *Inquirer* has sought to expand into the more politically conservative suburban areas (areas where the demographics are more to the liking of advertisers). Ed Herman, professor emeritus at the University of Pennsylvania and a noted media analyst and critic, suggests that the once liberal *Inquirer*, in an effort to woo readership, has been consciously trying to present a more conservative image. It has initiated, for example, a regular series of conservative guest columnists under the heading "The Right Stuff."

Cutbacks in staffing at the *Daily News* and the *Inquirer* by these papers' parent company, Knight-Ridder, according to one editor at the latter publication, have also contributed to the problem. Biased members of the paper's staff run inaccurate information about the case unhindered by fact checkers. That may explain how columnist Tom Ferrick Jr., a longtime writer and former desk editor at the paper who has attacked Abu-Jamal in print a number of times, was able to publish a column in June 2002 about his Third Circuit appeal that had more errors than accurate facts.[7] In his column, which attacked both Abu-Jamal's latest claim of innocence and his claim that the jury had been purged of blacks, Ferrick wrote that "there is no evidence that blacks were excluded." He also wrote that "there would have been more" than the three blacks who were selected for the jury, "except that several blacks were rejected" by Abu-Jamal.

As we saw in Chapter 7, the first claim by Ferrick is refuted by none other than the prosecution itself, which stipulated at the 1995 PCRA hearing that 10 of prosecutor McGill's peremptory challenges had been against black prospective jurors. And in fact, the defense had identified an 11th of his peremptory challenges as being a black woman.

Likewise, a reading of the trial transcript's *voir dire* makes it clear that Abu-Jamal only rejected a single black juror among his 20 peremptory challenges, and Judge Sabo was careful to call attention to the race of that one black juror.

Ferrick, in a third error, asserted that state Supreme Court Justice Ron

Castille had had "nothing to do with" Abu-Jamal's case. This is a ludicrous assertion, given that Castille had been elected Philadelphia's district attorney in 1986, and in that position oversaw the office's challenge to Abu-Jamal's appeal of his conviction, and also the preparations for Abu-Jamal's post-conviction hearing.

Finally, Ferrick claimed that Abu-Jamal's argument about the training video for new young prosecutors made by assistant D.A. Jack McMahon was irrelevant. This was the video discussed earlier that tells prosecutors how to "get around" the U.S. Supreme Court's 1986 and earlier restrictions on keeping blacks and other racial groups off of juries. It had no relevance to Abu-Jamal's claim of race-based jury selection, Ferrick argued, because it had been made in 1987—years after Abu-Jamal's trial.

Again false. McMahon has since publicly stated that the tape he made (which was financed and authorized for use by D.A. Castille), was merely an explanation of methods which had been in effect for years in the D.A.'s office. Those methods, he said, had been in effect both during Castille's tenure, and under his predecessor, Ed Rendell—D.A. at the time of Abu-Jamal's trial.

These errors in Ferrick's column were pointed out by me in a formal complaint to the paper's ombudsperson, Lillian Swanson. But, she denied that they were errors and refused to have the paper run a correction.

For whatever reasons, as Philadelphia's most influential media organization, the *Inquirer's* approach to the Abu-Jamal case has set the tone for the rest of the city's media. And, since the first thing any out-of-town reporter does in working on a story like this is to look up the clips from the local paper, the *Inquirer* also probably to a great extent sets the tone for the national media, on those occasions when the story gets such attention.

That may help explain why Abu-Jamal's story has been treated in such biased fashion outside of Philadelphia.

Consider the "20/20" ABC newsmagazine show's report on Abu-Jamal's case, which aired on December 9, 1998. Produced by Harry Phillips and narrated by the network's star correspondent Sam Donaldson, ABC telegraphs its slant on the story, headlined "Hollywood's Unlikely Hero," with Diane Sawyer' lead:

> We begin tonight with the story of a man who is sitting on death row for the murder of a police officer on this day in 1981. But what is it about this case? He has generated international fervor, support from all kinds of celebrities and politicians. Do they know the whole story? Are they in for a surprise?

Replies Donaldson:

> Well, Diane, they could be, because passions have run high on all sides of this case almost from the moment a rising young black journalist named Mumia Abu-Jamal was arrested on the scene of a vicious murder.[8]

In his recounting of the shooting, Donaldson makes the factually incorrect assertion that all three prosecution eyewitnesses—Scanlan, White and Chobert—"saw Jamal run from across the street and shoot the officer in the back."[9] In reality, only one of the prosecution witnesses claimed to have seen this happen. As we saw in Chapter 5, Chobert only claimed to have looked up from his logbook after hearing the first shot. Scanlan never actually said he'd seen Faulkner shot in the back. Furthermore, he was unable to identify Abu-Jamal at the scene as the shooter. Only White said she had seen Abu-Jamal run across the street and shoot Faulkner, and she was a witness whose credibility, as discussed in Chapters 1, 5 and 8, has been found seriously wanting.

In attempting to debunk defense witness Veronica Jones, Donaldson falsely claims that 14 years had passed before she first reported seeing two men jogging from the scene of the crime. He also quotes her as saying she had been "half a nickel bag high," at the time.[10] But in making that claim at the PCRA hearing some 14 years later to have seen people running from the scene of the shooting, Jones wasn't introducing a new revelation. Rather, she was actually returning to the original statement she had made to police, the very statement she made before changing her testimony on the stand at the trial. In his report, Donaldson pointedly accused Abu-Jamal's celebrity supporters of not bothering to study the transcripts of the trial and PCRA hearing. But his misstep here, in stating that 14 years had elapsed before Jones' first statement about seeing two men jogging from the scene, makes clear that either he himself never studied the transcripts—or if he did study them carefully, he chose to misrepresent the facts.

Donaldson's mention of Jones' being high brings up an important journalistic standard: fairness. If the intoxication of a witness is important, as it surely is, then the level of intoxication of all witnesses is important. But Donaldson fails to inform viewers that both Scanlan and Chobert had been drunk at the time they witnessed the shooting. As for White, a known drug addict who purportedly died of an overdose in 1992, she was almost certainly drunk or high or both the night of the shooting, as well.

Donaldson also characterizes the prosecution's three witnesses—White, Scanlan, and Chobert—as having given "essentially the same statement" to three different police investigators.[11] The truth: not only did their accounts vary widely from each other's, but what each said at different times to different investigators or on the stand also changed. Among the discrepancies ignored by Donaldson: Scanlan did not claim to have seen White, Chobert, or even Chobert's cab parked behind the victim's police car. White said she hadn't seen Chobert's cab until after police had arrived on the scene. And Chobert said he didn't see White. Furthermore, White reported seeing police beat Abu-Jamal. Chobert reported no such incident, an omission that clearly raises questions about the veracity of what he did claim to see.

In an interview with a staff writer for the *Philadelphia Inquirer* following the airing of the ABC documentary, Donaldson stated, "there were problems with the trial, no question about it." But in a comment that reveals the limits of what passes for investigative reporting at ABC and "20/20," Donaldson parrots the prosecution's claim that it was "open and shut":

> Everything that we looked at compellingly points to the fact that Mumia shot [Philadelphia police officer Daniel] Faulkner in cold blood…and was convicted properly, and was sentenced according to the laws of the state of Pennsylvania.
>
> And as far as I'm concerned, as long as it's on the books, the death sentence has to be carried out.[12]

Besides its many factual errors and evident bias towards the prosecution, the "20/20" team apparently misled some of those it approached on the defense side. In a 12-page letter to Donaldson and Philips, actor Mike Farrell blasted the program for its factual errors. He also accused Donaldson of lying to him for failing to include in the program "your own statement to Ed Asner and me at the taping session that you believed the confession story was phony."[13] In addition, Farrell took issue with the show's off-hand characterization of Abu-Jamal as "Hollywood's Unlikely Hero," and with the suggestion that his presumably ignorant celebrity supporters would be "in for a surprise" after seeing the program.

As Farrell (who is well versed on the details of this case, and who has made it clear from the outset that he is not claiming Abu-Jamal is innocent) wrote:

> Even you have to own that this is a cheap and inappropriate shot. I understand it helps raise your profile to drag Hollywood into the discussion whenever you can, but this must embarrass even you. A few names connected with show business, much as they provide glitz for your hype-machine, do not demonstrate ownership of a case you yourselves describe as having garnered "worldwide interest."

...

I'll give only a passing nod to the left-baiting references, "a who's who of the celebrity left" and "his supporters are a kind of radical left for the 90s," but ask you to be fair in acknowledging that you failed to include in your derisive litany of his "supporters" the category into which most of the "celebrities" you are so quick to name actually fit: namely, those who make no claim as to Jamal's innocence but believe it is clearly evident that he did not get a fair trial and, even if guilty, deserved one. (It's also quite clear here that you chose not to follow up on my suggestion that you contact Stuart Taylor, Jr., the author of the article in *The American Lawyer* entitled "Guilty and Framed.")

Of course, having included the above category would have made it much more difficult for you to lump all of those you branded into a single class of "dupes," so I understand why you chose to leave it out. But does that make you proud? I rather suspect including it (or talking to Mr. Taylor) would have also made for a lot more serious work on the part of those to whom you entrust your investigating. And that, I take it, is to be avoided.[14]

While it was the only documentary done on Abu-Jamal's case by one of the major broadcast networks, "20/20" was not the only time a national media outlet did a slanted report on it. The *Washington Post*, in a feature story published in 1995 on the eve of his PCRA hearing, went so far as to begin with a lead that propagated a falsehood still being peddled today by Maureen Faulkner. It began:

There is an image from Mumia Abu-Jamal's trial that stays with Maureen Faulkner, even now, 13 years later. Abu-Jamal was charged with killing Faulkner's husband, Daniel, a 25-year-old Philadelphia policeman, by shooting him first in the back and then pumping four bullets into his prone body. When the ballistics expert held up her husband's bloody shirt to display the bullet holes, Abu-Jamal, seated at the defense table, turned around and looked at Maureen Faulkner.

'He smiled at me,' she says.[15]

The reporter accepted this chilling image at face value. Had she bothered to review the trial transcript, however, she would have seen that only one bullet was fired into Faulkner when he was prone. The others all missed. Who can deny Faulkner's claim that Abu-Jamal smiled at her, though? After all, transcripts don't capture facial expressions. But transcripts do tell when a defendant or a witness is in the courtroom and when they are not. Had the reporter reviewed the transcript, she would also have seen that Faulkner's account of Abu-Jamal's smile was impossible: at the time the victim's shirt was displayed to the jury, Abu-Jamal wasn't present: he had been ejected from the courtroom by the judge.[16] The transcript of the trial refers to the defendant's remaining outside the courtroom at the start of that day of the trial, until he could meet with John Africa or his representatives.

Surely one of the most damaging examples of mainstream media bias in the coverage of Abu-Jamal's story came in 1999, however, when *Vanity Fair* magazine ran a lengthy piece on the case written by Buzz Bissinger, a well-known Pulitzer Prize-winning former *Philadelphia Inquirer* reporter. Bissinger conceded that the trial had "some potentially troubling developments," including the judge's reputation for being pro-police and pro-prosecution, whether the defendant's right to defend himself was unfairly denied, that he had not had the assistance of a ballistician or pathologist, and that no routine test had been performed on his hands to see if he had fired a weapon. But then he dismissed all these concerns by saying that they had all been appealed and rejected by the state's supreme court. Ignored by Bissinger was the role of Judge Sabo as factfinder at the PCRA; the arbitrary constraints placed on the defense's ability to discover evidence and subpoena witnesses; and the evidence of bias even on the state's high court. On the latter point, as mentioned, a former D.A. involved in the case had refused to recuse himself from considering the appeal. Also ignored was any mention of Gary Wakshul. What made this slanted article particularly damaging, though, was that it broke the story that a prison volunteer, who said he had befriended Abu-Jamal during the latter's incarceration, had come forward with a report that Abu-Jamal had confessed to him in 1992 that he had in fact slain Faulkner. Bissinger wrote that Philip Bloch, a 47-year-old substitute teacher and Prison Society volunteer, had told him the alleged confession had been inadvertent, in the course of a philosophical conversation about whether violence might be acceptable in the advancement of certain causes:

> ...It was in that context, Bloch says, that he asked Abu-Jamal if he had any regrets over killing Faulkner, and Abu-Jamal replied with a one-word answer of "yes."
>
> "There was a long pause," Bloch remembers. "I think we probably both realized what he had just done."[17]

This would not be the first time there had been reports of an inadvertent or blurted-out Abu-Jamal confession. He seems, to hear police investigators and then Bissinger tell it, as though he just can't stop himself from blurting out self-incriminating tidbits, and to the most unreliable of people. But in fact, besides sounding improbable, the story was probably a lie. Bloch claimed he had kept silent for seven years about the information he had, until in 1999 he grew "disgusted" with Abu-Jamal's supporters, whom he felt were going too far in lionizing him and attacking Maureen Faulkner. But a few weeks after the account appeared in *Vanity Fair*, Abu-Jamal destroyed the credibility of the account when he located a letter in his possession. Written to him by Bloch and dated July 17, 1993, well after the purported "confession" conversation, its contents were published in the *Philadelphia Tribune*, the city's main black-owned newspaper, on August 3 1999 (but not in the *Inquirer* or the *Daily News*, which both ignored the new information). It showed that after writing about how he had been inspired by the number of Native Americans who had been freed after first being jailed following the FBI assault on the Pine Ridge Reservation back in 1975, he had then concluded:

> So it is possible to get justice from the jury. Not always, but sometimes. So, when you get a new trial, I think there is a good chance of an acquittal.[18]

Hardly the words of someone who had heard a confession to murder only a few months before. Furthermore, in 1992 Bloch was a supporter of Abu-Jamal's, and by his own account believed in Abu-Jamal's innocence. It makes little sense in that context that Bloch would have asked the question about Abu-Jamal regretting killing Faulkner since the question assumed his guilt. Another member of the Pennsylvania Prison Society to which Bloch belonged, Karry Koon, later said that Abu-Jamal often said he believed he was constantly monitored and that rooms were bugged by prison authorities. "He wouldn't discuss anything about his case," she said—an account of his behavior that is far more likely accurate than the idea that Abu-Jamal just can't help but repeatedly confess to his crime. She also said that she'd lived in the same small western Pennsylvania town as Bloch through the mid '90s, and that "he always acted as if he believed in [Abu-Jamal's] innocence."

Suppose Bloch is telling the truth, that attacks on Faulkner's widow and excessive praise of Abu-Jamal by his supporters led him, in 1999, to go public with his confession claim. It doesn't explain why he would have tried in 1992 to entrap a man, with a loaded question, the way he claims to have done. This makes his whole story appear concocted. Bissinger, however, never asked Bloch about this.

As pointed out in Chapter 2, the magazine and the author should be faulted for not disclosing that Bissinger was a fan and promoter of former

Philadelphia Mayor Ed Rendell, who had been the District Attorney over-seeing the prosecution of Abu-Jamal. But it's not the *Vanity Fair* piece alone that highlights the bias of the mainstream media. How the rest of the media responded to its confession "scoop" is equally telling. When Bloch's tale hit, the mainstream media played it big. Nothing wrong with that—such an allegation is newsworthy. But when Abu-Jamal's follow-up news, released in the form of Bloch's letter, came out, it was either ignored or rel-egated to the back pages. As Temple University journalism professor Linn Washington said, following publication of the Bloch letter revelation:

> So there's continuing double standards in the coverage of the Mumia case—and this is something you could document year after year after year after year.[19]

As the *Philadelphia Tribune* demonstrated in its coverage of the Bloch affair, the black-owned media—print and radio—in Philadelphia and also in other jurisdictions has been a dramatic exception to the bias that has been manifest in most of the mainstream media coverage of this case. Washington, who himself is one of those black journalists who has attempted to fairly report on the story over the years, observes, "The black-owned media in Philadelphia has persistently carried articles examining this case since the arrest." One black-owned publication, the *Philadelphia New Observer*, has even run columns written by Abu-Jamal.

Even on the left, the journalism has not always been fair. Marc Cooper, a writer who frequently does stories for such important progressive news outlets as *The Nation* magazine and Pacifica radio, attacked Abu-Jamal and the movement that supports him with a venom more often seen in right-wing publications. In an article appearing in the *New York Press* on January 6, 2000 (and in several other versions in other venues, including the left-leaning *Mother Jones* magazine), Cooper pleaded:

> I make no New Year's resolution. Instead, I have a simple plea: Oh Lord, please make 2000 a year free of Mumia.
> That's right. That's no typo. I said free of Mumia. Not Free Mumia.
> I've had it. If I go to one more lefty event and see one more Free Mumia poster, I might just have to switch sides on this one. What collective affliction has overcome my fellow pinkos? You haven't had enough defeats and embarrassments these past two decades? Now you want to take the deathly serious issue of capital

punishment and tie it to some flaky cult-member like Mumia Abu-Jamal?[20]

Cooper concedes that Abu-Jamal "probably" didn't get a fair trial. But then he buys into the thesis that because Abu-Jamal was found slumped on the curb near the dead or dying Faulkner, and because his gun was found nearby with five spent cartridges, he also was probably guilty as convicted, of first degree murder. Cooper also refers to the bullets in Abu-Jamal's gun as hollow-points (which are designed to do maximum damage on impact, and as such are designed to kill, suggesting a certain premeditation to the act). But while it's true that the cartridges were for high-powered bullets, the claim that they were hollow points, which are specially soft shells with the core hollowed out so that they mushroom on impact causing greater damage, is false. Cooper also ignores the critical issue of who fired first, a core question that could make all the difference in whether this was a case of self-defense or manslaughter or a capital crime. Indeed, he doesn't even mention that Abu-Jamal had been shot by Faulkner's gun—something that was never adequately explained at the trial.

Instead, Cooper claims that somehow by supporting Abu-Jamal, whom he describes as, "wigged out," those in the movement for his freedom are somehow betraying the thousands of others on death row. In reality, every Abu-Jamal rally makes the case that the nation's death penalty system is a crime. (Moreover, celebrity death penalty prisoners have traditionally been the vehicle death penalty opponents have used in fighting against capital punishment. It would make little sense to campaign against the death penalty using only unknown and unappealing convicts.) Cooper's real ire seems to be directed at what he calls a "cult" surrounding Abu-Jamal, and at the MOVE organization, for which Abu-Jamal expresses affection and support. Surely he is correct that many of Abu-Jamal's supporters are uncritical worshipers of their imprisoned hero. But it hardly follows that because of this his case should be ignored as Cooper implores. Nor does he recall that it was that same "cult" which rescued Abu-Jamal's case from potentially fatal obscurity in the mid-'80s—a fact which might help explain this condemned prisoner's enduring loyalty to MOVE.

In the face of this kind of slanted, biased coverage, Abu-Jamal has nonetheless, with the help of alternative media, minority-owned media, the Internet, and various support organizations, managed to get his side of the story out. But he has not been able to reach the broader mass of Americans who get their news from mainstream newspapers and, especially, television. Among many people (when they are aware of Abu-Jamal's case at all and are asked about it), the common refrain is, "Well, he did it, didn't he?" For there to be such certitude with regard to a trial that was roundly criticized by the press during its unfolding, the media deserve much of the blame.

Chapter Twelve

No Conclusion

Unfair and damaging as it has been, the media can't take all the blame for the widespread antipathy this case generates, both in the general public and among normally knee-jerk liberals and progressives. One reason there has always been some skittishness about this case among the broader public is that, at least until 2001, twenty years after the shooting, there had been only one version out there of what happened on December 9, 1981. That was the version provided by District Attorney Joseph McGill at the 1982 trial. His account is as damning of Abu-Jamal as it is unambiguous: Abu-Jamal, seeing Officer Faulkner involved in an "interaction" with his brother William Cook, ran across the street, shot the officer in the back with his .38 revolver; he was then shot by the wounded and falling officer. Then, standing over his victim, he fired four more times, finally killing him with a shot to the head at close range.

As we have seen, Abu-Jamal finally, after two decades on death row, gave an account of what he says happened that night. But it is actually rather incomplete, as he says he was unconscious or semi-conscious through most of the incident. In his version of events, he heard shouting and then shooting while filling out his logbook in his parked taxicab. Seeing his brother screaming and staggering in the street, he says he ran to him. As he ran, he says he saw a uniformed police officer who turned towards him and fired, hitting him. He says he was rendered unconscious by the injury and awoke to find himself being assaulted by a group of officers. This account is linked by the defense with the account of Arnold Beverly, the self-described mob hit man who says he was hired to kill Faulkner. Beverly says while he was waiting for his chance, Faulkner, who had stopped William Cook's VW, was shot by an unidentified shooter firing from somewhere "east on Locust Street." He says he ran over and fired the fatal shot into Faulkner's face, and then saw Abu-Jamal shot by another uniformed officer who had "arrived on the scene."

We have gone at length into the problems with both of these scenarios, but let's summarize the basic points.

McGill's story suffers from the fact that no witness saw Faulkner shoot Abu-Jamal. Even Cynthia White, who in later accounts to detectives claimed it looked as if Faulkner was "grabbing for something" as he fell, never said she actually saw him pull out his service revolver and fire. To do so would have been a remarkable achievement for someone surprised by a shot in the back. In any case, there is also the problem of the trajectory of the bullet from Faulkner's gun, which was downward through Abu-Jamal's torso, despite having allegedly been fired by a falling shooter.

As for the Abu-Jamal/Beverly account, it suffers from a number of equally serious problems. Put aside for a moment the broader issue of whether it is even believable that corrupt police would have hired a mob hit man to kill a brother officer and, after actually helping him escape, would have allowed the killer to live on to eventually tell his story. There remain concrete factual difficulties. Put aside, too, the credibility problems of Beverly as a witness. His Pennsylvania rap sheet includes at least 19 arrests for everything from criminal trespass to kidnap, rape and "terrorist threats." He has six convictions for burglary, seven convictions for theft, two convictions for receiving stolen property, three convictions for criminal conspiracy, and one conviction for weapons possession, as well as at least six separate jail sentences, including two for up to 10 years.[*] Burglary and theft are considered *crimen falsci*, which any prosecutor would surely raise as an issue to diminish the credibility of the witness' testimony.[1]

Putting these aside, all the main witnesses in this case, for both the defense and the prosecution, say that all of the shooting happened *after* Abu-Jamal began crossing the street or as he was crossing it to come to his brother's aid. Abu-Jamal's version has the shooting (or sound of shooting) come first, *before* he crosses the street. Had that been the case, credible witnesses like Hightower might have had their attention riveted to the scene *before* Abu-Jamal began crossing the street and would have witnessed the whole shooting incident, rather than just its aftermath.

Secondly, the current evidence is that it was a bullet from Faulkner's gun which hit Abu-Jamal. If he were actually shot by a different police officer, either there is an error in the identification of the bullet and the gun that fired it, or the other officer was using Faulkner's gun. Third, the wound

---

[*] Of course, it might be argued that a man with this many criminal violations, up to and including aggravated assault, might well also be capable of premeditated murder as Beverly is claiming. But, when it comes to trying to overturn a conviction on appeal, where the person to be convinced is a federal judge, or panel of judges, not a jury, the major problem is likely to be the impact of that record on the witness's credibility. Especially when his story is so extraordinary and where there is so little in the evidence to support it.

suffered by Abu-Jamal, while serious, would not likely have caused him to immediately lose consciousness, since it did not hit any major arteries. His weakness, which was testified to by the doctor who treated him 45 minutes later at the hospital, would have grown over time as he continued to bleed internally from his wound. Even at the hospital, after having lost about one-fifth of the blood in his body, the doctor said Abu-Jamal was still conscious and able to communicate intelligibly.

There are other theories of what happened, some of which seem more likely than the two offered up by the prosecution and the defense.

One, suggested during his summation statement by Abu-Jamal's defense attorney at the trial, Anthony Jackson, was that William Cook was the actual shooter. Jackson, apparently on the basis of pure speculation and desperate to at least create some reasonable doubt in the mind of jurors about the confession, suggested to the jury that perhaps Abu-Jamal, if he had truly confessed to the shooting at the hospital, was actually covering up for his brother, thinking perhaps that he was in any case dying himself.

It is certainly conceivable that an enraged Cook could have taken his injured brother's gun from him and shot the officer on the ground. The one bit of evidence hinting at this is Scanlan's testimony. He identified Abu-Jamal in the paddy wagon as "the driver of the car," which could mean he thought the other man on the scene—Cook—was the shooter, though this is only an inference. All in all, though, while it might have been in character for Abu-Jamal to take the rap for his younger brother, it seems unlikely that the shooter was Cook, as no other witnesses suggested this.

Another theory is that the shooter was Billy Cook's stand partner, Kenneth Freeman. As we saw in Chapter 8, there is some evidence suggesting Freeman was in the car with Cook, as well as evidence that a man resembling Freeman, who sported an Afro hairstyle, fled the scene. Early police efforts to locate the owner of the license application found on Faulkner—and to conceal from the prosecution where that document was discovered—further suggest that someone, probably Freeman, was in that car. The main problem with this theory, as we also discussed in Chapter 8, is that Freeman himself didn't behave like a man who had killed a policeman and who knew his friend and partner, whose brother was on death row for the deed, had seen him do it. Another problem is that Cook's statement to police arriving at the scene was odd, if indeed it was Freeman who had shot Faulkner and fled. He is reported to have said, "I had nothing to do with it," not, "We had nothing to do with it."

The other theory is that Abu-Jamal was in fact the shooter, but not in the way McGill had described things. According to this theory, Abu-Jamal was shot first by Faulkner as he was running to help his brother, who was being beaten by the officer. This theory has the advantage of explaining the trajectory of the bullet from Faulkner's gun which wounded Abu-Jamal. At the time he was struggling with Cook, Faulkner, a tall man, was by most accounts standing on the curb, slightly elevated from the street level, and Abu-Jamal was described by some witnesses as running, with a slightly bent-over posture. Those two relative positions could have easily produced a downward-coursing injury. Put together with the Harkins' account of Faulkner being spun around and knocked forward onto the ground before he was shot, this scenario would explain the nature of Faulkner's first injury, too. If Abu-Jamal had then stood over the officer and fired more shots at him, this could be explained as an act of self-defense by a man who had been shot and who feared that the officer who shot him might well continue to fire at him. Both guns were found on the street by arriving officers, suggesting that Faulkner could have still been armed when he was on his back. Such a scenario would hardly qualify as first-degree murder, but might have ended up earning Abu-Jamal a conviction for manslaughter.

None of these stories is without problems. The two key prosecution witnesses—Chobert and White—provided testimony which contradicts both of the last two scenarios, though as we have seen, both those witnesses have grave credibility issues themselves, and indeed may not even have been real witnesses to the shooting. Still, what seems clear is that the two least likely accounts of what happened on December 9 are the official ones on offer by the prosecution and the defense.

The reason for all this uncertainty is that the original trial never fairly presented the evidence in the case to the jury. Furthermore, a flawed appeals process allowed Sabo, a clearly pro-prosecution judge, who had already severely limited the defense's ability to present its own evidence and to challenge the prosecution's evidence, to become the factfinder in establishing what could and could not be appealed in federal court. Finally, a federal judge, Yohn, who seems not to have carefully read the transcripts in the case and who declined to hold hearings on any claim, took a narrow and conservative view of his authority and, despite finding errors by the prosecution and the state courts—even *unreasonable* errors—failed to overturn the verdict on the basis of any of the defense's 20 claims.

Clearly, the only way to finally come to the truth of this troubling case, and to bring justice to both Mumia Abu-Jamal and to Daniel Faulkner, is a new trial. Whether that will happen now will be up to a three-judge panel of the Third Circuit Court of Appeals. Arguments will be made on both sides in this case, and eventually, a decision will be rendered, which will likely either:

- reinstate his death sentence, leaving Abu-Jamal with no more hope of reprieve (aside from a hopeless appeal to a Supreme Court now stacked with a majority of pro-death penalty conservative justices);
- reverse Judge Yohn on the jury selection issue, thus overturning the conviction and requiring a whole new trial; or
- uphold Judge Yohn's decision in full, thus leaving it to the District Attorney of Philadelphia to decide whether to let Abu-Jamal spend the rest of his life behind bars, or to request a new sentencing trial in the hopes of winning a new death sentence.

A new trial, before a fair and open-minded judge, could answer a lot of currently puzzling questions. Among them:

How did Abu-Jamal end up being gravely wounded by a bullet from Faulkner's gun—a bullet which, without ever contacting a bone or hard obstacle, coursed in a perfectly straight line from his right nipple down to a lower vertebra in his back. Prosecutor McGill came up with all kinds of bizarre explanations for how a falling officer could have pulled his gun from his holster and fired off a shot at a standing assailant and still managed to have such a trajectory result. His Herculean efforts, though, resemble the machinations of the Catholic Church as it tried to maintain the theory of a geocentric universe after the discovery that the planets all orbited the sun.

How did Faulkner, if he fell backwards to the ground, injure his knee and tear his pants leg and why did the shot to his back course upwards and exit through his neck near his Adams apple?

Was anyone else in the car with Cook?

There are other puzzling bits of information, too, which could be investigated in a new trial. Why did the police rush Cynthia White off to Homicide before bringing her over to the wagon to see if she could identify the suspect, the way they did with all their other "eye witnesses"? Why, if Abu-Jamal shot Faulkner in the back from inches away, was there no evidence of powder burns on the jacket Faulkner was wearing?

And why did Faulkner have a camera in his squad car at the time of the shooting? Mumia supporters allege that it was supplied by the FBI so he could get evidence of corruption on the force. That may be a reach on the available evidence, but there are other tantalizing hints. I obtained a copy of Faulkner's FBI file through a Freedom of Information Act request. [Fig. 6 p. 176d] Although Faulkner is dead and thus raises no privacy issues arise, it inexplicably had large sections blacked out. For example, on the first page, under the initial heading: Attention: Uniform Crime Reports, Room 7258, it says:

> [Deleted]; Daniel Faulkner, police officer, Philadelphia, PA., Police Department (PHPD) – victim – deceased, police killing:[2]

What could that first phrase before Faulkner's name have said? FBI informant?

After this, nine full lines are deleted entirely. The next two pages are also entirely deleted, except that on page two, at the top of the page, it says "new, unclas" and at the bottom, "Philadelphia strongly recommends letter to wife from director."[3] In the middle of page three, there is the short line saying, "Page Three, PH 184, UNCLAS."[4] These notes would suggest that some part of each page was unclassified, but that, by implication, other parts which are deleted, may remain classified. The official explanation for the deletions is that they:

> ...could reasonably be expected to disclose the identity of *a confidential source* [emphasis added], including a State, local, or foreign agency or authority or any private institution which furnished information on a confidential basis, and, in the case of record or information compiled by a criminal law enforcement authority in the course of a criminal investigation, or by an agency conducting a lawful national security intelligence investigation, information furnished by a confidential source. [5]

Another page of the file, an "airtel" [telex] from the Philadelphia FBI office to the FBI Director's office, Uniform Crime Reporting Section, is apparently a cover letter for a questionnaire pertaining to the analysis of law enforcement officers killed in the line of duty. Dated December 30, 1981, it carries the handwritten remark:

> Close #4 Destroy 12/87[6]

What is #4, and why was it destroyed in December 1987?

When I appealed to the agency to have all the deletions restored to the file, I received in response only a second version of the first page of the file, this time with four of the deleted lines restored and two lines partially restored. It now reads:

> At approximately 4:00 AM on 12/9/81, Officer Daniel Faulkner, Badge Number 4699, PHPD, made a car stop in the Center City area of Philadelphia [rest of line deleted]

[line deleted]
[line deleted]
[line deleted]
[line deleted]
Officer Faulkner fired one time, [deleted] in the chest area.
Officer Faulkner was rushed to a hospital where he died.

What is the FBI hiding here? Maybe nothing. The last deletion, for example, is obviously simply a reference to Mumia Abu-Jamal, whose name is deleted according to standard FOIA procedure because he is not the subject of the file. Maybe this is all just a case of just somebody with a black marker run amok—a not uncommon practice at the FBI where FOIA requests are concerned. But then, maybe there is something fishy going on. My second appeal for more information was denied.*

One person who is at least suspicious about that file is someone who is in a position to know—25-year FBI veteran I.C. Smith, a retired agent who served for years as head of the Bureau's Arkansas office. Smith, currently working on a tell-all book about the FBI titled *In Sunshine and In Shadows: An FBI Journey,* told me that the lengthy deletions in the deceased Faulkner's file "suggest that there is probably a good chance that the officer had a relationship with the FBI." He notes that the FBI has historically gone to great lengths to avoid revealing its confidential sources—even dead ones. "You may have hit on something here," he says.

While we're on the subject of the FBI, a new trial could finally consider just what the significance is of all those hundreds of pages of documents assembled and kept over the years on Mumia Abu-Jamal. There could also finally be discovery to learn what kind of files the Philadelphia Police had on him, and what period was covered by those files.

Meanwhile, other evidence continues to emerge further suggesting that Abu-Jamal's trial was never fair in the first place. The latest of these is the belated account by Yvette Williams, a former prostitute and small-time criminal. She states in a declaration taken by Abu-Jamal's attorneys on January 28, 2002, that she had been in jail in an adjacent cell at the same time as Cynthia "Lucky" White immediately after the shooting of Officer

---

*With Faulkner dead for over 20 years, there is no good reason for any deletions from the file except for the concern about the privacy of Maureen Faulkner where there is a reference to sending her a letter of condolence. But current FOIA guidelines issued by Attorney General John Ashcroft have reversed a long-standing federal policy on Freedom of Information Act requests. Instead of, as in the past, releasing all information which can be released except for that which involves national security secrets or the right to privacy, federal agencies are now instructed to withhold all information except that which is legally mandated to be released.

Faulkner. At that time, Williams says, White, very distraught, had told her the police were pressuring her into saying she had seen Abu-Jamal shoot Faulkner. She says of White:

> She was nervous and frightened and glad to have someone to talk to. She was always crying and sad. She told me she was scared for her life. I asked her, "Scared of who?" she stated, "The guards and vice." [a reference to vice squad officers]
>
> When Lucky told me she didn't even see who shot Officer Faulkner, I asked her why she was "lying on that man" (Mumia Abu-Jamal). She told me it was because for the police and vice threatened her life. Additionally, the police were giving her money for tricks.[7]

She continues:

> Lucky told me that what really happened that night was that she was "on the stroll" (looking for and serving customers) in the area of 13th and Locust when Officer Faulkner got shot, but she definitely did not see who did it. She also told me that she had a drug habit and was high on drugs when it happened. She tried to run away after the shooting, but the cops grabbed her and wouldn't let her go. They took her in the car first and told her that she saw Mumia shoot Officer Faulkner.[8]

Williams says she never came forward for twenty years out of fear. Coming from a black woman in Philadelphia who had been in trouble with the law in the past, such fear might well have been warranted. She says that, on reading about Abu-Jamal's case in December 2001, she felt she needed to let it be known that White had been lying at the trial.

In the workings of the American justice system, William's statement is not likely to have much impact. Her testimony would be termed hearsay. In any event, it could not be easily used to impeach White, since White is presumed dead. Yet put together with the testimony of Jones and Jenkins (the final defense witness to testify at Abu-Jamal's PCRA hearing, as described in Chapter 8), they tell a story of a police frame-up. Both of them claimed to have heard that police were pressuring and bribing White to give false testimony. Both of them claimed to have been pressured to give false testimony in this case themselves. It does tend to add to suspicions that all was not what it seemed in McGill's "open-and-shut case."

Unfortunately, Abu-Jamal's decision to go forward with Beverly as a potential witness, with his "I was the hit man" story, has probably soured judges like Yohn and whatever judges are appointed to his Third Circuit appeal on further new witnesses with stories to tell, however believable they might sound. This was precisely the concern that attorneys Williams and Weinglass—and seemingly Abu-Jamal himself—had about Beverly in the first place: that the outlandishness of his claim would tarnish other more credible defense witnesses. And both Weinglass and Williams say that originally, Judge Yohn was communicating with them about scheduling hearings—something that he evidently changed his mind about after the Beverly witness issue came up and after Abu-Jamal changed his legal representation.

It should not be surprising that this saga, which has dragged on now for over 20 years, is no closer to resolution than it was that dark morning back on December 9, 1981, when police came on the scene of a dead colleague and a gravely-wounded and well-known local newsman, each with a pistol close at hand. The machinery of the American judicial system has ground out a verdict. The creaky capital appeals process has lumbered along as that verdict was predictably appealed. Even in the most routine of circumstances the U.S. legal system can be cumbersome and grueling, and this has never been a routine case. Incorporating many of the major conflicts of modern American society—black versus white, police versus police critics, left versus right, law-and-order versus civil liberties, money and power versus street demonstrations—it was bound to be even more tortured and tortuous than usual. As a result, the *truth* of what happened remains disturbingly unclear. One man, a promising young police officer, is dead, cut down in the early morning hours of what promised to be a bright future. Another, a promising writer and social critic, has spent almost his entire adult life locked away behind bars in conditions that would not be tolerated in a modern zoo. But beyond that, there is no sense that justice has been done, the way there was (even among many of those opposed to the death penalty) when Timothy McVeigh was executed for the bombing of the Murrah Building in Oklahoma City.

It should not be surprising because the American justice system is not really just about getting to the truth (though that is certainly the claim). It is about getting results. The right of death row prisoners to appeal has been steadily chipped away. And every juror seated on a capital jury panel must be someone who supports the death penalty philosophically. These factors mean that justice in a case like this is not as certain or likely as it might be in a stolen car or a check-kiting case. Justice in America is affected by many factors: the resources of the defendant, the race of the defendant, the talent and integrity of the respective lawyers, the integrity of the judge, the courage and integrity of witnesses, the prevailing sentiment of the community, and many other things.

Sometimes, in the justice system, factors that appear to any layperson as critical and common sense are dismissed on technical grounds. These can include such things as the realization that a prostitute who is currently behind bars and who has outstanding warrants is not likely to be a truthful witness for the state. Or that the conviction for arson and subsequent parole violations of a witness ought to be disclosed to a jury whose task it is to evaluate the truthfulness of his testimony. Or that no experienced policeman, much less two, would wait for over two months to report hearing a confession by a suspect in the murder of one of their own. Just as alarming, newly discovered evidence of innocence or of trial error can be ignored after a verdict simply because an appellate judge decides in her or his wisdom that the jury wouldn't have been sufficiently swayed by it to have rendered a different verdict.

But those limitations of the justice system don't absolve us of the obligation to try to root out that elusive truth.

In attempting to do that in the case of Mumia Abu-Jamal, it becomes apparent that whatever the truth of December 9, 1981, justice has not been rendered. Any condemned prisoner is going to do her or his damnedest to escape execution, so it's important to be skeptical of the claims of innocence made by such persons. At the same time, since executions are irreversible punishments, it is even more important that any decent, fair system of justice be working at its best where the ultimate sanction is being considered. As we have seen, this is not what happened in Mumia Abu-Jamal's case. There are far too many loose ends, conflicts in testimony, recantations of testimony, examples of shoddy or deliberately inadequate police work, questions about political motivations, questions of bias on both the jury and the bench, and new evidence raising questions about guilt, for it to be possible to say with certitude that the official version of this story is the correct one. Especially when, for a conviction, it must be true beyond a reasonable doubt.

In this profoundly troubling case, we know the following:

The prosecution deliberately avoided having its star eyewitness demonstrate on the scene that she could identify the shooter of Officer Faulkner.

The prosecution hid from the defense at trial evidence of a passenger in Cook's car: specifically a license document that was found in a pocket of the dead officer.

The judge refused to let the defense call a police witness whose written statement taken the day of the shooting directly contradicted claims of a hospital confession, though the man—at the request of the police or prosecutor— was waiting at home during the trial expecting to be called.

The suspect, though labeled by the prosecutor as a cop-hating law-breaker, had a completely clean police record and a reputation for being peaceful.

The two reputed eyewitnesses to the shooting both had outstanding criminal records at the time they testified, and the jury was never told about it in one of their cases (Chobert).

The prosecutor used 11 of his 15 peremptory challenges to remove black jurors who had said they could support the death penalty, resulting in a jury that was ultimately composed of two blacks and 10 whites, plus three white alternates.

The defense did not have the resources to hire expert witnesses to examine and testify about the ballistics and forensics of the case.

The court allowed the prosecution to withhold all contact information for witnesses from the defense.

The judge improperly claimed that the defendant was belligerent, in removing his right to defend himself, forcing him to use an attorney in whom he had lost confidence.

The defense attorney made numerous critical mistakes, including:

- failing to raise the issue of cab driver Chobert's probationary status;
- failing to challenge jurors who had close ties to police officers;
- and failing to request delays. That first request should have come to prepare for trial when he was suddenly told at the start of the trial that he, and not the defendant, was to be the lead attorney. The second request should have been time to prepare for the sentencing phase of the trial, once a guilty verdict had been rendered.

The judge, despite abundant evidence of bias against the defendant, refused to recuse himself from sitting as factfinder at the defendant's PCRA hearing.

A former D.A. who had overseen the challenge to Abu-Jamal's appeal of his conviction refused to recuse himself as a supreme court judge and ruled on his state appeal, which was rejected in total.

The federal judge hearing Abu-Jamal's *habeas corpus* petition made a number of serious errors of fact.

- He failed to realize that witness Cynthia White was dead and thus couldn't have been called as a witness by the defense in 1995;
- he failed to realize that Veronica Jones never did approach the crime scene;
- he failed to realize that William Cook, unlike Chobert, had no reason to fear his brother sitting near the crime scene;
- as earlier discussed, he was also seriously confused about evidence presented to support the *Batson* claim of race-based jury selection by the prosecutor, and improperly rejected that evidence based upon false assumptions regarding its relevance and whether it could have been introduced earlier in the appeals process.

Beyond these, and many other known mistakes and errors in this case, there are reasons to be suspicious about many other aspects, among them:

- Do we even know who fired the first shot?
- Why did officers Bell and Wakshul, and hospital guard Durham, take two full months to tell police detectives they had heard an alleged confession by Abu-Jamal the morning of the shooting at the hospital?
- Why did Durham not mention, until she was on the stand six months after the shooting, that she had allegedly reported the confession to her supervisor?
- Why did prosecutor McGill make no effort to bring in Durham's boss to prove the authenticity of the typed version of Durham's purported report of a confession?
- Why did police use a polygraph test on defense witness Dessie Hightower, a young man with a clean record and no reason to lie about what he'd seen, and on no other witness?
- Why did police fail to conduct a routine test on Abu-Jamal's hands for gunpowder residue to see whether he had recently fired his pistol?
- Why did no witness report seeing Chobert's cab parked behind Faulkner's police car at the time of the shooting? Was he told by police on the scene to drive up closer and park behind Faulkner's cruiser after the shooting was over?
- Why did no witness see White at the scene of the shooting?

- Who was the person several witnesses saw running from the scene after the shooting?
- Why did police initially arrest Arnold Howard as a suspect, and then, after getting his alibi, cease pursuing the theory of a second suspect?
- What was the role of Kenneth Freeman? Was he in the car with Cook? Why was Freeman not questioned by police, or if he was questioned (as claimed by Arnold), why wasn't the defense informed?
- How could Abu-Jamal have been injured by a downward coursing bullet if Faulkner was falling at the time he fired at him?
- How could Faulkner have been injured by an upward coursing bullet fired into his lower back and exiting the front of his neck, by a running Abu-Jamal?
- Why did Faulkner have a torn knee in his pants and a bruised knee if he had fallen, as the prosecutor asserts, onto his back?
- Why, if Abu-Jamal shot Faulkner in the back from only 18 inches away, was there no powder burn evidence on Faulkner's coat?
- How could Chobert have seen Abu-Jamal fire a shot into Faulkner's face if that shot was fired from less than 18 inches away, but Faulkner was on the curb in front of his car while Chobert was seated at the wheel of his cab behind Faulkner's car? Wouldn't the body of the police car have completely obscured his view?
- Why did former Governor Tom Ridge's office monitor Abu-Jamal's mail with his attorneys on the eve of his filing of a request for a PCRA hearing?
- What kind of surveillance was the Philadelphia Police Department conducting on Abu-Jamal up to and at the time of the shooting? We know the department had spied on him in the past, because they were the source of much of the material in his 600-page FBI file. If the police weren't currently spying on him, when did they stop?

The problems and unanswered questions regarding this case go on and on. A new trial may not resolve all these issues or come to the truth either, but it is clear from a thorough examination of this case that it would have to lead to a fairer result than the current one.

It may even be that this case, as the defendant and his supporters have maintained all along, was rigged from the start.

Way back in June 1982, just as the Abu-Jamal trial was getting underway in Courtroom 253 in Philadelphia's City Hall, there was a chance meeting by two pairs of people in an unusual setting. Here is how the scene was described in a declaration taken by Abu-Jamal's defense attorneys on August 21, 2001:

> In 1982, a few months after I started working at the Court of Common Pleas, I was sent to a courtroom different than that I usually worked in because the judge I was assigned to was going to be doing "VOP" (Violation of Probation) and post-verdict motion hearings there that day. I went through the anteroom on my way to that courtroom where Judge Sabo and another person were engaged in conversation.
>
> Judge Sabo was discussing the case of Mumia Abu-Jamal. During the course of that conversation, I heard Judge Sabo say, "Yeah, and I'm going to help them fry the nigger." There were three people present when Judge Sabo made that remark, including myself.[9]

The defense obtained this damning accusation against the presiding judge of the Abu-Jamal trial from a courtroom stenographer, Terri Maurer-Carter. After years of sitting on the information, she had mentioned it to someone who turned out to be an Abu-Jamal supporter, who then brought it to the attention of his defense team. They sought out Maurer-Carter and took down her statement.

Abu-Jamal's lawyers then included her statement as part of their attempt, before state Common Pleas Judge Patricia Dembe, to have a new or reopened PCRA hearing called that would consider new evidence in the case—most notably the claim by Arnold Beverly that he and not Abu-Jamal had shot Faulkner.

When the story of Maurer-Carter's affidavit broke, the local media missed or deliberately ignored its real import. The *Philadelphia Inquirer* and the *Daily News* both chose to focus on the evidence of racism in the judge's alleged statement. But while the use of the term "nigger" would certainly indicate an element of racism in the judge's thinking, the bigger issue is clearly the alleged expression of the judge's intent to throw the trial and convict the defendant. Neither publication mentioned this—an indication of either the bias of the two papers or the inexperience of the reporters assigned to the story.

Judge Dembe, after a brief hearing at which the defense and the district attorney's office made arguments for and against a new PCRA hearing, ruled against any new hearing.

In rejecting the Terri Maurer-Carter evidence of alleged bias and judicial misconduct by Judge Sabo, Dembe wrote:

> The question before this court is not what attitudes and opinions the trial judge may have held, the question is whether the rulings he made were improper. Since this was a jury trial, as long as the presiding Judge's rulings were legally correct, claims as to what might have motivated or animated those rulings are not relevant. The legal propriety of Judge Sabo's rulings and courtroom conduct have already been examined on direct appeal, and on appeal from prior PCRA hearings. See, *Commonwealth v. Mumia Abu-Jamal*, 553 Pa. 485, 720 A.2d 79 (1998), and cases cited therein. There is no legal basis for this court to reexamine them at this time.[10]

While Dembe cited no precedents to support this portion of her ruling, her logic does rest on a powerful point—that jurors, not judges, decide outcomes in jury trials. However, as the judge surely is aware, it is also true that judges play a very influential role in trials. They help to shape the make-up of a jury by deciding which jurors may be dismissed "for cause." They rule on what evidence the jury sees. They permit or deny to various witnesses the right to testify. They sustain or overrule objections about material in opening and closing arguments. (It should be recalled here, for instance, that McGill got away—over Jackson's objection thanks to a decision by Sabo—with stating something that has in other cases been considered grounds for a mistrial. In his closing argument, he argued that a death penalty should not be considered final by jurors because there would be many appeals to come—an argument that improperly attempts to lessen the gravity of the jury's profound decision.) And, crucially, judges instruct jurors as to how to go about making their decisions regarding guilt and sentence. (Recall also that Judge Yohn ultimately overturned Abu-Jamal's death sentence, ruling that Judge Sabo had erred during the penalty phase by not telling jurors that they did not have to unanimously agree about any mitigating circumstances for those mitigating circumstances to be counted in settling on a penalty.)

It is important to distinguish between "bias" and a foregone conclusion, too. Surely it is human nature to be biased. A person hears some facts regarding a case and, whether judge or layperson, thinks, "sounds guilty to me" or "sounds innocent to me." But someone with either bias can still also say, "let's see what the evidence reveals." Then, based upon what that additional evidence is, the person's bias can either be supported or overcome.

The statement "Yeah, and I'm going to help them fry the nigger!" isn't just about bias, however; if true, it is a statement of intent to steer a trial in a certain direction, whatever the evidence. That would not be bias; it would be judicial misconduct.

Consider that a judge, besides setting a tone which is evident to jurors, and which could easily sway their evaluation as to the credibility of witnesses, also determines the amount of time available for attorneys to prepare their cases and their witnesses. Here, indeed, was a case where the defense was repeatedly damaged by Sabo's insistence on speed. Jackson was given no time to prepare when, at the end of jury selection, he was informed that he would be the lead attorney for the defense. Likewise, Sabo gave Jackson no time once the jury had convicted the defendant, to prepare for the sentencing phase of the trial, which he ordered to begin the following morning.

Even worse, Sabo's personal views became even more critical during the PCRA hearing, where there was no jury and where the judge's role was that of "factfinder." As became clear in Judge Yohn's rulings, those "facts," once established by Sabo, were then no longer open to question. Because of the law, Yohn had to base his decisions on the merits of Abu-Jamal's various constitutional claims for relief upon those very Sabo-validated "facts." Clearly then, if there is evidence that Sabo was not just unfair in practice, but by deliberate intent, as suggested by Maurer-Carter's statement, Abu-Jamal (and arguably the other 28 black and Latino convicts sent to death row by Judge Sabo during his career as Philadelphia's hanging judge) would deserve a new trial.

Even though Dembe's ruling might strike many as wrong or illogical, given the obvious influence judges have over the course of any trial, it is also true that Maurer-Carter's claim has little weight. She waited nearly 20 years to report what she had heard, and in any event, what she has to offer is hearsay, and thus counts for very little.

Moreover, Judge Sabo, contacted by the *Philadelphia Inquirer* about Maurer-Carter's allegation, denied ever saying what Maurer-Carter has alleged he said.

With this being just a case of a court stenographer's word against a retired judge's word, this story would likely not amount to much, particularly now that Sabo, who died on May 9, 2002, cannot be put on the stand and questioned under oath.

But there is more to this story.

Unknown to the Abu-Jamal defense team at the time they were presenting Maurer-Carter's affidavit to Judge Dembe, a far more significant person had also heard Judge Sabo's outrageous remark. In a series of interviews with Maurer-Carter, I managed to deduce the identity of the unidentified third person with her when the two pairs of people passed in the robing room of Courtroom 253. It was Judge Richard Klein, the jurist for whom she was at the time working as a stenographer. She explained that she had merely referred in her affidavit to three people being in the room with Sabo, leaving Klein's identity anonymous, because she did not want to subject the judge to embarrassment.

In fact, there was a logical reason for Maurer-Carter and Klein to have bumped into Judge Sabo and his court clerk. It turns out that back in mid-1982, at a time when Judge Klein was working as a civil court judge, he and a number of his colleagues were asked to help the criminal courts clear away a growing backlog of violation of parole (VOP) cases. These involved convicted criminals charged with violating the terms of their parole and who therefore were facing possible reincarceration. Many VOP defendants are potentially violent or prone to escape. Because the civil court building did not have any holding cells or security systems, the hearings had to take place in the criminal courtrooms, which at that time were located in Philadelphia's ornate but decidedly dilapidated City Hall. On a late afternoon in mid-June, 1982, Klein was assigned to Courtroom 253, the courtroom of Common Pleas Judge Albert Sabo, who was at that time just beginning the high-profile murder trial of Mumia Abu-Jamal. As Judge Klein and his court stenographer, Maurer-Carter, were walking into the robing room of Sabo's courtroom, Sabo was just leaving for the day.

Judge Klein is a bit of a character among Philadelphia judges. A reasonably talented jazz drummer, his band members have included some of the very people he has sent to prison. He is also a scion of a local Republican family and is a second-generation judge. Klein, who was elected in November 2001 to the Pennsylvania Superior Court, is respected among local attorneys for his integrity. He stands out in a jurisdiction where too many of the judges—all elected and subject to periodic reelection contests—are little better than political hacks and patronage beneficiaries who, with donations to the local ward leaders, bought their seats on the bench.

In contrast to all this judicial mediocrity, Klein takes his work seriously. One time, after he had sentenced someone and gone home, he called his court stenographer and asked that a portion of the trial be read back to him. Asked why, since the trial was already over, he reportedly said, "I don't know. The defendant seemed so stunned when he was pronounced guilty that I'm wondering whether maybe we made a mistake."

In September 2001, I confronted Klein over the phone at his office with Maurer-Carter's account of the incident, including her information that he had been present. He issued no denial. After I asked about it, he remained silent on the telephone for nearly half a minute—so long a time I began to worry that I had been cut off. Finally he said, "I won't say it did happen, and I won't say it didn't. That was a long time ago." He acknowledged having handled some VOP cases around 1982, but said he had no recollection what time of year it had been. A second attempt to talk with him two months later in November, right after his election to Superior Court, was rebuffed, and with good reason. His assistant said Klein couldn't talk "because he may be subpoenaed in this case." (It is interesting to note that the judge himself raised the possibility that he might end up being subpoenaed to testify. The defense has to date not contacted him, as Maurer-Carter did not include him in her official account of the incident. This alone would seem to suggest Maurer-Carter is telling the truth about who was there when Sabo spoke.)

A prominent defense attorney who has tried cases before Klein, and who therefore has an interest in remaining anonymous, says of the judge's initial response, "That's a confirmation in my mind. I think Judge Klein is too honest to lie and say it never happened, and that's why he's saying it that way."

The significance of Klein's having been present during Sabo's alleged comment to his clerk is enormous. Like Maurer-Carter, his account of the incident would be classified as hearsay, but it would be the hearsay of a sitting Superior Court judge. No one but Judge Klein himself knows what he would say if put on the stand under oath. But if he were to give the same account of the incident that Maurer-Carter has given, his words could be expected to carry some weight with any judge considering the matter, and could even lead to the calling of a mistrial.

As *American Lawyer* writer Stuart Taylor, who watched Sabo at work during Abu-Jamal's post-conviction hearing, says after learning about the judge's alleged comment, "I have always (since I researched the case in 1995), thought of Sabo as a rabidly biased, pro-prosecution judge. But if he made that comment, he was even worse than I thought."

But will Judge Klein ever be put on the stand to testify? At this point, unless the case is ordered back for a new trial, or for a new sentencing trial, the answer is almost certainly no.

That is a scandal.

Afterword
"So... Did He Do It or Not?"

Over the last several years, as I've worked on this project, whenever people have heard that I was writing on a book on Mumia Abu-Jamal, whether they were progressives, middle-of-the-road Democrats, or even conservative Republicans, the first question has always been the same: "So, did he do it or not?"

I'm baffled at what it is about this case that makes even the most committed civil libertarians forget that whether or not he "did it" is beside the point. Maybe he is entirely innocent of the crime of killing Officer Daniel Faulkner, and was, as a black friend from Philadelphia put it, "just a poor nigger who was in the wrong place at the wrong time." Maybe he did shoot Faulkner, but for some reason other than a mindless hatred of cops and a desire to kill, as Joseph McGill, the prosecutor who put him on death row, claimed to the jurors.

The question of course, is not whether he "did it," but whether he received a fair trial and a fair appeal of his conviction.

And this is what makes the story of Mumia Abu-Jamal and the shooting of Officer Daniel Faulkner important, and much more than just a who-done-it. This case, because of the race of the defendant and the race of the victim, because of the politics of the defendant and the profession of the victim, and because of the passions and the attention it has generated over the years, is nothing less than a test of the American justice system. The more high profile a case, the stronger the passions within the community, the more important it is that the legal system handle it with the highest degree of professionalism.

Instead, as we have seen, this case has suffered from poor defense resources, possible prosecutorial misconduct, judicial bias and misconduct, and juror bias. It doesn't get much worse than that.

After doing all the investigative reporting I could, interviewing all the people I could locate, and reading and rereading the thousands of pages of trial and PCRA hearing transcripts, evidence documents, affidavits and appeal petitions, I am not certain about what really happened on that December 9 morning in 1981.

But I am convinced beyond not just a reasonable doubt but beyond *any* doubt whatsoever, that Mumia Abu-Jamal did not receive even the approximation of a fair trial. I am equally convinced that his appeals process, which was fatally contaminated by the presence of the unabashedly biased Judge Sabo as factfinder at his PCRA hearing, has been a travesty of justice. I hope that my limited skills as a writer have by now convinced the reader that I am right in both of these convictions.

There are those in the Free Mumia movement who are absolutely convinced that they are fighting for the life and freedom of an innocent man. They are as powerfully convinced of the righteousness of their movement as Maureen Faulkner and her family, and many of her supporters in law enforcement are that the killer of her husband has just spent the last two decades dodging his just rewards for a vicious crime. One of those two bitterly opposed sides may be in the right, though I have my doubts about both.

If I had to lean in one direction, I'd certainly lean towards innocence. I don't think the evidence has ever been there that Mumia Abu-Jamal was a first-degree murderer. It's not consistent with his life up to the day of Faulkner's death, and aside from McGill's over-the-top rhetoric in his opening remarks and his two summations to the jury, the facts were never there to prove intent to kill. As we saw, both of the people who testified at the trial to having seen Abu-Jamal firing at the prone officer were highly questionable witnesses, who were subject to considerable pressure from police and prosecutor, whether real or perceived.

At the same time, I'm not convinced that Mumia Abu-Jamal was simply an innocent bystander. That he was framed on a first-degree murder rap, is, I think, almost certain. The confession he allegedly made at the hospital doesn't even sound like a well-done conspiracy by the police and hospital security guard who testified to it. (They are the only witnesses in this case who had completely matching stories, down to the exact wording of the confession). Both took two months to mention anything to police, which made even the prosecutor, if he was not involved himself, wonder what was going on in a case where his other witnesses were offering wildly varied versions of what happened.

But did he actually shoot Faulkner? The answer has to be maybe.

So that leaves me, at least, uncertain about what really happened. It could be Abu-Jamal is innocent, the victim of a frame up. It could be he shot Faulkner, but simply as a matter of self-defense. It could be he wounded the officer and someone else finished the job off. It could have been a case of several well-meaning but heavily armed people all doing what they thought was right--with tragic consequences for all of them.

If he was defending himself but overreacted after being shot, or after seeing his brother being beaten, it could be the charge should have been manslaughter.

Maybe (though I don't think the scenario claimed by Beverly makes sense), there is even something more to this story. Something darker—as suggested by the cryptic and wholly unjustified gaps in Faulkner's FBI file and some of the peculiar behavior of police investigators in this case, as well as by the never-explained evidence of other bullets having hit doors and windows remote from Faulkner's body, and the mysterious camera in his car.

The point is, without a fair trial, with evenly matched attorneys and resources to procure evidence—something that did not exist at Abu-Jamal's trial—we will never know the answer to this puzzle.

Meanwhile, a talented and potentially very influential black man sits on death row, convicted on a charge—first-degree murder—of which he is almost certainly innocent.

Selected Readings & Research Guide

History

Frank Rizzo: The Last Big Man in Big City America
    S.A. Paolantonio
    Camino Books, Philadelphia, 1993

On a Move: The Story of Mumia Abu-Jamal
    Terry Bisson
    Litmus Books, 2000

Protectors of Privilege: Red Squads and Police Repression in Urban America
    Frank Donner
    University of California Press, Berkeley, 1990

A Prayer for the City
    Buzz Bissinger
    Vintage Press, New York, 1997

25 Years on the MOVE
    Dubside
    Self-published by MOVE, Philadelphia, 1997

The Trial

Race for Justice: Mumia Abu-Jamal's Fight Against the Death Penalty
    Leonard Weinglass
    Common Courage Press, Monroe, ME, 1995

Executing Justice: An Inside Account of the Case of Mumia Abu-Jamal
    Daniel R. Williams
    St. Martin's Press, New York, 2001

Cop Killer: How Mumia Abu-Jamal Conned Millions Into Believing He Was Framed
> Dan Flynn
> Accuracy in Academia, Washington, D.C., 2000

The Case of Mumia Abu-Jamal: A Life in the Balance
> Amnesty International
> Seven Stories Press, New York, 2001

Newspaper Clippings and Trial & Appeals Hearings Transcripts

www.mumia2000.org
> (good source for recent briefs filed by the defense, also some of Abu-Jamal's writings)

www.justice4danielfaulkner.com
> (contains all transcripts of original 1982 trial, including jury selection, and PCRA hearing, as well as many pro-prosecution articles critical of the defense and the Free Mumia movement)

rwor.org/s/mumia_e.htm
> (offers many defense and some prosecution briefs, as well as well-written articles from a pro-defense advocacy stance)

www.mumia.org
> (website of the MOVE organization and International Concerned Friends and Family of Mumia Abu-Jamal. Contains many of Abu-Jamal's writings. Good source for curent activities of the Free Mumia movement)

www.fortunecity.com/meltingpot/botswana/509/inqarticles/inquirer-index.htm
> (This site has a long list of articles from the *Philadelphia Inquirer* on the case, going back to the original incident.)

Works by Mumia Abu-Jamal

Live From Death Row
Mumia Abu-Jamal
Avon, New York, 1996

Death Blossoms: Reflections of a Prisoner of Conscience
Mumia Abu-Jamal and Cornell West
Seven Stories Press, New York, 2000

All Things Censored
Mumia Abu-Jamal, Noelle Hanrahan and Alice Walker
Seven Stories Press, New York, 2000

Hardknock Radio Presents 175 Progress Drive (CD with early Abu-Jamal broadcasts)
Mumia Abu-Jamal
AK PR Distribution, New York, 2001

A Conversation on Death Row (CD of Abu-Jamal)
Mumia Abu-Jamal
Plough Publishing, 1997

Notes

Insert

1 *Philadelphia Inquirer*, "The latest theory, the latest sham," by Tom Ferrick, Jr., June 12, 2002, p. 1B

2 Batson v. Kentucky, U.S. Supreme Court, 476 U.S. 79 (1986) J. Powell's majority opinion

3 Baldus, David and Woodworth, George, et. al., "Race Discrimination and the Death Penalty in the Post-*Furman* Era: An Empirical and Legal Analysis with Recent Findings from Philadelphia," *Cornell Law Review* 1638 (1998)

4 Hardcastle v. Horn, No. 98-CV-3028 (E.D. Pa.)

5 Memorandum and Order, Mumia Abu-Jamal v. Martin Horn, Dec. 18, 2001, p. 219

6 Ibid., p. 220

7 Habeas petition, Mumia Abu-Jamal v. Horn, 99 Civ. 5089 (Yohn) October 14, 1999, p. 94

8 Ibid., p. 94

Foreword

1 Leonard Weinglass, *Race for Justice: Mumia Abu-Jamal's Fight Against the Death Penalty*, Common Courage Press, 1995

2 Apprendi v. New Jersey, U.S. Supreme Court No. 99-478, decided June 26, 2000. Antonin Scalia's concurring opinion

Chapter One

1 Exhibit C-20, Radio Tape Transmittal, Commonwealth of Pennsylvania v. Mumia Abu-Jamal, June 19, 1982

2 *Philadelphia Inquirer*, August 27, 1995, "How to Head off Police Corruption," by Peter F. Vaira, p, E5; and April 4, 1996, "Some Major Events of Corruption

Probe," p. 6

3 Trial transcript, Commonwealth of Pennsylvania v. Mumia Abu-Jamal, July 1, 1982, 8201-1357-59, p. 181

4 Donner, Frank, *Protectors of Privilege: Red Squads and Police Repression in Urban America*, University of California Press, Berkeley, 1990, p. 218

5 Pretrial hearing on a Motion to Suppress Evidence, Commonwealth of Pennsylvania v. Mumia Abu-Jamal, June 1, 1982, trial transcript, page 69

6 *Philadelphia Bulletin*, December 17, 1981, " Did Abu-Jamal Say Anything?", by columnist Adrian Lee

7 *Philadelphia Inquirer*, April 17, 1986, "Ex-Police Inspector Cooperating in Probe"

8 PCRA hearing transcript, Commonwealth of Pennsylvania v. Mumia Abu-Jamal, August 1, 1995, p. 61

9 Trial transcript, Commonwealth of Pennsylvania v. Mumia Abu-Jamal, June 24, 1982, p. 44

10 Trial Transcript, Commonwealth of Pennsylvania v. Mumia Abu-Jamal, June 19, 1982, p. 131

11 Declaration of Arnold Beverly, June 8, 1999, p. 2

12 Trial Transcript, Commonwealth of Pennsylvania v. Mumia Abu-Jamal, June 19, 1982, p. 179

13 *Philadelphia Daily News*, "A Subtle Anti-Gay Element Surfaces in the Mumia Case," by Mubarak S. Dahir, August 15, 1995, p. 24

Chapter Two

1 *Philadelphia Inquirer*, "Police got $2500 A Year in Payoffs From Bar and Game, Ex-Officer Says," by Tim Weiner, December 6, 1985, p. B8

2 Paolantonio, S.A., *Frank Rizzo: The Last Big Man in Big City America*, Camino Books, 1993, p. 62

3 Ibid., p. 67

4 Ibid., p. 67

5 Donner, Frank, op. cit., p. 205

6 Weinglass, op. cit., p. 216

7 Donner, Frank, op. cit., p. 208

8 Bisson, Terry, *On a Move: The Story of*

Mumia Abu-Jamal, p. 93

9   Donner, op. cit., p. 215

10 Philadelphia Bulletin, "Courtroom Drama Stars Rizzo, Weinrott and Young Lawyer," Sept. 1, 1970.

11 Donner, op. cit., p. 215

12 Ibid., p. 216

13 Philadelphia Weekly, "Mumia, up close and personal," by Linn Washington, August 30, 1995, p. 15

14 Philadelphia Weekly, op. cit., p.17

15 Bisson, op. cit., p. 166

16 Justice for Daniel Faulkner, www.danielfaulkner.com/indexmyth14.html

17 Cop Killer: How Mumia Abu-Jamal Conned Millions Into Believing He Was Framed, Dan Flynn, Accuracy in Academia, 2000, p. 25

18 Vanity Fair, "The famous and the dead," by Buzz Bissinger, August 1999, p. 72

19 Ibid., p. 72

20 Washington, Linn unpublished manuscript on police brutality

21 Bissinger, Buzz A Prayer for the City, Vintage Books, 1997. Note: Bissinger, a Pulitzer Prize-winning author, may or may not have pulled his punches in largely admiring portrait of Rendell, but he and Vanity Fair clearly should have made his unusual relationship with the former chief prosecutor known to readers in publishing his article on the Abu-Jamal case.

22 Vanity Fair, op. cit., p. 46

23 Philadelphia Magazine, "81 People to Watch in 1981," January 1981, p. 107

24 Commonwealth of Pennsylvania v. Mumia Abu-Jamal, transcript of PCRA hearing, June 26, 1997, p. 3

25 Transcript of PCRA hearing, Commonwealth of Pennsylvania v. Mumia Abu-Jamal, June 26, 1997, p. 44

26 Ibid., p. 259

27 Notice of Dismissal, Cert. U.S. Federal Court Cert. # 972753, Federal Archives, Philadelphia

28 Notice of Dismissal, Cert. U.S. Federal Court Cert. # 972753, Federal Archives, Philadelphia

29 Philadelphia Inquirer, "Battered cargo: The

costs of the police "nickel ride," June 3, 2001, p.1

30 Philadelphia Inquirer, "5 indicted in probe of vice payoffs cases called first in series against police," March 1, 1983

31 Affidavit of Donald Hersing, taken May 10, 1999, filed with the U.S. District Court of Eastern District of Pennsylvania, Case No. 99 Civ 5089 (Yohn), May 4, 2001, p. 3

32 Philadelphia Inquirer, May 1, 1983, "Corruption Probes Against Philadelphia Police Have a Long History," by Mike Leary, p. 11

33 Philadelphia Inquirer, "Focus of Police Probe Shifts to East Division," by Tim Weiner, November 30, 1985, p. B1

34 Philadelphia Inquirer, "15 ex-police officers enter not-guilty pleas," May 11, 1984

35 Transcript of PCRA hearing, Commonwealth of Pennsylvania v. Mumia Abu-Jamal, August 11, 1995, p. 211

36 Affidavit of Linn Washington, Mumia Abu-Jamal v. Martin Horn et. al., No. 99 Civ 5089 (Yohn), p. 2, filed May 4, 2001

Chapter Three

1   Trial transcript, Commonwealth of Pennsylvania v. Mumia Abu-Jamal, July 1, 1982, p. 169

2   Ibid., p. 172

3   Ibid., p. 186

4   Philadelphia Inquirer, "Did Abu-Jamal Want the Jury to Find Him Guilty?", July 11, 1982, p. 1

5   Williams, op. cit., p. 201

6   Trial transcript, Commonwealth of Pennsylvania v. Mumia Abu-Jamal, July 3, 1982, p. 56

7   Ibid., p. 63

8   Ibid., p. 64

9   Ibid., p. 66

10 Bisson, Terry, op. cit. p. 13

11 Ibid., p. 12

12 Mumia Abu-Jamal, Live From Death Row, Avon Books, 1995, p. 150

13 Bisson, op. cit., p. 37

14 Abu-Jamal, op. cit., p. 150

15 FBI Teletype message from New York to

San Francisco bureau, March 17, 1970, p. 1

16 FBI airtel from Special Agent in Charge, Albany, NY, bureau to Special Agent in Charge, Philadelphia bureau, 2/25/72, p. 1

17 Bisson, op. cit., 119

18 *Philadelphia Magazine*, "81 People to Watch in 1981," January 1981, p. 107

19 Ibid., p. 150

20 Dubside, *25 Years on the Move*, self-published booklet, 1996, p. 15

21 Bisson, op. cit. p. 157

22 *Philadelphia Bulletin*, "U.S. Jury acquits MOVE's founder," July 23, 1981, p. A6

23 Trial transcript, Commonwealth of Pennsylvania v. Mumia Abu-Jamal, June 30, 1982, p. 148

24 Williams, op.cit., p. 232

25 Trial transcript, Commonwealth of Pennsylvania v. Mumia Abu-Jamal, PCRA Hearing, July 26, 1995, p. 43

26 Trial transcript, Commonwealth of Pennsylvania v. Mumia Abu-Jamal, PCRA Hearing, July 26,1995, p. 51

27 Trial Transcript, PCRA, op. cit., p. 94

28 Trial Transcript, PCRA, op. cit., p. 97

29 Trial Transcript, PCRA, op. cit., p. 110

30 Trial Transcript, PCRA, op. cit., p. 156

31 Trial Transcript, PCRA, op. cit., p. 149

32 Associated Press, "Former Black Panther Freed On Bail In 1968 Murder Case," June 10, 1997.

33 Airtel from FBI Special Agent in Charge for Philadelphia to FBI Director, 12/3/1970, p. 1

34 Bisson, op. cit., p. 103

35 FBI Airtel from Special Agent in Charge, Philadelphia, to FBI Director, 4/4/1974, p. 1

36 Trial transcript, Commonwealth of Pennsylvania v. Mumia Abu-Jamal, July 1, 1982, p. 148

Chapter Four

1 Trial Transcript, Commonwealth v. Mumia Abu-Jamal a/k/a Wesley Cook, 7/1/1982, p. 48

2 Trial Transcript, Commonwealth v. Mumia Abu-Jamal a/k/a Wesley Cook,

7/1/1982, p. 34

3 Trial Transcript, Commonwealth v. Mumia Abu-Jamal a/k/a Wesley Cook, 7/1/1982. p. 33

4 *A Life in the Balance: the Case of Mumia Abu-Jamal*, Amnesty International, New York, Feb. 17, 2000, p. 4

5 *Philadelphia Inquirer*, "After a search for the truth behind the slogans, the sentence seems more troubling than the verdict," July 18, 1995, p. 6

6 *Philadelphia Inquirer*, "L'Affaire Mumia: In court, Judge Sabo is his own worst enemy," 8/13/1995, p. E4

7 *The American Lawyer*, "Guilty and Framed," by Stuart Taylor, December 1995, p. 83

8 Ibid., p. 1

9 *Philadelphia Inquirer*, "Judge Sabo is ousted in cutbacks: He is noted for his controversial role in the Mumia Abu-Jamal case. Two other senior judges were dropped as well," 11/26/1997, p. B1

10 Williams, Daniel, *Executing Justice: An Inside Account of the Case of Mumia Abu-Jamal*, p. 63

11 *Salon Magazine*, "The death penalty's other victims," by Dave Lindorff, January 4, 2001

12 *Philadelphia Inquirer*, "Jury Selection Completed for Abu-Jamal's Murder Trial," by Marc Kaufman, June 17, 1982, p. B3

13 Trial transcript, Commonwealth v. Mumia Abu-Jamal, June 7, 1982, p. 146

14 Ibid., p. 152

15 Ibid., p. 161

16 Ibid., p. 163

17 Trial transcript, Commonwealth v. Mumia Abu-Jamal, June 11, 1982. p. 93

18 Ibid., p. 94

19 Trial transcript, Commonwealth v. Mumia Abu-Jamal, 6/21/82, p. 130

20 Williams, op. cit., p. 90

21 Trial transcript, Commonwealth v. Mumia Abu-Jamal, June 9, 1982, p. 81

22 Trial transcript, Commonwealth v. Mumia Abu-Jamal, June 16, 1982, p. 135

23 Williams, op. cit., p. 96

24 Trial transcript, Commonwealth v. Mumia Abu-Jamal, 6/18/82, p. 40

25 *Philadelphia Inquirer*, "Lesser role sought for Abu-Jamal," by Marc Kaufman, Date June 9, 1982, p. B1
26 *Philadelphia Inquirer*, "Jury for Abu-Jamal may be sequestered," by Marc Kaufman, June 8, 1982, p. B6
27 Williams, op. cit., p. 98
28 Ibid., p. 99
29 Trial transcript, Commonwealth v. Mumia Abu-Jamal, June 9, 1982, p. 2
30 Ibid., p. 17
31 Trial transcript, Commonwealth v. Mumia Abu-Jamal, June 9, 1982, p. 19
32 Ibid., p. 21
33 Ibid., p. 23
34 Ibid., p. 23
35 Ibid., p. 44

Chapter Five

1 Williams, op. cit., p. 112
2 Trial transcript, Commonwealth v. Mumia Abu-Jamal, a/k/a Wesley Cook, June 19, 1982, p. 10
3 Ibid., p. 15
4 Ibid. p. 19
5 Williams, op. cit., p. 113
6 Trial transcript, Commonwealth v. Mumia-Abu-Jamal, June 28, 1982, p. 50
7 Trial transcript, Commonwealth v. Mumia Abu-Jamal, June 19, 1982, p. 210
8 Ibid., p. 211
9 Ibid., p. 216
10 Ibid., p. 217
11 Ibid., p. 231
12 Ibid., p. 234
13 Ibid., p. 235
14 Trial transcript, Commonwealth v. Mumia Abu-Jamal, June 21, 1982, p. 93
15 Ibid., p. 160
16 Ibid., p. 166
17 Ibid., p. 178
18 Trial transcript, Commonwealth v. Mumia Abu-Jamal, 6/29/82, p. 114
19 Ibid., p. 105
20 Trial transcript, Commonwealth v. Mumia Abu-Jamal, June 22, 1982, p. 107
21 Transcript, Hearing before Judge Ribner, January 11, 1982, p. 96
22 Trial transcript, Commonwealth v.

William Cook, 81-12-0272, March 29, 1982, p. 41
23 Ibid., p. 33
24 Trial transcript, Commonwealth v. Mumia Abu-Jamal, 6/25/01, p. 7
25 Ibid., p. 76
26 Ibid., p. 78
27 Ibid., p. 79
28 Ibid., p. 88
29 Trial transcript, Commonwealth v. Mumia Abu-Jamal, 6/19/82, p. 185
30 Trial transcript, Commonwealth v. Mumia Abu-Jamal, 6/18/82, p. 90
31 Trial transcript, Commonwealth v. Mumia Abu-Jamal, 6/23/82, p. 127
32 Trial transcript, Commonwealth v. Mumia Abu-Jamal, 6/24/82, p. 30
33 Ibid., p. 136
34 Ibid., p. 97
35 Ibid., p. 100
36 Ibid., p. 109
37 Investigation Interview Report, Philadelphia Police Department Homicide Div., December 9, 1981, p. 2
38 Investigation Interview Report, Philadelphia Police Department Homicide Div., December 16, 1981, p. 2
39 Trial transcript, Commonwealth v. Mumia Abu-Jamal, July 1, 1982, p. 173

Chapter Six

1 Trial transcript, Commonwealth v. Mumia Abu-Jamal, June 28, 1982, p. 123
2 Ibid., p. 126
3 Stuart Taylor, *The American Lawyer*, " Guilty and Framed," December 1995, p. 81
4 Trial transcript, Commonwealth v. Mumia Abu-Jamal, 6/29/82, p. 99
5 Ibid., p. 129
6 Ibid., p. 132
7 Ibid., p. 134
8 Ibid., p. 140
9 Ibid., p. 140
10 Ibid., p. 140
11 Trial transcript, Commonwealth v. Mumia Abu-Jamal, 6/30/82, p. 14
12 Trial transcript, Commonwealth v. Mumia Abu-Jamal, 7/01/82, p. 64
13 Ibid., p. 80

14 Ibid., p. 146
15 Ibid., p. 171
16 Ibid., p. 172
17 Ibid., p. 179
18 Taylor, op. cit., p. 82
19 Ibid., p. 82
20 Trial transcript, Commonwealth v. Mumia Abu-Jamal, 7/1/82, p. 180
21 Ibid., p. 153
22 Ibid., p. 180
23 Ibid., p. 185
24 Trial transcript, Commonwealth v. Mumia Abu-Jamal, 7/02/82, p. 5
25 Ibid., p. 77
26 Ibid., p. 77
27 Ibid., p. 77
28 Ibid., p. 78
29 Trial transcript, Commonwealth v. Mumia Abu-Jamal, 7/03/82, p. 16
30 Ibid., p. 15
31 Ibid., p. 17
32 Ibid., p. 18
33 Ibid., p. 20
34 Ibid., p. 20
35 Ibid., p. 22
36 Ibid., p. 22
37 Ibid., p. 22
38 Ibid., p. 25
39 Ibid., p. 25
40 Ibid., p. 31
41 Ibid., p. 32
42 Ibid., p. 55
43 Ibid., p. 57
44 Ibid., p. 64
45 Ibid., p. 65
46 Ibid., p. 69
47 Ibid., p. 72
48 Ibid., p. 73
49 Philadelphia Inquirer, "Slain Officer's Wife Praises the Jurors," July 4, 1982, p. B1
50 Ibid., p. 106

Chapter Seven

1 Letter from Mumia Abu-Jamal to Jane Henderson, dated June 3, 1998.
2 Salon Magazine "Planning for Martial Law?" by Dave Lindorff, February 20, 2002, cover story
3 Jamal v. Price, et. al., U.S. District Court, Case No. 95-618, June 6, 1996
4 Declaration of Rachel Wolkenstein, Commonwealth of Pennsylvania v. Mumia Abu-Jamal, CD# 1357-1358, September 5, 2001, paragraphs 70-72
5 Williams, op. cit., p. 215
6 PCRA hearing transcript, August, 11, 1995, p. 190
7 PCRA hearing transcript, August 2, 1995, p. 5
8 PCRA hearing transcript, July 12, 1995, p. 13
9 Ibid., p. 98
10 Williams, op. cit., p. 224
11 PCRA hearing, op. cit., p. 116
12 PCRA hearing transcript, July 26, 1985, p. 191
13 Transcript of PCRA hearing, July 27, 1995, p. 4
14 Salon Magazine, "The Death Penalty's Other Victims," by David Lindorff, p. 2.
15 Ibid., p. 3
16 Transcript of PCRA hearing, July 27, 1995, p. 9
17 Ibid., p. 77
18 The American Lawyer, "Guilty and Framed," by Stuart Taylor, Jr., December 1995, p. 83
19 Williams, op. cit., p. 249
20 Transcript of PCRA hearing, July 27, 1995, p. 45
21 Ibid., p. 46
22 Williams, op. cit.., p. 51
23 Ibid., p. 59
24 Williams, Daniel, Executing Justice, p. 244
25 Transcript of PCRA hearing, op. cit. p. 112
26 Transcript of PCRA hearing, July 28, 1995, p. 49
27 Ibid., p. 131
28 Ibid., p. 172
29 Transcript of PCRA hearing, August 1, 1995., p. 95
30 Williams, op. cit., p. 242

Chapter Eight

1 Notices of Suspension, City of Philadelphia, April 24, 1997, filed as evidence in Federal Court Case No. 972753, filed at the Federal Archives in

Philadelphia.

2   Notice of Dismissal, City of Philadelphia,
    June 18, 1986, filed as evidence in
    Federal Court Case No. 972753, filed at
    the Federal Archives in Philadelphia.

3   Investigative Interview Record,
    Philadelphia Police Department
    Homicide Div., December 9, 1981, p. 2

4   Investigative Interview Record,
    Philadelphia Police department
    Homicide Div., December 16, 1981, p. 2

5   Investigation Interview Record,
    Philadelphia Police Department,
    February 11, 1982, p. 3

6   Transcript of PCRA Hearing,
    Commonwealth of Pennsylvania v.
    Mumia Abu-Jamal, Aug. 1, 1995, p. 25

7   Ibid., p. 37

8   Ibid., p. 67

9   Investigative Interview Record,
    Philadelphia Police Department Internal
    Affairs Bureau, February 11, 1982, p. 5

10 Ibid., p. 78

11 Ibid., p. 80

12 Ibid., p. 102

13 Trial transcript, Commonwealth of
    Pennsylvania v. Mumia Abu-Jamal, July
    1, 1982, p. 33

14 Transcript of PCRA Hearing,
    Commonwealth v. Mumia Abu-Jamal,
    August 1, 1995, p. 114

15 Transcript of PCRA Hearing,
    Commonwealth v. Mumia Abu-Jamal,
    August 2, 1995, p. 72

16 Ibid., p. 60

17 Ibid., p. 62

18 Ibid., p. 226

19 Investigative interview record,
    Philadelphia Police Dept., 12/9/1981, p.
    1

20 Investigative interview record,
    Philadelphia Police Dept., 12/17/1981, p.
    1

21 Transcript of PCRA Hearing,
    Commonwealth v. Mumia Abu-Jamal,
    August 2, 1995, p. 201

22 Ibid., p. 209

23 Ibid., p. 211

24 Williams, op. cit., p. 360

25 Transcript of PCRA Hearing,
    Commonwealth v. Mumia Abu-Jamal,

August 3, 1995, p. 98

26 Transcript of PCRA Hearing,
    Commonwealth v. Mumia Abu-Jamal,
    August 3, 1995, p. 88

27 Ibid., p. 96

28 Transcript of PCRA hearing,
    Commonwealth v. Mumia Abu-Jamal,
    August 9, 1995, p. 6

29 Ibid., p. 7

30 Ibid., p. 8

31 Ibid., p. 9

32 Trial Transcript, Commonwealth v.
    Mumia Abu-Jamal, June 25, 1982, p. 45

33 Trial Transcript, Commonwealth v.
    Mumia Abu-Jamal, July 1, 1982, p. 179

34 Transcript of PCRA hearing,
    Commonwealth v. Mumia Abu-Jamal,
    August 15, 1995, p. 4

35 Ibid., p. 20

36 Ibid., 26

37 Transcript of PCRA hearing,
    Commonwealth v. Mumia Abu-Jamal,
    September 18, 1996

38 Ibid., p. 18

39 Ibid., p. 19

40 Ibid., p. 22

41 Ibid., p. 24

42 Ibid., p. 25

43 Ibid., p. 31

44 Ibid., p. 127

45 Ibid., p. 143

46 Ibid., p. 143

47 Ibid., p. 145

48 Ibid., p. 215

49 Memorandum and Order, Mumia Abu-
    Jamal v. Martin Horn, Commissioner
    Pennsylvania Department of Corrections,
    December 19., 2001, 99-civ-5089, p. 65

50 Transcript of PCRA hearing,
    Commonwealth v. Mumia Abu-Jamal,
    June 26, 1997, p. 59

51 Transcript of PCRA hearing,
    Commonwealth v. Mumia Abu-Jamal,
    June 30, 1997, p. 73

52 Declaration of Rachel H. Wolkenstein,
    op. cit., p. 2

53 Ibid., p. 5

54 Williams, op. cit., p. 305

55 Transcript of PCRA hearing,
    Commonwealth v. Mumia Abu-Jamal,
    August 11, 1995, p. 9

56 Williams, op. cit., p. 303
57 Ibid., p. 234
58 Ibid., p. 270
59 Declaration of Rachel H. Wolkenstein, op. cit., p. 2
60 Williams, op. cit., p. 307
61 Transcript of PCRA Hearing, Commonwealth v. Mumia Abu-Jamal, August 10, 1995, p. 68

Chapter Nine

1 Letter from Leonard Weinglass to Mumia Abu-Jamal, February 22, 2001
2 Memorandum and Order, Commonwealth vs. Mumia Abu-Jamal, November 21, 2001, 8201-1357-59, p. 11
3 Speech by Mumia's attorneys written for delivery at a May 23, 2002 fundraiser for Mumia Abu-Jamal's defense, by Marlene Kamish, Eliot Lee Grossman, Nick Brown and J. Michael Farrell, May 23, 2002.
4 Ibid.
5 Ibid.
6 Williams, op. cit., p. xii
7 The information on Kamish's and Grossman's legal backgrounds first appeared in an article I wrote in the online magazine *Salon*. The article ran on June 15, 2001, under the headline "Mumia's All-or Nothing Gamble."
8 Trial transcript, Commonwealth v. Mumia Abu-Jamal, July 3, 1982, p. 33
9 Declaration of Mumia Abu-Jamal, Mumia Abu-Jamal vs. Martin Horn, Commissioner, Pennsylvania Department of Corrections, and Connor Blaine, Superintendent of the State Correctional Institution at Greene, May 3, 2001, p. 2
10 Ibid.
11 PCRA hearing transcript, August 11, 1995, p. 7
12 Supplemental Declaration of William Cook, Mumia Abu-Jamal vs. Martin Horn, Commissioner, Pennsylvania Department of Corrections, and Connor Blaine, Superintendent of the State correctional Institution at Greene, April 29, 2001, p. 3
13 Ibid., p. 3
14 Ibid., p. 4
15 Hardcastle v. Horn, No. 98-CV-3028 (E.D. Pa.)

Chapter Ten

1 Memorandum and Order, Mumia Abu-Jamal v. Martin Horn, Commissioner, Pennsylvania Department of Corrections, et al., December 18, 2001, p. 41
2 Ibid., p. 41
3 Ibid., p. 41
4 PCRA hearing transcript, Commonwealth of Pennsylvania v. Mumia Abu-Jamal, August 4, 1995, p. 16
5 Memorandum and Order, op. cit. p. 45
6 Ibid., p. 45
7 Trial transcript, Commonwealth of Pennsylvania v. Mumia Abu-Jamal, June 22, 1982, p. 107
8 PCRA hearing transcript, Commonwealth v. Mumia Abu-Jamal, August 3, 1995, p. 171
9 Memorandum and Order, op. cit., p. 61
10 Ibid., p. 65
11 Petition for Habeas Corpus, Mumia Abu-Jamal v. Martin Horn, Commissioner, Pennsylvania Department of Corrections, et. al., Oct. 17, 1999, p. 27
12 *Philadelphia Inquirer*, "Timony Defends Decision," by Mark Fazlollah and Robert Moran March 27, 2001, p. 1, and Philadelphia Daily News, "'Tough on Crime' Unless Perp is a Cop," March 27, 2001. P. 19
13 PCRA hearing transcript, Commonwealth of Pennsylvania v. Mumia Abu-Jamal, August 1, 1995, p. 61
14 Memorandum and Order, op. cit., p. 84
15 Ibid., p. 84
16 Ibid., p. 100
17 *Chicago Tribune*, "Ryan Suspends Death Penalty, Illinois First State to Impose Moratorium on Executions," by Ken Armstrong, Steve Mills and Ray Long, January 31, 2000, p. 1
18 Memorandum and Order, op. cit., p. 119
19 Ibid., p. 160
20 Ibid., p. 187
21 Amnesty International, "A Life in the

Balance: The Case of Mumia Abu-Jamal," February, 17, 2000, p. 17

22   Memorandum and Order, op. cit., p. 195

23   Ibid., p. 195

24   Memorandum and Order, op. cit., p. 215

25   thenation.com, online edition of *The Nation*, "Aiming for a Conviction," Dave Lindorff, May 2, 2002

Chapter Eleven

1   *Extra!*, September-October 2000, "Witness for the Prosecution," by Jim Naureckas

2   *Philadelphia Inquirer*, June 15, 1998

3   *Extra!*, September-October 2000, "Hometown Hostility" by Ed Herman

4   Amnesty International, "USA: A Life in the Balance: The Case of Mumia Abu-Jamal," February 2000, p. 23

5   *Philadelphia Inquirer*, "News Briefs," February 18, 2000, p. 2B

6   *Daily News*, "Let Mumia Rot in Darkness," December 19, 2001, p. 19

7   *Philadelphia Inquirer*, "The latest theory, the latest sham," by Tom Ferrick Jr., June 12, 2002, p. 1B

8   ABC's "20/20" newsmagazine, Transcript No. 1879, "Hollywood's Unlikely Hero", p. 2

9   Ibid., p. 9

10   Ibid., p. 9

11   Ibid., p. 9

12   *Philadelphia Inquirer*, "ABC's Sam Donaldson not among those who want to free Mumia," December 9, 1995, p. D12

13   Letter from Mike Farrell to Sam Donaldson and Harry Philips of ABC's "20-20" newsmagazine, December 22, 1998

14   Ibid.

15   *Washington Post*, May 18, 1995, "Condemned to Silence? Does a Man Lose His Right to Write if he Kills a Cop? A Widow Says Yes", by Megan Rosenfeld, p. C1

16   Trial transcript, Commonwealth of Pennsylvania v. Mumia Abu-Jamal, June 26, 1982, p. 26

17   *Vanity Fair*, August 1999, "The Famous and the Dead," by Buzz Bissinger, p. 76.

18   *Revolutionary Worker*, August 15, 1999, "Mumia: Blowing Away the Lies", by C. Clark Kissinger, p. 1

19   Ibid., p. 4

20   *New York Press*, "For a Free Mumia 2000," by Marc Cooper, January 5, 2000

Chapter Twelve

1   Court History printout for Arnold Beverly, Police No. 486108, Birth Date November 1, 1951.

2   FBI Freedom of Information/Privacy Acts section, Subject Daniel Faulkner, p. 1

3   Ibid., p. 2

4   Ibid., p. 3

5   FBI FOIA Explanation of Exemptions OPCA-16a (Rev 12-3-96), category (b)(7)(D)

6   FBI FOE/PA section, Subject Daniel Faulkner, p. 7

7   Declaration of Yvette Williams, January 28, 2002

8   Ibid.

9   Affidavit of Terri Maurer-Carter, August 21, 2001, p. 1

10   Memorandum and Order, Commonwealth v. Mumia Abu-Jamal, Judge J. Dembe, November 21, 2001, p. 15

Index

childhood friend of Abu-Jamal and William Cook, 230
driver's license application found in Faulkner's pocket, 15, 58, 230–32
early suspect in shooting, 230–32
loaned driver's license application to Freeman, 15, 232
questioned by Weinglass at PCRA hearing, 231–32
Howlett, Charles, 55
Humoresque, 37

I

In Sunshine and In Shadows (I.C. Smith), 331
International Concerned Family and Friends of Mumia Abu-Jamal, 178, 314

J

Jackson, Anthony, 21, 28, 32, 59
Abu-Jamal's concerns about abilities, 94
affected by case, 29
called no character witnesses during penalty phase, 164
closing arguments at trial, 156–58, 172
cross-examined at PCRA hearings, 201–204
death penalty experience, 30, 91, 144, 206
defense of Abu-Jamal, 144–76
did not request delay of trial, 113
disbarred, 92–93, 197
during penalty phase of trial, 164, 172
experience, 91
failed to advocate for Abu-Jamal's life, 73
failed to challenge "blurt-out" confession, 92
failed to notice misidentified slug, 26
filed police brutality complaint, 136–37
handled *voir dire*, 99
hired by Abu-Jamal's family, 26, 91
insufficient funds for defense, 153
Judge Sabo ordered him to lead defense, 71
no help from progressive legal commu-

nity, 91–92
had organizational problems, 92
as part of alleged conspiracy, 109–10
possible substance abuse problem, 92, 197
risked jail during jury selection, 109
shortcomings as attorney, 92
stopped preparing for Abu-Jamal case, 95
submitted suspicious Durham document, 139–40
testimony at PCRA hearing, 198–200
Jackson, Reverend Jesse, 186, 266
Jamal, Mydiya, Wadiya, 68
Jefferson Hospital confession, *see* "blurt-out" confession
Jenkins, Pamela
credibility as witness, 244–45, 262
pressured into giving false testimony, 58, 244
relationship with Ryan, Baird, 48–50, 244, 245
testimony about White, 49, 244
Jones, Veronica, 147, 161
arrested during PCRA hearing, 29, 241–42
cross-examined at PCRA hearing, 240–43
denied seeing fleeing suspect, 148
described deal White received from police, 239–40
as defense witness, 145, 148–53
intimidated by Judge Sabo, 237
left crime scene, 125
possible deal with police, 149–53, 207
pressured as witness, 58, 236–41
testimony at PCRA hearing, 236–43
threatened by police, 238–40
jury, trial
composition, 111
convicts Abu-Jamal of first-degree murder, 162–63
impact of character witnesses on, 72–73
included Dominic Durso, 111
included Edward Courchain as alternate, then juror, 103–105
never heard of police corruption, 34

Z

About the Author

Award-winning investigative reporter Dave Lindorff has been working as a journalist for 30 years. He ran the *Daily News* bureau covering Los Angeles County government, spent several years as a correspondent in Hong Kong and China for *Businessweek*, and has written for such publications as *Rolling Stone, The Nation, In These Times, Mother Jones, Village Voice, Salon, The London Observer* and the Australian *National Times*. He is also the author of *Marketplace Medicine: The Rise of the For-Profit Hospital Chains* (Bantam, 1992), an investigative report on the for-profit hospital industry. A 1975 graduate of the Columbia University Graduate School of Journalism, he earned his B.A. in 1972 in Chinese from Wesleyan University. In 1991 he was a Fulbright Scholar in Shanghai, China. For the past six years he has lived with his family just outside Philadelphia.